John Forster

The debates on the grand Remonstrance

John Forster

The debates on the grand Remonstrance

ISBN/EAN: 9783337043056

Printed in Europe, USA, Canada, Australia, Japan

Cover: Foto ©ninafisch / pixelio.de

More available books at **www.hansebooks.com**

THE DEBATES

ON THE

GRAND REMONSTRANCE,

NOVEMBER AND DECEMBER,
1641.

WITH

AN INTRODUCTORY ESSAY

on *Englifh Freedom under Plantagenet & Tudor Sovereigns.*

BY JOHN FORSTER, LL.D.

LONDON:
JOHN MURRAY, ALBEMARLE STREET.
1860.
[*The right of Tranflation is referved.*]

LONDON:
BRADBURY AND EVANS, PRINTERS, WHITEFRIARS.

CONTENTS.

INTRODUCTORY ESSAY ON ENGLISH FREEDOM UNDER PLANTAGENET AND TUDOR SOVEREIGNS, pp. 1—109.

PAGE

§ I. THE PLANTAGENETS . . . . 1—64
Purpofe of this Effay. Pofition taken up by Charles the Firft's opponents. Records and Titles of Englifh freedom, 1. Burke on our hiftory. Precedents in older time. Charter of Henry the Firft (1100). Difficulty of fuppreffing a charter, 2. HENRY THE FIRST. Royal conceffions not refumable. Imperfect judgments in hiftory. Strength and weaknefs of Norman kings, 3. Bafis of Saxon conftitution. Adopted by the Conqueror and his fons. Origin of Feudality. Its burdens and modes of tenure, 4. Natural confequences of Feudal Syftem. Its development. Hereditary Succeffion. Extinction of Vaffalage. The Crufades, 5. Feudal Inftitutions improved. Influences of Chriftianity. Seeds of Commerce and Literature. HENRY II, 6. Firft Plantagenet King (1154). Gains to civil freedom. Difpute of Henry II and his Primate. Becket's fcheme, 7. Henry's oppofition. What the ftruggle involved. Character of Henry. Complete victory to either not defirable, 8. What was due to the Church. What Henry II gained. Ranulf de Glanville, *Tractatus de Legibus et Consuetudinibus Regni Angliæ*. Appointment of circuits for judges (1176), 9. RICHARD I (1189). New relations between throne and barons. Independent oppofition to Crown. Beginning of ftruggles of party, 10. ARTHUR'S claim to the fucceffion: fought only in French provinces. The Englifh Crown not heritable property. Sovereignty elective. Normans defer to Saxon principle, 11. Coronation of JOHN (1199). Treafons the feed-plot of Liberty. Legitimacy or Election? Why John preferred to Arthur, 12. Henry II's policy unfettled by his fons. Monarchy and ariftocracy in conflict. People chooſe their fide alternately, 13. Character of John. His defertion of both fides. Ufes of a bad king. What the triumph of the Barons involved, 14. Party fpirit and its refults. Englifh King ftripped of French conquefts. Conduct of the Barons.

Contents.

Growth of national feeling, 15. Common caufe againft foreigners. Alliance of lords and citizens. King's furrender to Pope (1213). Freedom's debt to John, 16. Confederacy againft King. Character of Langton. His fervices to Englifh freedom. Firft day at Runnymede (Tuefday 16th of June, 1215), 17. Faith in Langton. Fourth day: CHARTER figned. Its general character. Confirmation of exifting liberties. Principles latent in it, 18. Remedial provifions. Guarantees of franchifes. Redrefs of perfonal wrongs, 19. Central courts of law. Levies of aid limited. Conftitution of Great Council. Forms of fummons thereto: hateful to fucceeding princes, 20. Minor provifions. Securities for liberty and property. Juftice not to be denied or fold. "*Nullus liber homo*," 21. All freemen to be tried by their peers, 21, 22. Extenfion of relief to fub-vaffals. Effect of Charter in later times. Its power of expanfion, 22. Subftance fhaping Forms. Violations and reaffertions of Charter. HENRY III (1216), 23. EARLIEST COUNCIL NAMED AS A PARLIAMENT. Supply conditional on redrefs. Control of money by Parliament. Appeal of Henry III to People. Similar appeal from Barons, 24. Jealoufy of French favourites. Struggle for power transformed to war of principles. Rife of merchants and tradefmen. Guilds and Charters, 25. Privileges and rights ceded to middle clafs. King's fummons for parliament not obeyed (1233). Political ballads. Attack upon the Favourite, 26. General difcontent. Grievances reported and Redrefs demanded (February, 1234). Parliament affembled and Favourite difmiffed (April, 1234). Minifterial refponfibility and Parliamentary control, 27. Diftrefs, Redrefs, and Supply. Securities for public faith. Law fyftematifed (*Bracton*, 1250). Curia Regis, 28. Cabinet of the King. A memorable affembly (2nd of May, 1258). The Great Council under Normans: not a Houfe of Lords: not hereditary, but reprefentative, 29. Germs therein of larger fyftem. Break-up of elements of Council. Diftinctions and grades of rank. Varieties in writs of fummons, 30. Peculiarities of feudal reprefentation. Aid for Protection. Leffer tenants reprefented by larger, 31. Tranfition from feudal to real rights, 31, 32. Language of writs of fummons. Fictions forefhadowing truths. Forms conveying Subftance, 32. Commiffions of inquiry in fhires. Old inftitution adapted to new ufes (1223). County reprefentation begins. Collection of taxes (in 1207 and 1220), 33. Beginning of the end. Vague formation of authority of Commons. Gradual fteps thereto (1214). Scheme to obtain money from fhires (1254), 34. Knights to anfwer for their counties. Reprefentatives to impofe taxes. One chamber at Weftminfter: feparate fittings elfewhere, 35. Admiffion of third eftate, 35, 36. Knights fit with Lords. Lords pay, fitting in their own right. Knights are paid, fitting for others. County rates, 36. Wages of knights levied on entire county. Election by full County Court. All freeholders com-

Contents.

prised: and represented by knights of shire, 37. Results of such representation. Ages prepare what the hour produces. Six eventful years. Writs for FIRST HOUSE OF COMMONS (14th of December, 1264), 38. Rights gained once, gained always. Power of Commons ever growing. EDWARD I (1271). Election of Sheriffs, 39. Great Statute of Winchester (1284), 39, 40. EDWARD II (1307). Creation of Royal Boroughs. Equal power claimed for Commons. Provision for assembling of Parliaments, 40. Confirmations of Great Charter. Attempts to impose taxes without Parliament. Money supplies made conditional. EDWARD III (1327). Statute of Treasons. Acts against Conscription, 41. No forced pressing of Soldiers. Character of Edward III. Victorious in peace as well as war. First man in the realm. Intellectual influences of his reign, 42. Chaucer (1328). Improvement of the language. English adopted in Parliament rolls. RICHARD II (1377). Results of Richard's deposition, 43. People's power to alter the succession: sole claim of House of Lancaster. Terms of Richard's submission. His abdication made compulsory, 44. Popular principle accepted. Adhesion of the people. Soliciting the Throne. Shakespeare's *Bolingbroke*. HENRY IV (1399), 45. King Bolingbroke. Elevation of the people. Parliamentary assumptions. Precedent for Hanoverian succession (1406), 46. No judge to plead King's orders. Claim to make supplies conditional on redress (1401). Officers of Household removed (1404). Law for regulating County Elections, 47. All Freeholders to vote. The lack-learning Parliament (1406). Accumulation of Church property. Its unequal distribution, 48. Proposal to seize it for better appropriation. Failure of attempt. Thirty articles for regulation of King's affairs. Ministerial responsibility established (1410), 49. Interference with Taxation by the Lords resisted. Changes since the Conquest. Petitions and Bills. Royal evasion of Parliamentary control, 50. Bills substituted for Petitions. HENRY V (1413). Good out of evil. Advantage to Commons from Henry V's wars. Further restraints on the prerogative, 51. Admission of rights of legislature. Law against tampering with petitions. Exemptions claimed for members of the Commons, 52. PRIVILEGE OF PARLIAMENT. Thorpe's case. Established against the courts. Right of IMPEACHMENT won. Liberal gains intercepted, 53. Freedom outraged but not lost, 53, 54. Concessions to force. HENRY VI (1422). Differences in quarter of a century, 54. Voting of all freeholders in counties: limited to forty-shilling freeholders, 54, 55. Greater importance of the people. Feudality declining. Villenage passed away. Changes in Society, 55. Higher developments of feudal principle. A contrast. *Tyler's Rebellion*: Popular demands (1381). *Cade's Rebellion*: Popular demands (1450), 56. Rapid fall of Feudal System: as the People rose. Levelling of distinctions. Comforts of labouring claſſes, 57. Reſpective condition of England and of France, 57, 58. Contraſts of the two Nations. Teſtimony of Sir John Forteſcue: and of Philip de Comines, 58. *De Laudibus Legum Angliæ* (1465). Reſtraints on prerogative. Conſtitution of Parliament. Rights of the ſubject. Reſponſibility of the Crown, 59. Encroachments of Executive. Checks of Parliament. Control of the purſe. Loans and Benevolences, 60. Source of ſtrength to Commons: derived from other powers. Aſſiſted from above and from below. The People the ſupreme force. Expedients to keep it down, 61. *Wars of the Roſes.* EDWARD IV: EDWARD V: RICHARD III (1461—1483). Legiſlation during Civil Wars. Richard III's ſtatute againſt forced loans, 62. Advances in commerce, learning, and the arts. Loſs of the French provinces. War on ſurface of the land, Peace beneath. Commercial guilds replacing great families, 63. Break-up of ſyſtem of Middle Ages. Kingcraft ſucceeds. Its chief profeſſors. French, Spaniſh, and Engliſh kings. Reſults in England, 64.

§ II. THE TUDORS . . . . 65—92

HENRY VII (1485). Uneaſineſs as to ſucceſſion. Parliamentary ſettlement, 65. Pope's reſcript on Henry's title: tranſlated for the people: and firſt printed in broadſide by Caxton, 65, 66. Lord Bolingbroke's view of the reign. Loſſes to public liberty. Defection of parliament, 66. Maintenance of legal forms. Peculiarity of Tudor deſpotiſm. Indications of ſocial change. Power changing hands, 67. Neceſſity for a Poor Law. Houſe of Lords: 29 in number. Commons weakened by weakneſs in Lords. Influences unſeen, 68. Unconſcious law-making. Star Chamber created. A keen but narrow viſion. Lord Bacon's character of Henry VII, 69. Leading acts of his ſovereignty. What was intended by his legiſlation. What was effected beyond his intention, 70. Interval between feudal and popular agencies. Firſt Expedition to America (1496). Viſit of Eraſmus to England. Sebaſtian Cabot in the New World, 71. Eraſmus in Oxford. Revival of ſtudy of *Homer.* Greek Profeſſorſhip at Oxford (1497). Diſlike of the new learning, 72. A good old Engliſh complaint: againſt Letters and Poverty. Part taken by Eraſmus. Diſciples of Aquinas, 73. Syſtem of the Schoolmen doomed. Language an enſlaver as well as liberator. Connection of words and things. Eraſmus's great weapon. "A Second Lucian," 74. Firſt pure text of the Teſtament. The way prepared for Luther. Complaint againſt Eraſmus. Harbinger of the Reformation. Titles of Eraſmus to reſpect, 75. His example. His achievements. His connection with Oxford. Henry's Statutes. Commerce and learning indirectly aſſiſted, 76. Uſes of the Printing Preſs. Legiſlating for the future. Diſfavour to nobles. Favour to Churchmen and Lawyers, 77. Throne guarded from Treaſon: and enriched

Contents.

PAGE

by Forfeitures, 77, 78. New methods of extortion. Empſon and Dudley. Uſes to which they were put, 78. Plunder under forms of law. HENRY VIII (1509). Execution of Empſon and Dudley. Tudor characteriſtics, 79. Cauſes of ſucceſs: yielding to people, repreſſing nobles. Taſk of each ſovereign, 80. HENRY'S (1509). EDWARD'S (1547). MARY'S (1553). ELIZABETH'S (1558), 80, 81. Tudor deſpotiſm exceptional. Its checks and limits, 81. Elizabeth's conceſſions. Mary's weakneſs. Poſition of Houſe of Commons. Acts of parliament edged tools. Parliamentary reſiſtance to Mary, 82. Three diſſolutions in two years. Privileges won from Henry VIII. Thirty members added to Commons. Safeguards of an armed people, 83. Obligation for martial exerciſe. Power beyond the Sovereign. All legiſlation in name of Commons. Subſtance as well as form claimed by them, 84. Elizabeth's reign. Character of the Queen: a ſovereign demagogue. Advantages of the people. Reſults of the Reformation. Oxford leſſons complete, 85. Change impending. Riſe of religious diſcontent. The newly eſtabliſhed Church. Impulſes of Reformation reſtrained. A danger overlooked, 86. Cartwright's Lectures at Cambridge (1570). PURITAN PARTY FORMED. Its leaders in Houſe of Commons. Vain attempts to ſubdue them, 87. Laſt act of the greateſt Tudor. Elizabeth's antipathy to Puritans: Puritan ſympathy with Elizabeth, 88. Champion and leader of the Reformation. Puritaniſm in a new form: joined with political diſcontent. A Queen's Serjeant coughed down, 89. Cecil's warning to Commons. Elizabeth's laſt appearance in Parliament. JAMES I (1603). Two kingdoms united under the Stuarts, 90. Opportunity loſt by Cecil. No conditions made at Acceſſion. No check on overſtrained prerogative. Provocation to Rebellion, 91. Penalties to be paid, 92.

§ III. FIRST STUART KING . . . . 92—109

Character of James. His learning. His cunning and ſhrewdneſs, 92. Wiſeſt fool in Chriſtendom. What he did with learning. Uſes of his knowledge. Too confident an aſſumption, 93. Early career in Scotland. His excuſes. A ſchool for king-craft. His poſition between Puritan and Papiſt, 94. Formation of his character. His attachments. Family of James. Princeſs Elizabeth born (1596). Prince Charles born (1600), 95. The Gowrie Conſpiracy. Prince Charles's boyhood. Phyſical defects, 96. Proſpect of Engliſh throne. Joy of laity in Scotland. Indignation of clergy. Elizabeth's death announced, 97. Journey ſouthward begun (April, 1603), 97, 98. Novelty of a King after half a century of a Queen. Perſonal characteriſtics of the new monarch. Face and figure. Slobbering ſpeech, 98. Shuffling gait. Abſence of ſelf-ſupport. A fence to monarchy thrown down. Courtiers confounded. Royal progreſs to London, 99. Entertainments. At Hinchinbrook:

PAGE

OLIVER CROMWELL (æt. 4) firſt fees a king. Interview with Francis Bacon. Arrival in land of promiſe, 100. Interview with Cecil: at Theobald's (3rd May), 100, 101. Unfavourable impreſſion on the miniſter. Foreign policy. Death of Cecil (1612). Riſe of Somerſet, 101. King's manner to favourites. Somerſet's fall. Riſe of Villiers, 102. A prime miniſter at a maſque. Scenes and actors in the Court. Unreſtrained indulgences. Bribes taken by women, 103. Sports of the Cockpit. Profligate expenditure. Debts of the King. Shameful neceſſities, 104. Buckingham's extravagance. Expedients for money. Benevolences and fines. Patents and monopolies. Knighthood exhauſted. Baronetcies invented. Peerages put up to ſale, 105. Tariff of titles. James's theological diſplays. Hampton Court Conference. King's conduct to Puritans, 106. Delight of the Biſhops. Chancellor Elleſmere's ideal. James's religious perſecutions, 107. Retribution in ſtore. A parallel to James's creed. Alleged darker traits: not eſtabliſhed. *Lambeth MSS.* (930, *f.* 91), 108. Innocent as to Overbury and Prince Henry. Opinions of the people. Contempt of the perſon of the ſovereign. Legacy to Charles I, 109.

THE DEBATES ON THE GRAND REMONSTRANCE, NOVEMBER AND DECEMBER, 1641. pp. 110—421.

Fac-simile of Two Pages of Sir Simonds D'Ewes's Journal of the Parliament, begun November 3rd, 1640. From the Original MS. in the Britiſh Muſeum . . . . To face the Title-page

§ I. PREFATORY . . . . 110—114

Moſt exciting incident before the war. Moſt neglected by hiſtorians, 110. Remonſtrance printed in *Ruſhworth*. Miſleading of Clarendon. Falſification of Debates. Misſtatements followed by all, 111. Sir Philip Warwick's account. Extraordinary ſcene. Hampden's influence, 112. Various references to Great Remonſtrance. Clarendon generally followed. Purpoſe of the preſent work. Written from MS. records, 113.

§ II. WHAT THE GREAT REMONSTRANCE WAS . . 114—117

Caſe of the Parliament againſt the King. Moſt complete juſtification of Great Rebellion. Religion and Politics in union, 114. Hume's falſe diſtinctions: refuted by the Remonſtrance, 114, 115. Character of its contents. Warnings againſt Court. Appeal to the country, 115. No diſreſpect to King or Church. States what the war put in iſſue. Occupies 15 folio pages in Ruſhworth. Difficulty of reproducing it, 116. Its various and minute detail. Purpoſed illuſtration by MS. records. Teſt for Clarendon's honeſty, 117.

Contents. xi

PAGE

§ III. SIR SIMONDS D'EWES AND HIS MANUSCRIPT JOURNAL
OF THE LONG PARLIAMENT . . . . 117—125

Text. Authority for new facts in this work, 117. Journal by D'Ewes in Harleian MSS. Writers acquainted with it, 118. Neceffity of ftudying the original MS. Account of D'Ewes. Born (1602). At Cambridge (1618), 119. Leaves Cambridge, 1620-1. Quits Weftminfter Hall. Delight in old records. Marriage (1626). Buys his rank, 120. Projects a Hiftory. High Sheriff of Suffolk (1639). Sympathy with Puritans. Returned to Long Parliament for Sudbury, 121. Lodgings at Weftminfter. Firft fpeech in Houfe. Affiduous attendance. Takes Notes of debates, 122. Fruit thereof: in five volumes of Journal, 122, 123. Condition of the original MS. Pages fac-fimilied. Component Parts of MS., 123. Confufed prefent ftate, 124. Example of importance of their contents. Why not earlier made ufe of, 125.

Notes. Notes by D'Ewes characterifed. *Edinburgh Review* (July, 1846), 118. Self-painted portrait. Jealoufy of Note-taking. Old Vane objects, and D'Ewes replies, 124.

§ IV. ATTAINDER OF THE EARL OF STRAFFORD . 126—152

Text. The Attainder made a teft of opinions. A fallacious one. Unwife comparifons and contrafts, 126. The "Proteftation" to defend Parliament and Religion, 127. Royalift fupporters of Attainder. Falkland, Culpeper, Capel, and Hyde, 128. Danger of believing in Clarendon. Conduct of Hyde. Why he declined office. Strange felf-expofure, 129. Hyde chairman of a committee. Encounters a "tempeftuous" perfon. Mr. Cromwell "in a fury." Sir Ralph Verney's *Notes*, 130. Reports debate on Strafford. Speech by Hampden : on queftion not material to the Bill, 131. Attainder not in difpute. Hampden fuppofed favourable to it, 132. Correcter judgment by Macaulay : *Effays* (i. 467), 132, 133. Line really taken by Hampden. Evidence of D'Ewes. Doubts fet at reft. Procedure by Bill originally propofed. Pym and Hampden for Impeachment, 133. Difpute of the 10th April. Diffatisfaction with the Lords. Bill of Attainder revived. Oppofed by Pym and Hampden, 134. Elder Vane's Notes of Council, 134, 135. Objection to their production. Excitement thereon. Conference with Lords propofed, 135. Pym and Hampden outvoted. Sitting of the 12th April, 1641. Reported in D'Ewes's MS. Two pages in fac-fimile, 136. Pym and Hampden acting together. Why they oppofed Attainder. Pym fuggefts conference. Maynard recites points for fettlement, 137. Houfe will make facrifices to prevent delay. Others guilty with Strafford. Their guilt not to be infifted on. The Notes of Council, 138. Laud

PAGE

and Cottington involved. Hotham for Attainder. Pym
againſt. Maynard for. Rudyard doubtful. Tomkins for,
139. Culpeper for. D'Ewes againſt. Urges judgment on
Impeachment. Explanation aſked from old Vane. Refuſed,
140. Glyn explains. Marten for Attainder. Hampden
againſt. Vane and his Son. Subſequent courſe of ſupporters
of Attainder. Conduct of Glyn and Maynard, 141. Line
taken by Falkland: excuſed by Clarendon. What excuſe
for Mr. Hyde? 142. Takes ſame line as Falkland. Too
much faith in ſhort memories. Pym and Hampden confiſtent
throughout, 143. Their belief in Strafford's guilt. Queſtion raiſed whether to hear his counſel? Refiſted by Falkland and Culpeper. Supported by Hampden and Pym, 144.
Speech of Maynard againſt. Pym in reply. Advocates
Strafford's claim to hearing. His appeal ſuccefsful, 145.
His ſuggeſtions as to Attainder. Engliſh compared to
French Revolution. Folly and falſehood of compariſon, 146.
Obſolete views. Opinions of the better informed. Agreement up to Arreſt of Five Members. Parliament's juſtification, 147. General character of the ſtruggle. More wealth
with the Commons than with the King. No terroriſm,
148. Origin of the intereſt ſtill inſpired by the war, 148,
149. A war without an enemy. D'Ewes as to acts and
motives, 149. Strafford. Greateſt man on the King's ſide,
149, 150. Where his ſtateſmanſhip ſucceeded. Where it
failed. His ſyſtem in Ireland, 151. The good implied in
it. The danger that proved fatal. Bad faith of the King,
151. Moral of Strafford's government, 152.

Notes. "Story of Corfe Caſtle," 126. D'Ewes to Lady
D'Ewes. King's ill-fated ſtep. Agitation in the Houſe
and in the City, 127. "Proteſtation"drawn up. Taken by
all, 128. Verney's Notes, 130. As to fac-ſimile, 140.
Strafford's contempt for old Falkland, 142. Hyde and Falkland's agreement. Sitting as well as voting together, 143.

§ V. REACTION AFTER STRAFFORD'S DEATH . . 152—163

Text. Parties altered after Strafford's death. Remonſtrance a
freſh ſtarting-point, 152. What Cromwell ſaid to Falkland,
152, 153. Alleged narrow eſcape for Charles. Hyde's new
policy. Reaction for the King, 153. Chances of ſucceſs.
Old poſitions reverſed. Daily defections from Popular ranks,
154. Character of the King. His view as to invalidity of
ſtatutes. Aſſenting with purpoſe to revoke. Hyde's complaint. Sources of danger to Parliament, 155. Signs of
wavering. Abatement of Popular enthuſiaſm, 156. Charles's
advantages. A warning needed. Threatenings of force,
157. Freedom or Deſpotiſm? Reſolution to appeal to the
People. Origin of the "Remonſtrance." Firſt moved by
Lord Digby, 158. The King receives Warning: on Eve of

Contents.

journey to Scotland, 158, 159. Bifhop Williams advifes conciliation. King confents. Scheme baffled. Intended diftribution of offices, 159. Friday, 30th July, 1641. : New Miniftry expected. Saturday, 7th Auguft : Remonftrance formally brought forward, 160. Bifhop Williams's labour loft. Remonftrance openly difcuffed. King quits London : 9th Auguft. Hyde's previous interview, 161. Why Charles was grateful to him. His fervice againft Epifcopacy Bill. Engagement to defeat it, 162. Hopes from the Scottifh journey. Hyde's promife, 163.

Notes. Miftake of Richard Baxter, 153. Only lawyers feceded on the Attainder, 154. The Clergy and Univerfities. Ficklenefs of the people, 156. Impatience of waiting. Cure more painful than difeafe, 157. Excitement as to Scotch journey, 160.

VI. REASSEMBLING OF PARLIAMENT, OCTOBER, 1641 . 163—168

Text. 20th of October, 1641. Houfes meet. Defaulters from the Commons, 163. Strode's propofition againft the abfent without leave, 163, 164. Liberal party weakened. Forebodings coming true. Report from the Recefs Committee, 164. Another plot. Letters produced from Hampden. The "Incident," 165. Hyde and Falkland outvoted. Pym's refolutions carried, 166. Alarm of Secretary Nicholas. King's friends difheartened. Arrival of Hampden, 167. Bifhops' Bill under difcuffion. Speakers for and againft. Hampden's furprife. Falkland's avowal, 168.

Notes. Charge againft Montrofe. 30th October. Pym's fpeech on Army defigns, 165. Confpiracy tracked out, 166. Character of Edward Nicholas, 166, 167. Indirect ways of the Court, 167.

VII. LORD FALKLAND . . . . . . 169—181

Text. Beliefs as to Falkland's character. Suppofed type of moderation. Errors and misjudgment, 169. Never zealous for the King, 170. Clarendon's defcription, 171, Opinions held by Falkland : as to Court and Parliament. Influence of Hyde. Faith of the old Cavalier, 172. Sentiment not judgment. Eafy prey to Hyde's perfuafion. Falkland's ftronghold, 173. View taken by Macaulay, 174. Objections thereto. Excitability of temper. Anecdote by Clarendon. Emphafis overdone, 175. Similar trait of Danton. Strange refemblances. Stranger contrafts, 176. Diflike of the war. Laft appearance in Houfe of Commons. More like delinquent than Minifter. Regret or felf-reproach? 177. Falkland's nobler qualities. Services to men of wit, 178. Open houfe at Oxford : to men of all opinions, 179. A college in purer air, 180. Three fpecial

Contents.

PAGE

characteriftics: *love of truth*; *hatred of spies*; *reverence for private letters*, 180, 181.

Notes. Tribute by Hyde. Gratitude of the Poets to Falkland. His Eclogue on Jonfon's death, 170. On Jonfon's learning. His vogue in theatres. His felf-raifed fortune, 171. As to lawfulnefs of refiftance, 172. Macaulay's *Effays* (i. 160). A public man unfit for public life. What if he had lived to Revolution, 174. Hyde's happy eulogy, 178. Exquifite delicacy. Picture of Falkland's houfe. Intolerant only of intolerance. Difcourfes againft Popery, 179.

§ VIII. THE SECESSION AND ITS DANGERS . . 181—190

Text. Falkland's new leader: not Hampden but Hyde, 181. Liberal phalanx broken up. Its achievements, 182. Defertion by feceders: never accounted for, 182, 183. The King unaltered. Old caufe ftill hateful to him. Danger of lofing all, 183. Reappearance of plague, 183, 184. King's defire for adjournment of Houfes. Pym's refiftance. Attempt on Pym's life, 184. Letter delivered by the Serjeant, 184, 185. Handed to Mr. Rufhworth. Its contents. Mr. Rufhworth's alarm. Further attempts againft Pym, 185. His affailants in the Houfe, 186. Refolution moved: againft King's appointments to office, 186, 187. Strode's violence, 189. Hyde's opportunity. Irifh Rebellion. Pym's opportunity, 190.

Notes. A Judge arrefted on the bench, 182. Allufions to Pym in Queen's letters. Attempts to bring him into fufpicion. Caufes of his popularity. Tribute by Covenanter Baillie, 186. Clarendon's attack on Strode: not applicable to Strode of James's reign, 187. Probable confufion between two Strodes, 187, 188. The later Strode a young man. Evidence of D'Ewes's Journal. Scene at Arreft of Five Members, 188. Counter teftimony in favour of identity, 188, 189. The other view ftrengthened: in letter to Lady D'Ewes. Another Hyde: more decidedly royalift than Edward, 189.

§ IX. THE NEW PARTY AND THE OLD . . . 190—200

Text. 5th November, 1641. Pym's fpeech on Evil Counfellors, 190. Excitement in Houfe. Edmund Waller's reply. Compares Pym to Strafford, 191. Pym rifes to order. Cries for Waller. Reparation made, 192. Dramatic changes: reported to the King: Royal thanks to managers. Hyde fent for by Nicholas, 193. Is fhown a letter from the King. Old leaders unmoved. Majority ftill fufficient, 194. Meafures againft Bifhops: propofal to make five new ones, 194, 195. Cromwell's counter motion. Bifhops' demurrer.

Holborne fupports Bifhops, 195. D'Ewes replies to Holborne: raifing laugh againſt him. Beginning of the end, 196. Moves and counter moves. Prudence and fagacity of Pym. Gives effect to fuggeftion of St. John, 197. Pofition of Houfe as to Irifh Rebellion, 197, 198. Hope of the King thereon. Baffled by Pym. Speech to the Lords againſt Evil Counfels, 198. Refolution paffed. A Motion by Oliver Cromwell. Germ of the Parliamentary Army. Ominous claim put forth, 199. Ordinances *minus* the King. Alarm thereat. Preparations for conflict, 200.

Notes. Value of preparation in Oratory, 191. Commons' Journals, 5th November. Waller's apology, 192.

§ X. CONFLICT BEGUN . . . . . . 200—202

Text. 8th November (1641). Rough Draught of Remonftrance fubmitted, 200, 201. Nicholas writes to the King. Mr. Secretary's trouble, 201. Urges King's inftant return, 201, 202. King's anfwer: Stop the Remonftrance! Forces organized for the ftruggle, 202.

§ XI. THE OPENING DEBATES: 9TH, 10TH, 12TH, 15TH, AND 16TH NOVEMBER . . . . 202—210

Text. Firſt Debate: Tuefday, 9th November, 202. Procedure fettled. Movers of amendments. Report of Nicholas to King. King's order thereon, 203. Second Debate: 10th November. No copies to be given out. 11th November, Speech by Strode. Deftination of Remonftrance avowed: to go to the people, 204. To be printed and circulated. Third Debate: 12th November, Motion for Candles, 205. D'Ewes in favour of Candles. Private reports to the King, 206. Tenacity of his Majefty's oppofition. Fourth Debate: 15th November. As to Bifhops favouring idolatry. Speech by Dering, 207. Falkland's former attack on Bifhops. Prefent vehement defence. Fifth Debate: 16th November, 208. Claufe againſt Bifhops carried. Compromife as to Liturgy. Conceffions to Oppofition. Unauthorifed reports. Suppreffion of printed and MS. diurnals, 209. Refolutions to Second Army Plot, 210.

Notes. Strode's manner of fpeech. Avowal as to Scotch Army, 205. Shilling fines. Orders as to bufinefs: as to reading of Bills, 206. Dering fneered at by Clarendon, 207.

§ XII. PREPARATIONS FOR THE FINAL VOTE, 19TH NOVEMBER AND 20TH NOVEMBER . . . 210—215

Text. Nicholas's fear for the King. Progrefs of Remonftrance reported, 210. Nicholas as to printing: the defign avowed. Sixth Debate: 19th November, 211. Amend-

ments and verbal changes, 211, 212. Hyde's urgent appeal.
Pym's reply: and vindication. A home thruſt, 212. Order
for engroſſment. Complaint of Mr. Speaker. Lenthal
relieved. Seventh Debate: 20th November. Final Debate
fixed. Cromwell and Falkland, 213. Preparations for laſt
Debate. Remonſtrance lying on table, 214. Propoſed hiſtorical illuſtrations. Dering on the Remonſtrance, 215.

Notes. A bold Mechanick, 211. Statement by Clarendon:
charge againſt Pym: a miſrepreſentation, 214.

ABSTRACT OF THE GRAND REMONSTRANCE . 215 273

1. *The Preamble: Purpoſe aimed at* . . . . 215—218

Text. Struggle of paſt twelve months, 215. Why Remonſtrance introduced. Neceſſary to completion of Reforms,
216. Court Conſpiracy: to ſubvert laws; to degrade Pro-
teſtantiſm; to diſcredit Parliament, 216, 217. Upholders
of right nick-named Puritans, 217. Popery the chief Con-
ſpirator, 218.

Notes. Falkland againſt Laud. Propoſed Pope at Lambeth,
217. Engliſh livings and Romiſh opinions, 218.

2. *Firſt, Second, and Third Parliaments of Charles* . 218—223

Text. Clauſes 1—6. Incidents of Firſt Parliament, 218. Clauſes
7—10. Incidents of Second Parliament, 219. Clauſes
11—16. Incidents of Third Parliament, 220. Violation
of Petition of Right. Impriſonment of Members, 222.
Heavy Fines. Sufferings and death of Eliot. His blood
crying for vengeance, 223.

Notes. Billeting grievances. Liſts of recuſants. Yonge's
Diary, 219. Proceedings to get money. How ſpent.
Amendments by J. C., 220. Addition by Strode.
Moundiford MSS. Billeting ſoldiers. Sheriffs and ſhip-
money. Projects for plunder of ſubject, 221. Atro-
cities of the Court. Authors of Amendments, 222.
Eliot's uſage in Tower, 223.

3. *Government by Prerogative: from Third Parliament to Pacification of Berwick* . . . . . 224—244

Text. Clauſes 17—60. Government by Prerogative. Clauſes
17, 21, 22, 31, 44, 45, and 49. Revival of feudal ſtatutes, 224.
Ancient Charters broken, 225. Packed juries and robberies
by law. Clauſes 18, 19, 20, and 24. Monſtrous taxation of
commerce. Pretence of guarding ſeas, 226. Ship-money,
227. Seas wholly unguarded, 228. No laws to appeal to.
Caſe of Richard Chambers, 229. Clauſes 27, 28, 29, 30,
33, 34, and 35. Monopolies revived: all neceſſaries of life pro-

Contents. xvii

PAGE

tected and debafed. Reftraints on enterprife, 230. Debafement of currency. Courts of law become courts of Royal revenue, 231. Claufes 23, 24, 25, 26, and 32. Gunpowder monopoly: Trained Bands difcouraged thereby, 232. Favours to Papift projectors. Seizures under Crown Commiffions. Commons taken from people, 233. Claufes 38, 39, 40, 41, 42, 43, 46, and 47. Patents of the Judges altered. Juftice intercepted, 234. Law and lawyers degraded. Old jurifdictions abufed, 235. New courts created. Rules of law unfettled, 236. Claufes 37, 51, 52, 53, 54, and 55. Ecclefiaftical tyranny, 236, 237. Star Chamber. High Commiffion and Council Table. Bifhops' Courts. People driven beyond feas. Extent of the Emigration, 238. Claufes 48, 50, 56, 57, 58, 59, and 60. Church preferments. Pulpit doctrines. Ufe and abufe of fheriffs, 239. Treatment of Patriots: excluded from offices and honours, 240, 241. Terrorifm and corruption, 241. Strafford's and Laud's predominance at Council, 241, 242. Claufes 61—67. Defign of the Court. Puritans the partition againft Rome: to be flung down, 242. Scotch Rebellion. Claufes 68—75. Strafford at the Council Board. His reafons for a Parliament, 243. His Irifh levies againft the Scots, 244.

Notes. Proclamation againft talking of a Parliament, 224. Wardfhip extortions. Coat and conduct money. Schedule of grievances (April 1640), 225. The tax leaft fupportable, 226. Hardfhips of Ship-money affeffment. Prifons filled. Hampden one of many recufants. Lord Saye's refiftance: decifion in his cafe, 227. Pym on Shipmoney. Not a light tax. Piracies in the Channel. Infults to Englifh flag, 228. Captures by Turks. Popular fympathy for Judge Hutton. Hyde's fpeech againft the Judges, 229. Bulftrode Whitelocke, 230. Project for brafs money, 1638. Falkland's reference thereto. Grimfton on denials of juftice, 231. Culpeper on protection of gunpowder, 232. Wilde and Clotworthy. Plunder of the poor, 233. Commiffions. Alleged defects in title deeds. Anecdote of a Judge, 234. Council Board tyranny. Policy of Keeper Finch. Courts of the houfehold. *Verney Papers*, 235. Death for ftealing Royal difh. Notices for infertions in Remonftrance, 236. Tragedies of Baftwick, Burton, and Prynne, 236, 237. Mutilations for confcience' fake. Rous's *Diary.* Cafe of a hat, 237. Wentworth on political fermons. Royalift preachers, 239. Hyde on the Council of the North, 239, 240. Anecdote of Hyde at York. Trouble at his lodgings. Landlady curfes and abufes him. The myftery explained, 240. Travelling between London and York, 241. Who were called Puritans, 242. *Diary* of Rous (March 1639). Prayers for a Parliament, 243.

b

4. *The Short Parliament and the Scottish Invasion* . 244—253

Text. Claufes 76—78. Claufes 79—84. Strafford's fatal Counfel, 244. Its refults. Diffolution of Short Parliament, 245. Claufes 85—87. Laud ftill moving to Rome, 246. Crown above the laws: Mitre above Crown, 246, 247. Church oppreffion, 247. Claufes 88—94. Defigns and power of Papifts, 247, 248. Secret meetings, 248. Agencies at Court and in Council. *Imperium in imperio*, 249. Claufes 95, 104. Prifons full. Non-parliamentary fupply exhaufted, 250. Difcontent of Lords: petitions for Parliament, 250, 251. The Scotch invafion. Parliament fummoned (3rd November, 1640), 253.

Notes. Strafford's advice (5th May, 1640), 244. Arrefts of Parliament men. Riots at Southwark and Lambeth. Allufions by Clarendon, 245. An honeft Judge. Sir Benjamin Rudyard, 246. Grimfton. Falkland, 247. Mafs connived at: conventicles made criminal, 247, 248. Favour to Papifts. Matters fubject to monopoly, 248. Speech by Rudyard. State and Church grievances infeparable, 249. Ruin of Old Monarchy. Yonge's *Diary*, 250. The York Declaration. Dangers to State and Church. Grievances of fubject. Innovations in religion, 251. Taxation without reprefentation. Parliament the only remedy. Story by Shaftefbury, 252. Firft refolve of the Court: fecond thoughts. Shaftefbury Papers, 253.

5. *Acts of the Long Parliament* . . . . . 253—258

Text. Claufes 105 and 110. Heroes of the Long Parliament, 253, 254. Their tafk. Claufes 106—9 and 111—124. Two armies paid. Twelve fubfidies raifed. Grievances redreffed, 254. Monopolies abolifhed, 255. Taxation reftored to Commons. Delinquents punifhed, 256. Claufes 127—136, 125 and 126, and 137—142. Overthrow of tyranny: ecclefiaftical and civil, 256, 257. How accomplifhed, 257. Two famous ftatutes. Other acts prepared: titles and objects thereof, 258.

Notes. Culpeper againft projectors. Swarm of monopolift vermin. Speech by Pym: fmall gain to King from large lofs to fubject, 255. Ralph Verney to James Dillon (1634), 256. Prynne's punifhment defcribed. Court of Requefts divifion, 257. Horror of impreffment, 258.

6. *Practices of the Court Party* . . . . . 259—265

Text. Claufes 143—153. Obftructions expected. Preferment of evil Counfellors. Reproach againft Houfe: of refufing to fupport the Crown, 259. A million and a half voted for the King. Claufes 154—161. Popular Bills paffed by King.

Contents.

Four great Acts recited, 260. No intention to weaken Crown by them. Restraints neceffary to fafety, 261. Claufes 162—168. Slanders againft the Parliament, 261, 262. Danger of hafty judgments. Comparifon with former Parliaments. Alleged excefs of privilege, 262. Claufes 169—180. The party hoftile to Parliaments. Intriguers with army. Promoters of Rebellion, 263. The Irifh tragedy, 264. Intended prologue to tragedy in England, 265.

Notes. Privileges from fuits at law, 262. Maffacres of Irifh Proteftants. Narrative by May, 264. Narrative by Rufhworth. Clarendon's account, 265.

7. *Defence of the Popular Leaders* . . . . 265—269

Text. Claufes 181—191. Hopes of Leaders of Commons, 265, 266. Reply to their affailants, 266. Champions of Epifcopacy : their flanders, 266, 267. Defign of the Bifhops' Bill. No intention to relax juft difcipline, 267. Conformity defired, 268. Suggeftion for a Synod : to fettle Church Government, 269 Defire to advance Learning : by reforming Univerfities, 269.

Notes. Idolatry in the Church, 267. Authorfhip of Remonftrance. Afcribed to Pym. Parallel paffages from Pym's *Vindication*, 268.

8. *Remedial Meafures demanded* . . . . 269—273

Text. Claufes 192—206. Demands made, 269, 270. Settlement of Monarchy with limitations. (i.) Safeguards againft Roman Catholic Religion, 270. Suggefted Commiffion, 271. (ii.) Securities for adminiftration of laws. (iii.) Protection againft evil Counfellors. Parliament to be confulted in choice of minifters, 272. Minifters to be made fubject to laws. Clofing prayer of Remonftrance, 273.

Notes. Pym's view as to Popery : diflike of the Statefman, not the Bigot, 270. The King's tendencies to Rome. Compact for reftoration of Epifcopacy. Propofed invitation to the French, 271. Englifh Statefmen : and foreign penfions, 273, 274.

XIII. THE HOUSE AND ITS MEMBERS : 22ND NOVEMBER, 1641 . . . . 273—285

Text. Monday, 22nd November. King approaching London, 273, 274. Ten o'clock A.M. Speaker late. Petition from Moniers, 274. Diftinction between Commonwealth and King. Pym on Ireland. Twelve o'clock A.M. Dinnerhour. Cries for Order of the Day, 275. Hyde's motion to gain time. The Old Houfe of Commons. Weftminfter

xx   *Contents.*

PAGE

Hall. Famous Affociations, 276. Pym and Hyde. Shops
in the Hall. Place of refort: for M.P.'s, lawyers and clients,
277. St. Stephen's Chapel. Its old interior. Officers of
Houfe. Honourable Members, 278. Pofition of Mr. Speaker.
Richard King's attack on Lenthal, 279. Hon. Mr. John
Digby: his difrefpect to Houfe: rebuked by Lenthal, 279,
280. Mr. Speaker's powers, 280. Lenthal's weaknefs, 281.
Magifter Venter. Houfe emptied by dinner-bell, 282. Where
leading Members fit. Sir Simonds D'Ewes: taking his
notes, 283. Marten and Pym, Culpeper, Hyde, Falkland
and Palmer. Vane and King's Minifters, 284. Independent
Members. Hampden, Waller, Cromwell, Hollis, and Selden.
The lawyers, 285.

Notes. Efcape of Weftminfter Hall from fire, 277. Selden
and the Digbys. Digby on his ladder and the ape on
houfe-top. D'Ewes and Lenthal, 280. A quarrel on
point of order. D'Ewes lectures Mr. Speaker. Lenthal's fubmiffion, 281. Pym's dinner parties. An evening ride, 282. Places of Members in Houfe, 283.
Mode of referring to Members, 284, 285.

§ XIV. SPEECHES OF HYDE, FALKLAND, DERING, RUDYARD,
AND BAGSHAW . . . . 286—299

Text. Eighth Debate: Monday, 22nd November. Hyde
fpeaks. Doubts Houfe's right to remonftrate, 286. Objections to form and language: unjuft to King, 286, 287. Lord
Falkland fpeaks. King's right to name his own Minifters,
287. Defends Laud. Dangers of Remonftrance, 288.
Apology for Bifhops: and Popifh Lords, 288, 289. Sir
Edward Dering fpeaks: not difcreetly, 289, 290, 291. Urges
importance of Remonftrance. But why carry it to the people? People want only good laws, 291. Remonftrate to
King: but not downward to people. Agrees with Falkland. Church regulation no fubject for Parliament, 292.
Advocates Prizes in Church. Would not fplit moons into
ftars. Final reafons for adverfe vote, 293. Rudyard fpeaks.
His Character by May. Favourable to a Declaration, 294.
Great acts of the Parliament. Neceffity to defend it againft
libels. States one objection to Remonftrance, 295. Would
only mention Acts paffed: not Bills in progrefs or intended.
Subfequent attacks on Rudyard. A poet and friend of poets,
296. Joins the Parliament. Unfit for all its duties, 297.
Sayings and doings. Conduct in old age. No apoftate, 298.
Acting in Houfe till his death (æt. 87). Mr. Bagfhaw fpeaks:
againft the Remonftrance, 299.

Notes. Hyde's wordinefs in fpeaking, 286. Allufion to Eliot
in Remonftrance: incorrectly quoted by Hyde, 287.
Dering's publication of his fpeeches. Ordered to be

Contents.

burnt. Origin of penny-a-lining, 289. Reported speeches never spoken: Royalist petitions forged: work of poor scholars in ale-houses. Verney's *Notes*, 290. Sydney Smith anticipated, 293. Poem to Rudyard by Ben Jonson, 296. Epigrams addressed by Jonson, 297.

XV. SPEECHES OF CULPEPER, PYM, BRIDGMAN, WALLER, AND HAMPDEN . . . . . . 300—308

Text. Sir John Culpeper speaks. Manner of speaking, 300. Objects to Remonstrance: not necessary: and dangerous in form. People not to be addressed alone. Pym speaks, 301. Answers preceding speakers, 301, 302. Replies to Hyde: replies to Falkland. Claim of Parliament to advise King, 302. Right to control Ministers. Replies to Culpeper. Replies to Dering. Slanders against Parliament, 303. As to Church Prizes. Remarks on Rudyard. Replies to Bagshaw. Opposes Lords' claim to share in Remonstrance, 304. An act of Commons, not of Lords or King. Appeal to people from representatives. Orlando Bridgman speaks. Replies to Pym, 305. Edmund Waller speaks. Laws not to yield to Orders. Why control the King? John Hampden speaks, 307. Why object to declaration? Replies to Dering. Quotes and applies Revelations, 307.

Notes. Character of Culpeper. Remark by Hyde: more applicable to Pym, 300. Hampden's quotation, 307.

XVI. THE SPEECHES UP TO MIDNIGHT . . . 308—313

Text. Hampden resumes seat (9 o'clock P.M.). Why D'Ewes had left at 4 o'clock. Attempts at compromise resisted, 308. Two divisions, 309. (i.) 187 to 123. (ii.) 161 to 147. Denzil Hollis speaks. People to be influenced. Power of House to declare singly, 310. Right to control King's advisers. Glyn speaks. Precedents for Remonstrance. Reasons in its favour, 311. Mr. Coventry speaks. Geoffrey Palmer speaks. Maynard speaks, 312. Midnight approaching. Secretary Nicholas retires. Writes to the King. Reveals Hyde's purpose, 313.

Notes. Subject of first division. Remark by D'Ewes. Tellers, 309. Second division, 310. Speaker's eye, rule of precedence, 311.

XVII. QUESTION PUT, AND PALMER'S PROTEST . 314—322

Text. Resistance to putting question. Which side gained by delay, 314. Hyde's statement: Whitelocke's: reasons to the contrary, 315. Truth of the case. Numbers on first division (310): on second division (308), 316. Numbers on third division (307). New question raised. Clarendon's

Narrative, 317. As to Hyde's proteſt: as to Palmer's: as to others: as to cloſe of debate: as to incidents in its progreſs. A tiſſue of misſtatements, 318, 319. Real mover of printing, 319. Mr. Peard, 320. True objeƈt of "Proteſters." To divide and deſtroy authority of Houſe, 321. Why ſo reſolutely reſiſted. Exiſtence of Houſe involved. Unexampled ſcene, 322.

Notes. Whitelocke's *Memorials*: not reliable, 315. Numbers commonly preſent in Houſe, 316. Change by Clarendon's firſt editors, 317. Hyde and Hampden. D'Ewes on Hampden. Art of making uſe of others: open to misjudgment, 320. Clarendon's charaƈter of Hampden. A governor of men, 321.

§ XVIII. VALLEY OF THE SHADOW OF DEATH . . 322—327

Text. Remonſtrance carried (by 159 to 148), 322. Denzil Hollis aƈting with Pym. Peard moves printing. Hyde oppoſes. Confuſed debate. Members proteſting, 323. Palmer moves to take down names: of all claiming to proteſt, 323, 324. Cries of "All, all." Palmer proteſts for "All." Sudden fury of excitement. "I thought we had all ſat in "the Valley of the Shadow of Death" (Philip Warwick), 324. Swords ready for miſchief. Parallel from Saul's Wars. Calmneſs of Hampden. Shows Palmer's preſumption, 325. How ſhould he anſwer for "all." The Houſe calmed. Printing to be left unſettled, 326. Fourth diviſion: 124 to 101. Houſe riſes (2 A.M.), 326, 327. What Cromwell ſaid of the Vote. Turning-point of freedom or deſpotiſm, 327.

§ XIX. SITTING OF TUESDAY, THE 23RD NOVEMBER . 327—331

Text. Tueſday, 23rd November. Houſe meets at 10 o'clock, 327, 328. Buſineſs in hand. Four, P.M. Pym refers to laſt night's ſcene, 328. Miſchievous claim put forward: to be diſcuſſed next day, 328, 329. The truth, and Clarendon's verſion of it. As to party counſels. Impoſſible as ſtated, 329. As to a purpoſe againſt himſelf: rejeƈted by Northern men. As to diſputes among the leaders. Not confirmed by D'Ewes or Verney, 330. Why not credible. Refuted by MS. of D'Ewes, 331.

Notes. D'Ewes correƈts Clarendon, 329. Clarendon's diſtinƈtion between himſelf and Palmer, 330, 331.

§ XX. DEBATE ON PALMER'S PROTEST . . . 331—343

Text. Ninth Debate: Wedneſday, 24th November. Pym denounces ſcandalous prints, 331. Complaints of Pamphleteers. Referred to Committee for abuſes of printing. Pym ſpeaks againſt "Proteſt," 332. Shows its danger. Hyde defends it:

Contents. xxiii

PAGE

amid clamour. Why not Commons as well as Lords? 333.
Repeats proteft againft printing. Suggeftion by Strode: difregarded. Mr. Hotham fpeaks, 334. Attacks Palmer: as
leader of a mutiny, 334, 335. Moves to have him fent for.
Palmer enters. Conflict of friends and foes, 335. Hyde
fupports Palmer. Too late to require him to anfwer. Culpeper on fame fide. Members to be queftioned only at
fpeaking, 336. Denzil Hollis makes new charge. D'Ewes
fpeaks. Replies to Hyde. Exhibits precedents, 337. Members not queftionable elfewhere: but by the Houfe at any
time. Judgment of Houfe never avoidable. Error in Culpeper's argument, 338. Future parliament may queftion
paft. Houfe unchanged by abfence of members. D'Ewes's
own abfence at midnight of Monday, 339. Would have
Palmer fpeak. D'Ewes proud of his logic. Palmer's
friends prevent his rifing. A divifion called for, 340.
Hyde moves addition to queftion, 340, 341. Defeated by
192 to 146. Original queftion carried by 190 to 142.
Palmer required to fpeak, 341. His defence. Hampden's
queftion. Apology. Whitelocke fupports Palmer. Mr.
Speaker cannot fee hon. members. Subject to be refumed to-
morrow. Adjournment at dark (4·30), 343.

Notes. Clarendon's account of opening of debate, 332.
Hyde and Palmer, 333. Hyde reported by himfelf, 336.
A correction not legible, 337. Pym's vigilance, 343.

§ XXI. PALMER'S PUNISHMENT AND SUBMISSION . 343—355

Text. Tenth Debate: Thurfday, 25th November, 343. Petition
to accompany Remonftrance, 343, 344. Referred to Committee. Tonnage and Poundage Bill. Palmer's Debate
called for, 344. Speeches on either fide. In aggravation of
offence. Scene it had occafioned. In extenuation of offence,
345. Interference of Hampden. Palmer's previous fervice.
Delays reforted to. Refolution of majority to punifh, 346.
Gravity of the act attempted: to place minority above
majority, 346, 347. Punifhment demanded. Hotham and
others for expulfion, 347. Speeches by friends of Palmer:
Strangways and Bagfhaw. Crew comes to refcue, 348.
Suggefts reprimand by Mr. Speaker. Reminds Houfe of
Palmer's fervices. Waller on fame fide: lefs difcreet, 349.
Too many penalties for fmall offences. Do not punifh tem-
perance. Anger of Hotham. Suggeftion by Sir Ralph
Hopton, 350. Replied to by D'Ewes. Ufages of the Houfe.
Queftions put, 351. Shall Palmer be fent to Tower? Yes:
by 169 to 128. Shall he be expelled? No: by 163 to
131. Houfe adjourns, 351, 352. Friday 26th Nov. Palmer
appears at Bar, 352. Is committed. 8th December fends in
petition and is releafed. Refults of Palmer's punifhment.

Contents.

Clarendon's *History* (ii. 61-2). Series of misstatements, 353. Alleged ground of hostility to Palmer. No truth therein, 354. False averment as to printing, 354, 355. *Notes.* Clarendon "letting himself loose," 347. Pembroke Lord Steward. Crew at Uxbridge, 348. Clarendon's account of Palmer's committal, 354.

§ XXII. PETITION TO ACCOMPANY REMONSTRANCE . 355—366

Text. Eleventh Debate: 27th November. King's arrival. Impolitic acts. Order as to religion, 355. Guard to Parliament dismissed. Excitement in House. Hampden speaking, 356. Oliver Cromwell. Suggestion for defence of kingdom. Referred to Committee, 357. Remonstrance Petition brought in. Abstract of its contents. Why King's presence desired. Zeal of evil Counsellors, 359. Declaration prepared: to point out dangers to State and King. Why such warnings necessary, 360. Three closing requests: (i.) To abridge Bishops' power. (ii.) To remove ill Counsellors. (iii.) To apply Irish forfeitures to public needs, 360, 361. Pym answers objections. A point of order. Hampden restores quiet. D'Ewes explains usage of House, 362. Culpeper in fault, not Pym. "Well moved." Pym answers Culpeper. Petition read again: and debated in detail, 364. D'Ewes attacks Bishops. House adopt his views. Further objections by Hyde: and Mr. Coventry, 364. Replied to by D'Ewes. Urges study of Rolls. Pym's moderation, 365.

Notes. Question as to Guard. King's message, 356. Tuesday, 20th November. King's design as to Guard, 357. Personal reasons. Pym's counter reasons. Plots in progress. Attack on Parliament expected, 358. Unsafe without their own Guard, 358, 359. Changes proposed in Petition, 361. Unaltered Petition sent to Court, 365. Secret communication with the King, 366.

§ XXIII. THE KING RECEIVES REMONSTRANCE AND PETITION . . . . 366—372

Text. Tuesday, 30th November. Petition engrossed. Committee named to wait on King, 366. Its members. Several King's friends. Pym withdraws his name. Dering to read Petition to King, 367. Declines, and Hopton chosen. Thursday, 2nd December. Hopton's report. Reception by Charles. Hopton reading Petition, 368. Interruptions by King. The Bear and the Bear's skin. Committee questioned: "Do you mean to *publish?*" King's answer to Petition, 369. Close of interview. Message before departure. No pledge *not* to publish. Incitements to publication, 370. Hostile acts against House. King's purpose unmasked. Hyde and friends invited to office, 371.

Notes. D'Ewes's remark on deputation, 368.

Contents.

§ XXIV. RETALIATION AND REVENGE . . 372—375

Text. Tamperings with command of Tower. Popular commotion, 372. New King's Guard. People fired upon. 30th November, A.M. Houſes difmifs King's Guard, 373. Ominous precaution. The end approaching. Witty remark by Selden, 374. Doctor Chillingworth's difcloſure, 375.
Notes. Preparing for act of violence, 372. Lord Dorſet, 373. *Commons' Journals* (30th November). Selden's *Table Talk*, 374.

§ XXV. ALLEGED INTIMIDATION OF PARLIAMENT . 375—384

Text. Hyde's plot. Parliament "not free." King's plea of coercion, 375. Minority againſt majority. 30th November, P.M. Charge againſt Citizens. Charge againſt Members. Shall we not give votes freely? 376. Strangways afks for committee. Is required to ſtate complaint. Story of an apprentice, 377. Some members to be overawed by others. "Name! Name!" Kirton names Ven. Houſe prevents Ven's anſwer, 378. Pym's queſtion to the Speaker. 2nd and 3rd December. Debates on popular gatherings. Waller, Strode, and Culpeper. D'Ewes defends the citizens. Culpeper interrupts, 379. Earle and D'Ewes to order. Culpeper explains. D'Ewes replies. Houſe ſupports D'Ewes, 380. Culpeper filenced. Pym's motion againſt Upper Houſe. Stoppage of uſeful bills, 381. Will minority of Lords join majority of Commons in a proteſt? Counter propoſition by Godolphin, 382. Hopes of Court party. Views of Mr. Speaker, 383. Monday, 6th December. Cromwell on breach of Privilege, 383, 384. Peers' interference with elections. Tueſday, 7th December. A ſtartling propoſal, 384. Dangers from army intrigues. Diſtruſt of the King, 385.
Notes. D'Ewes's MS. A ſcene in "Gracious" Street, 377. Obſtructions in Upper Houſe, 381. Pym's appeal to Lords: Do not leave us to ſave the country alone, 382. *Commons' Journals* (3rd December and 7th December), 383.

§ XXVI. AN OMINOUS PROPOSAL . . . . 385—393

Text. Tueſday, 7th December. Bill preſented by Haſelrig: for ſettling the Militia, 385. Account in the D'Ewes MS. Bill angrily received. Culpeper moves its rejection. Barrington againſt. Strode and D'Ewes for. Cook cites precedent againſt, 386. Mallory would have bill burnt. Cook called up: ordered to withdraw. Had miſquoted precedent, 387. D'Ewes expoſes and laughs at him, 387, 388. Cook admoniſhed. Bill read a firſt time (158 to 125), 388. Same

Contents.

PAGE

incident told with ſtrange variations, 388, 389. Clarendon's *Hiſtory* (ii. 76, 80). Motion made as to Militia: how treated, 389. Hyde replied to by Solicitor General. St. John brings in a bill, 390. Clarendon's *Hiſtory* (i. 486): ſame incident again told, 390, 391. Quite different account of ſame faƈts, 391. Bill brought in by Hazelrig: drawn by St. John: who defends and explains it, 391, 392. Never read ſecond time. Alleged rejeƈtion. Error as to firſt reading. Carried (by 158 to 125), 392. Miſtakes and confuſion. Hiſtorians miſled. Nalſon no authority, 393.

Notes. Commons' Journals (ii. 334). Verney's *Notes* (p. 132), 388.

§ XXVII. THE CITY PETITION . . . . . 393—401

Text. Wedneſday, 8th Dec. Friday, 10th. New Guard on Houſes, 393, 394. Agitation thereat. By whom placed. Writ from Lord Keeper, 394. Voted breach of privilege. Halberdiers removed. Lords ſtartled as well as Commons, 395. " Shut the door!" Member quits Houſe without leave, 395, 396. Rebuked by Pym. 11th Dec: Sheriff and Magiſtrates reprimanded. The City petition, 396. Its arrival announced. Brought by twelve citizens, 397. Received by Clerk. Its dimenſions. Addreſs to the Chief of Deputation. Reply of Mr. Speaker, 398. Debate as to Ireland. Queſtion of printing Remonſtrance revived. Reſolve thereon, 399. Tueſday, 14th Dec., Meſſage from King: reſpeƈting bill under diſcuſſion, 399, 400. Voted breach of privilege. Proteſt carried to King, 400. Reſolve taken, 401.

Notes. Points of form and order, 393, 394. *Commons' Journals* (ii. 338), 395. The City 220 years ago, 396. Source of its power. Its ſupport of popular cauſe, 397. Charge againſt St. John. Not credible, 400. Curious notices from the D'Ewes MS., 400, 401. Deputation preſent proteſt. Archbiſhop Williams reads it, 401. King's anſwer: read by Nicholas, 401, 402. Anger of the King, 402.

XXVIII. THE LAST DEBATE . . . . . 402—408

Text. Twelfth and laſt Debate: 15th Dec. Pureſoy moves printing. A great ſilence, 402. Argument for printing: will recover People to Houſe, 402, 403. Surpriſe of D'Ewes and others. Peard ſeconds Pureſoy. Waller oppoſes, 403. Debate prolonged to evening. Candles called for. Sir Nicholas Slanning oppoſes. An eager royaliſt, 404. Forces diviſion: on queſtion for candles, 405, 406. Candles brought (152 to 53). Diviſion for printing. Carried (135 to 83), 406. Printing ordered. Slanning revives claim to

protest. Storm allayed by Pym, 407. Monday, 20th Dec.
Debate on right to protest, 407, 408. Ominous remark by
Holborne. Resolution against Hyde's party, 408.
Notes. Great men of little size. Hales of Eton. Chillingworth. Sidney Godolphin. Falkland, 405. Picture by Clarendon (*Life*, i. 43, 44), 405, 406. Right to protest rejected, 408.

§ XXIX. IMPOSSIBILITY OF COMPROMISE . . . 408—414

Text. Result of Remonstrance Debates. Popular leaders averse to war. Indecision of Charles. Bankes (C.J.) attempts to mediate with King, 409. Like attempts of leaders in both Houses. Lord Wharton. Denzil Hollis. Lord Say and Seale, 410. Lord Essex. Lord Northumberland. Objects of Court party. To weaken and degrade Parliaments, 411. Small part in a great scene: creditably played. Character of Bankes (C.J.) unwisely compared with Coke (C.J.), 412. Coke's claims. The Institutes and the Petition of Right. Party views for and against Charles. A plain case up to the war, 413. A case more perplexing, 414.

§ XXX. CONCLUSION . . . . 414—421

Text. Limited scope of present work : to restore an effaced page in History, 414. Object of Notes appended. Clarendon's *History*. Its beauties. Its demerits, 415. Its author confronted with contemporaries. Result decisive against him. Misstatements no longer possible. Ludicrous errors, 416. D'Israeli's *Commentaries* (ii. 294). Effect of Remonstrance on the people: its vindication: and measure of its importance, 417. Its subsequent influence. Confessed by Hyde. Recruiting-serjeant for Civil War. Motives of its authors: in so appealing to the people. To save the ancient monarchy, 418, 419. Civil and religious freedom not separable. Rights demanded by' Remonstrance. Leaders of the Long Parliament, 419. Their genius and greatness. Their patience and endurance. Their respect for old precedents and laws, 420. Reverence due to them, 421.

INDEX . . 423

THE DEBATES

ON THE

GRAND REMONSTRANCE.

INTRODUCTORY ESSAY.

§ 1. The Plantagenets.

I PROPOSE to introduce an attempt to re-describe, with greater fullnefs and accuracy, fome leading events in the political ftruggle of the Seventeenth Century, by a fketch of the earlier efforts for freedom in the Plantagenet and Tudor reigns. From the circumftances that attended the gradual growth of our liberties, were drawn ever the moft powerful arguments for their maintenance and defence; and it is impoffible clearly to underftand the pofition in this refpect taken up by Charles the Firft's opponents, without fome knowledge of the grounds on which they refted their claim to connect with the old laws and ufages of England, their refiftance to the tyranny of the Stuarts.

One of the nobleft images in the writings of Burke, is that in which he fays of the fpirit of Englifh Freedom that, always acting as if in the prefence of canonifed forefathers, it carries

Purpofe of this Effay.

Pofition taken up by Charles the Firft's opponents.

Records and titles of Englifh Freedom.

2   *Introductory Essay.*

Burke on our History.

an impoſing and majeſtic aſpect. "It has "a pedigree and illuſtrating anceſtors. It has "its bearings and its enſigns armorial. It has "its gallery of portraits, its monumental in- "ſcriptions, its records, evidences, and titles." For collecting and producing them, Selden was thrice impriſoned by James the Firſt and his Son; and the part which they played in that ſtruggle with the Stuarts, was but the revival, in more powerful form, of an influence they had exerted over the Plantagenets and the Tudors. As in later, ſo it had been in the

Precedents in older Time.

earlier time. The Petition of Right, enacted in Charles the Firſt's reign, was but the affirmation and re-enactment of the precedents of three foregoing centuries; and in the reign of John, when the Barons were in treaty for the Great Charter, Langton put forward, as the baſis and title of their claims, a charter of a hundred years' earlier date.

Charter of Henry I. 1100.

That was the enactment of the firſt year of Henry Beauclerc, the firſt of the name, and the third of our Norman kings. It was ſuppoſed to be the only copy then in exiſtence; ſo aſſiduous Henry's officers had been, in the more ſecure years of his reign, to deſtroy the evidence of his recognition of popular rights at

Difficulty of ſuppreſſing a Charter.

the outſet of his uſurpation. But he could not depreſs the people for his pleaſure, when already he had raiſed them for his gain. They are edged tools, theſe popular compacts and conceſſions; and not ſo ſafe to play the game of diſſimulation with, as a friendly nod or greeting to the friend you purpoſe to betray. "Does he ſmile and ſpeak well of me?" ſaid

§ 1. The Plantagenets: Henry I.

one of the chief justiciaries of this King. "Then I am undone. I never knew him praise a man whom he did not intend to ruin." It was truly said, as the speaker soon had occasion to know; but it is more difficult so to deal with a people. A charter of relief from onerous and unreasonable burdens, once granted, is never more to be resumed as a mere waste piece of parchment. The provisions of which men have lost the memory, and are thought to have lost the proof, reappear at the time of vital need; and the prince into whose violent keeping a people's liberties have fallen, is made subject to a sharp responsibility. For the most part, unhappily, history is read as imperfectly as it is written. Beneath the surface to which the obscurity of distant records too commonly restricts us, there lies material to be yet brought to light, less by laborious research than by patient thought and careful induction. Conceding to the early chroniclers their particular cases of oppression, subjection, and acquiescence, let us well assure ourselves that these will not prevail for any length of time against an entire and numerous people. If ever rulers might have hoped to measure their immunities and rights by the temper and strength of their swords, it should have been these early Norman princes; yet at every turn in their story, at every casualty in their chequered fortunes, they owe their safety to the fact of flinging down their spoil. A something which, under various names, represents the People, is still upon their track; and thus, over our rudest history, there lies at

Henry I.

Royal concessions not resumable.

Imperfect judgments in History.

Strength and weakness of Norman Kings.

4 *Introductory Essay.*

leaſt a ſhadow of the ſubſtance which fills our later and nobler annals.

<small>Baſis of Saxon Conſtitution.</small> The baſis of the Saxon Conſtitution reſted wholly on the mutual correction, and relative ſuſtainment and ſupport, of two oppoſite powers; that of the King exerted through a prerogative juriſdiction, and that of the People expreſſed through their various courts and guilds. Nor does it admit of queſtion that, ſubſtantially, <small>Adopted by the Conqueror and his ſons.</small> the Conqueror and his ſons adopted the Saxon juriſprudence, and that it continued to be the baſis of the common law. Every ſubſequent alteration operated upon it; and though the action of time and circumſtance made thoſe alterations conſiderable, there was little direct change by poſitive enactment. The notion which long prevailed that the Feudal Syſtem was firſt introduced into England at the Conqueſt has been diſproved by modern inquiry. <small>Origin of Feudality.</small> All the rudiments and germs of the feudal ſervices exiſted in the Germanic nations; and whether theſe were grown in their foreſts, or had been derived in any degree from what they ſaw of the ſyſtem of the Empire, is not very material. As early as Tacitus, every chieftain had his band of retainers, who honoured him in peace, and followed him in war; and that an artificial connection ſhould gradually have ariſen, reciprocally binding the lord to his vaſſal, and the vaſſal to his lord, renders it eaſy to underſtand the growth of <small>Its burdens and modes of tenure.</small> the entire ſyſtem of feudality. In what way its more onerous incidents and obligations aroſe opens up wider conſiderations. But there is reaſon to believe that even theſe had made

§ 1. *The Plantagenets: Henry I.*

considerable advance under the Saxons, though not to the exclusion of other modes of tenure, before the subtle and elaborate Norman devices were grafted on them. The Saxon king certainly claimed the right of wardship, though less often, and in simpler and less oppressive form, than in the Norman time; and the acknowledgment, by oath, of the obligation in a feud as reciprocal and binding on both parties, is known as early as Alfred's reign. As that obligation took more settled shape, the system developed itself in largely civilising and humanising forms. The compact implied on both sides fixed rights and settled duties, and made Protection as sacred as Service. It led gradually, in short, to the feud becoming a life-estate; from which, as an almost natural consequence, the principle of hereditary succession arose; every new occupant making still his acknowledgment of vassalage, and binding himself as fully as the first grantee. Nor did it require much forethought to discern, that the perfect development of this system would end in a mutual arrangement of legally binding obligations and legally maintainable rights, in the course and action of which the very life of the relation of vassalage would expire. {.sidenote Natural consequences of the Feudal System. Its development. Hereditary Succession. Extinction of Vassalage.}

Contemporaneous with Henry the First's charter were the first great victories of the Crusades, which led to the sacrifice of many millions of lives, and had the effect not only greatly to increase the temporal power and ecclesiastical domination of the Popedom, but to begin the terrible story of religious wars. Yet {.sidenote The Crusades.}

they had alfo good refults, to which the exifting condition of the world gave a preponderating influence. What there was of merit in the feudal inftitutions had here taken a higher and more fpiritual character, largely abating their ferocity and fomewhat leffening their injuftice. A troubadour of the century now begun called Jerufalem a fief of Jefus Chrift; and in the expreffion may be traced the origin of the Crufader's fenfe of his bond and vaffalage to the Son of God. To his fancy, he was now firmly eftablifhing a reciprocity of obedience and protection between himfelf and heaven. The union alfo, which the Crufades effected, of different countries in a common object, had a tendency to diffipate many narrow hindrances to a common civilifation; and the intercourfe of eaftern and weftern nations by degrees introduced into religion, as well as into government, larger and more humane views. The pecuniary obligations incurred by the feudal chiefs, led at the fame time to a wider circulation of money, and made further gradual but fure encroachment on the ftricter domains of feudalifm. Finally, we owe it mainly to the Crufades, that the enrichment of the ports of Italy, by fuch fudden avenues to trade, became an important element in the advance to a higher and more refined fyftem of fociety; and that, fcattered through the wandering paths of Troubadour or Dominican, the feeds of eloquence and fong fprang up in later days, and in many countries, into harvefts of national literature.

Feudal Inftitutions improved.

Influences of Chriftianity.

Seeds of Commerce and Literature.

Henry II. Some of thefe advantages began to be felt

§ 1. *The Plantagenets: Henry II.*

even so early as under the first and greatest of the Plantagenet kings. It was in Henry the Second's reign that personal services of the feudal vassals were exchanged for pecuniary aids; that, by the issue of a new coinage of standard weight and purity, confidence was given to towns and cities, then struggling into importance by the help of charters and fiscal exemptions; that it was made the duty of the itinerant judges to see that all free men were provided with competent arms and means of defence; that the most oppressive baronial tyrannies received a check from the Crown; and that further settled guarantees for internal tranquillity were given by a more orderly, equal, and certain administration of the laws. Yet even such services to civilisation yield in importance to that which was rendered by this great prince in resisting the usurpations of the Church. His dispute with his Primate involved essentially little less than the ultimate question of the entire arrangement of human society. Not seventy years had passed since the voice of Hildebrand had declared the papal throne to be but the temporal emblem of a universal spiritual authority, holding absolute feudal jurisdiction over the lesser authority of kings and nobles; and Becket stood upon the claim so put forth by Hildebrand. Like him, he would have turned human government into a theocracy, placing the Church at its head, unquestioned and supreme. He would have drawn together the whole of Christian Europe under one sole Suzerain authority, and, through all the wide and various extent of civilised

[marginal notes:] First Plantagenet King. 1154. Gains to civil freedom. Dispute of Henry II. and his Primate. Becket's scheme.

nations, would have made the ſpiritual tyranny of Rome the centre and metropolis of dominion. To Henry Plantagenet, on the other hand, it ſeemed that any ſuch centraliſation of eccleſiaſtical power would be fatal to the peace, the happineſs, and the liberty of the world. He had laboured hard, with his Chancellor Becket, to reduce all autocracies and tyrannies within his kingdom; and againſt his Primate Becket, he now reſolutely declared that this work ſhould ſtill go on. Whether ſpiritual intereſts were, or were not, of higher importance than temporal intereſts, was not neceſſarily the queſtion implied; any more than whether a firm belief in Chriſtianity ſhould involve a total ſubjection of the underſtanding, of the heart and the will, of the active and the intellectual powers, to eccleſiaſtical domination. Not ſo, happily for the people whom he governed, was this reſolute prince diſpoſed to renounce his ſocial and civil duties. In events that aroſe as the conteſt went on, he was rude, paſſionate, and overbearing; and perhaps much of the work he was called to do, by more delicate ways could hardly have been done: but, though what he had nobly gained was thus at times in danger of being ignobly loſt, there ſeldom fails to be viſible, throughout all the reckleſs impulſes of that really majeſtic though ill-regulated nature, a ſtrong comprehenſion of the vital truth which was afterwards wrought out with ſuch breadth and potency in England. And on the whole it was certainly well that Henry the Second's triumph ſhould not have been on all points complete.

Henry's oppoſition.

What the ſtruggle involved.

Character of Henry.

Complete victory to either not deſirable.

§ 1. *The Plantagenets: Henry II.*

Notwithstanding the spiritual despotism which the Church would fain have established, we cannot forget what the Church in those rude times represented and embodied; and for the utter discomfiture and overthrow of which, any absolute supremacy of the State and the sword would have been but a poor compensation. What it was well that the King should retain, he did not lose; and though neither did Becket entirely forfeit what his arrogance too rashly put in peril, substantially the victory remained with Henry. Asserting the necessary rights of temporal princes, and upholding the independent vigour of civil government, he defended and maintained, in effect, religious liberty and equal laws; and the soil was not unprepared to receive that wholesome seed, even so early as the reign of the first Plantagenet. *What was due to the Church. What Henry II. gained.*

The most distinguished associate of Henry in his civil labours was the famous Ranulf de Glanvile, in whose name is written the most ancient and memorable treatise of the laws and customs of England; and the greatest act they jointly performed was to give authority, universality, and settled form and circumstance, to a practice which was only very imperfectly introduced in the time of Henry Beauclerc, and had been, since then, carried out still less perfectly. In a Great Council at Northampton, Henry formally divided the kingdom into six districts, to each of which he assigned three itinerant judges, and from that time circuits have never ceased in England: carrying gradually with them (in consequence of other improvements introduced by this great and sagacious *Ranulf de Glanvile, Tractatus de Legibus et Consuetudinibus Regni Angliæ.* 1176. *Appointment of circuits for judges.*

prince) the general adoption of juries, an elevation of the character of the judges, and other settled advantages in jurisprudence as well as in legal administration, felt to this hour.

Richard I. 1189. The reign of the second of the Plantagenet family supplies to our constitutional historian, in the sentence passed on the Chancellor of the absent King by the convention of barons, the earliest authority on record for the responsibility of Ministers to Parliament. The incident, however, important as it is, seems rather to take its place with others in the same reign, *New relations between throne and barons.* which mark the springing up of a new condition of relations between the baronage and the throne. In the obstinate absence of Cœur-de-Lion on his hair-brained enterprises, the inaptitude and imbecility of his brother had thrown all the real duties of government into the hands of a council of barons; these again *Independent opposition to Crown.* were opposed by men of their own class, as well for self-interest as on general and independent grounds; and the result of a series of quarrels thus conducted between equals, as it were, in station, between forces to a great degree independent of each other—the Crown striving to maintain itself on the one hand, but no longer with the prestige of power it had received from the stronger kings; the Aristocracy advancing claims on the other, no longer overborne or overawed by the present pressure of the throne *Beginning of struggles of party.* —led to what, in modern phrase, might be called a system of unscrupulous party struggle, in which royalty lost the exclusive position it had been the great aim of the Conqueror's family to secure to it, and became an unguarded

§ 1. *The Plantagenets : Arthur.*

object of attack, thereafter, to whatever hostile confederacy might be formed against it.

What there was of evil as well as of good in the contest became strongly manifest in the two succeeding reigns.

In the strict order of hereditary succession the crown, which on Richard's death was conferred on John, would have fallen to Arthur, the orphan of John's elder brother. But though the subsequent misfortunes and sorrowful death of this young prince largely excited sympathy in England, there was never any formidable stand attempted, here, on the ground of his right to the throne. The battle was fought in the foreign provinces. In England, while some might have thought his hereditary claim superior to his uncle's, there was hardly a man of influence who would at this period have drawn the sword for him, on any such principle as that the crown of England was heritable property. The genius of the country had been repugnant to any such notion. The Anglo-Saxon sovereignty was elective; that people never sanctioning a custom by which the then personal and most arduous duties of sovereignty, both in peace and war, might pass of right to an infant or imbecile prince; and to the strength of this feeling in the country of their conquest, the Normans heretofore had been obliged to yield. At each successive coronation following the defeat of Harold, including that of the Conqueror, the form of deferring to the people's choice had been religiously adhered to; nay, of the five Norman kings on whom the English crown had now descended, four had

Arthur's claim to the succession:

fought only in French provinces.

The English Crown not heritable property.

Sovereignty elective.

Normans defer to Saxon principle.

been conſtrained to reſt their ſtrongeſt title on that popular choice or recognition: but its moſt deciſive confirmation was reſerved for the coronation of John. Till after the ceremony, his right was in no particular admitted. He was earl, until he aſſumed the ducal coronet; and he was duke, until the Great Council, ſpeaking through the primate, inveſted him at Weſtminſter with the Engliſh crown, accompanying it with the emphatic declaration that it was the nation's gift, and not the property of any particular perſon. Speed, with his patient induſtry and narrow viſion, calls this latter condition, "a ſecond ſeed-plot of trea-"ſons;" but for the moſt part it has happened, throughout our Engliſh hiſtory, that treaſons have been the ſecond ſeed-plot of liberty. Other hiſtorical critics imagine John's coronation to have been a mere arrangement of conditional fealty ſpecially reſtricted to him; the ſole temptation to elect him, in preference to his nephew, being the conſideration that leſs was to be looked for in the way of civil reſtitution from a legitimate monarch, than from one who held by elective tenure. But theſe reaſoners overlook, not only the fact that the law of ſucceſſion as between a living brother and a dead brother's child was by no means ſettled at this time, but that, as has juſt been pointed out, the choice of a monarch on grounds excluſively hereditary would have been the exception and not the rule. If anything beyond the objection to entruſting ſovereignty to a child and a woman, induced the preference of John, it very probably was ſome anticipation

[marginalia:]
Coronation of John. 1199.

Treaſons the ſeed-plot of Liberty.

Legitimacy or Election?

Why John preferred to Arthur.

§ 1. *The Plantagenets: John.*

of a poffible and not diftant ftruggle between the throne and its feudal dependencies, and the fenfe of how much the latter would be ftrengthened by an incompetent and feeble King. For, how ftood the government of England, when placed in John's keeping?

The balance of power between the various grades of feudal fociety, as in a great degree eftablifhed by the difcreet and powerful policy of Henry the Second, had been wholly relaxed and unfettled by the lawlefs adminiftration in Cœur-de-Lion's abfence. The powers which Henry centered in the throne for good purpofes, were proftituted to evil by both his fons. The weaknefs which an able king, for wife and prudent purpofes, had fought to introduce into the ariftocratic element of the kingdom, had fince been ufed for the fuppreffion of all reftraint upon monarchical tyranny. If fuch a fovereign as Henry could have continued to reign, until a forced repreffion of the baronial feuds might have permitted a gradual and free reaction of the popular on the kingly power, the eftablifhment of rational liberty would have been haftened by at leaft two centuries. But even as it was, there ftood the People between the two oppofing forces; alternately recognifed in the neceffities of each, and by both made confcious of their power. In the Church queftions, and that of refiftance to invafion, which arofe in the earlier portion of the reign, they took part with John; in the queftions of civil freedom which immortalifed its clofe, they joined the grand confederacy of his enemies. Of the character of this prince it is needlefs to fpeak.

<small>Henry II.'s policy unfettled by his fons.</small>

<small>Monarchy and ariftocracy in conflict.</small>

<small>People choofe their fide alternately.</small>

Introductory Essay.

Character of John. It belongs to the few in hiſtory or in human nature of which the infamy is altogether black and unredeemed. The qualities which degraded his youth grew with his years; combined with them, he had juſt enough of the ambition of his race to bring forth more ſtrongly the puſillanimity of his ſpirit; and thus he was inſolent and mean, at once the moſt abject and the moſt arrogant of men. The pitileſs cruelties recorded of him ſurpaſs belief; and the reckleſs madneſs with which he ruſhed into his quarrels, was only exceeded by his impotent cowardice when reſiſtance ſhowed its front. **His deſertion of both ſides.** He deſerted the people when the people joined him againſt the church, and he deſerted the church when the church joined him againſt the people. Yet, what reſulted from the very vice and falſehood of ſo deſpicable a nature was in itſelf the reverſe of evil. A man more able, though with an equal love of tyranny, would have huſbanded, **Uſes of a bad king.** and kept, his power; this man could only feel that he exiſted when he knew that he was trampling on his fellow-men, and, making his power intolerable, he riſked and loſt it. The concluſion which would infer that with the barons, and not with the people, the ſubſtantial benefit remained, is far too haſtily formed. **What the triumph of the Barons involved.** What, in its beginning, was the claim of one powerful faction in the realm as againſt its feudal lord, became in the end a demand for rights to be guaranteed to the general community. It was but a month before the gathering at Runnymede that an unavailing attempt was made to detach the greater barons

§ 1. *The Plantagenets: John.*

from the national confederacy, by offering to themselves and their immediate followers what the Great Charter was to secure to every freeman.

I have shown that party spirit had now arisen in England. From it have sprung scenes and compromises often neither just nor honourable; but with it have been associated, in very memorable periods of history, the liberties and political advances of the English people. The determined wish of a large section of the nobles to degrade the position and humble the pride of their sovereign, became obvious at the outset of John's reign. When he began his continental wars, he was master of the whole French coast, from the borders of Flanders to the foot of the Pyrenees; when three years had passed, the best portion of that territory was irrevocably lost to him, and, after a separation of three hundred years, Normandy, Anjou, Maine, and Touraine, were reannexed to the French crown. Nor were any of his complaints so loud and bitter, during the progress of these events, as that which was implied in his reproach that the English nobles had forsaken him. They certainly saw pass into subjection to France those large and opulent provinces so long won and guarded by the swords of their fathers, and they made no sign of resistance. But this had also a deeper significance than mere disgust with John. They had elected their country. They were no longer foreign proprietors on a soil which was not their own; they were Englishmen, resolved to cast their fortunes and their fate with England. Soon after this,

Party spirit and its results.

English King stripped of French conquests.

Conduct of the Barons.

Growth of national feeling.

indeed, they raifed a counter-cry to that of their recreant King, accufing him of foreign favouritifm. With the name, opprobrious now, of *foreigner*, they branded the Angevin, the Norman, and the Poitevin nobles whom he had brought into England at the clofe of his French wars; and whom he now delighted to parade about his perfon, to load with dignities and wealth, and to encourage in their vigorous efforts to plunder and opprefs the native population. Even the French hiftorian of the Norman Conqueft is here fain to admit that the conquering lord and the conquered peafant had found a point of contact and a common fympathy. He can no longer refift the conclufion, that in the foil of England there was at length germinating a national fpirit common to all who traverfed it. Without doubt it was fo. Nor was there a new fine now levied on one of the old domains, or a new toll on one of the old bridges or highways, that did not bring the Englifh baron and lord of the manor nearer in his interefts and rights to the Englifh farmer and citizen.

<small>Common caufe againft foreigners.</small>

<small>Alliance of lords and citizens.</small>

<small>King's furrender to Pope. 1213.</small>

The next ftep in John's degradation completed the rupture with his barons and carried over the people to their fide. From the attempted overthrow of all government, by the furrender of England to the Pope, dates the firft fenfible advance in our annals to anything like a government under general and equitable forms of law. There is not an Englifh freeman living in this nineteenth century, who may not trace in fome degree a portion of the liberty he enjoys to the day when

<small>Freedom's debt to John.</small>

§ 1. *The Plantagenets: The Great Charter.*

King John did his beſt to lay his country at the feet of a foreign prieſt, and make every one of her children as much a ſlave as himſelf. From that day the grand confederacy againſt the King took its really formidable, becauſe now unwavering ſhape; and what was beſt in England joined and ſtrengthened it. The concentration of its purpoſes was mainly the work of Stephen de Langton, and forms his claim to eternal memory. Rome never clad in her purple a man of nobler nature, or one who more reſolutely, when he left the councils of the Vatican, ſeemed to have left behind him alſo whatever might impinge upon his obligations as an Engliſhman. No name ſtands upon our records worthier of national honour. In an unlettered age, he had cultivated with ſuccefs not alone the higheſt learning, but the accompliſhments and graces of literature; and at a time apparently the moſt unfavourable to the growth of freedom, he impelled exiſting diſcontents, which but for him might have waſted themſelves in caſual conflict, to the eſtabliſhment of that deep and broad diſtinction between a free and a deſpotic monarchy, of which our hiſtory, through all the varying fortunes and diſaſters that awaited it, never afterwards loſt the trace. Even while he perſonally controlled the treacherous violence of the King, he gave ſteady direction to the ſtill wavering deſigns of the Barons; and among the ſecurities obtained on the firſt day at Runnymede for due obſervance of the bond or deed which the King was to be called upon to ſign, probably none inſpired greater confidence than that which

Confederacy againſt King.

Character of Langton.

His ſervices to Engliſh freedom.

Tueſday 16th of June, 1215. Firſt day at Runnymede.

18   *Introductory Essay.*

<small>Faith in Langton.</small> configned for a certain specified time to Langton's cuftody the Tower and the defences of London. This and other guarantees conceded, the various heads of grievance and propofed means of redrefs were one by one difcuffed; and, the document in which they were reduced to legal fhape having <small>Fourth day: Charter figned.</small> been formally admitted by the Sovereign, on the fourth day from the opening of the conference, Friday the 19th of June, 1215, there was unrolled, read out aloud, and fubfcribed by John, the inftrument which at laft embodied, in fifty-feven chapters, the completed demands of the confederacy, and is immortalifed in hiftory as the Great Charter.

<small>Its general character.</small> The Great Charter, it is hardly neceffary to fay, had nothing to do with the creation of our liberties. Its inexpreffible value was, that <small>Confirmation of exifting liberties.</small> it corrected, confirmed, and re-eftablifhed ancient and indifputable, though continually violated, public rights; that it abolifhed the worft of the abufes which had crept into exifting laws; that it gave an improved tone, by giving a definite and fubftantial form, to future popular defires and afpirations; that, without attempting to frame a new code, or even to inculcate any grand or general principles of legiflation, it did in effect accomplifh both, becaufe, in infifting upon the juft difcharge of <small>Principles latent in it.</small> fpecial feudal relations, it affirmed a principle of equity which was found generally applicable far beyond them; that it turned into a tangible poffeffion what before was fleeting and undetermined; and that, throughout the cen-

§ 1. *The Plantagenets: The Great Charter.* 19

turies which fucceeded, it was violated by all our kings and appealed to by every ftruggling fection of our countrymen.

To very many of its provifions no reference needs to be made, beyond the mention that they redreffed grievances of the military tenants, hardly intelligible fince the downfall of the fyftem of feuds, but then very feverely felt. Reliefs were limited to a certain fum, as fixed by ancient precedent; the wafte committed, and the unreafonable fervices exacted, by guardians in chivalry, were reftrained; the difparagement in matrimony of female wards was forbidden; and widows were fecured from compulfory marriage and other wrongs. Its remedies on thefe points were extended not to the vaffals only, but to the fub-vaffals of the Crown. At the fame time the franchifes, the ancient liberties and free cuftoms, of the City of London, and of all towns and boroughs, were declared to be inviolable. Freedom of commerce was alfo guaranteed to foreign merchants, with a provifo to the King to arreft them for fecurity in time of war, and keep them until the treatment of our own merchants in the enemy's country fhould be known. The tyranny exercifed in connection with the Royal Forefts was effectively controlled; and a remedy was applied to that double grievance of expenfe and delay, long bitterly felt, to which private individuals were fubjected when profecuting fuits in the King's court, by the neceffity of following the King in his perpetual progreffes. "Common Pleas fhall not "follow our court," faid this memorable pro-

Remedial provifions.

Guarantees of franchifes.

Redrefs of perfonal wrongs.

vision of Magna Charta, "but shall be held in some certain place."

As striking a provision had relation to the levy of aids and scutages, and this, which was not in the articles first submitted to the King, appears to have originated during the four days' conference at Runnymede. The frequency of foreign expeditions had given a very onerous character to these aids; always liable to be farmed out with peculiar circumstances of hardship, and lately become of nearly annual recurrence. But the provision in question now limited the exaction of them to the three acknowledged legal occasions—the King's personal captivity, the knighthood of his eldest son, and the marriage of his eldest daughter; and in case aid or scutage should be required on any other grounds, it rendered necessary the previous consent of the Great Council of the tenants of the crown. It proceeded then to enumerate the constituent parts of this Council, as to consist of archbishops, bishops, abbots, earls, and greater barons, who should be summoned personally by writ; and of all other tenants in chief of the crown, who should be summoned generally by the sheriff: and it ordered the issue of summons forty days beforehand, with specification of time and place, and intended subject of discussion. Nor did anything in the Charter, notwithstanding the careful limitation of the article to royal tenants and to purposes of supply, prove so hateful to succeeding princes as this latter stipulation. It was soon formally expunged, and was never formally restored; yet in its

§ 1. *The Plantagenets: The Great Charter.*

place arofe filently other and larger privileges, fuch as no one was found daring enough in later years to violate openly.

Upon many fmaller though very falutary provifions which, relating to the better adminiftration of juftice, to the ftricter regulation of affize, to mitigation of the rights of preemption poffeffed by the Crown, and to the allowance of liberty of travel to every freeman excepting in time of war, took a comparatively narrow and local range, it is not neceffary to dwell. I proceed to name thofe grander provifions which proved applicable to all places and times, and were found to hold within them the germ of our greateft conftitutional liberties.

Thefe were the claufes which protected the perfonal liberty and property of all freemen, by founding acceffible fecurities againft arbitrary imprifonment and arbitrary fpoliation. "We will not fell, we will not refufe, we will not defer, right or juftice to any one," was the fimple and noble proteft againft a cuftom never thenceforward to be practifed without fecret crime or open fhame. In the fame great fpirit, the thirty-ninth claufe, beginning with that rude latinity of *nullus liber homo* which Lord Chatham thought worth all the Claffics, ftipulated that no freeman fhould be arrefted or imprifoned, or diffeifed of his land, or outlawed, or deftroyed in any manner; nor fhould the King go upon him, nor fend upon him, but by the lawful judgment of his peers, or by the law of the land. And a fupplementary claufe, not lefs worthy, provided that earls and

Minor provifions.

Securities for liberty and property.

Juftice not to be denied or fold.

"Nullus liber homo."

All freemen to be

tried by their peers.

barons should be amerced by their peers only, and according to the nature of their offence; that freemen should not be amerced heavily for a small fault, but after the manner of the default, nor above measure for a great transgression; and that such amerciaments—saving always to the freeholder his freehold, to the merchant his merchandise, and to a villein his implements of husbandry—should be imposed by the oath of the good men of the neighbourhood. It was at the same time provided that every liberty and custom which the King had granted to his tenants, as far as concerned him, should be observed by the clergy and laity towards their tenants, as far as concerned them; thus extending the relief generally, as before remarked, to the sub-vassals as well as vassals, but restricting it still to the freeman.

Extension of relief to sub-vassals.

Manifest as were such restrictions and omissions in the Charter, however, and limited as the bearing seemed to be even of its greatest remedial clauses, these did not avail against its mighty and resistless effect through the succeeding centuries. Its framers might have paused, could they wholly have foreseen or known what it involved; and that under words intended only to be applicable to the relations of feudal power, lay concealed the most extended truths of a just and equitable polity. By the very right they claimed to deny protection to serfs, the bonds of serfdom were for ever broken. By the authority they assumed of protesting against the power of taxation in a prince, they forfeited the power of taxation in a like case which they believed they had re-

Effect of Charter in later times.

Its power of expansion.

§ 1. The Plantagenets: Henry III.

served to themselves. They could not assert a principle, and restrict its operation and consequences. They could not insist upon regular meetings of the Great Council with the purpose of controlling the King, and prevent the ultimate admission into it of forms of popular election which were most effectually to control the Nobility. If required to convey by a single phrase the truth embodied in the Great Charter, it might be simply and sufficiently expressed as resistance to irresponsible tyranny; and this substantially is the same, under the stuff jerkin of the peasant and under the coat of mail of the baron. In all the struggles of freedom, therefore, which filled the centuries after Runnymede, it played the most conspicuous part; and from the solid vantage ground it established, each fresh advance was always made. Never, at any new effort, were its watchwords absent, or its provisions vainly appealed to; although, when old Sir Edward Coke arose to speak in the third parliament of James the First, the necessity had arisen no less than thirty-two times to have them solemnly reaffirmed and re-established. Thirty-two several times had they then been deliberately violated by profligate ministers and faithless kings.

Already twice had this wrong been suffered in the reign succeeding John's, when, six years after the Regent Pembroke's death, and while the person of the young King was under the guardianship of a Poitevin bishop, Peter des Roches, formerly a tool of John's, there was summoned the earliest Great Council which

Substance shaping Forms.

Violations and reassertions of Charter.

Henry III. 1216.

Earliest council named as a Parliament.
bore the ominous name of Parliament. The Court's urgent necessities had called it together: but, upon the demand for a subsidy, fresh violations of the Charter were made broadly the ground for refusing to give; and it was only at length conceded, in the shape of a fifteenth of

Supply conditional on redress.
all movables, upon receipt of guarantees for a more strict observance of the Charter, and with the condition that the money so raised should be placed in the treasury, and none of it taken out before the King was of age, unless for the defence of the realm, and in the pre-

Control of money by parliament.
sence of six bishops and six earls. As far as I am aware, this is the first example of parliamentary control brought face to face with the royal prerogative, and the transaction contained in the germ whatever has been worthiest of a free people in our history.

Appeal of Henry III. to people.
Indirectly may be traced to it, among other incidents very notable, that proclamation from Henry the Third, summoning his people to take part with him against the barons and great lords, which was one of the most memorable of the precedents unrolled by Sir Robert Cotton and Sir Edward Coke when the struggle with the Stuarts began. It was then late in the reign; but Henry was only seeking to better the instruction received in his nonage

Similar appeal from Barons.
from appeals exactly similar addressed to the people by the Barons, while their conflict still continued with Peter des Roches. The wily Poitevin, galled by the conditions attached to the subsidy, precipitated the young King into further disputes; in the course of which, offices of trust were gradually taken from the English

§ 1. *The Plantagenets: Henry III.*

barons and filled by foreigners brought over into England. The men of old family, wedded now to the land of their fathers as jealously as the Saxon had been, saw themselves displaced for the French jester, tool, or pander; and these so-called Norman chiefs turned for sympathy and help to a people no longer exclusively either Norman or Saxon, but united inseparably on their English soil. Jealousy of French favourites.

Historians have been very reluctant to admit so early an intrusion of the popular element into the government of the Plantagenets; and it is still the custom to treat of this particular reign as a mere struggle for the predominance of aristocracy or monarchy. But beneath the surface, the other and more momentous power is visible enough, as it heaves and stirs the outward agencies and signs of authority; and what might else have been a paltry struggle, easily terminable, for court favour or military predominance, was by this converted into a war of principles, awful and irreconcilable, which ran its course with varying fortune through all subsequent time. The merchants and tradesmen of the towns are now first recognisable as an independent and important class. They have been enriched by that very intercourse with foreigners which was so hateful to the class above them. They are invested with privileges wrung from the poverty of their lords. They are no longer liable to individual services, but in place of them are paying common rents. They have guilds and charters inviolable as the fees of the great proprietors; and, incident to these, the right, as little now Struggle for power transformed to war of principles. Rise of merchants and tradesmen. Guilds and Charters.

to be difputed as that of the feudal fuperior had been, to hold fairs and demand tolls, to choofe their own magiftrates and enact their own laws. On the hearing of fuch men, the provifions of the Great Charter, read aloud from time to time in their County Courts, could not have fallen as a mere empty found. What was fo proclaimed might be but half-enfranchifement; it could indeed be little more, while ferfdom remained in the claffes directly beneath them; but it pointed to where freedom was, accuftomed them to its claims and forms, and helped them onward in the direction where it lay. They joined the Barons againft the foreign favourite.

Privileges and rights ceded to middle clafs.

The conflict had continued fome time, and Henry was twenty-fix years old, when his neceffities again compelled him to call together a parliament; but twice his bidding was refufed, and the meffengers who bore the refufal might have added the unwonted tidings, that fongs fung againft the favourite, and filled with warnings to the fovereign, might daily be heard in the ftreets. Amid other figns and portents of focial change had now arifen the political ballad. In it fhone forth the firft *vera effigies* of the Poitevin bifhop of Winchefter; nimble at the counting of money as he was flow in expounding the gofpel; fitting paramount, not in Winchefter, but in Exchequer; pondering on pounds, and not upon his holy book; poftponing Luke to lucre; and fetting more ftore by a handful of marks than by all the doctrines of their namefake faint. Would the King avoid the fhipwreck

King's fummons for parliament not obeyed, 1233.

Political ballads.

Attack upon the Favourite.

§ 1. *The Plantagenets: Henry III.*

of his kingdom ? afked the finger. Then let him fhun for ever the ftones and rocks (Roches) in his way. Quickly, too, were thefe warnings followed up. By no lefs a perfon than Pembroke's fon, the ftandard of rebellion was let loofe in the Welfh diftricts; the clergy, oppreffed by tax and tallage from Rome, began to take part in the general difcontent; and in midft of a feaft at the palace, Edmund of Canterbury (Langton's fucceffor) prefented himfelf with a ftatement of national grievances and a demand for immediate redrefs. He reminded the King that his father had well-nigh forfeited his crown; he told him that the Englifh people would never fubmit to be trampled upon by foreigners in England; and for himfelf he added that he fhould excommunicate all who any longer refufed, in that crifis of danger, to fupport the reform of the government and the welfare of the nation. That was in February, 1234. In April, a parliament had affembled, Peter and his Poitevins were on their way home acrofs the fea, the minifters who had made themfelves hateful were difmiffed, and the oppofition barons were in power.

General difcontent.

Grievances reported and Redrefs demanded. February, 1234.

Parliament affembled and Favourite difmiffed. April, 1234.

This will read like the language of a modern day; but if fuch events have any hiftoric fignificance, they eftablifh what in the modern phrafe can only properly be defcribed as minifterial refponfibility and parliamentary control. Nor were they the folitary or ifolated events of their clafs which marked the feeling of the time. Again and again, during this prolonged reign, the fame incidents recur, in precifely

Minifterial refponfibility and Parliamentary control.

the same circle of resistance and submission. There is an urgent request for money, which is contemptuously refused; but on a promise to redress grievances, the subsidy is given. Then, Court coffers being full, Court pledges are violated; until again distress brings round the old piteous petition, and, with new conditions of restraint and constitutional safeguards before undemanded, assistance is rendered again. In five years from the incident I have named, the money so granted by Parliament was paid into the hands of selected Barons, with as strict proviso for account as modern parliaments have claimed over public expenditure; and in two years more, on the payment of certain monies to the Exchequer, the City of London exacted a stipulation that the Justiciary, Chancellor, and Treasurer might thereafter be appointed with the consent of Parliament, and hold their offices only during good behaviour. And, at the very time when public faith was thus beginning to be exacted and recognised, law was taking the form of a system. It was now that Bracton produced that treatise which went far in itself to establish uniformity of legal practice, and so create our common law; nor had the reign for which this might have sufficed as the sole distinction, reached its close, before the same great lawyer found himself able to reckon as superior to the King "not "only God and the law by which he is made "king, but his Great Court (Curia Regis); "so that if he were without a bridle, that is, "the law, they ought to put a bridle upon "him." This Court, this Curia Regis, con-

§ 1. *The Plantagenets: First House of Commons.* 29

fifting of Chief Jufticiary, Chancellor, Con- Cabinet of
ftable, Marfhal, Chamberlain, Steward, and the King.
Treafurer, was what in modern time might be
called the Cabinet of the King.

But the achievement which moft connects
this thirteenth century with the ftruggles of
the feventeenth, and with the affociations of
modern time, remains to be commemorated.
Beyond doubt or queftion, and after due allowance for differences in a difcuffion where the
moft learned and calm of antiquarians have
not been able wholly to diveft themfelves of A memo-
party zeal, in the Great Council which met at $\substack{\text{rable af-}\\\text{fembly:}}$
Weftminfter on the 2nd of May, 1258, ori- 2nd May,
ginated the Houfe of Commons as a feparate 1258.
branch of the State.

Under the earlieft Norman kings, what was The Great
called the Great Council appears to have been $\substack{\text{Council}\\\text{under}}$
only another form of the Saxon Witan. A Normans:
greater mifapprehenfion of our conftitutional
hiftory can hardly exift than that which would
affect to difcover in it any actual commencement of our modern Houfe of Lords. The
idea of an hereditary Houfe of Lords did not Not a
at that time exift in England. A barony $\substack{\text{Houfe of}\\\text{Lords:}}$
confifted of fo many knights' fees; in other
words, of fo many eftates from which the
fervices of a knight were due; and a baron
claimed his barony not as a lord (even the
coronet was not worn until much later), but
as a proprietor. The Council, in fhort, was Not here-
diftinctly reprefentative. The dignity was $\substack{\text{ditary, but}\\\text{reprefen-}}$
territorial, refulting from the poffeffion of fiefs tative.
of land; and if thofe fiefs were forfeited,
alienated, or loft, the dignity departed with

them. But it is not difficult to difcern how a larger parliamentary fyftem would almoft neceffarily arife out of fuch baronial tenures. Through all the differences and diffenfions of the many learned perfons by whom thefe matters have been difcuffed, and without touching the vexed queftions which their learning has left ftill unfolved, it feems tolerably clear that, whether or not tenure by knight's fervice in chief was originally diftinct from tenure by barony, they had become fo feparated fome time before the reign of John. Tenants in chief appear to have comprifed, in the firft inftance, only the King's immediate vaffals; but as time wore on they could not fo be reftricted. Many of the greater baronies fplit up and became divided; while the name of baron, no matter what number of fees it reprefented, or for the feudal fervice of how few or how many knights it may have been refponfible, was ftill retained.

But this led to a natural jealoufy on the part of the greater proprietors; and in time to a broad diftinction, in name at leaft, between the more important of thofe barons who held by their honours or baronies, and the leffer proprietors whom grants of efcheated honours might newly have created, or whofe ancient rights had been reduced by efcheat or decay. A tenant in chief was now not neceffarily a baron; or he might be a baron of inferior grade. It is more difficult to determine what regulated the iffue of writs of fummons; but it feems probable that the fame jealoufy to which allufion has been made, brought about

Germs therein of larger fyftem.

Break-up of elements of Council.

Diftinctions and grades of rank.

Varieties in writs of fummons.

§ 1. *The Plantagenets: First House of Commons.*

the distinction first observable in John's reign, between the greater baron summoned by his special writ, and the inferior tenants in chief called together by a summons directed to their sheriff. It is clear also, that, though all were entitled to summons, the mere right of tenure could not dispense with its forms; and an unsummoned tenant, without resorting to such remedies as might compel the issue of the writ, could not take his place in the Council.

Up to this point, it will be observed, the principle is distinctly that of feudal representation. The immediate vassals of the Crown, representing certain land, possess the personal right to be present in parliament. They are the liegemen of the Sovereign; and by the universal feudal compact, though aid could be asked of the liegeman, the man's consent was necessary to legalise the aid; while the same relation, implying protection from the lord, conveyed a further right to insist upon corresponding guarantees. In this view, the presence of both larger and lesser tenants was required, and was even exacted by the Crown as needful to the authority and execution of a law. But, as the inferior tenants increased in number, the tax for parliamentary attendance on men of smaller fortunes became intolerable; and their consent and attendance came to be implied in that of the greater barons. Still, they were supposed to be in the Council; and it seems to me that to the mere form and legal fiction thus resorted to, may be traced the gradual transition from a feudal to a real representation. The sure though silent power, with which a

Peculiarities of feudal representation.

Aid for Protection.

Lesser tenants represented by larger.

Transition

growing fociety of men will modify and adapt old inftitutions to new neceffities, at once widening and ftrengthening their foundations, is for the moft part happily unknown to thofe who might otherwife not unfuccefsfully ftrive to control it.

from feudal to real rights.

As the inferior tenants in chief withdrew gradually from the Council, its component members became reftricted to the bifhops and abbots, the earls and barons, the minifters and judges, and neighbouring knights holding of the Crown. But the language of the writs continued to imply a much larger attendance. When, for example, the Great Charter was confirmed in the ninth year of Henry's reign, the roll informs us that at the fame time a fifteenth had been granted in return by the bifhops, earls, barons, knights, free tenants and all of the kingdom (*et omnes de regno noftro Angliæ*); and when a fortieth was granted feven years later, there is put forth, as having concurred in the grant, the ftrange and ominous combination of bifhops, earls, barons, knights, freemen *and villeins.* This was indeed a fiction, but with an expanding germ of truth. The confent of particular claffes was to be underftood, as a matter of courfe, to have been included in that of others. But the very emptieft acknowledgment of a right is precious. The right itfelf waits only its due occafion to affume the fubftance and importance of reality.

Language of writs of fummons.

Fictions forefhadowing truths.

Forms conveying Subftance.

Nor had the Englifh freeman, even under his earlieft Norman kings, been wholly without the means of knowing what reprefentation meant. When the Conqueror or his fons had

§ 1. *The Plantagenets: First House of Commons.* 33

any special reason to make inquiry into their own rights; when particular wrongs of the people reached them, or when peculations were charged against their barons or officers; nothing was more common than a commission of knights in each shire, not simply named by the Sovereign (as when the Conqueror issued an inquiry into the details of the Saxon law), but quite as frequently elected in the County Court, whose business it was to proceed from hundred to hundred, to make the investigation upon oath, and to lay its result before the King in council. The Great Charter contained a provision for the election of twelve knights in the next court of each county to inquire into forest abuses. In the seventh year of the reign now under notice, every sheriff was ordered to inquire, by means of twelve lawful and discreet knights, what special privileges existed in his shire on the day of the first outbreak between John and his barons. And in the year of the assembling of the Great Council to which these remarks apply, a commission of four knights in each county received it in charge to inquire into certain excesses committed by men in authority. In relation to the levy of subsidies also, the same rule came to be adopted. The most ancient example on record of a subsidy (that of 1207) is found to have been collected by the itinerant judges; but only thirteen years later, the office of collection is seen to be deputed to the sheriff, in conjunction with two knights to be chosen in a full court of the county, with the consent of all the suitors.

Commissions of inquiry in shires.

Old institution adapted to new uses. 1223.

County representation begins.

Collection of taxes in 1207 and 1220.

D

Beginning of the end.

Was it not obvious that such usage as this must grow as the people grew? Were not the collection of taxes, and reports of grievances, manifest steps to a power over the money collected, and to a right of petition against the grievances exposed? Is it difficult to discern, throughout these efforts of Norman royalty to check the excess of its ministers, and obtain the co-operation of its people, the vague formation of that authority and house of the Commons, which was to prove more formidable than either of the powers it was called into existence to control?

Vague formation of authority of Commons.

Soon what was vague became more distinct. It wanted yet two years of the date of the Great Charter, when a writ was issued marking the first undoubted transition towards the change so vast and so memorable. This contained a summons for military service, with an order that four discreet knights of the county should be sent to Oxford without arms to treat with the King concerning the affairs of the kingdom. In other words, it was a summons to Parliament, in terms the same as those of a later period; and it was followed, after an interval of forty years, by another and more decisive instance. While Henry the Third was on the continent in 1254, his Queen and Regents summoned the tenants in chief to sail to his assistance; and gave order, in the summons, that "besides these, two lawful and discreet " knights should be chosen by the men of " every county, in the place of all and each " of them, to assemble at Westminster, and " to determine with the knights of the other

Gradual steps thereto. 1214.

Scheme to obtain money from shires. 1254.

§ 1. *The Plantagenets: First House of Commons.*

"counties what aid they would grant to their Sovereign in his present necessity, so that the same knights might be able to answer, in the matter of the said aid, for their respective counties."

Of the meaning of such a writ and its return, there cannot surely be a question; nor is it easy to understand the discussion it has provoked. Call it singular, anomalous, or by what name may most suitably express its irregular character; except it from ordinary parliaments, and call it a convention; still the undeniable fact remains, that it was a scheme to obtain money from the Commons of the various counties, and that to this end it prescribed the election of representatives whose deliberation and assent should control those of their constituents. The language of the writ connects itself undoubtedly with that of its predecessor in the fifteenth of John; and it is quite immaterial whether or not the barons, and higher tenants in chief, were summoned to sit with these knights. Enough that the Commons of the shires were thus admitted to a co-ordinate share in the imposition and voting of taxes; for, whatever antiquarians may urge as to Parliament's use of one chamber at Westminster up to the middle of the third Edward's reign (abundant proof exists of separate sittings in other parts of England), it is sufficiently clear that the voting must always have been by each order separately, and without interference from each other. The mere circumstance of the different proportions of taxation would establish this.

In the thirty-eighth of Henry the Third,

Knights to answer for their counties.

Representatives to impose taxes.

One chamber at Westminster: separate sittings elsewhere.

Admission

then, the principle of a real reprefentation had become part of the conftitution of England, and the third eftate of the realm took a direct fhare in its government. Yet, momentous as the conceffion was, it had been obtained by no violent effort, but fimply as the unavoidable refult of the increafing importance of the people. From leffer they had rifen quietly to higher duties. The knight, whofe bufinefs it had been to affefs fubfidies, had found gradual admiffion by the fide of the earls and barons, to help in the difpofition and diftribution of the money obtained; and that he and his fellows were fo received diftinctly as the deputies of others, appeared even in the remuneration fet apart for them. Great men, fuch as earls and barons, who attended in their own right, paid their own charges; but men of fmaller fubftance, who had undertaken merely to tranfact bufinefs for others, were held to have a title to compenfation from thofe in whofe behalf they acted. As they were paid for their labour in affeffment, fo for their facrifice of time and labour in reprefentation they were paid. Wherefore a rate levied on the county difcharged their expenfes for fo many fpecified days, in " going, ftaying, and returning."

On another branch of this inquiry, too, which has been fadly encumbered with needlefs learning and mifplaced vehemence of difcuffion, the county rate would feem to have an important bearing. It has been affumed, by thofe antiquarians who would narrow as much as poffible the bafis on which our freedom is built, that the reprefentative knights, as reprefenting

§ 1. *The Plantagenets: First House of Commons.* 37

simply the inferior tenants in chief from whose reluctance to attend in Parliament they first derived importance, are not to be taken to have had relation to the county at large. But this assumption is negatived by every reasonable supposition. The wages of the knights were levied on the whole county (*de communitate comitatûs*); and the mesne tenant could hardly have been denied a right, to the support of which he was obliged to contribute. That what concerned all should be approved by all, was a maxim not unused by even Norman kings. The language of the writs of election, also, cited with pardonable exultation by Prynne in the early sittings of the Long Parliament, is clear and specific. The tenants in chief are never mentioned in them; while tenants of the Crown implied tenants both by free and by military service. The condition required of the candidate, was to be discreet and lawful; of the electors, to be suitors of the county; and of the election, to be made in a full court. A full County Court was always the least feudal of the modified feudality that lingered in England. It comprised all freeholders; whether of the King, of a mesne lord, or by military or any free service; and in the reign of Henry the Third therefore, not less certainly than in that of Victoria the First, the knights of the shire represented, without regard to the quality of tenure, the whole body of freeholders.

<small>Wages of knights levied on entire county.</small>

<small>Election by full County Court.</small>

<small>All freeholders comprised:</small>

<small>And represented by knights of shire.</small>

Still, they were knights. Their station associated them with the earls and barons. They were part of what in feudal institution was held to be a lower nobility. They ranked above the ordinary burgefs or citizen. They reprefented the power of the Commons, but they were not commoners; even when the commoners fat apart, they continued to fit with the barons; and as yet no man feems to have dreamt that the clafs even lower than theirs could ever be raifed to the national councils, whether in feparate, co-ordinate, or fubordinate rank. Though the principle which by eafieft preffure expanded to admit them, had been winning its gradual way for centuries to the acknowledgment it had at laft obtained, yet that lower clafs were ftill fhut out. But, what ages and generations are needed to prepare, the man and the hour accomplifh; and both were at hand when the Great Council, having met at Weftminfter on the 2nd of May, 1258, yielded to the demand of Simon de Montfort that a parliament fhould meet at Oxford in June. The ftruggle which then began, filled more than fix eventful years; but at laft the day arrived, never to be forgotten in Englifh ftory, and on the 14th December, 1264, writs went forth calling together reprefentatives from the counties, cities, and boroughs, to meet the prelates and great lords: and the firft enactment of that moft memorable affemblage, giving folemn confirmation to charters and ordinances, ran as by common confent " of the King, his fon Edward, the prelates, earls, barons, *and commonalty of the realm.*"

That, from the pofition thus gained, the commonalty never again were diflodged, is the fuffi-

Marginalia:
Refults of fuch reprefentation.
Ages prepare what the hour produces.
Six eventful years.
Writs for firft Houfe of Commons, 14th Dec. 1264.

§ 1. *The Plantagenets: Edward I.*

cient anfwer to thofe who would afcribe the victory lefs to the caufes I have retraced than to the fudden needs of a faction of the barons. As of right the commonalty took, and they kept, the place to which they were called; and we may difmifs as of the leaft poffible importance the queftion whether the power was ufurped that called them. Their exiftence once recognifed, no man was found to gainfay it; their pofition and place once difcovered, everything helped to make it more decifively plain. In the reigns of the firft and fecond Edwards, and their fucceffors, we find them in actual efficiency as a branch of the State; and in fpite of the weaker princes, as with the help of the wifer and ftronger, their power was ftill to grow. *Rights gained once, gained always. Power of Commons evergrowing.*

Edward the Firft had not occupied his father's throne three years, when a ftatute was paffed that forafmuch as election ought to be free, no man by force of arms, nor by malice or menacing, fhould difturb any to make free election. It was in this reign alfo (when fo many great improvements in the laws were effected that to Edward has been afcribed the too lofty title of the Englifh Juftinian) that the refidents of the various counties, in which the Jury Syftem had been finally confolidated, obtained the power, afterwards furrendered and loft, of electing their own fheriffs. In the thirteenth of the fame prince, what proved to be one of the heavieft blows to the fyftem it was meant to guard was ftruck by the arming of all claffes: for then was paffed the Great Statute of Winchefter, by which every man in *Edward I. 1271. Election of Sheriffs. Great Statute of*

Winchef-ter, 1284. *[margin]*

the kingdom, according to the quantity of his lands and goods, was affeffed and fworn to carry weapons. The leffon had now been taught to two eftates of the realm, that in the third, as yet unknown to itfelf, the fupreme force lay; and the ability or power moft effectively to make common caufe with the third, was hereafter to be the meafure of gain or lofs to either of the other two. A curious example prefents itfelf in the fucceeding reign. Under Edward the Second, when beyond all queftion the Commons fat, as well as voted, apart from the temporal and fpiritual Barons, numerous boroughs were expreffly created with the defign of ftrengthening the regal as oppofed to the ariftocratic influences; and it was alfo then that, in a very remarkable ftatute, equal legiflative power with the other eftates was claimed for the commonalty, not as a new pretenfion, but as a fundamental ufage of the realm. " The matters," they faid, " to be eftablifhed " for the eftate of the king and of his heirs, " and for the eftate of the realm and of the " people, fhall be treated, accorded, and eftab- " lifhed in parliament, by the king, and by the " affent of the prelates, earls, and barons, " and the commonalty of the realm, *according* " *as hath been before accuftomed.*" Then, too, the Great Charter was again confirmed, with the ftriking addition of " forafmuch as many " people be aggrieved by the king's minifters " againft right, in refpect of which grievances " no one can recover without a common par- " liament, we do ordain that the king fhall " hold a parliament once in the year, or twice,

[margins:] Edward II. 1307. Creation of Royal Boroughs. Equal power claimed for Commons. Provifion for affembling of Parliaments.

§ 1. *The Plantagenets: Edward III.* 41

"if need be." In the succeeding reign six different statutes confirmed and still more enlarged its provisions; and when both the first and the third Edward, in the plenitude of their power and their success, attempted without direct authority from Parliament to impose taxes on the people, they both had to suffer defeat. Edward the First struggled long to reverse that decision; and in the end had but to enter into more special covenants that he would never again levy aid without the assent and good-will of the estates of the realm. From the weak government of his son and successor, the power was decisively wrested; and money supplies were almost always afterwards, or at least with rare exceptions, made conditional, not merely that the specific services for which they were voted might be secured, but that, as the voluntary gift of lords and commons, they should not by any pretence be drawn into precedents as of right or force.

<small>Confirmations of Great Charter.</small>

<small>Attempts to impose taxes without Parliament.</small>

<small>Money supplies made conditional.</small>

The long and remarkable reign of Edward the First's grandson is the date of the Statute of Treasons, one of the greatest gains to constitutional freedom. It limited the crime, before vague and uncertain, to three principal heads; the conspiring the King's death, the levying war against him, and the adhering to his enemies; and, if any other cases for question should arise, it prohibited the judges from inflicting the penalty of treason without application to Parliament. Then also were passed those memorable acts against arbitrary conscription and compulsory pressing of soldiers, so repeatedly cited in the conflict with Charles

<small>Edward III. 1327.</small>

<small>Statute of Treasons.</small>

<small>Acts against Conscription.</small>

the Firft, which faved to every man, except upon "the fudden coming of ftrange enemies into the realm," the obligation to arm himfelf only within his own fhire. Without a ftruggle of which our records have kept the trace, thefe popular gains were won. What weaker fovereigns would have perilled life to hold, the third Edward conceded freely. He was too clear-fighted to grafp at a fhadow when already he held the fubftance, and he was too powerful to fear conceffions that had a tendency without danger to the throne to conciliate the other authorities of the realm. Peace had her victories for him, therefore, not lefs renowned than thofe which he obtained in war. He could compofe or amufe his reftless Lords by a politic foundation of the order of the Garter, as he propitiated his difcontented Commons by a frank redrefs of the complaint or grievance. No manlier prince, and none more prudent or fuccefsful, ever occupied the Englifh throne. No influence from the throne having plainer tendencies to popular cultivation, was ever left to a fucceeding age. He had played with confummate genius the part of the firft man in the realm. He had interefted men in himfelf for no apparently felfifh reafons, had juftified his own ambition by the ambition of a common country, and had aggrandifed his own glory as the fummit of the nation's greater glory. Even his palaces gave the feeling of elevation to his people. The magnificent ftructures of Weftminfter Hall and Windfor rank juftly with the intellectual influences that were then diffufed ; and, as though an era of

[margin notes: No forced preffing of Soldiers. Character of Edward III. Victorious in peace as well as war. Firft man in the realm. Intellectual influences of his reign.]

§ 1. *The Plantagenets: Depofition of Richard II.* 43

fo much that was great fhould not pafs without a mark to diftinguifh it among even the greateft of all future time, the poet Chaucer arofe to charm and inftruct his countrymen, and, by the purification of their native tongue, to complete the national fame. Nor was this (perhaps the higheft diftinction of Edward the Third's reign) to pafs without leaving traces in his ftatute-book. With much appropriatenefs it was enacted, in the thirty-fixth year of his government, that the Englifh language which had been thus ennobled, fhould in future be ufed as the language of legiflation.

Chaucer: 1328.

Improvement of Englifh:

Adopted in Parliament rolls.

The greateft of the Edwards governed England for fifty years, and called together feventy parliaments. He was fucceeded by a prince of qualities in all refpects the reverfe of his, and whom Parliament depofed. Yet not more certainly in the enforced refignation of the crown which clofed the reign, than in the rebellion of the ferf-clafs which fignalifed its commencement, did Richard the Second's rule bear teftimony to the ftrength and efficacy of principles promoted equally by the rule of Edward. Placed even on the inferior ground of a conflict between the higher powers of the State; calling it mere gain to the King when he broke down the exclufive pretenfions of the great lords by forcing their Houfe to recognife his writs of fummons, and counting it but as a new privilege to the Barons when they led Henry of Lancafter to the throne; the confequences of this reign were momentous. With at leaft the nominal co-operation of the conftituted authorities of his empire, a legitimate

Richard II. 1377.

Refults of Richard's depofition.

King had been depoſed; and never was it afterwards diſputed, that the ſolid and ſingle claim of the dynaſty which took his place, reſted upon the ability of Parliament, or of the power which thoſe Lords and Barons with all England armed behind them repreſented, ſo to alter the ſucceſſion. By the wording of the acts of ſettlement connected with the change, that moſt eſſential principle of popular right was fully admitted; and from them were derived the hiſtorical and legal precedents which, down to our own time, have proved moſt advantageous to the people.

{margin: People's power to alter the ſucceſſion: Sole claim of Houſe of Lancaſter.}

The people's political importance was in fact eſtabliſhed by it. It ſtruck out from the dictionary of the State the terms of 'divine right,' and 'indefeaſible power.' "I confeſs," ſaid the humbled prince to the men who had withdrawn their allegiance, "I recogniſe, and, from certain knowledge, conſcientiouſly declare, that "I conſider myſelf to have been, and to be, "inſufficient for the government of this king- "dom, and for my notorious demerits not "undeſerving of depoſition." Nor was the voluntary abdication held ſufficient. The Houſes of Lords and Commons, in ſolemn conclave in the hall at Weſtminſter, made Richard the Second's renunciation of his crown their own compulſory act, and, amid the ſhouts of the common people who had there aſſembled, Henry of Lancaſter was conducted to the vacant throne.

{margin: Terms of Richard's ſubmiſſion. His abdication made compulſory.}

Hardly at any preceding period, even among the Saxons, had the popular principle taken more viſible ſhape than on that momentous

§ 1. *The Plantagenets: Henry IV.*

occasion. It was only some few years before that the exclusive pretensions of the barons had been invaded, by admission of regal writs of summons into their house; and here they were now themselves inducting a new sovereign to the seat of supreme power, with less guarantee that he would found his future pretensions on the fidelity of their swords, than that he would rest it rather on the adhesion of the people. From those approving shouts, in which the old Saxon liberty might again seem pealing through the air, there doubtless fell more safety on the ear of Bolingbroke, than from the mailed tread of the barons who led him to Richard's chair. May we not even accept the fancy of the poet whose genius takes rank with history, and suppose the new sovereign of the house of Lancaster, for years before this crowning day, a suppliant candidate for the popular cries that at length hailed the downfall of the family of York? *[side: Popular principle accepted. Adhesion of the people. Soliciting the Throne.]*

> Ourself, and Bushy, Bagot here, and Green,
> Observ'd his courtship to the common people.
> How he did seem to dive into their hearts,
> With humble and familiar courtesy;
> What reverence he did throw away on slaves,
> Wooing poor craftsmen with the craft of smiles,
> And patient underbearing of his fortune,
> As 't were to banish their affects with him.
> Off goes his bonnet to an oyster wench;
> A brace of draymen bid . . God speed him well. .
> And had the tribute of his supple knee,
> With . . ' Thanks, my countrymen! my loving friends!'
> As were our England in reversion his,
> And he our subjects' next degree in hope.

[side: Shakespeare's Bolingbroke.]

Nor did these crafty courtesies cease, on attainment of their first great object. Every popular limitation of his right was accepted *[side: Henry IV. 1399.]*

ungrudgingly by the firſt prince of the houſe
King Bo- of Lancaſter. Wary as he was bold, the policy
lingbroke. of Bolingbroke continued to be the policy of
Henry the Fourth. The parliamentary autho-
rity which had given him power, and the
popular ſympathies which had confirmed his
title, were in every poſſible way promoted by
him during the fourteen years of his great
though ſtill diſputed rule; and no one who
examines the preambles and other wording of
the ſtatutes that were paſſed in his reign, can
Elevation fail to be ſtruck with the ſenſe of how much
of the
people. the commoneſt orders of the people muſt have
riſen ſince the date of the reign of John, in
all that, with the feeling of perſonal power,
brings the hankering after political privilege,
gradual means to eſtimate freedom at its value,
and ſtrength ultimately to win it. Henry's
firſt Houſe of Commons re-aſſerted the right on
which his title was baſed, by taking on itſelf to
recogniſe his ſon as prince of Wales and heir
Parlia- apparent to the throne. This proceeding was
mentary revived and confirmed in the year 1404, when
aſſump- the ſovereign obtained from the parliament a
tions. formal permiſſion that the right of ſucceſſion
to the crown ſhould be veſted in the prince's
brothers, if he himſelf ſhould die without
heirs. In 1406 another and greater ſtep was
taken, the Commons themſelves in that year
carrying up a petition to Henry, to limit the
Precedent ſucceſſion to his ſons and their heirs male.
for Hano- This was in effect a precedent for the ſettle-
verian ſuc-
ceſſion. ment of the crown in after years on the houſe
1406. of Hanover.

Other precedents, ſcarcely leſs important,

§ 1. *The Plantagenets: Henry IV.*

date from this reign. In the firſt ſeſſion of Henry the Fourth, a law was paſſed that no judge ſhould be releaſed from the penalty affixed to the ſanction of an iniquitous act, by pleading the orders of the king, or even danger to his own life from the ſovereign's menaces. In the ſecond year of the reign, the practice which was afterwards one of the ſtrongeſt bulwarks of popular privilege, and which had now been for ſome time ſubſtantially operative, was formally inſiſted on as a right; and a neceſſary ſupply was propoſed to be withheld from the prince until he had anſwered a petition of the ſubject. The Commons in perſon, headed by their Speaker Sir Arnold Savage, formally proffered this bold claim. Three years later, the king was deſired to remove from his houſehold four officers, one of them his own confeſſor, who had given offence to the Commons; and Henry complied with the requeſt, that he might not, as he ſaid, leave the wiſhes of his faithful ſubjects unſatisfied. At the ſame time he informed them that he knew of no offence which the perſons complained of had committed. In the ſixth year of the ſame reign, while the Commons voted the king ſupplies, they appointed treaſurers of their own to make ſure that the money was diſburſed for the purpoſes intended. In that year, alſo, new laws to regulate parliamentary elections atteſted the rapidly increaſing ſtrength of the third eſtate. A ſtatute on "the grievous complaints of the Commons "againſt undue elections for ſhires from the " partiality of ſheriffs," and directing " that in

Marginal notes: No judge to plead King's orders. Claim to make ſupplies conditional on redreſs. 1401. Officers Houſehold removed. 1404. Law for regulating County Elections.

All Freeholders to vote.

"the next County Court, after writs for parliament are delivered, proclamation shall be made of the day and place of the parliament, and that all they that be there present, as well suitors duly summoned as others, shall proceed to the election freely and indifferently, notwithstanding any request or command to the contrary"—bears date in the year 1406.

The lack-learning Parliament. 1406.

That was the year, too, in which the House of Commons having been asked to grant supplies, startled the King with a plain proposal that he should seize all the temporalities of the Church, and employ them as a fund reserved for the exigencies of the State. It is needless to describe what the Church was then, or the extent to which the ill-gotten wealth of the regular clergy had attained. Its accumulation had been checked by statutes of mortmain under the first and third Edwards, but these again were eluded by licences of alienation; and the competent evidence of Bishop Burnet permits us to add that the hand of a churchman is not very ready to let go what once it has firmly grasped. Even more objectionable than the extent of this wealth, was its unequal apportionment. While such abbots as those of Reading, Glastonbury, or Battle, lived with the riotous pomp of princes and passed their days in feasting, thousands of monks, learned and laborious, were struggling with sordid poverty in its lowest and most degrading forms. The project of the Commons included, therefore, a general and reasonable endowment of all the clergy, to precede any state appropriation of

Accumulation of Church property.

Its unequal distribution.

§ 1. *The Plantagenets: Henry IV.* 49

the enormous furplus of ecclefiaftical revenues. The argument they urged for it, and again and again repeated, was, that fuch exorbitant riches no lefs than fuch too fcanty earnings could tend only to difqualify all fections of the Church for the due difcharge of minifterial functions; and though they failed in their immediate purpofe, and had a heretic or two burned in their faces by way of archiepifcopal revenge, and were dubbed by the higher clergy in fcorn a lack-learning parliament, they might have felt that, by the very agitation of fuch a queftion, the feeds were fown of no partial gain for pofterity. The Church itfelf had moft reafon to regret its immediate failure. But it led to fome important checks on clerical privilege; and the thirty articles which, two years later, were not only propofed but conceded, for the regulation of the King's houfehold and government, have been declared by Mr. Hallam, an authority well entitled to refpect, to form a noble fabric of conftitutional liberty, hardly inferior to the petition of right. The Sovereign was required to govern by the advice of a permanent council; and this council, together with all the judges and the officers of the royal houfehold, were bound by folemn oath to parliament to obferve and defend the amended inftitutions. It eftablifhed in effect the principle of minifterial refponfibility; and it is a remarkable evidence of the fame fpirit, and of the ftrong popular impulfe favoured, if not created, by the acceffion of the Houfe of Lancafter, that an attempt made by the Lords to interfere with the taxation of the people, in the year after the

Propofal to feize it for better appropriation.

Failure of attempt.

Thirty articles for regulation of King's affairs.

Minifterial refponfibility eftablifhed. 1410.

County Elections Bill paſſed, was ſtrongly reſented and reſiſted by the Lower Houſe, as in great prejudice and derogation of their liberties.

Interference with Taxation by the Lords reſiſted.

To this, then, had been brought, at the opening of the fifteenth century, that claim of a Sovereign Authority which in the older time had certainly been conceded to the Norman King. For it would be as idle to doubt in what diviſion of the State the Conqueſt temporarily veſted ſuch authority, as to deny that many forms of it ſtill were retained long after its ſubſtance and vitality had departed. Still, for example, the courſe of legiſlative procedure retained veſtige of excluſive kingly rule. Petitions were ſtill preſented by the Commons, conſidered by the Lords, and replied to by the King; which, being entered on the parliament roll, formed the baſis of legiſlation by the monarch himſelf. Even down to Henry the Fifth, indeed, on the authority of a ſomewhat remarkable remonſtrance found on the roll, we find it alleged as a not unuſual practice for the King, taking advantage of the cuſtom which had ſo ariſen of leaving ſtatutes to be drawn up by the judges from the Petition and Anſwer during the parliamentary receſs, to induce or compel the judges to miſrepreſent and falſify the intentions of parliament, by producing ſtatutes to which it had not given aſſent. But how ſtrikingly it proves that the ſovereign authority, as a real working power, had declined, and that the Houſes, repreſenting the power which ſtood in arms behind them, had riſen, when ſuch artifices were thought

Changes ſince the Conqueſt.

Petitions and Bills.

Royal evaſion of Parliamentary control.

§ 1. *The Plantagenets: Henry V.*

worth reforting to; and how fignificant the form difappeared altogether, and, in place of the old Petitions, the introduction of complete ftatutes under the name of Bills was effected. {Bills fubftituted for Petitions.}

What the fword had won the fword fhould keep, faid Henry the Fifth on his acceffion; but what was meant by the faying has its comment in the fact that in the year which witneffed his victory at Agincourt, he yielded to the Houfe of Commons the moft liberal meafure of legiflative power which until then it had obtained. The dazzling fplendour of his conquefts in France had for the time caft into fhade every doubt or queftion of his title, but the very extent of thofe gains upon the French foil eftablifhed only more decifively the worfe than ufeleffnefs of fuch acquifitions to the Englifh throne. It is a ftriking example of the good which is wrought out of evil by an all-wife and over-ruling Providence, that the very mifchiefs incident to thefe wars, the neceffity for unufual fupplies, and the unavoidable burdens thrown upon the people, led to fuch legiflative conceffions of a popular kind as till then had not been obtained. The neceffities of the fovereign were fupplied, but the full equivalent was demanded and received in a maintenance of the reftraints upon his prerogative. The diftinction of Henry's reign in conftitutional hiftory will always be, that from it dates a power, indifpenfable to a free and limited monarchy, of which not only were the leading {Henry V. 1413. Good out of evil. Advantage to Commons from Henry V.'s wars. Further reftraints on the prerogative.}

safeguards now obtained, but at once so firmly established, that against the shock of incessant resistance in later years they stood perfectly unmoved.

<small>Admission of rights of legislature.</small> They had followed, as a kind of inevitable consequence, from that formal admission of legislative rights in the Commons, just adverted to, which led to the change from Petitions to Bills. An Act had been passed, providing that "from this time forward, by complaint " of the Commons asking remedy for any mis- " chief, there be no law made thereupon, which " should change the meaning by addition or " by diminution, or by any manner of term " or terms;" and a formal grant, in the name of the King, was at the same time appended <small>Law against tampering with petitions.</small> to it, stating that from thenceforth, nothing " be enacted to be petitions of his Commons " that be contrary to their asking, whereby " they should be bound without their assent." It was hardly to be expected, therefore, that when subsequently, in the same reign, the Commons claimed certain rights and exemptions needful to the discharge of their trust, to last as long as the trust lasted, and to cease when it was laid down, such a demand could safely <small>Exemptions claimed for members of the Commons.</small> be resisted. Among other things, they required personal release from such judicial proceedings as might impede parliamentary functions. They asserted the right to an absolute despotism concerning every thing that passed within their own walls. They exacted the exclusive jurisdiction of offences which tended to impair their powers or obstruct their public duties. In a word, they achieved what was thenceforward

§ 1. *The Plantagenets: Henry V.* 53

known by the formidable name of Privilege of Parliament; the fhield and buckler under which all the battles of liberty and good government were fought in the after time. An attempt to drag the adjudication of the privilege into courts of law followed; when, in the famous cafe of Thorpe the Speaker, the judges declared "that they would not deter- "mine the privilege of the High Court of "Parliament, of which the knowledge be- "longeth to the Lords of Parliament, and not "the juftices." Nor will it be hazardous to predict that when this privilege is in any material point abandoned, political freedom is at an end. When deputed rights are fuccefsfully affailed, abfolute rights are no longer fafe; and parliaments without parliamentary liberties, as Pym nobly faid, will be but a fair and plaufible way into bondage. Not many years afterwards, another moft momentous claim was conceded, for which the prefent right had ferved to herald the way. This was the awful power of Impeachment, which, alfo won in the fame reign, was never again loft.

For let it not be thought that all the fruits of the hard-fought liberal victories were at once gathered in and ftored for peaceful and uninterrupted enjoyment. What moft impreffes the careful ftudent of early Englifh hiftory, is the marked diftinction he finds it neceffary to keep before him, between the fecurities of civil freedom as generally exifting and in fubftance recognifed, and their violation as frequently and flagrantly permitted. Still the violation, when it occurred, was feen

Privilege of Parliament.

Thorpe's cafe.

Eftablifhed againft the courts.

Right of impeachment won.

Liberal gains intercepted.

Freedom outraged

to be such. "So when the Lion preyeth," as brave old Sir Edwin Sandys told the House of Commons early in James the First's reign, " no cause to think it his right." So when James claimed a privilege of the Plantagenets as a flower of the Crown, "the flower hath had "a long winter, then," quaintly interposed Sir James Whitelocke, the father of Bulstrode, " since it hath not budded these two hundred " years!" Of a mingled character in this respect were the results of the long and bloody contest, now about to begin, between the rival branches of the Plantagenet family; but it does not admit of doubt that the final predominance of the house of Lancaster was, like its accession, favourable to popular liberty. The influence from which it first derived authority, still imparted power. The right of parliament to alter the succession was the title on which that house rested, and in its continuance the popular sanction was implied. The legislation of Henry the Sixth was less popular than that of Henry the Fourth, but the very fact marks the progress which had been made in the interval. Henry the Fourth's statute " against undue Elections for Shires from " the partiality of Sheriffs," gives the power of voting to every one present at the place of election, as well suitors duly summoned as others. Henry the Sixth's statute "for the " due Election of Members of Parliament in " Counties," limits the right to such as possessed forty shillings a year in land free from all burthens within the county, but offers priceless proof, in the very terms of its pre-

§ 1. *The Plantagenets: Henry VI.* 55

amble, of how great had been meanwhile the advance among the commoneſt orders of the people in at leaſt a knowledge of their ſtrength and their pretenſions to power. "Whereas," it ran, "the election of knights has of late, "in many counties of England, been made "by outrageous and exceſſive numbers of "people, many of them of ſmall ſubſtance "and value, yet pretending to a right equal "to the beſt knights and eſquires, &c." As the period of the acceſſion of the family of Tudor approaches, the full effect of influences that had led to ſuch legiſlation is diſtinctly ſeen. *Limited advance to forty-ſhilling freeholders.*

Greater importance of the people.

The heavieſt blow had been ſtruck unconſciouſly at the feudal ſyſtem in England when the third eſtate of the realm obtained a formal place in the legiſlature, and with the acceſſion of Edward the Firſt the feudal tenures and privileges had begun rapidly to decline. Domeſtic and prædial ſervitude had alſo been aboliſhed, or had fallen to diſuſe; and though villenage was never repealed by any regular enactment, the peaſantry had gradually been emerging from it into the ſtate of hired labourers and copyholders. During the interval up to the wars of the Roſes, without expreſs external aid, ſociety had been finding for itſelf a more eaſy level throughout its various gradations. The few ariſtocratic privileges that remained were no peculiar burden on the knight, the gentleman, or the yeoman, the burgeſs, or the labourer; and, what is very important to keep in mind, theſe ſeveral particular claſſes had obtained their form and *Feudality declining.*

Villenage paſſed away.

Changes in Society.

place in simple obedience to the working of general laws. Servitude or villenage was no part of feudalism; and the tendency of the feudal system itself was to decay, in proportion to the higher development of that principle of mutual rights and duties, and of the corresponding obligations thereby engendered, on which feudalism was founded.

A more striking illustration of this truth could not perhaps be afforded than by the contrast, which has not escaped observation, between the insurrections of Wat Tyler and Jack Cade. It is the remark of Sir Frederick Eden, in his excellent book on The Poor, that in the earlier of these popular tumults, which, notwithstanding the atrocities that attended it, very materially contributed towards the extinction of servitude, the language of the rebels, who were chiefly villeins, bespeaks men not unacquainted with the essential requisites of rational liberty. They required the abolition of slavery, freedom of commerce in market towns without tolls or imposts, and a fixed rent on lands instead of services due by villenage. But more remarkable and worthy of notice is the advance which, after the comparatively short interval of three quarters of a century, Jack Cade's rebellion proclaimed. Here there is nothing to connect the movement with any forms of serfdom. What rebels now claimed with arms in their hands, was the redress of such public wrongs as the King's profligate expenditure, and the subject's exposure to illegal exactions in order to maintain it; the preference of foreigners over

§ 1. *The Plantagenets: Henry VI.*

Englishmen in the offices of State; the gross wrongs committed by sheriffs and the collectors of taxes; the imperfect and uncertain administration of justice; and finally (most memorable grievance of all) the unwarrantable interference of the nobles in elections for the House of Commons. Nothing could more strongly show how rapid must have been the fall of the feudal system when once the change began; or how naturally the classes immediately below the noble, had become parties to a league offensive and defensive against him. The good old Fuller so hated all rebellions, except rebellions against popery, that he finds in these popular insurrections a reason why the better sort of people, to avoid being confounded with levellers and rabble, set up a variety of nice social distinctions: but the truth lies exactly the other way. Less and less were the distinctions marked, as the Tudor time came on. Commerce and intelligence level by exalting. And Mr. Hallam has pointed attention to the very unpleasing remark, which everyone who attends to the subject of prices will be disposed to think not ill-founded, that the labouring classes engaged in agriculture were generally better provided with the means of subsistence in the reign of Henry the Sixth than at the period when he wrote.

Evidence more direct and positive, indeed, is not wanting, of the comparative happiness and freedom of the people generally under the latter years of the Plantagenet rule. Two very trustworthy writers have sketched, from personal observation, the respective condition

[margin:] Rapid fall of Feudal System:

[margin:] as the people rose.

[margin:] Levelling of distinctions.

[margin:] Comforts of labouring classes.

[margin:] Respective condition of England

of England and of France at this time; and both have directed attention to the fact that while, in France, there exifted only the two divifions of a powerful governing nobleffe and a fervile peafant population, in England, on the other hand, a third and middle clafs had been able to make good its independence, becaufe the nobles wifely had retained no privileges that prevented their mixing and marrying freely with other claffes of the realm. So while in France the principle of the Civil Code, that the will of the monarch is law, prevailed, the people in England lived under protection of laws of their own enacting; while the French people were plundered at the fole difcretion of their Prince, who gave immunity only to the nobles, the Englifh people paid taxes of their own impofing; and while an Englifhman upon any charge of crime had the benefit of trial by a jury of his peers, confeffion was extorted from a Frenchman by the rack. When thus, twenty years before Henry the Seventh afcended the throne, Sir John Fortefcue wrote in praife of the Englifh laws, he placed all thefe advantages on the diftinct ground of the fpecial limitation of the power of the Sovereign, and of the non-exclufive character of the privileges of the Lords; and when his yet more travelled and experienced contemporary, Philip de Comines, turned to England from the contemplation of other States, as the country where the commonwealth was beft governed, it was becaufe he had reafon to believe that there the People were " leaft oppreffed."

§ 1. *The Plantagenets: Henry VI.*

What the main guarantees againſt oppreſ- *De Lau-*
ſion were, Henry the Sixth's learned Chan- *dibus Legum*
cellor enables us to ſtate in detail with tolerable *Angliæ.*
exactneſs. In the firſt place, the " ſole will of 1465.
" the prince " could not enact a law, nor make
alterations in exiſting laws, nor " burthen men
" againſt their wills with ſtrange impoſitions,"
nor " lay taxes or ſubſidies of what kind
" ſoever upon the ſubject," but with the con- Reſtraints
current conſent of the whole kingdom through on prerogative.
their repreſentatives in Parliament. Theſe
repreſentatives conſiſted of the lords ſpiritual
(biſhops and mitred abbots), and lords temporal (in right of property, by hereditary Conſtitu-
claim, or, after Richard the Second, by ſum- tion of Parlia-
mons), who voted in the upper houſe ; and of ment.
individuals choſen by the freeholders of counties, and the burgeſſes of towns, who formed
the lower houſe. In the next place, no man Rights of
could be thrown into priſon, but under ſanc- the ſub-
tion of a legal warrant which ſpecified his ject.
offence, and with the right of demanding
ſpeedy trial. That trial, moreover, muſt be
heard in a public court, in the diſtrict where
the alleged offence was committed, and be
determined concluſively by the verdict of
twelve men ; which in like manner decided
queſtions of fact, as affecting the civil rights of
the ſubject. Finally, the ſervants and officers
of the Crown were liable to actions of damage, Reſpon-
or to criminal proceſs, when the ſubject ſuf- ſibility of theCrown.
fered unjuſtly at their hands in perſon or
eſtate ; nor could they plead in anſwer or juſtification, even the direct order of the Sovereign.

How far theſe guarantees, and eſpecially the

Encroachments of Executive.
last, were reduced or evaded in practice, it would not be difficult to show. Lord Macaulay has remarked on the facility with which a prince who reserved to himself a pardoning power might overstep the limits that separate executive from legislative functions, by so remitting or so enforcing penalties as virtually to annul or create the statute imposing them. But, in theory at least, no one ventured to dispute the law; and when judges were honest, and juries intelligent and brave, an effective restraint was not seldom put upon the Crown.

Checks of Parliament.
The checks of Parliament had invariable recognition. In affairs of peace and war, in the marriages of princes, in control of the domestic government, Parliament had now for centuries claimed and obtained the privilege of advising, and not seldom of restraining, the Sovereign; and in one momentous question, it had completely succeeded, as we have seen, in establish-

Control of the purse.
ing its paramount authority. The formal tenure and absolute control of the public purse had at length been finally yielded by the Crown. The struggle lasted long; but more than a century before the first Tudor, no prince had even attempted to impose a tax without the consent of Parliament. Happily for the prince, indeed, when such consent involved any great difficulty, he had the show of begging and borrowing to resort to; but the very name of the

Loans and Benevolences.
Loan or the Benevolence, the mere pretence that he would borrow and beg, kept alive his formal abandonment of the right to take, and at last strengthened the people to destroy it for ever.

One consideration should be added, which in

§ 1. *The Plantagenets: Henry VI.*

every retrospect of English constitutional history it is safe not to lose sight of. In reviewing the course of events through which the Commons' house of parliament obtained recognition, it is important not to attach too great a weight to their single unassisted authority. They profited less by power to which they could of themselves lay claim, than by power or weakness in other sections of the State. They were stronger after the rebellion of the serfs, which struck the blow at villenage; they were stronger after the rebellion of the barons, which crowned the first Lancastrian king. Deriving help alternately from the powers above and below themselves, it would have fared ill with the third branch of the legislature at any difficult crisis, if, unsupported by the people, they had been unassisted by the lords. Nor might it be unjust to measure the relative value of such support and of such assistance, by a comparison of the less perfect maintenance of the national liberties, with the absolute victory in taxation. In the first, the Commons were often deserted by the Barons; in the last, they were never deserted by the People.

There the supreme force lies. None exists that can be compared with it, when moved into action. The bodily fetters of the feudal system, the mental bondage of the Roman Catholic priesthood, were expedients to keep the People at rest; but they could not last for ever. The doom of feudalism had gone forth, before the preaching of Wickliffe began. It only remained that the aristocratic factions should throw themselves into a self-exhausting strug-

Source of strength to Commons.

Derived from other powers.

Assisted from above and from below.

The People the supreme force.

Expedients to keep it down.

gle, and, underneath the very ſtorm, provide for thoſe principles which they muſt elſe have refiſted, and might have overthrown, an unconſcious but efficient ſhelter.

Wars of Roſes. Edward IV. Edward V. Richard III.
1461.
1483.

During the wars of the Roſes there was no leiſure to perſecute the Lollards; and commerce and the arts, unobſtructed by any intermeddling, were left to their natural development. Even when there was intermeddling, it ſhowed how Commerce had been riſing. The few legiſlative enactments of this ſingular period, paſſed when parliaments were at leiſure from raiſing or putting down the rival ſovereigns, ſufficiently prove its importance, and that of its cultivators.

Legiſlation during Civil wars.

It was a parliament of Edward the Fourth, which, after confirming the ſtatutes of the fourth, fifth, and ſixth Henries (with the impolitic and dangerous diſtinction of " late, in fact, but not of right, kings of " England") prohibited the importation of foreign corn; it was in parliaments of Edward the Fourth and Richard the Third, that importations of foreign manufacture were forbidden, where the like articles could be produced at home; and it was by Richard the Third him-

Richard III.'s ſtatute againſt forced loans.

ſelf (who had the ſtrong inducement of all uſurpers to invite popularity from every ſource) that the practice of extorting money from merchants and citizens, on pretence of loans and benevolences, was aboliſhed, for which the uſurper has obtained the praiſe of Lord Bacon as "a prince in militar virtue approved, jealous " of the honour of the Engliſh nation, and " likewiſe a good law maker, for the eaſe and " ſolace of the common people." Thus the

§ 1. *The Plantagenets: Richard III.*

marked increase and growing respect of commerce, the sudden reawakening of learning, advances made in the useful arts, and the earliest great endowments for the foundation of grammar-schools and places of popular education (after the 25th of Henry the Sixth, these foundations increased rapidly everywhere),—are the incidents which also signalise the time, when the chiefs of the great families, ejected finally from those provinces of France which had fed their appetites for plunder and power, had been impelled to that conflict with each other, on their own soil, of which all the sufferings and all the retribution were to fall upon themselves alone. For though this was a strife which lasted incessantly for thirty years, though twelve great pitched battles were fought in it, though eighty princes of the blood were slain, it raged only on the surface of the land, and the peaceful current beneath was free to run on as before. The desolation of the bloody conflict never reached the heart of the towns, except in awakening such instincts of danger as are the primary sources of safety. Hence, on the one hand, for precaution and defence, guilds, commercial brotherhoods, and municipal safeguards silently arose, to grow more hardy and to flourish; while, on the other, ancient baronies, all-powerful families, names that had overawed the crown and overshadowed the people, sank in the conflict, never to rise again. The storm that swept the lofty, spared the low. It was the beginning of a vast social change, now accomplished apparently without the aid of those whom principally it was to

Advances in commerce, learning, and the arts.

Loss of the French provinces.

War on surface of the land, Peace beneath.

Commercial guilds replacing great families.

Break-up of syftem of Middle Ages. affect; and not limited to England. Over the whole continent of Europe its manifestations might be seen. The syftem of the Middle Ages was everywhere breaking up. The sway of a feudal chiefdom, in all modifications of its form still fitful and turbulent, was ending; *Kingcraft succeeds.* and there was rising, to take its place, a predominance of kingship in personal attributes, a calm concentrated individual cunning, or, as it was called in after years, when it had lost the subtle qualities that justified the name, a Kingcraft, which in two great monarchies was destined to overpower Freedom, and in the third to fall before it.

Its chief professors. The *tres magi* of kings, renowned for possession of this supreme craft, have been celebrated by Lord Bacon. Louis the Eleventh had arisen in France, and Ferdinand in Spain; yet the lesson for which Machiavelli waited was incomplete, until Henry Tudor took possession of the *French, Spanish, and English kings.* English throne. To the French and Spanish kings, with standing armies at their back to silence their States General and their Cortes, the task of tyranny was not very difficult; but an insular kingdom, protected from its neighbours by the sea, had no pretence to indulge in such a sovereign luxury as the professional Soldier, and the more difficult problem awaited our English king of predominating over parliament by sheer *Results in England.* force of the prerogative. Favoured by circumstances, it succeeded for a time; but it left to a later time that forced readjustment of the balance, which, by raising parliament far above the prerogative, preserved for us finally the old Constitution of the realm.

§ II. THE TUDORS.

THOUGH the last living representative of the house of Lancaster, Henry Tudor was not its legitimate heir; but from his marriage with the heiress of the house of York, he derived a strong title. His own dissatisfaction with it nevertheless, and his uneasy desire to surround it with other guarantees, are among the indications of a state of feeling in England, at the time, which further distinguishes the position of Henry the Seventh from that of the other of the *tres magi*. The act of settlement passed by the two Houses upon his accession, taking great pains to avoid either the assertion or contradiction of any pretensions of lineal descent, had created strictly a parliamentary title; but he afterwards obtained a rescript from Pope Innocent the Third, setting forth all the other conditions on which he desired it to be known that the crown of England also belonged to him. It was his, according to this document, by right of war, by notorious and indisputable hereditary succession, by the wish and election of all the prelates, nobles, and commons of the realm, and by the act of the three estates in Parliament assembled; but nevertheless, to put an end to the bloody wars caused by the rival claims of the house of York, and at the urgent request of the three estates, he had consented to marry the eldest daughter and true heir of Edward the Fourth: and now, therefore, the supreme Pontiff, being called to confirm the dispensation necessary to such mar-

Henry VII. 1485.

Uneasiness as to succession.

Parliamentary settlement.

Pope's rescript on Henry's title:

riage, declared the meaning of the act of settlement passed by Parliament to be, that Henry's issue, whether by Elizabeth, or, in case of her death, by any subsequent marriage, were to inherit the throne. More remarkable than the rescript itself, however, were the means taken to carry it directly to the classes it was meant to address. It is the first similar document of which we have any evidence that it was translated into English and circulated in a popular form throughout England. A broadside containing it, printed by Caxton, is one of the most interesting of modern discoveries in matters of this kind.

Such indications may at least satisfy us that Henry Tudor would not very gravely have resented the description which has been given of him by Lord Bolingbroke, as a creature of the people raised to the throne to cut up the roots of faction, to restore public tranquillity, and to establish a legal government on the ruins of tyranny. The same writer, however, who doubts if he succeeded in this design, is undoubtedly wrong when he supposes that he failed in establishing what by all the customs of historical courtesy must be called a legal government. It is not of course to be disguised that in spite of many great principles asserted in it, and advantages achieved, his reign was not in its immediate course favourable to liberty. But the fact, as little to be questioned, that during its continuance, risings in the Commonalty were far more frequent than remonstrances in the Commons, and that upon questions where the people proved most

Marginal notes: translated for the people. and first printed in broadside by Caxton. Lord Bolingbroke's view of the reign. Losses to public liberty. Defection of parliament.

§ II. The Tudors: Henry VII.

ſtubborn, parliament generally was moſt compliant, ſufficiently ſhows that the defection did not ſo much lie with the people themſelves, as with their proper leaders in the State. It was neverthelefs the peculiarity of Henry's defpotifm, as diſtinguiſhed from that of his more violent predeceſſors, that he bottomed it ſtrongly on the precedents and language of law, ſcreening the violation of liberty by artful employment of its forms; and though this may have made the deſpotiſm more odious while it laſted, it eſtabliſhed more certainly a limit to its duration. Relatively to what is called the State, circumſtances had thrown an overbalance of power into the hands of Henry; but to the maſs of the people, theſe very circumſtances rendered him unconſciouſly the inſtrument of great ſocial and political change. The poſition he occupies in hiſtory, and the rights he exerciſed, began and ended with his race.

Maintenance of legal forms.

Peculiarity of Tudor deſpotiſm.

Everything at once ſhowed ſigns of deep and permanent alteration. The immediate reſult of the battle of Boſworth, which left victory in the hands of Henry and the ſmaller baronial faction of the Lancaſters, was the commencement of a ſyſtem by which the more numerous nobles of the oppoſite faction were as much as poſſible depreſſed, by which ſevere ſtatutes againſt the further prevalence of armed retainers were freſhly enacted or revived, reſtrictions on the deviſing of land in effect removed, and all things directed towards an ultimate transfer of the old baronial ſtrength into entirely new channels. Poverty itſelf

Indications of ſocial change.

Power changing hands.

became the herald and forerunner of change. While large numbers of the baronial vaſſals took refuge in the towns, increaſing their power and privileges, large numbers unhappily ſtill remained upon the ſoil; and theſe, no longer neceſſary for the ſhows of pomp or the realities of war, ſuffered the worſt horrors of deſtitution, were driven to its laſt reſources, became incendiaries or thieves, overran the land as beggars, and, in the end, rendered neceſſary that great ſocial revolution, which took the name of a Poor Law in the reign of Elizabeth.

Neceſſity for a Poor Law.

Of the ſhattered ariſtocracy of England only twenty-nine repreſentatives preſented themſelves when Henry called his firſt Parliament, and ſeveral of theſe were recent creations. Doubtleſs it was well, for the ultimate advance of liberty, that the old feudal power had thus been ſo completely ſubdued, and the way by ſuch means prepared for the deciſive ſtruggle with the Stuarts; but for the immediate progreſs of liberty, it was certainly leſs beneficial. The Houſe of Commons, ſuddenly wanting in an old and habitual ſupport, was too ready an inſtrument for the mere uſe and convenience of the King; and to avail themſelves, in ſuch circumſtances, of every attainable advantage and turn it to the beſt account, in each caſe holding it for religion that craft might ſuperſede force, conſtituted the very art and genius of the *tres magi*. But though ſuch circumſtances worked well for the Mage upon the Engliſh throne, he did not, with all his craft, penetrate influences around him that were

Houſe of Lords: 29 in number.

Commons weakened in by weakneſs in Lords.

Influences unſeen.

§ 11. *The Tudors: Henry VII.*

less obvious; nor suspect that, by a purely selfish legislation, he might yet be advancing higher hopes and more comprehensive designs. Surrounded, and no longer assailable, by the impoverished and broken power of the past, he was unconscious of a more formidable power which was silently and insensibly replacing it. He thought only of himself and his succession. When, by the statute enlarging and extending the old Consilium Regis, and creating the Star Chamber, he raised the judicial authority of the King in Council to a height at which the fiercest of his Norman predecessors would not have dared to aim, he did it to support the Throne. That a rallying cry against the Star Chamber might one day bear the Throne into dust was not to him within the sphere of possibility. What was near him, in short, he never mistook or marred, and no man so clearly saw what would help or might obstruct himself. As Lord Bacon says, he went substantially to his own business; and, to the extent of not suffering any little envies or any great passions to stand in its way, he was a practical and sagacious statesman. But he was not a great king, though he might be called an able, a crafty, and a prudent one. *Unconscious lawmaking.*

Star Chamber created.

A keen but narrow vision.

So much, even in the midst of eulogy that might itself have preserved his name, would seem to be admitted by his incomparable biographer. " His wisdom," says Lord Bacon, " by often evading from perils, was turned " rather into a dexterity to deliver himself from " dangers when they pressed him, than into a *Lord Bacon's character of Henry VII.*

"providence to prevent and remove them afar
"off. And even in nature, the fight of his
"mind was like some sights of eyes; rather
"strong at hand, than to carry afar off. For
"his wit increased upon the occasion; and so
"much the more, if the occasion were sharp-
"ened by danger." It will be a sufficient
comment on these pregnant sentences merely
to enumerate his leading acts of sovereignty.
Heresy he thought dangerous, and he burnt
more followers of Wycliffe than any since the
first Lancastrian king. Winner of a successful
stake in battle, he knew the chances of war to
be dangerous, and he favoured strenuously the
arts of peace. Served by men whom his
death or discomfiture might suddenly attaint
with rebellion, he thought it dangerous to
leave those friends without security against the
possible vengeance of future faction; and he
passed a law which made possession of the
throne the subject's obligation to allegiance,
and justified resistance to all who should dispute
it. Incessant suits for alienated lands he thought
dangerous, in a country torn with revolutionary
quarrel; and his famous statute of fines barred,
after certain conditions, all claims of ancient
heritage. But not to him, therefore, belongs
any part of the glory of those greater results
which flowed indirectly from these measures of
precaution. It was with no intended help
from him that the Wycliffe heresy struck
deeper root; that more eager welcome was
given to the studies which in England marked
the revival of learning; that the civil duties
of allegiance were placed on a just foundation;

Leading acts of his sovereignty.

What was intended by his legislation.

What was effected beyond his intention.

§ 11. *The Tudors: Henry VII.*

and that the feudal reftrictions of landed property were finally broken.

On the other hand, with relation to the progrefs of conftitutional freedom, or to the prevalence of juft views in government and popular legiflation, this reign of Henry the Seventh muft be regarded as the opening of a middle or tranfitional ftate. The feudal ftrength had been broken, and the popular ftrength had not made itfelf felt; power was changing hands, and confcience was about to be fet free, and both were to be meanwhile committed, almoft unrefervedly, into the keeping of the Tudors. The intereft of the fucceeding reigns, up to the very middle of Elizabeth's great career, is lefs political than focial; and it is not in the ftatute book or the parliament roll that we are to look for what fmoothed and made ready the way. Early in the fummer of the eleventh year after Henry the Seventh's acceffion, a Venetian feaman and pilot who had fettled in Briftol during the impulfe given to Englifh commerce in the wars of the Rofes, fet fail from that city, accompanied by his three fons, with the firft European expedition that ever reached the American continent. Later in the fame fummer, Lord Mountjoy brought over Erafmus into England, to take part in the new ftudy of which Oxford had become the unaccuftomed fcene. Of commerce, as of learning, it was the reawakening time. The Cabots difcovered the Ifland of Newfoundland and St. John, and, with their five fhips under the Englifh flag, crept along the coaft of Florida; while Erafmus, in the Greek clafs at

Interval between feudal and popular agencies.

Firft Expedition to America. 1496.

Vifit of Erafmus to England.

Sebaftian Cabot in the New World.

Oxford, was making difcoveries not lefs rich
or ftrange. "The world," exclaimed the
ftudent-fcholar, "is recovering the ufe of its
" fenfes, like one awakened from the deepeft
" fleep." The civilifation fo beginning, whatever ftruggle it had ftill to encounter, was to
reft finally on freer intercourfe and interchange
of the labours of men's hands as well as
thoughts ; and fingularly rare was the felicity
that befel the great Greek poet, whofe glory,
identified with nigh two thoufand years of the
hiftory of the paft, was to be alfo moft promi-
nently affociated with a frefh dawning and
reawakening of the world. As with the old,
fo with the new civilifation, which, through
all its heats and viciffitudes of quarrel, civil and
religious, was to find him ftill, as at firft,
driving along the Sigæan plain his temperate
and indefatigable horfes, making the Gods
themfelves his charioteers and minifters, and
keeping them, alike in the ardour of combat
and the tranquillity of Olympus, obedient to
his will.

<small>Erafmus in Oxford.</small>

<small>Revival of ftudy of Homer.</small>

<small>Greek Profeffor- fhip at Oxford. 1497.</small>

That Greek Clafs at Oxford was formed,
and in healthy vigorous action, when the
fecond fovereign of the Tudor race, to whom
even learned and intelligent inquirers have
exclufively attributed the improvement in lite-
rary ftudies and purfuits which was one of the
redemptions of his reign, was barely fix years
old. It is wonderful with what alarm it was
viewed at the very outfet. Thus early public
attention directed itfelf to what were called the
growing Oxford herefies. Lovers of exifting
fyftems and inftitutions lifted warning voice

<small>Diflike of the new learning.</small>

§ 11. *The Tudors: Henry VII.*

against them. Grave misgivings found utterance in many quarters; and for the most part in the tone of that good old English gentleman whose lamentations found later record in one of the writings of Richard Pace. "These foolish letters will end in some bad "business. I fairly wish all this learning at "the devil. All learned men are poor; even "the most learned Erasmus, I hear, is poor, "and in one of his letters calls the vile hag "Poverty his wife. By'r Lady, I had rather "my son were hanged than that he should be-"come a man of letters. We ought to teach "our sons better things."

A good old English complaint:

against Letters and Poverty.

Happily it was too late, for the mischief was done, and "the most learned Erasmus" had been its principal promoter. His brief sojourn at Oxford in his youth prefigures almost the whole of his illustrious career. The revival of learning—the re-awakening of the great writers of Greece and Rome—was to bring with it the downfall of the schoolmen; to whom the worst corruptions of the Church, and a large share of the vice and barbarism of monkery, were due. They had long banished from the studies of churchmen all pretence to a scriptural foundation. The honest pursuit of truth, they had replaced by argumentative subtlety; by methodical niceties of disputation; by scholastic distinctions, to the rest of the world unintelligible; by foul-killing lies, and "truths that work small good." It was the secret of the fierce opposition to the new learning, that it boded the ruin of this system sooner or later; and on the day when Erasmus

Part taken by Erasmus.

Disciples of Aquinas.

74   *Introductory Essay.*

System of the Schoolmen doomed.

and Colet met at Oxford, its doom had been pronounced. With the jargon of the old learning still dominant around them, with perhaps audible sounds of hideous dispute from monks and friars beneath their college windows, it was natural (though all to which it would eventually lead might not be seen) that their first interchange of thought should have been on language and style. Language

Language an enslaver as well as liberator.

has been called the liberator of mankind, but has also proved itself hardly less their enslaver; for almost as often as it has freed them from ignorance, it has handed them over to prejudice, or rebound them in the chains of custom. If the success of the schoolmen, and their strength in the Romish church, had arisen out of the confusion and imperfect understanding of language which their barbarous disputations engendered, it was fairly to

Connection of words and things.

be inferred that out of clearer and correcter notions of words would follow closer insight into things.

Even if not at first, however, the entire intention of Erasmus, it is not the less his

Erasmus's great weapon.

chief exploit and glory. With the mere weapon of style he was enabled to scourge the Dominicans from one end of Germany to the other. His exposure of the frauds and credulities of his age would have passed with comparatively little heed, if made less gracefully; and the printing-press of his friend Frobenius would have worked but heavily, if his easy and familiar wit had not lent it wings.

"A Second Lucian."

" Beware a second Lucian ! " cried the startled monks; " the fox is abroad that layeth waste "the vineyard of the Lord." And if that was the vineyard of the Lord, it was indeed laid waste by Erasmus. "He presumes to correct the Holy Spirit!" was the next note of alarm, as he presented to the world the first pure Greek text of the New Testament. But his gift was beyond recall; and what was thus by Erasmus made familiar to the learned, a stronger and more resolute spirit was at hand to make familiar to the people. The great scholar, in a word, taught by Grocyn and advised by Colet, was now, during the reign of our first Tudor sovereign, preparing minds at Oxford for the work which, even more than the unexampled compass of his learning and the vast number of his writings, immortalised his name. "Erasmus knows very well how to point out errors," said Luther in after years, "but he knows not how to teach the truth. He can do nothing but cavil and flout," he added; when in temper even less tolerant of that friend and fellow-workman, whom not long before he had called his glory and his hope, *decus nostrum et spes nostra*. It might be so; but the cavilling, and flouting, and rooting out of error, were in these early days the sowing of the seeds of truth. He who is to gather in the harvest, is as yet but a poor Franciscan schoolboy at Madgeburg, singing songs in the street for bread; and, meanwhile, this devotion so single hearted, this real hatred of hypocrisy and ignorance, this pure love of learning, this exalted spirit of labour, sacrifice, and self-denial, which made Erasmus the harbinger of a change whose extent he could not

First pure text of the Testament.

The way prepared for Luther.

Complaint of Erasmus.

Harbinger of the Reformation.

Titles of Erasmus to respect.

meaſure, and by which he conſtituted others, men of knowledge and eminence, unconſcious agents in a democratic revolution which of themſelves they would ſtrenuouſly have reſiſted, are ſurely entitled to large veneration and reſpect. It avails little againſt the claim, that the man who outran his time in thought, lagged behind it in action; and that, having borne the heat of a conteſt, he ſhrank from the reſponſibilities of a victory. What work was appointed him to do, he did with a ſingular ſucceſs. Superſtition and barbariſm had their firſt reſolute foe in him; the Scriptural foundations of truth and of morality had in him their great reſtorer; and it ſhould be matter of pride to Engliſhmen that it was here in Oxford, and by intercourſe with their countrymen, theſe glorious undertakings were canvaſſed, begun, and cheriſhed.

The ſtatute-book of Henry the Seventh, however, will be vainly ſearched for any attempt to ſtrengthen, govern, or direct ſuch agencies, whether material or moral. It was his policy to favour commerce for his own advantage; but moſt aſſuredly his proviſions againſt lending money on intereſt, againſt letting in foreign commodities, and for the ſuppoſed enrichment of the country by over-enrichment of himſelf, would have altogether failed to promote it. Among his legiſlative exploits none will be found to favour learning, nor did any of his acts of State ſuggeſt toleration for the new opinions; but nevertheleſs he could not burn a Lollard, without more widely diffuſing what men were ſo readily found calmly

His example.

His achievements.

His connection with Oxford.

Henry's Statutes.

Commerce and learning indirectly aſſiſted.

§ 11. *The Tudors: Henry VII.*

and even cheerfully to die for. To print an occasional pope's bull, or one of the acts of his own parliament, was the sole use to which he cared to put the types of Caxton or Wynkin de Worde; but there was sitting at the time, in those beggarly rooms of Oxford colleges, another parliament composed of such men as Grocyn, Linacre, Colet, More, Wolsey, and Erasmus, on whom that printing press was to confer an irresistible power, and who were legislating for the reign of his successor. Indeed, to that following reign, everything which marked out this from its predecessors had a singular and special reference; and not an opportunity in it, improved or not by Henry for himself, failed with tenfold increase to reach his son. Upon his two most prominent designs, of fencing the throne against conspiracy, and making it rich and independent, he suffered no doubt to rest. Of the few great nobles that remained, not one ever found favour from him; out of churchmen and lawyers exclusively, he chose his friends and counsellors; and "ever," as Bacon says, "having an eye to "might and multitude," there was not a gathering of common men, whether with the citizen's cap or the peer's badge, which was not watched by him so closely and unceasingly, and with so much caution, adroitness, and success, that of all the thick brood of treasons which marked the opening of the reign, not one existed at its close to vex its successor. That, even without his aid, the revenues of the Crown should at the same time have largely increased, was one of the consequences of the civil wars,

Uses of the Printing Press.

Legislating for the future.

Disfavour to nobles.

Favor to Churchmen and Lawyers.

Throne guarded from Treason;

which had difperfed the annuitants and cre-ditors who previoufly crowded the door of the Exchequer; but thefe revenues were handed down not merely unimpaired, but free from incumbrances, increafed by forfeitures, and with the enormous addition of his own ill-gotten exactions.

and enriched by Forfeitures.

" Belike he thought to leave his fon," fug-gefts Lord Bacon apologetically, " fuch a " kingdom and fuch a mafs of treafure, as he " might choofe his greatnefs where he would:" but nothing can palliate the iniquity by which fuch wealth was amaffed. Every means of extortion tried by the Plantagenet kings having been exhaufted, he fought out other and more fcandalous methods; and when, in his Courts at Weftminfter, he had found two learned lawyers fufficiently able, fupple, eloquent, and unfcrupulous, he was in poffeffion of what he fought. " As kings," fays James the Firft's experienced Chancellor, " do more eafily find " inftruments for their will and humour than " for their fervice and honour, he had gotten " for his purpofe, or beyond his purpofe, two " inftruments, Empfon and Dudley." Thefe men revived dormant claims of the Crown, founded on obfolete pretenfions of feudal tenure, and made them a means of frightful oppreffion. They difcovered forgotten cafes of forfeiture; invented falfe charges againft innocent men, from which releafe was only given on payment of what were termed mitigations; dragged forward arrears of old amercements, alleged to be unfatisfied; and, with the help of a fort of informers and plaintiffs who were called " pro-

New methods of Extortion.

Empfon and Dudley.

Ufes to which they were put.

§ 11. *The Tudors: Henry VIII.*

" moters," made the ordinary courfe of law an enormous engine of plunder. Unremembered penal ftatutes of profligate times were revived, to the end that, by intolerable exactions for offences unknown, unconfcious offenders might be dragged into the Exchequer; where Empfon and Dudley fat as barons, where packed dependents of the Crown difcharged the functions of juries, where juries with any fenfe of fhame were made docile by imprifonment and fine, and from whofe clutches the unhappy victims could only efcape by exorbitant compofition or hopelefs imprifonment. But, horrible as all this was, not a little was it owing to fuch atrocities that Henry the Eighth fucceeded to a better filled exchequer than any of his predeceffors fince the Conqueft, and to fo many greater facilities for the work it was appointed him to do. *Plunder under forms of law.* *Henry VIII. 1509.*

They did not indeed pafs without fome retribution. Though new honours had been largely heaped upon their perpetrators in the laft year of Henry the Seventh's reign, in the firft year of Henry the Eighth's both Empfon and Dudley were led to the fcaffold. The popular wrath demanded them as victims; and, it being more convenient that death fhould wipe out their debt, than that by any worfe accident the royal exchequer fhould be called to make reftitution, the new King gave them up to the executioner. Strong-willed as the Tudors were, they were generally able to put a prefent rein upon their paffions, when by fuch means they could make more fure of their ultimate fafe indulgence. They reigned in *Execution of Empfon and Dudley.* *Tudor characteriftics.*

England, without a successful rising against them, for upwards of a hundred years: but not more by a studied avoidance of what might so provoke the country, than by the most resolute repression of every effort, on the part of what remained of the peerage and great families, to make head against the Throne. They gave free indulgence to their tyranny only within the circle of the court, while they unceasingly watched and conciliated the temper of the people. The work they had to do, and which by more scrupulous means was not possible to be done, was one of paramount necessity; the dynasty uninterruptedly endured for only so long as was requisite to its thorough completion; and to each individual sovereign the particular task might seem to have been specially assigned. It was Henry's to spurn, renounce, and utterly cast off, the Pope's authority, without too suddenly revolting the people's usages and habits; to arrive at blessed results, by ways that a better man might have held to be accursed; during the momentous change in progress, to keep in necessary check both the parties it affected; to persecute with an equal hand the Romanist and the Lutheran; to send the Protestant to the stake for resisting Popery, and the Roman Catholic to the scaffold for not admitting *himself* to be Pope; while he meantime plundered the monasteries, rooted out and hunted down the priests, alienated the abbey lands, and glutted his creatures and his own coffers with that enormous spoil. It was Edward's to become the ready and undoubting instrument of Cranmer's design; to accept the

§ II. *The Tudors: Henry VIII.*

Reformation as it was so presented to him; in his brief reign, really to establish Protestantism on our English soil; but, with all the inexperience and more than the obstinacy of youth, so harshly, unsparingly, and precipitately to force upon the people Cranmer's compromise of doctrine and observance, as to render possible, even perhaps unavoidable, his elder sister's reign. It was Mary's to undo the effect of such precipitate eagerness of the Reformers, by lighting the fires of Smithfield; and opportunely to arrest the waverers from Protestantism, by exhibiting in their excess the very worst vices, the cruel bigotry, the hateful intolerance, the spiritual slavery, of Rome. It was Elizabeth's finally and for ever to uproot that slavery from amongst us, to champion all over the world a new and nobler faith, and immovably to establish in England the Protestant religion. *Mary's. 1553.* *Elizabeth's. 1558.*

But though the tasks thus appointed to this imperious and self-willed family, had the effect of imparting an exceptional character to their style and course of government, it is not to be inferred that even they dared openly to violate those old fundamental English laws of which it has ever been the nature, in all cases, adopting the fine expression of Fortescue, "to declare "in favour of liberty." Henry sent to the scaffold whomever he pleased, from within the precincts of the Court; but when, without the intervention of parliament, he would have taken the money of the people, he had to retreat before the resistance offered, and publicly to disavow the intention of breaking the laws *Tudor despotism exceptional.* *Its checks and limits.*

of the realm. Elizabeth's rule had been not less imperious than her father's, yet one of her latest acts was freely to surrender to the House of Commons her demand for certain monopolies, which had raised a fierce resistance in that house. Mary was able to burn, at her pleasure, the alienators of the abbey lands; but over the lands themselves, invested by forms of law in their new proprietors, she discovered that she was powerless. Unworthy as the position was, indeed, in which the House of Commons consented to place itself in these reigns, what survived of independence and courage still was able to find expression there; and the meanest-spirited of its assemblages had yet gleams of popular daring, which show how little might have served, even then, to put substance into the forms of liberty, and how ready was even a Tudor King, " as he would " sometimes strain up his laws to his preroga-" tive," to let down not the less, as Lord Bacon said of the founder of the race, " his " prerogative to his parliament." In truth it can never be too often repeated that tyranny can only reign in England through the pretences of freedom. Acts of Parliament are, with us, the weapons of despotic rule ; and at times they will recoil with danger to the user, or break in the despot's hand.

Of this the unhappy Mary had painful experience when she saw the very House she had packed with her creatures turn against her in the matter she had most at heart. They went with her in re-establishing over the kingdom the authority of Rome; but when she would have had them concede to her hufband an authority within the realm that might involve danger to the native privileges and laws, thofe very tools and creatures deferted her. Within two years fhe had to fummon and diffolve three Parliaments, and informations were pending againft recufant members at the time of her death. Nor will the fame kind of incidents fail to be noted in her ftronger father's reign. He found it not poffible to reduce the lower Houfe to the utterly dependent condition in which a conftant reaction of hope and dread (the choice between confifcation and the fcaffold, or church property and royal favour), foon placed what remained of the upper Houfe. The difficulty was not effentially very great, indeed, in dealing with the lower, but certain forms had to be obferved; and it is curious that in Henry the Eighth's reign, not only (in the cafe of Ferrers) was one of the moft valuable confirmations of privilege obtained by the Commons, but upwards of thirty members were added to their houfe, upon the principle expreffed in the preamble to the act for fo extending reprefentation to the principality of Wales, that it is difadvantageous to any place to be unreprefented, and that thofe who are bound by the laws are entitled to have a voice in their enactment. Thus, whatever ufes the Houfe of Commons might lend itfelf to, the idea of that higher function of reprefentation was at leaft never loft; and even the Tudors had to remember, in common with all princes to whom as yet the luxury of a ftanding army was unknown, that

<small>Three diffolutions in two years.</small>

<small>Privileges won from Henry VIII.</small>

<small>Thirty members added to Commons.</small>

<small>Safeguards of an armed people.</small>

Introductory Essay.

Obligation for martial exercise.

the people so represented, being freemen, were trained universally to bear arms, and were under penalties to present themselves, at stated periods, for martial exercise in their counties and shires. Only because he wielded an authority, therefore, not strictly his, and for the use of which he was not directly responsible, could the sovereign in such case ever assume to

Power beyond the Sovereign.

be all-powerful. There was a power beyond, which the people had now for two centuries uniformly recognised, and which alone could be the instrument, whoever might be the immediate agent, of changes affecting themselves. They saw the lower House continue to grant subsidies, not to be raised by any other means; and they saw it continued to be used in the proposal of statutes, which without

All legislation in name of Commons.

its consent could never become binding. It gave their sole validity to the bills of attainder which struck down the guilty, or shed the blood of the innocent; and only by its sanction had one-fifth of the landed property of the nation been transferred suddenly to new proprietors. As the times of the Tudors wore on, too, and left the character of their work, and its results, more visible, the members of that House began to claim for it worthier

Substance as well as form claimed by them.

associations. "I have heard of old Parlia-"ment men," said Peter Wentworth from his place there, in the latter half of Elizabeth's reign, "that the banishment of the Pope and "Popery, and the restoring of true Religion, "had their beginning from this house, and "not from the bishops."

Few were the opportunities directly obtained

§ 11. *The Tudors: Elizabeth.*

by the people, however, either through themselves or their reprefentatives, in this great reign. The authority of the two Houfes had been reduced, at her acceffion, to a point fo low that not a barrier any longer interpofed itfelf between the fovereign authority and the popular allegiance. But in placing herfelf freely amongft her fubjects, in making their interefts hers, in condefcending to their amufements and their prejudices, as if they were her children, they were yet made to feel that they muft fubmit themfelves to the difcipline of children. Defiring rather the fame of a fovereign demagogue than a fovereign prince, the afpiring tendencies found no countenance from her, and the mayor and the alderman had better chances of her favour than the man of literature or genius. But the people had their Spenfers and their Shakefpeares, in her defpite; they had their tranflation of the Bible, with its leffons of charity and brotherhood; they had as free accefs to the literature of the ancient writers as to that of the living and furpaffing genius which furrounded them; adventure and chivalry moved, in well-known forms and living realities, through the land; and the commoneft people might lift caps, as they paffed along the ftreets, to Drake, to Sidney, or to Raleigh. The work was thus far accomplifhed which Erafmus and his friends at Oxford had begun; and it was only neceffary that thofe rifing influences that had marked the acceffion of the Tudor family fhould appear in full and active operation on the minds of the Englifh people, to fentence to

Elizabeth's reign.

Character of the Queen:

A sovereign demagogue.

Advantages of the People.

Results of the Reformation.

Oxford leffons complete.

Change impending.

a gradual but certain downfall the half-political half-patriarchal fyftem of this famous woman, by far the greateft of her race. The fons and daughters of the Arcadia were the parents of the men of Charles and Cromwell.

Rife of religious difcontent.

The Queen had been twelve years upon the throne when difcontent took an ominous and threatening form. An effential feature in the Tudor fyftem had been that the framework of the ancient hierarchy of Rome fhould be left untouched. At a time when politics were fuddenly become fubordinated to religion, the idea of unlimited fpiritual dominion was too valuable to be furrendered, carrying with it, as it did by a very fimple analogy, unlimited temporal dominion alfo. This dominion had moreover been placed, by the aids of fupremacy and uniformity, at the abfolute ufe and difpofal of the fovereign; and in thus formally affuming the caft-off robes of the Pope, Elizabeth rivalled her father in the even partiality of her perfecutions. Indeed, her antagonifm to the Romanift was in fome refpects lefs keen and perfonal than to the Proteftant non-conformift. She loved to the lateft moment of her life the gorgeous ceremonials of religion, as fhe cherifhed all that placed in fubjection to authority the fenfes and the faith of men; and while, with this feeling, fhe adhered to forms and ceremonies which her mafculine fenfe would elfe have put afide in fcorn, and clothed her own bifhops with the fupreme authority fhe had ftruck down from thofe of Rome, fhe unhappily overlooked altogether the poffibility of danger from fuch reftraints to the impulfes

The newly eftablifhed Church.

Impulfes of Reformation reftrained.

A danger overlooked.

§ 11. *The Tudors: Elizabeth.* 87

of the Reformation. But this danger was now at hand.

In the year 1570, the inftitution of epif- copacy in the Proteftant church was openly affailed by the Lady Margaret's profeffor of divinity at Cambridge. There had been an active difcuffion going on for fome years, on matters of minor confideration. Tippets had been violently contefted, and fad and ferious had been difputes upon the furplice. But now, to the amazement of the imperious Parker, who had declared that he would maintain to the death thefe effentials of the new religion, all further mention of fuch matters ceafed, and the archbifhop was fummoned to maintain to the death neither tippet nor furplice, but the whole ecclefiaftical hierarchy of England. Cartwright's lectures were as a match to a train, and a formidable party of puritans ftarted up in England. It is not, however, neceffary to dwell on the ftruggle that enfued. It was fo far conducted with fpirit by individual members of the Houfe of Commons, as to achieve feveral folid acceffions to the privileges of that houfe, and to leave on lafting record a valuable proteft againft the Tudor fyftem as one which centuries of Englifh liberty rejected and difclaimed. Indeed, if Elizabeth had been lefs wife and prudent, if her perfonal expenditure had been wafteful or her exchequer ill fupplied, it might have gone hardly with her. In vain fhe packed the houfe with placemen, and flooded the country party with upwards of fixty new members. Still the Stricklands and the Wentworths remained, and ftill in every feffion there was

Cartwright's Lectures at Cambridge. 1570.

Puritan party formed.

Its leaders in Houfe of Commons.

Vain attempts to fubdue them.

at least placed on record the duty and right of parliament to inquire into every public matter and to remedy every proved abuse. The cry of English liberty was never raised more piercingly, though it remained for later days to send back to it a louder and more terrible echo.

<small>Last act of the greatest Tudor.</small> Elizabeth herself, in the closing years of her reign, showed that she had not remained unconscious or unmoved by the vehemence and sharpness of that cry. Greatest of the Tudors as she unquestionably was, it was when her authority might seem to have been most weakened, that she bequeathed to the race which succeeded hers, by her last act of sovereignty, an example which might have saved them the throne, if they could have profited by it. Unhappily they could only imitate her in the qualities which provoked, and not in those which subdued or turned aside, resistance.

<small>Elizabeth's antipathy to Puritans.</small> It is a striking fact in the career of this great Queen, that she could put aside her hatred and contempt even of Puritanism itself, when she saw it had become so transfused with the desires and wants of the people as to represent no longer a religious discontent alone. While she believed it to be confined within that limit, the prison and the rack were the only replies <small>Puritan sympathy with Elizabeth.</small> she made to it: because she knew that from all serious attacks to maintain it, the cause she championed then protected her most effectually; and that from the very dungeons into which she might throw the Puritan leaders, they would yet be ready to offer up, as they did, their prayers for the safety of herself and

§ II. The Tudors: Elizabeth.

the stability of her government. For to all the world it had become notorious, that the destinies and fate of the Reformation had for the time fallen exclusively into her hands; and that not in England only did she animate every effort connected with the new faith, but that, in her, centred not less the hopes of all who were carrying on the struggle, against overwhelming numbers, in other lands. Of the movement, however, of which she was thus the heroine, she unhappily never recognised the entire meaning and tendency; and instead of disarming Puritanism by concession, she had strengthened and cherished it by persecution.

Champion and leader of the Reformation.

But, towards the close of her reign, when, after that subduement of the Roman Catholic power on the continent to which she had devoted so many glorious years, she found leisure to investigate patiently the domestic concerns of her kingdom, the old Puritan remonstrance presented itself to her under a new form, and in ominous conjunction with very wide-spread political dissatisfaction. Everywhere voices had become loud against royal patents of monopolies; and not only was her first minister's coach mobbed in the streets when he went to open her parliament of 1601, but, when Mr. Serjeant Heyle rose in that parliament to express his amazement that a subsidy should be refused to the Queen, seeing that she had no less a right to the lands and goods of the subject than to any revenue of her crown, the House universally " hemmed and " laughed and talked " down the learned

Puritanism in a new form:

Joined with political discontent.

A Queen's Serjeant coughed down.

Serjeant. Nor was the aspect of affairs become less grave or strange, when, a little later in that same assembly, Cecil thought it right to warn the lower House of dangers which had particularly declared themselves to his ripe and experienced judgment. "I must needs give "you this for a future caution, that whatso- "ever is subject to public expectation cannot "be good, while the parliament matters are "ordinary talk in the street. I have heard "myself, being in my coach, these words "spoken aloud : *God prosper those that further* "*the overthrow of these monopolies!*" It had not then seemed possible to the Secretary's experience, that the Queen herself might think it safer to attract this prayer to her own prosperity than to let any one else reap the benefit of it; but a very few days undeceived him. Elizabeth in person went to the House, withdrew all claim to the monopolies which had excited resistance, redressed other grievances complained of, and quitted Westminster amid the shouts and prayers of the people that God might prosper their Queen. Within two more years she died, bequeathing the Crown to her cousin of Scotland.

Cecil's warning to Commons.

Elizabeth's last appearance in Parliament.

James I. 1603.

To this point, then, the Tudor system had been brought, when Scotland and England became united under one sovereignty, and the noble inheritance fell to a race, who, comprehending not one of the conditions by which alone it was possible to be retained, profligately misused until they completely lost it. The calamity was in no respect foreseen by the statesman, Cecil, to whose exertion it was mainly

Two kingdoms united under the Stuarts.

due that James was seated on the throne; yet
in regard to it he cannot be held blameless.
Right he undoubtedly was, in so far as the
course he took satisfied a national desire, and
brought under one crown two kingdoms that
could not separately exist with advantage to
either; but it remains a reproach to his name
that he let slip the occasion of obtaining for
the people some settled guarantees which could
not then have been refused, and which might
have saved half a century of bloodshed. None
such were proposed to James. He was allowed
to seize a prerogative, which for upwards of
fifty years had been strained to a higher pitch
than at any previous period of the English
history; and his clumsy grasp closed on it
without a sign of remonstrance from the leading statesmen of England. "Do I mak the
"judges? Do I mak the bishops?" he
exclaimed, as the powers of his new dominion
dawned on his delighted sense: "then, God's
"wauns! I mak what likes me, law and gos-
"pel!" It was even so. At a time when it was
manifest that the prerogative had outgrown
even the power of the greatest of the Tudors
to retain it, when the conflict long provoked
was about to begin, when the balance of popular right had to be redressed or the old constitution to be utterly surrendered, this licence
to make gospel and law was given, with other
far more questionable powers, to a man whose
personal appearance and qualities were as sug-
gestive of contempt, as his public acts were
provocative of rebellion. It is necessary to
dwell upon this part of the subject; for it is

Opportunity lost by Cecil.

No conditions made at Accession.

No check on overstrained prerogative.

Provocation to Rebellion.

only juſt to his leſs fortunate ſon and ſucceſſor to ſay, that in it lies the ſource of not a little for which the penalty was paid by him. What is called the Great Rebellion can have no comment ſo pregnant as that which is ſuggeſted by the character and previous career of the firſt of the Stuart kings. Upon this, therefore, and upon the court with which he ſurrounded himſelf in England, though they do not otherwiſe fall ſtrictly within my purpoſe, I ſhall offer a few remarks before cloſing this Eſſay.

Penalties to be paid.

§. III. FIRST STUART KING.

That James the Firſt had a decidedly more than fair ſhare of learning is not to be denied; but it was of no uſe to anyone, and leaſt of all to himſelf. George Buchanan was reproached for having made him a pedant, and replied that it was the beſt he could make of him. Learning the great teacher could communicate, but neither objects nor methods for its uſe, nor even a knowledge of its value. Probably no ſuch fooliſh man, in ways of ſpeech and life, as James the Firſt, was ever in fairneſs entitled, before or ſince, to be called a really learned one. Nevertheleſs the greater marvel is, that not only, being thus fooliſh in language and conduct, was he undoubtedly a ſcholar, but that he had alſo an amount of native ſhrewdneſs which ſcholarſhip had neither taught him, nor tamed in him. He poſſeſſed, to a quite curious extent, a quick natural cunning, a native mother wit, and the art of circumventing an adverſary; and it was to this Henri Quatre alluded when he called

Character of James.

His learning.

His cunning and ſhrewdneſs.

him the wifest fool in Christendom. That what he had acquired ever helped him to a useful thought, or a suggestion of practical worth, it is impossible to discover. Mystically to define the prerogative as a thing set far above the law; to exhibit king-craft as his own particular gift, directly vouchsafed from heaven; to denounce Presbytery as the offspring of the devil; to blow with furious vehemence what he called counterblasts to tobacco; to deal damnation to the unbelievers in witchcraft, and to pour out the wrath of the Apocalypse upon Popery; were its highest exploits. He had been busy torturing and burning old women for the imaginary crime of witchcraft, while Elizabeth was preparing a scaffold for his mother; and it was to make the rest of the world as besotted with superstition as himself, that he wrote his *Demonologie*. Before he was twenty, with an astonishing display of erudite authorities, he had conclusively shown St. Peter's descendant to be Anti-Christ; but his real objection to the Pope was his holiness's inconvenient rivalry to the royal supremacy, and James, who at other times seems to have contemplated even the setting up of a Scotch Cardinal, was not more eager to set fire to a witch than to burn seditious priests who might presume against his own Anti-Christ to rebel. To him it was, in all conditions, the climax of sin to resist any settled authority. He would have been right if settled authority had found in himself, as he appears to have verily believed it had, its highest exponent and noblest representative that the earth could

Wisest fool in Christendom.

What he did with learning.

Uses of his knowledge.

Too confident an assumption.

94   *Introductory Essay.*

afford. But it was far from being so; and his conduct, with all its gross inconsistencies, sinks to the mere selfish level. To seditious priests he owed his Scotch throne, there could be no doubt; but as little had he the courage to take open part against them, as the honesty to refrain from intrigues with his mother's turbulent faction. The only allegiance he was always true to, was that which he gloried in avowing he implicitly owed to himself.

It may nevertheless not be denied that, at least in that outset of his life, he had some excuse for such self-saving instincts, in the straits through which he then passed. Alternately swayed between the two contending forces; his person now seized by the Nobles, and the Presbytery now governing by his name; he fell into the habit of making unscrupulous use of either, as occasion happened to serve. And hence the skill in outwitting people, the sly ways of temporising, the studied deceit and cunning, which he formed gradually into a system under the misused name of kingcraft, and in which his whole idea of government consisted. Of course neither party could trust him. The condition of king *de facto* he owed to the presbyterians who placed him on the throne, but it was only from the papists he could obtain concession of the title of king *de jure* which he coveted hardly less; and if he detested anything more than the Jesuit who preached the pope's right to release subjects from their allegiance, it was the Presbyter who claimed a power to control the actions of his prince. And so his character was formed:

Margin notes: Early career in Scotland. His excuses. A school for kingcraft. His position between Puritan and Papist.

§ III. *First Stuart King.*

without an opinion to rest upon, or a principle to guide it; devoid utterly of straightforward- ness or self-reliance; incapable, in any manly sense, of either friendship or enmity; and, above and in spite of all, with a sort of intellectual activity, real in itself and often of a consummate shrewdness, which threw only into greater relief and more mischievous prominence those grave defects of character. He never formed an attachment which was perfectly creditable to him, or provoked a contest from which he did not run away. In this respect he was always the same, and the early Scotch days of Arran but prefigured the later English ones of Somerset and Buckingham.

Formation of his character.

His attachments.

Before he inherited the English throne, James had three sons and two daughters born to him. Of these, two sons and a daughter died before they reached maturity; but to the surviving daughter and son, a memorable part in English history was assigned. At Falkland, in the autumn of 1596, was born Elizabeth, afterwards Queen of Bohemia: whose name became identified on the continent with the Protestant cause, and through the youngest of whose ten children, the Electress Sophia of Hanover, the House of Brunswick finally displaced the House of Stuart. At Dumferline, in November 1600, was born Charles, his second son, who succeeded him as Charles the First: and shortly before whose birth, Sir Henry Neville had written to Sir Ralph Winwood that out of Scotland rumours were abounding of no good agreement between the King of Scots and his wife; and that "the discovery

Family of James.

Princess Elizabeth born, 1596.

Prince Charles born, 1600.

"of some affection between her and the Earl of Gowrie's brother, who was killed with him, was believed to be the truest cause and motive of all that tragedy." The tragedy referred to was the murder, in their own castle, of the grandson of the Ruthven who first struck at David Rizzio; and the condition of James's mother, when she witnessed the assassination of her favourite, was the same as that of his wife, when she heard the fate of Alexander Gowrie. Not even in the blood-stained Scottish annals is an incident to be found more dark or mysterious than this; and, on the day when the bodies of the two brothers were sentenced to ignominious exposure, the second son of James and Anne was born. His baptism was sudden, for he was hardly expected to outlive the day; and it was through an infancy and boyhood of almost hopeless feebleness, he struggled on to his ill-fated manhood. There is a complexional weakness imparted at birth, which nothing afterwards will cure; and this, disqualifying alike for resolved resistance or for manly submission, was unhappily a part of Charles the First's most sad inheritance. He was nearly six years old before he could stand or speak, his limbs being weak and distorted, and his mouth mal-formed; nor did he ever walk quite without difficulty, or speak without a stammer. Who shall say how far these physical defects carried also with them the moral weaknesses, the vacillation of purpose and obstinacy of irresolution, the insincerity and bad faith, which so largely helped to bring him to the scaffold?

§ III. *First Stuart King.* 97

James's last year as the King of Scots was probably the quietest he had passed in that troubled sovereignty. As his succession to the English throne drew nearer, his authority in his hereditary kingdom grew more strong. Many of his enemies had perished, others had become impoverished; and all began to think it more profitable game to join their king in a foray on the incalculable wealth of England, than to continue a struggle with him for the doubtful prizes of his barren and intractable Scotland. But his disputes with his subjects survived his dangers from them. What tamed the laity, had made more furious the clergy; who already, in no distant vision, saw their sovereign seated on the English throne surrounded by the pomps of prelacy, and armed newly with engines of oppression against themselves. Never was Kirk so rebellious, in flaming up, synod after synod, against the sovereign's unprincelinefs and ungodliness; and never was King so abusive, in protesting before the great God that highland caterans and border thieves were not such liars and perjurers as these "puritan pests in " the church." He was in the thickest fury of the contention, when the sycophants who had bribed Elizabeth's waiting-woman for earliest tidings of her last breath, hurried headlong into Scotland to salute him as English King. Quieting, then, some ill-temper of his wife's by shrewdly bidding her think of nothing but thanking God for the peaceable possession they had got, James set out upon his journey southward on the 5th of April, 1603.

Prospect of English throne.

Joy of laity in Scotland.

Indignation of clergy.

Elizabeth's death announced.

Journey southward

H

Introductory Essay.

begun: April, 1603.

It was indeed something to be thankful for, that peaceable possession of the land to which his very progress was a sort of popular triumph. Doubly wonderful had Kings grown to us, says old Stowe, so long had we, fifty years or more, been under Queens. Racing against each other as for life or death, rushed statesmen and courtiers, lawyers, doctors, and clergy, civic corporations, mayoralties, officialities of every description and kind, all classes and conditions of public men,—eager to be shone upon by the new-risen sun. And surely never from stranger luminary darted beams of hope or promise upon expectant courtiers.

Novelty of a King after half a century of a Queen.

Personal characteristics of the new monarch.

The son of a most unhappy mother, by a miserable marriage, and even before birth struck by the terror of the murder of Rizzio, James was born a coward, and through life could never bear even the sight of a drawn sword. He was of middle stature, and had a tendency to corpulence, which the fashion of his dress greatly exaggerated. He had a red complexion and sandy hair, and a skin softer, it was said, than taffeta sarsenet, because he never thoroughly washed himself, but was always rubbed slightly with the wet end of a napkin. His sanguine face had only the scantiest growth of beard; and his large eye rolled about unceasingly with such suspicious vigilance, that it put fairly out of countenance all but the most experienced courtiers. He had a big head, but a mouth too small for his tongue, so that he not only slobbered his words when he talked, but drank as if he were eating his drink, which leaked out on either side again

Face and figure.

Slobbering speech.

§ III. *First Stuart King.*

into the cup. His clothes formed a woollen rampart around him, his breeches being in large plaits and full stuffed, and his doublets quilted for stiletto proof; and so weak and ricketty were his legs that his steps became circles, and he was well-nigh helpless when he would walk alone. "He likes," says the astonished chaplain of the Venetian embassy, "in walking, to be supported under the arms "by his chief favourites." It was in truth a necessity, as the favourites were. His body had as little in itself to sustain it, as his mind. Both shuffled on by circular movements, and both had need of supports from without. *[Shuffling gait. Absence of self-support.]*

But, if the time has now come in England for any serious conflict between the Subject and the Crown, where any longer is that fence or barrier to the monarchy which the personal qualities and bearing of English sovereigns have heretofore thrown up; and which in past years, even when its privileges were most onerous, has been no inconsiderable protection to it? This clumsy, uncouth, shambling figure, with its goggle eyes, shuffling legs, and flobbering tongue, confounded even an eager congregation of courtiers; and by the time it reached London, a witness not prejudiced takes upon himself to avouch, "the admiration of "the intelligent world was turned into con-"tempt." *[A fence to monarchy thrown down. Courtiers confounded.]*

Up to the close of the journey, nevertheless, the contempt had been decently disguised. At Newcastle and York, magnificent civic entertainments awaited his Majesty. With splendour not less profuse, Sir Robert Cary received *[Royal progress to London.]*

<small>Entertainments.</small> him at Widdrington, the Bifhop of Durham at Durham, Sir Edward Stanhope at Grimfton, Lord Shrewfbury at Workfop, Lord Cumberland at Belvoir Caftle, Sir John Harrington at Exton, the Lord Burghley at Burghley, and Sir Thomas Sadler at Standen. With princely <small>At Hinchinbrook:</small> hofpitality, Sir Oliver Cromwell regaled him at Hinchinbrook ; and, there, the fturdy little nephew and namefake of Sir Oliver received <small>Oliver Cromwell (æt. 4) firft fees a King.</small> probably his firft impreffion of a king, and of the fomething lefs than divinity that hedged him round. At Broxbourne, too, where Sir Henry Cox had provided noble entertainment, greeting as memorable was in ftore for him; for here the greateft man then living in this univerfe, fave only one, waited to offer him <small>Interview with Francis Bacon.</small> homage. "Methinks," faid Francis Bacon after the interview, "his Majefty rather afks "counfel of the time paft than of the time "to come;" and, clofing up againft the time to come his own prophetic vifion, that wonderful genius took his employment in the fervice of the time paft. Nearer and nearer London, meanwhile, the throng fwelled more and more; and on came the King, hunting daily as he came, inceffantly feafting and drinking, creating knights by the fcore, and everywhere receiving <small>Arrival in land of promife.</small> worfhip as the fountain of honour. Vifions of levelling clergy and factious nobles, which had haunted him his whole life long, now paffed for ever from him. He turned to his Scotch followers, and told them they had at laft arrived in the land of promife.

<small>Interview with Cecil:</small> But he had yet to fee the moft important man in this promifed land. He was waiting

the royal advent at his feat of Theobalds, within a few miles of London, on the 3rd of May: and ftrange muft have been the firft meeting, at the gate of that fplendid manfion, between the broad, fhambling, fhuffling, grotefque monarch, and the fmall, keen, crookbacked, capable minifter; between the fon of Mary Queen of Scots, and the fon of her chief executioner. We are not left to doubt the nature of the impreffion made upon Cecil. During the years he afterwards paffed in James's fervice, he withdrew as far as poffible from the control he might have claimed to exercife, and the refponfibility he muft have affumed, over the home adminiftration; and did his beft, to the extent of his means, by a fagacious policy abroad, to keep England ftill refpected and feared in her place amid foreign nations. No one ferved the King fo ably, or, there is reafon to believe, defpifed him fo much. In her latter years, Elizabeth had exacted of her minifters that they fhould addrefs her kneeling, and fome one congratulated Cecil that thofe degrading conditions were paffed away. "Would to God," he replied, "I yet fpake upon my knees!"

At Theobalds: 3rd May.

Unfavourable impreffion on the minifter.

Foreign policy.

On the death of Cecil, in the tenth year of the reign, James found himfelf firft free to indulge, unchecked, his lufts of favouritifm. Though already the Ramfays, Humes, and Marrs, had contrived to fatten themfelves upon him, it is not until Cecil has paffed away that we get full fight of the Somerfets and Buckinghams. Robert Car was a poor but handfome young Scot, younger fon of one of

Death of Cecil: 1612.

Rife of Somerfet.

the ſmall lairds of Teviotdale, ſtraight-limbed, well-favoured, ſtrong-ſhouldered, and ſmooth-faced, when the King's eye fell upon him. Within a few weeks he was created Knight, Lord-treaſurer, Viſcount, Knight of the Garter, and Earl; and everywhere about the Court, according to Lord Thomas Howard, the King was to be ſeen leaning upon him, pinching his cheek, ſmoothing his ruffled garment, and, while directing his diſcourſe to others, looking ſtill at him. He attended him at his rooms in illneſs, taught him Latin, beggared the beſt to enrich him; and, when the wife of Raleigh knelt at his feet to implore him not to make deſtitute the hero he had impriſoned, ſpurned her from him with the words, " I mun ha' the land! I mun ha' it for " Car." On the eve of Car's arraignment as a murderer, the king is deſcribed, by one who was preſent at their parting interview, to have hung lolling about his neck, ſlobbering his cheeks with kiſſes; and their ſtrange connection was not even unlooſed by Car's conviction of the crime. The life of Overbury's murderer was ſpared; he had ſubſequent glimpſes of favour; and he received no leſs a penſion than 4000*l.* a year when his offices were transferred to a ſucceſſor certainly better entitled to favour than himſelf, and a man of greater ability, but whoſe riſe had been hardly more honourable. Never any man, exclaims Clarendon of George Villiers, in any age, or in any country or nation, roſe in ſo ſhort a time to ſo much greatneſs of honour, fame, or fortune, upon no other ad-

§ III. *First Stuart King.*

vantage or recommendation than of the beauty and gracefulnefs of his perfon. Nor was it in a lefs degree the amazement of the grave fignors and ambaffadors of Venice, when received at a court mafque, to fee the prime minifter Buckingham, for the delectation of the King, cut a fcore of lofty and very minute capers, and the King, for the reward of his prime minifter, pat him on both cheeks with an extraordinary affection. {A prime minifter at a mafque.}

Such entertainment had of courfe little to recommend it to Italian vifitors, who feem rightly to have judged, of all the ordinary actors in it, that not only were they odious and profligate, but in fome fenfe or other defpicable. The likings of James's court were indeed thofe of Comus and his crew; and even the genius it engaged in its fervice, it degraded to that level. Nakedly to indulge every grofs propenfity, became the daily purfuit and higheft qualification of all admitted to its precincts. The circle that furrounded Elizabeth had been no very exact model of decency; but there was ftrength of underftanding in the Queen, and it conftrained the vices of thofe around her, as it veiled her own. When James became chief of the revels, this check paffed wholly away. Everything was in wafteful excefs; and in the foul corruption which alone could fatisfy it, the men were not more eagerly engaged than the women, who drank alfo freely as they, and played as deep. Lady Glenham took a bribe of a hundred pounds for fome difhonourable work to be done by her father; and even the King's {Scenes and actors in the Court.} {Unreftrained indulgences.} {Bribes taken by women.}

coufin, poor Arabella Stuart, intrigued to get one of her uncles a peerage, for a certain fum to be paid to herfelf. The dead Queen had gradually difufed, and at laft ftrictly prohibited, *Sports of the cockpit.* the brutal fports of the cockpit; but her fucceffor revived, and at leaft twice every week took part in them. Daily, from morning until evening in the chafe, the bear-garden, or the cockpit, and from evening until night in grofs fenfual pleafures, the Court paffed its life; and to what extent fuch life took precedence of every other, may be partly meafured *Profligate expenditure.* by the fact that the fee of the Mafter of the Cocks exceeded the united falaries of two Secretaries of State. The fecond year of the reign had not paffed, when Cecil had to write to Lord Shrewfbury that the expenfe of the royal houfehold, which till then had not exceeded thirty thoufand a year, had rifen to a hundred thoufand; "and now think," added the minifter of Elizabeth, "what the Country "feels; and fo much for that." In the feventh year of the reign, the furplus of outlay above revenue continued, and, according to *Debts of the King.* the then value of money, James's debts were half a million; or at our prefent value, fomething more than a million and a half. The fhame of his neceffities became flagrant. His treafurer, Buckhurft, was feized in the ftreet for wages due to his fervants; the very purveyors ftopped the fupply to his table; and *Shameful neceffities.* fome years afterwards, when the embaffy from Venice came to London, fuch wants of the royal houfehold were ftill common talk. They went on increafing further. The hungry and numerous family of the favourite had to be provided for as well as himself, and of all the favourites none had been so profuse as Buckingham. As yet among rare luxuries was the coach, unheard of till the preceding reign, and then with two horses only; but James's prime minister, to the general amazement of men, drove six, and even eight horses. Hard would it be to say which was most degrading, the extremity of the waste, or the desperation of the means of meeting it. Benevolences were tried, and exorbitant fines were imposed by the Star Chamber on those who resisted them or who counselled resistance. Impositions by prerogative were laid in every form, and were backed by suborned and scandalous decisions in the courts. Patents were granted on all sides to greedy projectors, creating monopolies the most intolerable, and eating the life out of trade. Fees had been got from knighthood, until nobody more would incur the cost; men of gentle birth had been exhausted, till, as the saying went, not an untitled Yorkshire squire was left to uphold the race; and Lord Bacon, at even *his* wits' end after Lord Montgomery's barber and the husband of the Queen's laundress had been knighted, suggested knighthood with some new difference and precedence. Hereupon baronetcies were thought of; and, being offered for a thousand pounds each to any who consented to be purchasers, for a time they made the King richer by some hundred thousand pounds. This new branch of industry turning out so well, the peerage had been next put up to sale, and not

Buckingham's extravagance.

Expedients for money.

Benevolences and fines.

Patents and monopolies.

Knighthood exhausted.

Baronetcies invented.

Peerages put up to sale.

lefs openly. For fix thoufand pounds a man became a baron; for twenty thoufand an earl; and, if Mr. John Hampden, of Great Hampden in Bucks, had not preferred a lefs perifhable title, his mother would have given ten thoufand pounds to make a vifcount of him.

Yet the fcenes of extravagance and riot which fo marked the Court of the firft of our Stuart kings, may be characterized as even decent and refpectable, by the fide of thofe more deteftable exhibitions in which its chief actor claimed to be regarded as furnifhed forth with fparkles of divinity, and the lieutenant and vicegerent of God. James had written a treatife to prove that inafmuch as Monarchy was the true pattern of the Godhead, it could in no refpect be bound to the law; for as it was atheifm and blafphemy to difpute what God could do, fo it was prefumption and high contempt to difpute what a King could do, or fay that a King could not do this or that: and an unimpeachable witnefs, who was prefent at the Hampton Court Conference, has fhown with what peculiar emphafis, upon occafion, he could recommend thefe principles by his graces of fpeech. At that Conference (a memorable one, for in it the thing called Englifh Puritanifm firft openly made good its claims to obtain a hearing from majefty itfelf) he affected to fit in judgment as moderator between the High Church Party and the Puritans; and it was after having heard the high churchmen at great length, and with much gracioufnefs, that he interpofed with fcurrilous abufe as foon as the

§ III. *First Stuart King.*

Puritans began to fpeak. He "bid them "awaie with their fnivellinge; moreover, he "wifhed thofe who would take away the fur- "plice might want linen for their own breech. "The bifhops," it is added naively, "feemed "much pleafed, and faid his majeftie fpake by "the power of infpiration." One of the bifhops prefent, indeed, Bancroft of London, flung himfelf on his knees, and protefted his heart melted for joy "that Almighty God had, "in his fingular mercy, given them fuch a "King as had not been feen fince Chrift's "time." Chancellor Ellefmere cried out that for his part he had now feen what he had never hoped to fee, King and Prieft united fully in one perfon; and Archbifhop Whitgift affeve- rated that his Majefty fpoke by the Spirit of God. "I wift not what they mean," adds the reporter of the Conference, "but the fpirit "was rather foul-mouthed." It was cruel alfo; for the character in which this deified Scotch pedant next prefented himfelf was one that might well have been fuggefted and juftified by fuch obfequious blafphemy. He fent two Unitarian minifters, Bartholomew Legat and Edward Wrightman, to perifh by the ftake at Smithfield; he fent to the fcaf- fold, after torturing, the white-haired old puritan Peachem; and he perfecuted to the death the Dutch reformer Vorftius, againft whofe tolerant and pious teaching he had penned the memorable declaration which was infcribed to "our Lord and Saviour Jefus "Chrift by his moft humble and moft obliged "fervant James." In the prefence of fuch

Delight of the Bifhops.

Chancellor Ellefmere's ideal.

James's religious perfecutions.

acts and utterances, and of the utter impoffibility of difcovering for them any reafonable
mitigation or excufe, it is not harfh to James's
memory to fay that the blood of his unhappy
fon only half expiated thefe and fimilar fins.
The records of civilifed life, and of rational
men, offer no other inftance of fuch pretenfions.
We have to turn for a parallel to the peftilen-
tial fwamps of Africa, where one of thofe prodigious princes whom we bribe with rum to
aflift us in fuppreffing the flave-trade, announced
lately to an Englifh officer, "God made me
" after His image: I am all the fame as God:
" and He appointed me a King." This was
James's creed precifely; and after delivering it
to his fubjects in words exactly fimilar, he
might be publicly feen of them, as Harrington
defcribes him at a mafque given by Cecil,
" wallowing in beaftly delights."

It will neverthelefs be barely juft to add,
even of this revolting picture, that it has been
darkened by touches of a more infamous complexion of which there is no proof. In the
Overbury proceedings much muft ever remain
inexplicable; but agitation under threat of
an accufation unnamed, confifts unfortunately
with innocence quite as much as with guilt.
A weak man is even likelier than a guilty one
to be difturbed as James was, when Somerfet's
dark threats were brought to him by the
Lieutenant of the Tower; and there exifts a
letter of his at Lambeth, replying to the
Earl's remonftrance againft inquiry into the
murder, which, though earlier than the dif-
clofures of the Lieutenant, renders incredible

§ III. *First Stuart King.*

the inference they might elfe have led to. In plain words I believe James to have had as little to do with Overbury's death as with Prince Henry's, and that fufpicions even more deteftable reft upon no fair evidence. Enough otherwife has here been faid to explain the contempt and diflike, which, feveral years before his death, had faftened upon his name, and were the inheritance of his race.

[margin: Innocent as to Overbury and Prince Henry.]

Let an intelligent foreigner defcribe for us the opinion of their ruler, which had become generally prevalent among the Englifh people. "Confider for pity's fake," fays M. de Beaumont, in one of his defpatches, "what muft be the ftate and condition of a "prince, whom the preachers publicly from "the pulpit affail; whom the comedians of "the metropolis covertly bring upon the ftage; "whofe wife attends thofe reprefentations in "order to enjoy the laugh againft her hufband; "whom the Parliament braves and defpifes; "and who is univerfally hated by the whole "people." The Frenchman's great mafter, Henri Quatre, fhortly before he fell by the hand of an affaffin, had fpoken of the effects of fuch contempt when directed againft the perfon of a Sovereign, as marvellous and horrible: and in this cafe alfo they were deftined to prove marvellous and horrible, *in the fecond generation.*

[margin: Opinions of the people. Contempt of the perfon of the fovereign. Legacy to Charles I.]

THE DEBATES ON THE GRAND REMONSTRANCE.

November and December, 1641.

§ 1. Prefatory.

Moſt exciting incident before the war.

If the queſtion were put to any thoroughly informed ſtudent of our Great Civil War, into what ſingle incident of the period before the actual outbreak would appear to have been concentrated the largeſt amount of party paſſion, he could hardly fail at once to ſingle out the Grand Remonſtrance. And if he were then aſked to name, out of all the party encounters of the time, that of which the ſubject matter and antecedents have been moſt unaccountably ſlurred over by hiſtorians, he muſt perforce give the ſame anſwer. It follows that the writers of hiſtory have in this caſe thought of ſmall importance what the men whoſe deeds they record accounted to be of the greateſt, and it will be worth inquiring how far the later verdict is juſt.

Moſt neglected by hiſtorians.

Happily, the means exiſt of forming a judgment as to the particular ſubject, on grounds not altogether uncertain or unſafe. The Grand Remonſtrance itſelf remains.

§ 1. *Prefatory.*

Under maſſes of dull and lifeleſs matter heaped up in Ruſhworth's ponderous folios, it has lain undiſturbed for more than two centuries; but it lives ſtill, even there, for thoſe who care to ſtudy its contents, and they who ſo long have turned away from it unſtudied, may at leaſt plead the excuſe of the dreary and deterring companionſhip around it. The truth, however, is, that to the art and diſingenuouſneſs of Clarendon it is really due, in this inſtance as in ſo many others, that thoſe who have written on the conflict of parties before the civil war broke out, have been led off to a falſe iſſue. He was too near the time of the Remonſtrance when he wrote, and he had played too eager a part in the attempt to obſtruct and prevent its publication to the people, not to give it prominence in his Hiſtory; but he found it eaſier to falſify and miſrepreſent the debates concerning it, of which there was no publiſhed record, than to paſs altogether in ſilence the ſtatements made in it, diffuſed as they had been, ſome ſcore of years earlier, over the length and breadth of the land. Indeed it alſo better ſerved the purpoſe he had, ſo to garble and miſquote theſe; and from the fragment of a ſummary he gave, filling ſome ſix pages of the octavo edition of his book, Hume and the hiſtorians of the laſt century derived manifeſtly the whole of what they knew of the Grand Remonſtrance. But even the more careful and leſs prejudiced hiſtorians of our own century have not ſhown that they knew much more.

Upon the debate in the Houſe before it was

[Sidenotes:] Remonſtrance printed in Ruſhworth. Miſleading of Clarendon. Falſification of Debates. Miſſtatements followed by all.

put to the vote, as referred to by Hyde, all writers have dwelt; and of courfe every one has copied and reproduced thofe graphic touches of Philip Warwick, the young courtier and follower of Hyde, afterwards the faithful fervant of the King, in which he gives his verfion of what the Remonftrance was, how it originated, and what an exciting debate it led to. How fome leading men in the Houfe, as he fays, jealous of the propofed entertainment to be given by the City to the King on his return from Scotland, had got up an entertainment of their own in the fhape of a libel (the Remonftrance, that is), than which fouler or blacker could not be imagined, againft his perfon and government; and how it paffed fo tumultuoufly, two or three nights before the king came to town, that at three o'clock in that November morning when they voted it, he thought they would all have fat in the Valley of the Shadow of Death : for they would, like Joab's and Abner's young men, all have catched at each other's locks, and fheathed their fwords in each other's bowels, had not the fagacity and great calmnefs of Mr. Hampden, by a fhort fpeech, prevented it, and led them to defer their angry debate until the next morning.* Doubtlefs a fcene to be remembered, and which naturally has attracted all attentions fince; but that out of the many who have fo adopted it, and, from the mere reading it, felt fome fhare in the excitement it pourtrays, not one fhould have been moved to make clofer

Sir Philip Warwick's account.

Extraordinary fcene.

Hampden's influence.

---

* *Memoires of the Reign of King Charles the Firft*, by Sir Philip Warwick, Knight, (Ed. 1702) 201-2.

§ 1. *Prefatory.*

inquiry into what the fo-called "libel" really was that fo had roufed and maddened the partifans of the King, may fairly be matter of furprife. Hallam is content to give fome eight or nine lines to it, in which its contents are not fairly reprefented. Lingard difpofes of it in fomething lefs than a dozen lines. Macaulay has only occafion incidentally to introduce it, and a fimple mention of it is all that falls within the plan of Carlyle. Godwin paffes over it in filence; and fuch few lines as Difraeli (in his Commentaries) vouchfafes to it, are an entire mif-ftatement of its circumftances and falfification of its contents. It is not neceffary to advert fpecifically to other hiftories and writings connected with the period; but the affertion may be confidently made, that in all the number there is not one, whatever its indications of refearch and originality in other directions may be, which prefents reafonable evidence of any better or more intimate knowledge of the Grand Remonftrance than was derivable from the garbled page of Clarendon. The purpofe of this work is to remove that reproach from the ftudy of this period of hiftory; not merely by endeavouring to prefent in fome detail, and with explanatory illuftration from manufcript and contemporary papers, an abftract of the contents of the Remonftrance, but by reproducing, from records as yet untouched, fuch accurate and detailed defcriptions of the debates that attended its paffage through the Houfe, as may perhaps alfo reproduce, and reanimate with their old truth and vividnefs, the actual circum-

Various references to Great Remonftrance.

Clarendon generally followed.

Purpofe of the prefent work.

Written from MS. records.

stances of the time. Only so may the eagerness and passion displayed on both sides become again intelligible to the modern reader.

§ II. WHAT THE GRAND REMONSTRANCE WAS.

Case of the Parliament against the King.

THIS most memorable State Paper, commonly so garbled and almost invariably so misrepresented as I have had occasion to remark, remains nevertheless a fact living and accessible to us; a solid piece of actual history, retaining the form which its authors gave to it, and breathing still some part of the life which animated them. It embodies the case of the Parliament against the Ministers of the King. It is the most authentic statement ever put forth of the wrongs endured by all classes of the English people, during the first fifteen years of the reign of Charles the First; and, for that reason, the most complete justification upon record of the Great Rebellion. It possesses, for the student of that event, the special interest which arises from the fact, that it demonstrates more clearly than any other paper of the time, by its close and powerful reasoning, how inseparable Religion and Politics had become, and how each was to be stabbed only through the side of the other. If we would satisfy ourselves that wherever any writer such as Hume has sought to put a distinction between the modes of regarding these subjects pursued by the statesmen of this Parliament, and that where he has contrasted their profound capacity, undaunted courage, and largeness of view in Civil Affairs, with their supposed narrowness

Most complete justification of the Great Rebellion.

Religion and Politics in union.

Hume's false distinctions:

§ II. *What the Grand Remonstrance Was.*

and bigotry in Religion, he has fimply fhown how imperfect and narrow had been his own ftudy and preparation for the tafk of doing juftice to fuch men, we have but to turn to the Grand Remonftrance. For the prefent I can only dwell upon it briefly. *refuted by the Remonftrance.*

It defcribes, then, the condition of the three kingdoms at the time when the Long Parliament met, and the meafures taken thereon to redrefs ftill remediable wrongs, and deal out juftice on their authors. Enumerating the ftatutes paffed at the fame time for the good of the fubject, and his fafety in future years, it points out what yet waited to be done to complete that neceffary work, and the grave obftructions that had arifen, in each of the three kingdoms, to intercept its completion. It warns the people of dangerous and defperate intrigues to recover afcendancy for the court faction; hints not obfcurely at ferious defections in progrefs, even from the popular phalanx; accufes the bifhops of a defign to Romanize the Englifh Church; denounces the effects of ill counfels in Scotland and Ireland; and calls upon the King to difmifs evil counfellors. It is, in brief, an appeal to the country; confifting, on the one hand, of a dignified affertion of the power of the Houfe of Commons in re-eftablifhing the public liberties, and, on the other, of an urgent reprefentation of its powerleffnefs either to protect the future or fave the paft, without immediate prefent fupport againft papifts and their favourers in the Houfe of Lords, and their unfcrupulous partizans near the throne. There *Character of its contents.*

Warnings againft Court.

Appeal to the country.

is in it, nevertheless, not a word of difrespect to the person or the just privileges of royalty; and nothing that the fair supporters of a sound Church Establishment might not frankly have approved and accepted. Of all the State Papers of the period, it is in these points much the most remarkable; nor, without very carefully reading it, is it easy to understand rightly, or with any exactness, either the issue challenged by the King when he unfurled his standard, or the objects and desires of the men who led the House of Commons up to the actual breaking out of the war.

No disrespect to King or Church.

States what the war put in issue.

Essential as the study of it is, however, to any true comprehension of this eventful time, the difficulty of reproducing it in modern history must doubtless be admitted. It is not merely that it occupies fifteen of Rushworth's closely printed folio pages, but that, in special portions of its argument, it passes with warmth and rapidity through an extraordinary variety of subjects, of which the connection has ceased to be always immediately apparent. Matters are touched too lightly for easy comprehension now, which but to name, then, was to strike a chord that every breast responded to. Some subjects also have a large place, to which only a near acquaintance with party names and themes can assign their just importance, either as affecting each other, or making stronger the ultimate and wider appeal which by their means was designed. The very heat and urgency of tone, the quick impatience of allusion, the minute subdivision of details, the passionate iteration of topics, everything that made its

Occupies 15 folio pages in Rushworth.

Difficulty of reproducing it.

narrative so intense and powerful once, and gives to it in a certain sense its vividness and reality still, constitutes at the same time the difficulty of presenting it in such an abstract, careful and connected, not without detail and yet compressed, as would admit of reproduction here. It will be well worth while, nevertheless, to make the trial; which, however short it may fall of success in the particular matter, may have some historical value independently. For, by the use of those manuscript records to which I have referred, as yet unemployed by any writer or historian, it will at least be possible to illustrate the abstract to be given by an account of the Debates respecting it in the House of Commons, and these with relation as well to itself as to its antecedents and consequences, far more interesting, because more minute and faithful, than any heretofore given to the world. And in this will be the undoubted additional advantage, that thereby will be supplied a not inefficient test for Clarendon's accuracy and honesty of statement in the most critical part of his narrative of these affairs.

Its various and minute detail.

Purposed illustration by MS. records.

Test for Clarendon's honesty.

§ III. SIR SIMONDS D'EWES AND HIS MANUSCRIPT JOURNAL OF THE LONG PARLIAMENT.

ONE preliminary to the task I have undertaken seems to be required of me. To establish for myself the claim to authenticity of statement which it is proposed to dispute in others, it will be necessary to describe the

Authority for new facts in this work.

authority from which the moſt part of the faƈts given in this paper are derived, and now firſt contributed to hiſtory. They are the reſult of much tedious and painful reſearch into the blotted manuſcripts of Sir Simonds D'Ewes, preſerved in five bound volumes in the Britiſh Muſeum,* and entitled, "A Journal of the Parliament begun November 3d, "Tueſday, Anno Domini 1640." To the exiſtence of ſuch a journal attention has been lately drawn more than once by alluſions in Mr. Carlyle's writings in conneƈtion with Cromwell;† and from a manuſcript abſtraƈt made for him when he contemplated writing a Hiſtory of the Puritans (a projeƈt which it is a matter of great regret that he abandoned), a very intereſting notice of D'Ewes, with ſome account of his Journal, was publiſhed ſeveral years ago in the *Edinburgh Review*.‡ Mr. Carlyle kindly placed this

Journal by D'Ewes in Harleian MSS.

Writers acquainted with it.

---

* Harleian MSS. Nos. 162, 163, 164, 165, 166.

† " We call theſe Notes the moſt intereſting of all manu-
" ſcripts. To an Engliſh ſoul who would underſtand what
" was really memorable and godlike in the Hiſtory of his
" country, diſtinguiſhing the ſame from what was at bottom
" *un*-memorable and devil-like; who would bear in everlaſting
" remembrance the doings of our noble heroic men, and ſink
" into everlaſting oblivion the doings of our low ignoble
" quacks and ſham-heroes,—what other record can be ſo
" precious?"—Carlyle's *Miſcellanies*, iv. 338-9.

‡ For July, 1846. I do not betray any confidence in ſtating that this paper was by that very learned and agreeable writer, Mr. John Bruce, whoſe deſcription of D'Ewes's original manuſcript may here be ſubjoined, in confirmation of what is ſaid in the text. "For ſome part of the time, the
" Notes have been copied and written out in a narrative form,
" in a reſpectable hand; in other places, we have nothing
" but the rough jottings-down of D'Ewes's own pen. At
" firſt, when we begin to read them, all is obſcurity, as dull
" and denſe as that which overclouds the pages of Ruſhworth,

Notes by D'Ewes characterised.

Edinb. Review, July, 1846.

§ III. *Sir Simonds D'Ewes and his MS. Journal.*

manuscript at my disposal on my commencing some years since, at the request of the Messrs. Longman, what I have found to be the not very easy task of preparing for a library edition, and making less unworthy of the favour extended to it, a work entitled *The Statesmen of the Commonwealth* written several years before. On comparing, however, its abstract of D'Ewes with the original, it proved to be so entirely imperfect and deficient even as an index to the larger collections, that there was no alternative but to begin the research anew. I will preface what I have to relate as the result of such more careful inquiry with a brief account of the writer. *[Necessity of studying the original MS.]*

Simonds D'Ewes was the eldest son of Paul D'Ewes, one of the Six Clerks of the Court of Chancery, who had married the daughter of his chamber-fellow in the Temple, Richard Simonds, whose Dorsetshire estate, inherited by his daughter, went afterwards to enrich her son. He was born in December 1602; and, after a childhood passed with his mother's family in Dorsetshire, lived with his father alternately in Suffolk and in Chancery Lane; went in his fourteenth year to Bury School, and in his sixteenth to St. John's in Cambridge, from which, after a residence of little more than two years, he was very glad to get back to his father, out of, as he tells us, the swear- *[Account of D'Ewes. Born 1602. At Cambridge, 1618.]*

" Nalson, and the Journals ; but as we go on, the mist
" gradually grows less dense,—rays of light dart in here and
" there, illuminating the palpable obscure ; and in the end,
" after much plodding, and the exercise of infinite patience,
" we may come to know the Long Parliament as thoroughly
" as if we had sat in it."

ing, drinking, rioting, and luftful indulgence, abounding generally in Cambridge at that time. So long previously as his ninth year he had been entered of his father's Inn, fo that now, on going into commons at the Temple, he found himfelf, lad as he was, "ancient" to above two hundred elder Templars. But, though deftined for a working lawyer, he did not take kindly to the practical ftudy of the profeffion. True to his firft childifh affociations with the Chancery Rolls and Records in his father's houfe, he went fuddenly back to the purfuit thus favoured moft, and became a confirmed Antiquary. He had not mis-fpent his time at Cambridge. He was a fair claffical and Englifh fcholar, had got himfelf well up in Ariftotle, and was accuftomed to recreate his leifure with Spenfer's *Fairy Queen*. But the grand purpofe of all ftudy now prefented itfelf in other and more abforbing fhapes; and from this to the clofe of his life he found " in records and other " exotic monuments of antiquity, the moft " ravifhing and fatisfying part of human " knowledge."

Fortune befriended him. As his father had married an heirefs, he thought he might look out for one himfelf; and he found one. In his twenty-fourth year he married a Suffolk heirefs who had not quite completed her fourteenth, and five years later he added greatly to her eftate by inheriting his father's. He bought a knighthood and afterwards a baronetcy, worked hard at the tranfcription of records, collected valuable manufcripts and parchment rolls, amaffed materials for what he flattered himfelf would be "a more exact history of Great Britain that remaineth of any nation in the Christian world," compiled his really valuable Journals of Elizabeth's Parliaments, and brought together a library of some rarity and worth. The growth of his importance had been marked meanwhile by his nomination as High Sheriff of Suffolk in 1639. He had not in former years been unmindful of public affairs, nor had the study of antiquity dulled a somewhat sharp sight for what was actually passing around him; but not until the time of his official experience had he realised all the wrongs under which his countrymen were labouring. He was not long now in publicly declaring himself of the Puritan party, his natural leaning to which had been further strengthened by his affection for his wife's cousin, Sir Nathaniel Barnardiston, afterwards member for the county; and the end of it was that upon his humbly bringing before the Council, in his character of High Sheriff, certain ancient records showing the illegality of ship money, and proving other acts of the Board to be unwarrantable, Laud incontinently made a determined patriot of him by flinging him into the Star Chamber. Resolved upon this to get a hearing for his records in Parliament, since elsewhere they were silenced, he offered himself twice before he secured a seat, but was at length returned to the Long Parliament for Sudbury. He came up to London laden with the manuscripts, books, and parchment rolls, that were to proclaim his knowledge of the ancient liberties;

Projects a History.

High Sheriff of Suffolk, 1639.

Sympathy with Puritans.

Returned to Long Parliament for Sudbury.

took a lodging firſt in Millbank Lane, and then in "Goate's Alley, a little beyond the "White Lyon Taverne, near the Pallace Yard"; took his feat on the day when the committee of feven were appointed to fearch for precedents in the contemplated proceedings againſt Strafford; and on that night wrote off to his wife, whom he had left behind him in Suffolk, "I ſpake thrice this morning in the Houfe, "and at my fecond ſpeech vouched a record, "which not onelie gave great fatisfaction, but "ended a waightie and perplexed difpute it was "then controverting."

Lodgings at Weſt-minſter.

Firſt ſpeech in Houſe.

Daily from that day onward, for upwards of four years, Sir Simonds D'Ewes attended in the place he had felected for himſelf, on the front bench at the left of Mr. Speaker, juſt oppofite the end of the Clerk's table, with the regularity and precifion of one of his own precedents. "Vouching" them almoſt every day thenceforward, having fomething to ſay from them on almoſt every queſtion, and, what is moſt to our prefent purpofe, never failing for a fingle day, when not ſpeaking himſelf, to be feen bufily writing in a note-book as others fpoke around him, there fat the learned and felf-fatisfied member for that ſmall Suffolk borough, taking no unimportant part in the making of hiſtory. His love for ſtudying records had fortunately extended to a paſſion for creating them, and the fruit of his daily taking of notes was the manufcript "Journal of the Parliament begun November "3d, Tuefday, Anno Domini 1640," which ſtill continues for us, as I have ſtated, a record

Aſſiduous attendance.

Takes Notes of debates.

Fruit thereof:

§ III. *Sir Simonds D'Ewes and his MS. Journal.*

of inappreciable value. Even as Sir Simonds had actually written them in the House, with note-book on his knee and ink-bottle hanging at his breast, great portions of them remain, confusedly bound up with duplicate copies and other portions more fairly transcribed; and hence, arising from their very claim to implicit acceptance, the impossibility of accepting them from any but the original manuscript. in five volumes of Journal.

I soon found, indeed, on beginning the enquiry before adverted to, that without strictly honest and earnest examination of D'Ewes's actual handwriting, it was impossible to make anything of the Journal. Whatever in it is most valuable, is in the roughest blurred condition; written often on the backs of letters, mere *disjecta membra* of Notes for a Diary, often all but illegible, now and then entirely so; and the reader will better understand the full force of this remark who turns to the careful facsimile made for me of two of its pages, and given as an illustration to the present volume. Many portions, certainly, are more legibly written, a secretary or transcriber having been called in for the purpose; but these are found upon examination to be also the less valuable, consisting often of illustrations drawn from contemporaneous printed records, of prodigiously lengthy expansions of somewhat pedantic orations by D'Ewes himself, or of extracts from the Journals or other documents supplied by the Clerk of the House. Other parts, again, appear in duplicate, as mere expansions of preceding notes. On the other hand, wherever the blotted writing of Condition of the original MS.

Pages facsimiled.

Component parts of MS.

D'Ewes recurs, there springs up again the
actual and still living record of what he had
himself heard, and himself noted down, with
pen and ink, as he sat in that memorable parliament;* and these Notes, extending from
1640 to 1645, and in which the fourth or
fifth of those years is found jumbled up with
the first, second, or third, the one perhaps
written on the reverse of the other, have been
thrown together and bound with such equally
small regard to succinct arrangement, that the

Confused present state.

Self-painted portrait.

* I quote a passage from the original manuscript under date November 13th, 1641. The plea and demurrer put in by the bishops was then in debate, and Mr. Holborne, member for St. Michaels, was speaking. "I was then about to with-
"draw a little out of the house, and went down as far as the
"place where he was speaking; and finding a seat empty
"almost just behind him, I sat down, thinking to have heard
"him a little, before I had gone out. But finding him en-
"deavour to justify the plea and demurrer, I drew out again
"my pen and ink, and took notes, intending to answer him
"again as soon as he had done." Between four and five

Jealousy of Note-taking:

months later (March 5, 1641-2) a special instance occurred of the jealousy very frequently exhibited by members of the house in regard to the practice of note-taking. Sir Edward Alford, member for Arundel, had been observed taking notes of a proposed Declaration moved by Pym. Sir Walter Earle, member for Weymouth, upon this objected that he had seen "some at the lower end comparing their notes, and one of "them had gone out." Alford was thereupon called back, and his notes required to be given up to the Speaker. D'Ewes then continues: "Sir Henry Vane senr. sitting at that time
"next me, said he could remember when no man was allowed
"to take notes, and wished it to be now forbidden. Which
"occasioned me, being the principal note-taker in the house,
"to say, &c. That the practice existed before he was born.
"For I had a Journal, 13th Elizabeth. For my part I shall
"not communicate my journal (by which I meant the entire

Old Vane objects, and D'Ewes replies.

"copy of it) to any man living. If you will not permit us
"to write, we must go to sleep, as some among us do, or go
"to plays, as others have done." For further illustrations I may perhaps refer the reader to the *Arrest of the Five Members*, § xxiii.

record of the same week's debates may occasionally have to be sought through more than one, or even two volumes. The pages in facsimile prefixed to this work, which express fairly the condition of the rest, were selected not for that reason, but because they were found to contain a fact of such great historical importance, and to set at rest, in a manner so startling and unexpected, discussions relating to it which have divided the writers of history, that it seemed desirable to present them in a specially authentic form. Yet the very pages so containing it were found entirely separated from the main part of the debates of which they form the connected portion, and mixed up, in a different volume of the MS., with the quite disconnected records of three years later. All this, at the same time, while it explains the obscurity in which D'Ewes's Notes have until now been permitted to rest, gives us also striking proof of the genuineness of the record. Its extraordinary value and exactness will appear in the section I am about to devote to the subject of Strafford's Attainder, as well for more detailed explanation of the new fact referred to, as for the better understanding of the position of parties during the Remonstrance debates. The reader, who afterwards pursues with me the subject of the Great Remonstrance itself, will have less reason to doubt the scrupulous veracity of what is here about to be contributed to its illustration.

Example of importance of their contents.

Why not earlier made use of.

§ IV. Attainder of the Earl of Strafford.

<small>The Attainder made a teſt of opinions.</small>

The Bill for Strafford's Attainder has been generally employed as a teſt of opinion upon the occurrences of this great period. To have oppoſed, or to have ſupported it, is even to this day put forth for proof, in either partizan, of the temperate love of freedom or of the unreaſoning paſſion for revolution. The folly of adopting ſuch a teſt, and the grave contradictions it involved, have been often pointed out; but it has neverthelefs been ſtill repeated and infiſted on, with no abatement of confidence.

<small>A fallacious one.</small>

The laſt perſon of any pretenſion who made uſe of it, a privy councillor and county member, himſelf a lineal defcendant of Charles the Firſt's Chief Juſtice of the Pleas,* claſſes the Attainder with what he calls the revolutionary, the "fatal" act, for perpetuation of the Parliament, to which the royal aſſent was given

<small>Unwife comparifons and contraſts.</small>

on the ſame day; and he contraſts the reckleſs ſupporters of ſuch legiſlative abominations in the perſon of Mr. Pym, with the conſtitutional ſupporters of a limited monarchy reprefented by my lord Clarendon. It is neverthelefs more than doubtful whether Mr. Edward Hyde did not vote for the attainder,

---

<small>"Story of Corfe Caſtle."</small>

* The late Mr. George Bankes of Dorſetſhire, who made uſe of the expreſſions quoted in the text, in remarking on ſome family papers of his anceſtor Sir John Bankes, Charles the Firſt's Chief Juſtice of the Common Pleas, which he publiſhed a few years ago.

§ IV. *Attainder of the Earl of Strafford.*

and it is very certain that he *did* vote for the bill to perpetuate the parliament. The fame ingenuous admirer of Clarendon ſtrongly denounces the celebrated Proteſtation on behalf of Parliamentary liberty and the Reformed religion, brought forward at the time by Pym with fo furpriſing an effect upon the people, without appearing to be in the leaſt aware that the ſecond name affixed to the Proteſtation was Edward Hyde's.* He can find nothing better than Robeſpierre's Reign of Terror wherewith to compare the excitements and "pretended" plots that forced on Strafford's execution; though it reſts on authority

<small>The "Proteſtation" to defend Parliament and Religion.</small>

---

* In a letter to Lady D'Ewes, Sir Simonds thus deſcribes the ill-fated interference of the King which directly led to the Proteſtation, and deſtroyed the laſt hope entertained by Strafford. "On Saturday morning wee underſtood that the
" King was come to the Upper Houſe and expected us. Some
" feared a diſſolution; but Mr. Maxwell came in with his
" white ſticke, and looking cheerfullie, ſaied, Feare not; noe
" harme, I warrant you. But trulie wee heard there what
" aſtoniſht us all; for in ſumme the King told us, that the
" Earle of Strafford was not guiltie of treaſon in his conſcience,
" but of miſdemeanors onlie, and ſoe would not have him
" ſuffer death, but onlie bee removed from his places.—Upon
" our returne to the Houſe, wee refuſed to proceede in anie
" buſineſs, but ſate ſilent, yet ſome ſpake ſhortelie of our
" calamitie. When I dreamt of nothing but horror and
" deſolation within one fortnight, the conſideration of your-
" ſelfe and my innocent children drew teares from mee. At
" laſt, manye having often cried *Riſe, Riſe,* betweene eleven
" and twelve wee roſe. Sunday was paſſed over with much
" affliction and ſadneſs. On Monday morning, the third day of
" this inſtant May, ſome ſeven thouſand citizens came downe
" to Weſtminſter; manie of them Captaines of the Cittie and
" men of eminent ranke. They ſtaied each Lord almoſt as hee
" came by, and deſired they might have ſpeedie execution
" upon the Earle of Strafford, or they were all undone, their
" wives and children. Wee ſhut upp our doores, and though
" ſome went in and out, yet kept private what wee weere
" about, and ſtaied from eight in the morning till eight at

<small>D'Ewes to Lady D'Ewes.

The ill-fated King's ſtep.

Agitation in the Houſe and in the City.</small>

beyond difpute that the man who carried up to the Lords the firft meffage as to the army plot which precipitated the execution, was no other than Edward Hyde. Its refolute promoter to the laft, by fpeeches as well as votes, was Falkland, Hyde's deareft friend. Culpeper, his other confidential and intimate ally, fupported eagerly every ftep that led to it. The laft thing his affociate Lord Capel recalled, as he laid his own head down upon the fcaffold raifed by Cromwell, was his vote in favour of it. And Hyde himfelf was the man who expofed and defeated the final defperate attempt of Strafford's perfonal friends, by means of an efcape from the Tower, to avert what Clarendon had afterwards the face to call Strafford's " miferable and never to be enough " lamented ruin." Such are the inconfiftencies and contradictions incident to almoft every attempt, founded on the hitherto recognifed fources which alone were open to the ftudent, to adjuft and apportion correctly the fhare taken in thefe momentous proceedings by the leading men in the Commons.

Much of the confufion is undoubtedly due to Clarendon, the affiduous efforts of whofe later life, to blacken the characters of the

---

" night, and fo concluded of a Proteftation for the defence " of the true religion, the King's perfon, the Priviledges of " Parliament and our Liberties. The Speaker read the Pro-" teftation firft, and then everie man in the Houfe, even the " Treafurer of the King's Houfehold himfelf, fpoke to this " effect, holding the faid Proteftation in his hande.—'Mr. " 'Speaker, I, —, doe willinglie make the fame Proteftation " ' that you have made before me, according to what is con-" ' tained in this paper, with all my heart.' "

§ IV. *Attainder of the Earl of Strafford.* 129

leading men of the parliament, are read with implicit belief by fo many to whom it never occurs to remember that at the outfet of his life Mr. Hyde had acted cordially with thofe men. The privy councillor I have quoted at once fatisfied himfelf that Clarendon could not have had any poffible complicity with the Attainder, becaufe in that cafe his language to Lord Effex, fet down in his own memoirs, would involve an incredible inconfiftency. But unhappily the entire conduct of Hyde at this period is now proved to have been an inconfiftency (to ufe no ftronger word), deliberately as well as elaborately planned, and carried out with a view to the ufes to be made of it towards the fervice of the King. When he declined to take office with Culpeper and Falkland, it was becaufe " he fhould be able to " do much more fervice in the condition he " was in, than he fhould be if that were im-" proved by any preferment." In other words, he ftayed as an independent member among the patriots, to make the better royalift ufe of his knowledge of their plans. Even in his own hiftory he does not fcruple to fay as much, though his firft editors had not the filial courage to print it. By the favour of more authentic editing it ftands there now, a fhamelefs avowal, on the fame page which perpetuates his fame. When he had himfelf affented to a particular ftate paper iffued by the Houfe of Commons, he does not hefitate to inform us that the anfwer, iffued fome days later by the King, was copied from a draft prepared and privately forwarded

Danger of believing in Clarendon.

Conduct of Hyde.

Why he declined office.

Strange self-expofure.

by himſelf ; and when, in grand committee on the bill againſt epiſcopacy, he was choſen chairman, he expreſſly tells us that he uſed the advantage it gave him to "enſnare" and "perplex" the advocates of the meaſure. Somewhat earlier, it may not here be out of place to add, he had ſat alſo as chairman of a committee to hear witneſſes in ſupport of certain complaints brought before the Commons, on which occaſion he ſeems to have found it extremely difficult to enſnare or perplex a particular member who ſat with him. This was a gentleman whom he had "never before" heard ſpeak in the Houſe, but whoſe whole carriage in the committee was ſo tempeſtuous, and his behaviour ſo inſolent, that Mr. Hyde found himſelf under the painful neceſſity of reprehending him. A rebuke which neverthelefs appears to have had ſmall effect on the honourable member, who "in "great fury reproached the chairman for being "partial ;" which, having regard to the confeſſion juſt made in a preciſely ſimilar caſe, I am difpoſed to think that the chairman decidedly may have been. The honourable member who came ſo tempeſtuouſly on this occaſion between the witneſſes ("who were a "very rude kind of people ") and Mr. Hyde's ſenſe of decorum, was Mr. Cromwell, lately returned for the town of Cambridge.

But a more reliable reporter than Mr. Hyde was at length found when the *Notes* of Sir Ralph Verney were difcovered.* Among them

---

* Quoted originally by Serjeant Onſlow, and afterwards by Mr. Hallam, they were firſt publiſhed in detail by Mr. Bruce.

§ IV. *Attainder of the Earl of Strafford.* 131

was one of a speech by Hampden, in debate upon the propriety or otherwise of the Commons attending the upper House to hear Strafford's counsel on the matter of law, which, on being made public by Serjeant Onslow, was thought generally to have established the fact that Hampden had separated himself, as to the Attainder, from the friends with whom he usually acted, and had been against proceeding by bill. Verney's words are these. "HAMPDEN. The bill now pending doth not "tie us to goe by bill. Our Councill hath "been heard; *ergo*, in justice, we must hear "his. Noe more prejudice to goe to hear "Councill to matter of law, than 'twas to "hear Councill to matter of fact." No doubt the implication seemed to be that Hampden would rather not have been tied to go by bill.

<small>Reports debate on Strafford.</small>

<small>Speech by Hampden:</small>

On the other hand it was to be remarked that the resolution to which Verney's note relates, was upon a question in no respect vital to the Bill of Attainder. Culpeper voted with St. John against it, Sir Benjamin Rudyard joining with Lord Digby for it; and Hampden, in voting as he is supposed to have done, would have separated himself quite as much from the Hyde and Culpeper party as from the friends with whom he invariably acted. Nor was there really sufficient ground for supposing that up to this point any grave dispute or dissension had arisen in the lower House upon the course to be pursued against Strafford. As yet he had few friends there: his hottest enemy, Lord Digby, not having yet become his friend. And it is entirely a

<small>on question not material to the Bill.</small>

K 2

misapprehension to argue as though the alternative were raised by the point to which Hampden spoke, either to hear Strafford's counsel at the bar, *or* to proceed with the bill; and for this plain reason, that both were ultimately done. Hampden's opinion and vote prevailed, and the Bill of Attainder neverthelefs proceeded.

Attainder not in difpute.

It appeared to me, for thefe reafons, that nothing had been fettled conclufively by Verney's note beyond the fact of his having defired that Strafford's counfel fhould be heard in the manner propofed, with full fanction of the Houfe: both becaufe it contained no opinion diftinctly adverfe to the Attainder, and alfo becaufe, believing Pym to have originated that meafure, I found it difficult to imagine that in a proceeding of fuch importance Hampden could have feparated himfelf from the friend with whom, through the whole courfe of thefe eventful times, he certainly had no other known difference. I was, however, but partly right; and to the great hiftorian whofe lofs we all deplore, to Lord Macaulay alone, of all who have varioufly commented on Verney's note, muft be given the praife of having conftrued it, not indeed altogether correctly as to the fpecial matter in debate, but, as to the general and more important queftion of a defire ftill to ftand on the Impeachment, with a fingular correctnefs. "The opinion of Hampden," he had remarked, not permitting himfelf to be influenced, in the plain conftruction of the words, by any confideration of the courfe which Pym might have preferred to take, "as far as it

Hampden fuppofed favourable to it.

Correcter judgment by Macauley.

§ IV. *Attainder of the Earl of Strafford.*

"can be collected from a very obscure note *Essays, i.*
"of one of his speeches, seems to have been 467.
"that the proceeding by Bill was unnecessary,
"and that it would be a better course to ob-
"tain judgment on the Impeachment." This,
I shall proceed to show, was exactly the opinion Line
which Hampden had formed; and it is yet really
more startling to add that in adopting it he Hampden.
was only following Pym's lead. Not to
Macaulay, or to any one, had it occurred as
within reasonable probability, that Pym himself, upon the mere ground of policy, might
also have opposed the Attainder. Such nevertheless was the fact. The evidence of D'Ewes Evi-
is decisive. It sets at rest, at once and for dence of
ever, such personal statements and charges D'Ewes.
connected with this great fact in history as
have been variously disputed and long contested by historians; and it apportions at last, Doubts
with some degree of correctness, the respon- set at rest.
sibilities of blame and praise incurred by the
men who abandoned the way of Impeachment
they had themselves originated, in order to
proceed by Bill.

That mode of procedure, it seems, had Procedure
been canvassed at the opening of the session; by Bill
and having been strongly advocated by St. proposed.
John, Glyn, and Maynard, a Bill of Attainder
was actually prepared. But Pym and Hampden were so bent the other way, and so convinced that their proofs would establish the
charge of treason under the statute of Edward, Pym and
that the Impeachment went on. Nor in this Hampden
belief did they ever waver for an instant. Up for Im-
to the close of the proceedings on the trial, ment.

The Grand Remonſtrance.

they had an invincible perſuaſion that in the ſeveral hearings before the upper Houſe both the facts and the law had been eſtabliſhed; and when the ſitting of the thirteenth day, Saturday the 10th of April, had cloſed abruptly in violent diſſatisfaction at a deciſion of the peers which allowed Strafford to reopen the evidence on other articles provided the demand of the Commons to give additional proofs of the twenty-third article were conceded, they returned to their houſe, not to throw up the Impeachment, but to prepare the heads of a conference with the Lords for ſettlement of ſuch matters of difference as had ariſen. But with them returned a more diſcontented ſection, numbering among its members not only ſuch men as Haſelrig and Henry Marten, Oliver St. John and Glyn, but alſo a group compriſed of Falkland, Culpeper, the Hothams, Tomkins (member for Weobly), and others, all of whom afterwards either openly embraced the cauſe of the King, or ſecretly conſpired to further it. And by theſe men it was that the project of proceeding by Bill, formerly laid aſide, was now ſuddenly revived and preſſed. "Divers," ſays D'Ewes, "ſpake "whether we ſhould proceed by way of Bill "of Attainder, or as we had begun; but "moſt inclined that we ſhould go by Bill." The principal opponents were Pym and Hampden.

The additional evidence ſought to be given before the Lords, upon the twenty-third article, was that copy of the Notes taken at the Council Board by the elder Vane on the day

Diſpute of the 10th April.

Diſſatisfaction with Lords.

Bill of Attainder revived.

Oppoſed by Pym and Hampden.

Elder Vane's

§ IV. *Attainder of the Earl of Strafford.* 135

of the diffolution of the Short Parliament, which had been abftracted from his cabinet by the younger Vane, and by him given to Pym, who had founded the twenty-third article upon them. They were publicly read for the firft time, after the tumultuous return of the Commons to their own houfe on that Saturday afternoon; and from them it appeared, not only that Strafford had given the King fuch traitorous advice as the article in queftion charged him with (that, having been denied fupply by his Parliament, the Sovereign was abfolved and loofe from all rule of government, and that he had an army in Ireland which he might employ to reduce "this king-" dom" to obedience), but that Laud and Lord Cottington alfo had taken part in the dangerous counfel. Amid the excitement confequent thereon, the Bill of Attainder was produced; and the propofal by which it was met on the part of thofe who objected to its introduction, was, that a narrative of the circumftances attending the difcovery and production of Vane's important Notes of Council fhould be drawn up and fubmitted to the Lords at a conference; and that if, upon deliberation, the Lords decided not to receive it except upon condition of permitting the accufed to reopen the evidence upon other articles, then that it fhould be waived, and immediate fteps taken to fum up the cafe on both fides, and demand judgment. Any other courfe, they argued, would involve not only the certainty of delay, but a ftrong probability of difagreement with the Houfe of Lords. So decided

Notes of Council.

Objection to their production.

Excitement thereon.

Conference with Lords propofed.

The Grand Remonſtrance.

was the feeling for the Bill, however, that for once theſe great leaders were outvoted, and it was introduced and read a firſt time ; a ſug-geſtion of Hampden's, for reſuming at Monday's ſitting the preparation of heads for a conference with the upper Houſe, being at the ſame time aſſented to.

Pym and Hampden outvoted.

What occurred in the latter part of this Monday's ſitting (the early part was occupied by the ſpeeches of Pym and young Vane in reference to the Minutes of Council, and by the examination of the elder Vane's ſecretary as to their abſtraction from his cabinet), the reader who turns to the facſimile given at the opening of this volume may ſtudy from D'Ewes's blotted record, taken down while yet the ſitting went on, and while the men named in it were buſy talking and writing around him. He will probably, however, elect to avail himſelf of the labour I have already given to the taſk of decyphering it, and prefer to read it in the plain print ſubjoined. Nor, having ſo enabled him to underſtand the exiſting condition of D'Ewes's manuſcript, and the cauſes which will continue to keep it a ſealed book from all but the moſt determined ſtudent, ſhall I think it neceſſary to recur to the ſubject in the frequent further references I am about to make, and in which everything required to render my extracts intelligible will be ſilently ſupplied.

Sitting of the 12th April, 1641.

Reported in D'Ewes's MS.

The report now to be quoted is of the rougheſt kind, as will be obſerved ; paſſing abruptly from one point to another without explanation, and leaving upon record things ſubſequently laid aſide. But its evidence is

Two pages in fac-ſimile.

§ IV. *Attainder of the Earl of Strafford.* 137

decifive as to the perfonal matters for which alone it is here introduced; and never more can be raifed the queftion, fo long and eagerly debated, of whether or not Hampden quitted Pym's fide during the difcuffion of the Bill of Attainder, and temporarily joined with the party whom he afterwards very determinedly oppofed. Upon this, as upon every other great incident of the time, the two friends held their courfe together, from firft to laft. It muft be kept ever in view, however, that they did not oppofe the introduction of the Bill of Attainder as having any doubt either of Strafford's guilt, or of the fufficiency of the proofs againft him. They oppofed it for the exprefs reafon that they held the proofs already placed before the Lords *to be* fufficient; and their fubfequent affent to it, when the majority finally determined on that courfe, involved no inconfiftency. *Pym and Hampden acting together.*

Why they oppofed Attainder.

" Mr. Pymme fhewed that the Committee
" appointed for the managing of the evidence
" agſt the Earle of Strafford had prepared cer-
" taine heads for a conference with the Lords.
" Mr. Maynard begann where Mr. Pymme
" ended & furth [further] fhewed that wee
" were to defire a conference. *Pym fuggefts conference.*

" 1. A Narrative of the evidence concerning
" the triall againft the Earle of Strafford,
" for which evidence wee had two mem-
" bers of the houfe readie to bee depofed
" & for wch the Committee advized with
" the houfe & intended to have pre-
" fented the fame to their Lor^{pps} on
" Saturday laft. *Maynard recites points for fettlement.*

Houfe will make facrifices to prevent delay.

"2. The houfe having taken confideration thereof doe conceive it verie materiall: yet in regard of the danger & diftraction of the kingdome being verie great & will admit noe delay, they are refolved to come to a generall replie & to waive the faied evidence, if the Lords fhall not permitt it to bee examined unleffe the Earle of Strafford [have] libertie to examine witneffes to other Articles; wch the houfe doth doe to avoid delay, which is now of extreame dangerous confequence.

Others guilty with Strafford.

"3. Others confederated. Archb^p & Lord Cottington are difcovered: when motion to bring in Irifh armie was made by Earle of Strafford: by this paper will appeare, if their Lor^pps will have the paper read."

At this point, as will be feen in the facfimile, D'Ewes puts a note in the margin, refpecting that third head of the propofed conference to which the preceding not very clear fentences, and the two following not much more luminous paragraphs, relate.

Their guilt not to be infifted on.

"This 3d head thus penned was rejected, and a new one brought in.

"Defire the L^ds to joine with us to prevent danger: which might enfue upon fuch counfels.

"Thofe Councellors removed.

The Notes of Council.

"3. That upon occafion of difcoverie of this evidence a paper was read in the houfe by wch it appeared that at the fame time when the Earle of Strafford

§ IV. Attainder of the Earl of Strafford.

" gave that dangerous counfell of bring- *Laud and*
" ing in the Irifh armie into England *Cotting-*
" others were prefent, deciphered by *ton*
" thefe letters Arch. & L. Cott. whome *involved.*
" wee conceive Lord Arch. & L. Cott.
" verie full of pernicious counfell to the
" King & flanders to the Commons
" houfe affembled in the laft Parliament.

" Mr. Hotham moved to have the bill of *Hotham*
" the Earle of Strafford's attainder read. *for Attainder.*

" Mr. Pymme would not have the bill read,
" but to goe the other way: becaufe this is
" the fafer, to fhew that wee & the Lords are *Pym*
" reconciled & not fundred: & foe we fhall *againft.*
" proceed the more fpeedilie by demanding
" judgment.

" Mr. Maynard one way doth not croffe
" another, but wee may goe by bill of attain-
" der if wee will, or by demanding judgment: *Maynard*
" wch wee may beft refolve upon when wee fee *for.*
" the end of the triall.

" Sir Benjamin Rudier [Rudyard] fhewed
" the great treafon of the Earle of Strafford,
" & yet faied that one full third parte of the *Rudyard*
" evidence was not heard, & that divers of *doubtful.*
" the Lords who weere prefent at the open-
" ing thereof weere not fatisfied that it was
" treafon."

So ends the firft page of the facfimile. On the reverfe page the debate is continued, the firft two fpeakers being men notorious afterwards for their royalift fervices, and the third being D'Ewes himfelf.

" Mr. Tomkins for bill of attainder to bee *Tomkins*
" read, for it is the old way. *for.*

Culpeper for.	" Sir John Culpepper not to lay bill afide: " the fafeft & the fpeedieft way to proceede by " bill: yet for the conference now.
D'Ewes againft.	" I faied that I was verie gladd of the motion " for a conference. Neceffitie to complie with " L^s [Lords] for timor bonorum fpes malorum " & the diftraction now foe great in the king- " dome as it threatens much hazard. Firft " to demand Judgment the moft ancient way " in evident cafes: Bill, when men dead, or " fledd, or cafes difficult. This the fhorte
Urges judgment on Impeachment.	" way. For nothing now but to demand " judgment. A bill will be long in paffing; " & all delaies incident to that as to this. " For the fumming upp, a narrative may bee " omitted or proceeded in. This the fafe " way. B^{pps} in bill ought to have voices. " Divers faied No. But I tolde them that " I fpake not by rote or tradition but what I " knew. That I had this morning been " fearching in the office of the clark of the " Lordes houfe touching the bill of attainder " of Sir Thomas Seymour Lord Sudeley, as in " paper pinned.*
Explanation afked from old Vane.	" Divers moved that Mr. Treafurour might " explaine himfelfe, whome hee meant by " L. Cott. whether hee did not meane Lord " Cottington.
Refufed.	" Mr. Treafurour [Vane] denied to make " any other or further explanation till he had " well advized therupon, though wee fent him " to the Tower.

* All that remains now of that " paper pinned," however, is the fpace it once occupied. The page fimply proceeds and clofes as in the text.

§ IV. *Attainder of the Earl of Strafford.* 141

" Mr. Glynne fhewed reafon, why the com- Glyn
" mittee named the Lord Cottington becaufe explains.
" [he] had fworne hee was there.

" Mr. Martin [Henry Marten] fpake to Marten
" have bill of attainder read againe and to for Attainder.
" proceede that way.

" Mr. Hamden anfwered him & moved
" the meffage might goe upp fpeedilie.

" Mr. Hamden fent with the meffage about Hampden
" 12 of the clocke, but the Lords weere againſt.
" rifen.

" Being returned wee fell into debate to
" vote the heads for the conference.

" Upon the firſt head before fett downe Vane and
" being read and debated, Mr. Treafurour his Son.
" upon fome motions, was twice drawen to
" declare concerning the faied paper found by
" his fonne, that hee firſt moved his Matie that
" hee might burne it, & foe he commanded
" him to doe it : & fecondly, that hee was not
" poffiblie able to fpeake further to it, till hee
" had confidered deliberatelie of it."

Of the men who, on that 12th of April, Subfe-
thus fupported the Attainder, Hotham was quent
afterwards executed for betraying the truſt ſupporters
repofed in him by the Houfe, Tomkins was of Attainder.
expelled for fimilar bad faith, and Culpeper
entered into the fervice of the King. Glyn
and Maynard feem not to have committed
themfelves on that day, but in the fubfequent debates they proved to be as eager
for the Attainder as St. John himfelf; though Conduct
both lived to take part at the Reftoration, of Glyn
to their eternal infamy, in bringing to the nard.
fcaffold men fuch ·as Henry Vane, whofe

only crime was to have borne a share, not more marked than their own, in these transactions. Of Falkland, in relation to the Attainder, it is needless to speak. Such was what Clarendon calls his sharpness of tone upon this subject altogether, " so contrary," he adds, " to his natural gentleness and temper," that his friend says those who knew him but imperfectly were wont to account for it by recalling the memory of some unkindnesses, not without a mixture of injustice, from Strafford to his father ;* while Clarendon himself, with the usual disingenuousness, attributes it to his having been " misled by the authority of those " who, he believed, understood the laws per- " fectly." If this indeed had been the fact, it is a pity that so accomplished a lawyer as Mr. Hyde was already become did not take the necessary pains to enlighten so intimate a friend, gone astray on a matter of such great importance ; but still more is it to be regretted that very considerable grounds should exist for believing that they actually went astray respecting it in each other's company. For if it be also true, as in his history he distinctly informs us, that upon no question had they ever had a single difference,† or given votes

Side notes:
Line taken by Falkland:
excused by Clarendon.
What excuse for Mr. Hyde?

---

* Strafford had undoubtedly a great contempt for the elder Falkland, his predecessor in the Government of Ireland ; and when the King referred to the new Lord Deputy sundry applications from Falkland for favours to be bestowed on relatives or connections of his own, Strafford always resolutely set his face against them. See *Letters and Dispatches*, passim.

† This is repeatedly said or implied in what is remarked of Falkland throughout the history, and when it occurs to the historian to describe the disagreement between himself and Falkland on the debate of the bill for taking away the

Side note: Strafford's contempt for old Falkland.

§ IV. *Attainder of the Earl of Strafford.* 143

oppofed to each other, until the day when, after Strafford's execution, the bill for taking away the bifhops' votes was firft debated, the inference is irrefiftible that Hyde, who affuredly did not at any time vote againft, muft have voted *for*, the Attainder. Certainly what he fays refpecting it in his book is an entire falfification of the facts, and could only have been written under the perfuafion that the erafure from the journals of both Houfes, at the Reftoration, of every trace of the proceedings connected with it, had equally obliterated them alfo from the recollections of men. He might have fhrunk from fuch confident mifftatement, if any vifion of D'Ewes's Notes had prefented itfelf, as likely ever to rife again.

Takes fame line as Falkland.

Too much faith in fhort memories.

So clear and ftraightforward, on the other hand, was the courfe taken by Pym and Hampden, that even by their fubfequent adoption of the Attainder not a fhadow of inconfiftency was thrown on their previous refiftance. They refifted it, becaufe, believing

Pym and Hampden confiftent throughout.

---

bifhops' votes, brought forward after Strafford's execution, he expreflly notes it as memorable that there arofe in this debate, " *between two perfons who had never been known to differ in* " *the houfe*," a difference of opinion (i. 412). Now nothing is fo certain as that Falkland ftrenuoufly, by votes and fpeeches, fupported the Attainder in every ftage; and it is utterly impoflible that Hyde could have made the remark juft quoted, which was written two years after his friend's death, with anything fo recent and fo marked in his memory as a difference on the Attainder muft have been. The friends fat, too, as they voted, together. "The Lord Falkland "always fat next Mr. Hyde, which was fo much taken notice "of, that if they came not into the Houfe together, as "ufually they did, everybody left the place for him that was "abfent" (i. 413).

Hyde and Falkland's agreement.

Sitting as well as voting together.

the guilt of Strafford to have been proved, they continued to have faith in the Impeachment; and afterwards they adopted it, becaufe, the Houfe having finally determined againft the Impeachment, the fame conviction as to Strafford's guilt left them only that alternative. Until the very laft, however, they clung to the Impeachment, and to the obligations it had impofed. St. John, Glyn, and Maynard, as foon as the bill was introduced, would have made it the pretext for refifting what had previoufly been refolved as to hearing counfel for Strafford before the Lords upon the matter of law; and this point was ftrenuoufly debated for two days. It was in relation to it that the fpeech was fpoken by Hampden of which Sir Ralph Verney kept the note. Both Falkland and Culpeper, as well as St. John, Maynard, and Glyn, infifted ftrongly that it would compromife both the dignity and the power of the Commons, if, at a time when they propofed to make themfelves judges in the cafe, they confented to hear or reply to counfel anywhere but at their own bar; and Culpeper went fo far as to affert his belief, that, by attending fo to hear and reply before the Lords, they would imperil their right to affume fubfequent legiflative action in the matter. But Pym and Hampden were not to be moved from the ground on which they ftood refolutely as to this part of the cafe. Why fhould not the lawyers of the Houfe, fuggefted Hampden in reply to Culpeper, fpeak to the points of law before the bar of the Lords, and then come back to their feats among the members of their

§ IV. *Attainder of the Earl of Strafford.*

own Houfe, and afterwards fpeak again at the Lords' bar if neceffary? To which Maynard fomewhat hotly replied, that he fhould hold fuch a running up and down from one place to another to be nothing lefs than a difhonour to the Commons. The word called up Pym, who appears to have made one of his moft effective appeals. He fubmitted to the Houfe that the queftion before it, of hearing and replying to Strafford's counfel before the Lords, did not bind them either to continue, or to abandon, the proceeding by bill. That might hereafter be fettled, according to the wifdom and pleafure of the Houfe; but what they had now to confider was the queftion, really involving honour, whether the pledge was to be kept or to be broken, which, at the time when their counfel firft rofe before the Lords to fpeak againft Strafford, they then undoubtedly gave that Strafford's counfel fhould be heard in his behalf before the fame tribunal. "If," continued Pym, according to the report in D'Ewes's manufcript of this remarkable fpeech, " if we did not go this way to have it heard " publickly in matter of law as well as it had " been heard for matter of fact, we fhould " much difhonour ourfelves, and hazard our " own fafeguards."

To this appeal the Houfe yielded, and the fame fpirit which fuggefted it prevailed in the fubfequent proceedings. It was upon Pym's motion, when the Impeachment was finally abandoned, that all its moft material articles were imported into the Bill; that the facts, under each article, were voted feparately; and

Speech of Maynard againft.

Pym in reply.

Advocates Strafford's claim to hearing.

His appeal fuccefsful.

that, before the third reading paffed to a queftion, the Houfe firft heard the "Gentlemen
"of the long robe" argue at great length
the feveral points of law, and then proceeded
judicially to vote upon them. It would tax
a greater ingenuity, I think, than that of
the privy councillor and county member to
whom · reference has been made, to difcover
in all this anything of Barrère or Fouquier
Tinville. It is a fchool of comparifon, however, to which recourfe is ever readily found
by unreafoning affailants of the parliamentary
leaders ; and Mr. Bankes has not fcrupled to
declare that "while the Englifh are thought
" to be lefs fanguinary in their days of political
" frenzy than the French, undoubtedly the
" hiftory of London in 1641 bears very many
" points of fimilarity with the hiftory of Paris
" from the year 1791 to 1793." Not the
lefs is it to be faid, of all fuch attempts
at parallel, that they are fimply and utterly
falfe. For a moment to fet up the affertion
that the hiftory of London, during the year
when the Commons impeached and beheaded
the moft capable minifter of the King, and the
King made a fimilar but lefs fuccefsful attempt
againft the moft capable members of the
Commons, bears even any points of fimilarity
with the hiftory of Paris at the time when its
guillotine reeked with the execution of its
harmlefs inoffenfive King and its poor fallen
Queen, while women and men were taken
daily by waggon loads to death, and while the
fwollen gutters of the wicked city foamed
over into the Seine with the beft blood of

§ IV. *Attainder of the Earl of Strafford.* 147

France, is to infult the fenfe of the reader to whom fuch folly is addreffed. Happily, few are now found to repeat it. It belongs to a hardihood of affertion that has long been paffed away, to compare the frenzied wretches who bore aloft the mangled body of the Princeffe de Lamballe with the calm felf-refolute men who kept the fword quietly fheathed till it flafhed out at Edgehill and Marfton Moor. It is now for the moft part the declared belief of every writer who has fhown himfelf familiar with this period of Englifh hiftory, that with anything approaching to its temper under wrong, its patience in long fuffering before the fword was drawn, its moderation in victory when the fword was finally fheathed, no fimilar movement in the world was ever begun and carried to its clofe. *[sidenote: Obfolete views.]* *[sidenote: Opinions of the better informed.]*

Upon this earlier portion of the ftory of our civil wars, indeed, nearly all intelligent inquirers might be thought to have laid afide their differences long ago. From whatever oppofite points of view, the faireft judgments have been able of late years to arrive at fubftantially the fame conclufion, on this firft ftage of the conflict; and, up to the Arreft of the Five Members at leaft, to agree that a power to difcriminate between good and bad faith is really all the inveftigation requires. That the Long Parliament had no defire permanently to ftrip the Crown of any of its effential prerogatives, and did abfolutely nothing, before the fword was drawn, which was not juftified by the King's perfonal character, or of which the fufficient reafon is not difcern- *[sidenote: Agreement up to Arreft of Five Members.]* *[sidenote: Parliament's juftification.]*

ible in a neceffary abfence of all belief or truft in his promifes, is an opinion which the moft uncompromifing high-church reafoners have not been afhamed to adopt from the late Mr. Coleridge; and it was the fcrupulous regard for truth and right by which the ftruggle was fo characterifed at its beginning, that imparted to it mainly what bore it in fuch honour and credit to its end. We have alfo to remember that much more of the real wealth of the kingdom was committed on behalf of the Parliament than at any time remained with the King, and that this alone would have rendered it impoffible that *fanfculottifm* fhould have got the upper hand amongft us. Some lives were fternly exacted, becaufe held to have been neceffarily forfeited; but no blood was ruthleffly or caufeleffly fpilt upon the fcaffold. No monftrous or unnational innovations difgraced the progrefs, and no infamous profcriptions marked the termination, of the war. The palaces of England ftood throughout as unrifled as its cottages; and, except where fortified refiftance had been offered, the manfions and manor-houfes remained as of old, through the length and breadth of the land. While the conflict continued, no fervile paffions inflamed or difgraced it; and when all was over, the vanquifhed fat down with the victors in their common country, and no man's property was unjuftly taken from him.

For thefe reafons it is that the various incidents and characters in the civil wars of the feventeenth century continue to be regarded with a living and active fympathy. Other

§ IV. *Attainder of the Earl of Strafford.* 149

events, hardly lefs momentous at the time of their occurrence, have left but a local and partial ftamp upon our annals; while even yet the intereft of thefe is national and univerfal. They do not concern particular neighbourhoods only, but addrefs themfelves ftill to every family and firefide in the kingdom; for under Heaven we owe it mainly to them that all Englifh homes are now protected and fecure. The refult has anfwered to their origin. They began in no fordid encounter of felfifhnefs or faction, they involved no vulgar difputes of family or territory, and perfonal enmities formed no neceffary part of them. They were a war, as one of their leaders faid, without an enemy. In the principles they put to iffue, we continue ourfelves to be not lefs interefted than were our forefathers; and hardly a queftion of government has arifen fince, affecting human liberty or the national welfare, which has not included a reference to this great conflict, and fome appeal to the precedents it eftablifhed. Nothing can be unimportant that relates to it, therefore, nor any fervice fmall that may explain the motives of its leaders; and it is well that the record by D'Ewes, to which we are about to be fo largely indebted, fhould have enabled us firft to difcern clearly the courfe they took upon the greateft queftion that arofe before the war began.

 One word as to Strafford himfelf may be added at this outfet of my narrative. Believing that juftice remained with the Parliament, I think not the lefs that high and noble qualities were engaged on the fide of the King; and

ftill infpired by the war.

A war without an enemy.

D'Ewes as to acts and motives.

Strafford. Greateft man on

The Grand Remonstrance.

the King's confide. Beyond all question they found their most conspicuous example, as, but for the event I have been describing, they would have found their most formidable development, in Strafford. His Irish administration is the signal proof that in some of the noblest qualities of statesmanship, and eminently in the supreme art of turning the resources of a country to profitable account, he stood alone in his age. But what should have been to such a man the highest object of ambition, he unhappily missed altogether; and, tried as it was in most advantageous circumstances in Ireland, and backed as it was by his own consummate power, his whole system of government broke down. It could not have sustained itself, indeed, without overthrowing the public liberties, because it was an attempt to establish the royal prerogative above them. Nevertheless it also included much that had no unpopular aspect, for it was the design of a man of courage and genius. He would have cleared the land, by foul means or fair, of the native possessors; he would have rooted out the idle, improvident, beggarly proprietor; and he would have planted everywhere English wealth and English enterprise. It is remarkable that a scheme which in its final development brought its author to well-merited ruin, should yet have involved so much that, in other hands, and with other ultimate aims, might have saved and regenerated Ireland. Every petty oligarchy would have been reduced by it to subjection before the monarchy, and it would have struck down all the tyrannies but

Where his statesmanship succeeded.

Where it failed.

His system in Ireland.

§ IV. *Attainder of the Earl of Strafford.*

its own. The mere forms of parliament would univerfally have been retained and refpected by Strafford, becaufe he knew that defpotifm has no fuch efficient ally as parliaments deprived of parliamentary power. While he made the Irifh Cuftoms more profitable by four times their annual amount, he would fo have employed this enormous increafe as again and again to multiply itfelf, through enlarged refources of commerce and trade. While he eftablifhed vaft monopolies for the Crown, he would have abolifhed private monopolies that had fimply gorged its fervants. And in the very act of impofing taxes arbitrarily, and levying them by military force, he fell with fo heavy a hand on wrongdoers of high rank, as made the oppreffed commonalty grudge lefs what they, too, had to endure. But here lay the danger that proved fatal to him. He created numerous enemies whofe power he defpifed, and he failed to fecure the fingle friend whofe conftancy and courage might have baffled them. Strafford's Irifh adminiftration had no fuch dire foe as the monarch whom it was meant to fave. Charles intrigued againft it himfelf, and favoured all the intrigues of others. Even the fervices it rendered to him were hateful for their connection with the reftraints it would have impofed upon him. It became thus of the very effence of Strafford's defign, comprehenfive as it was, that the good it might have wrought fhould perifh by the evil it could not but inflict. The fword he had provided for fafety turned and broke in his hand. A too vaft ambition, joined with a too

The good implied in it.

The danger that proved fatal.

Bad faith of the King.

152   *The Grand Remonstrance.*

narrow aim, deftroyed him. And his Irifh adminiftration is now chiefly memorable, not for the revenues and refources it fo largely developed and his mafter as miferably wafted; not for the linen trade it eftablifhed, which ftruck root and has faved the land; but becaufe it has fhown, by one of the greateft examples on record, of what fmall account is the ftatefmanfhip moft fuccefsful in providing for material wants, which yet refufes to recognife the moral neceffities of the people it affumes to govern.

Moral of Strafford's government.

§ V. Reaction after Strafford's Death.

THE altered pofition of parties after Strafford's death was firft publicly fixed and declared by the Grand Remonftrance. The Debates refpecting it are the commencement of the ftruggle which divided into two hoftile camps the very party heretofore impregnable in their unity and ftrength, and which directly brought on the war. It is natural, therefore, that the author of the *Hiftory of the Rebellion* fhould nowhere affect more particularity of detail than in defcribing the various incidents and circumftances of the difcuffion relating to it. It was, indeed, to the party of which he then firft affumed the lead in the Houfe, as to their opponents, the critical moment of their career. It was, to both, the turning point of all they had done heretofore, or might hope to do hereafter. Falkland told his friend Hyde, that, as he and Cromwell left

Parties altered after Strafford's death.

Remonftrance a frefh ftarting-point.

What Cromwell

§ v. Reaction after Strafford's Death. 153

the houſe together immediately after the laſt ſaid to Falkland.
diviſion, the member for Cambridge ſaid to
him, that, if it had gone againſt them in that
vote, he and many other honeſt men he knew
would have ſold all they had the next morning,
and never have ſeen England more; and,
without too readily accepting this anecdote, Alleged
or thinking "the poor kingdom," as Mr. narrow eſcape for Charles.
Hyde phraſes it, to have been half ſo near to
its deliverance in that particular as he affects to
believe, it would be impoſſible to overſtate the
gravity, to both parties, of the iſſue depending
on the vote which had juſt been taken.

Immediately after the execution of Strafford, Hyde's new policy.
which Hyde and his aſſociates, as we have
thus ſeen, helped more largely than any other
ſection of the Houſe to accompliſh, they began
ſteadily and ſecretly to employ every artifice,
and all the advantages which their poſition in
the Commons gave them, to bring about a
reaction favourable to the King. The one
formidable obſtacle had been removed, by
Strafford's death, to their own entry into
Charles's counſels; and without further gua- Reaction for the King.
rantees for the ſecurity of any one conceſſion
they had wreſted from the Crown, they were
prepared to halt where they ſtood, or even (as
in the caſe of the Epiſcopacy Bill) to recede
from ground they had taken up.* Nor was

---

* Richard Baxter (*Reliq. Baxt.* 19) has attributed "the Miſtake of Richard Baxter.
firſt breach among themſelves" to the deſire on the part of
Lord Falkland, the Lord Digby, and divers other able
men," to gratify the King " by ſparing Strafford's life."
But Baxter wrote long after the event, and was very imperfectly informed. Neither Falkland nor Hyde had at any
time a friendly feeling to Lord Digby, and though a difference

it to be doubted that the plan had some chances of succefs, in the particular time when it was tried. From the moment the Impeachment was carried againſt Strafford, thoſe old relative poſitions of King and Houſe of Commons, which in the memory of living men, had exiſted as if unchangeably, were ſuddenly reverſed. There was not a Parliament in the preceding reign that James had not lectured, as a ſchoolmaſter his refractory pupils; nor any in the exiſting reign that Charles had not bullied, as a tyrant his refractory ſlaves. But this was gone. The King was now, to all appearance, the weaker party, and the Houſe of Commons was the ſtronger; and how readily ſympathy is attracted to thoſe who are weak, however much in the wrong, and how apt to fall away from the ſtrong, however clearly in the right, it does not need to ſay. The popular leaders became conſcious of daily defections from their ranks; the Houſe of Lords unexpectedly deſerted them, on queſtions in which they had embarked in uniſon; the Army was entirely unſafe; and opinions began to be buſily put about, that enough had

Chances of ſuccefs.

Old poſitions reverſed.

Daily defections from Popular ranks.

no doubt aroſe as to the Bill of Attainder, the principal feceders who went with Digby on that queſtion were lawyers, ſuch as Selden, Holborne, and Bridgman, who went with him on no other; and undoubtedly the men who took afterwards the lead in forming a king's party, ſuch as Falkland and Culpeper (whom Selden refuſed to join), had taken the lead in promoting the Bill of Attainder. The evidence adduced in the preceding ſection ſhows that when the liberal leaders, who to this hour are ſuppoſed to have originated and moſt hotly urged forward the Bill, were in reality oppoſing it, and bent only on continuing and cloſing by way of Impeachment, Culpeper and Falkland ſtrenuouſly advocated the procedure by Bill.

Only lawyers feceded on the Attainder.

§ v. Reaction after Strafford's Death.

been conceded by the King, and that the demand for more would be ungenerous.

Never had a great cause been in peril more extreme. For most thoroughly was the character of their adversary known to its chiefs, and that not a single measure of redress had been extorted from him which was not yielded in the secret hope of finding early occasion to reclaim it. It was notorious that Charles the First entertained a belief of the invalidity of the most important of the measures already passed by the Long Parliament, on the ground that his own assent, having been given by compulsion, was *ipso facto* void. His Attorney-General had encouraged him in this notion;* and Hyde himself cannot help condemning the facility with which he assented to acts requiring grave deliberation, in reliance on this dangerous opinion that the violence and force used in procuring them rendered them absolutely invalid and void. This, says Hyde,† made the confirmation less considered, as not being of strength to make that act good which was in itself null. One of those great acts indeed could not so be dealt with. Strafford could not be raised from the dead, and therefore only had the concession in his case been obtained with greater difficulty than in the rest. Now, everything promised fairly for a resumption of all else. The Army had been widely tampered with; to save the bishops and their bishopricks, the Universities were moving

Character of the King.

His view as to invalidity of Statutes.

Assenting with purpose to revoke.

Hyde's complaint.

Sources of danger to Parliament.

---

* Clarendon: *Life and Continuation*, I. 206-211.
† *Hist.* ii. 252.

heaven and earth;* reliance could no longer be placed upon the Lords; concurrently with many figns of treachery among the Commons themfelves, in which Mr. Edward Hyde notably took part, were feen evidences elfewhere dangerous of the return of an unreafoning confidence in the King; even in the City, the ftronghold of liberal councils, a prominent royalift had been able to carry his election as lord mayor; and the patriots could not hope that their power, or their opportunities, would furvive any real abatement of zeal or enthufiafm in the people. It is more wearing to the patience to wait for the redrefs that is really near, than for what is wholly uncertain and remote; and thofe who had bravely and filently endured the wrongs of fifteen years without a parliament, were ready to refent a delay of half as many months in the reliefs which parliament had promifed them.† What Charles gained by

Signs of wavering.

Abatement of popular enthufiafm.

The clergy and univerfities.

* " Bifhops had been much lifted at," fays May (lib. i. cap. ix), " though not yet taken away, whereby a great party " whofe livelihood and fortunes depended on them, and far " more whofe hopes of preferment looked that way (moft of " the Clergy, and both the Univerfities), began to be daily " more difaffected to the Parliament; complaining that all " rewards of learning would be taken away. Which wrought " deeply in the hearts of the young and moft ambitious of " that coat."

Ficklenefs of the people.

† This point is admirably touched by the hiftorian May. " Some are taken off" (weaned from Parliament, he means) " by time and their own inconftancy, when they have looked " for quicker redrefs of grievances than the great concurrence " of fo many weighty bufineffes can poffibly admit in a long " difcontinued and reforming Parliament, how induftrious " foever they be, diftracted with fo great a variety. Thofe " people, after fome time fpent, grew weary again of what " before they had fo long wifhed to fee; not confidering that

§ v. Reaction after Strafford's Death.

secrecy, the popular leaders loft. It was impossible that they should make public all the reasons and motives for their proceedings, while yet such enforced concealment on their part told strongly to the advantage of the King. If ever warning for future guidance were needed, the time for it was now come; and there was nevertheless no way, consistent with safety, of showing the people in whose cause they were labouring, the present perils and pitfalls that beset them, without turning frankly and boldly to the lessons of the past. With even so much semblance of amended administration, and such pretences of half popular measures, as the ingenuity of Hyde could furnish (if Charles could be brought to concede only so much), there was yet the means, in the absence of that indispensable warning against reposing confidence in the sovereign, of striking a heavy blow for recovery of the old prerogative. Nor were nearer dangers wanting. Pym's life had been aimed at repeatedly; and more than one attempt had been tried to overawe deliberation by the display of force.

Charles's advantages.

A warning needed.

Threatenings of force.

" a prince, if he be averse from such a Parliament, can find
" power enough to retard their proceedings, and keep off for
" a long time the cure of the State. When that happens,
" the people, tired with expectation of such a cure, do usually
" by degrees forget the sharpness of those diseases which before
" required it; or else—in the redressing of so many and long
" disorders, and to secure them for the future, there being for
" the most part a necessity of laying heavy taxes, and draining
" of much money from the people—they grow extremely
" sensible of that present smart; feeling more pain by the
" cure, for a time, than they did by the lingering disease
" before; and not considering that the causes of all which
" they now endure were precedent, and their present suffering
" is for their future security." Lib. i. cap. ix. 115.

Impatience of waiting.

Cure more painful than disease.

158   *The Grand Remonſtrance.*

<small>Freedom or deſpotiſm?</small> Something was in peril beyond the abſtract freedom of parliament or debate; nor was it more to ſecure the permanence of proviſions already achieved for the public liberty, than to guard againſt ſudden ſubſtitution of a naked deſpotiſm, that the parliamentary chiefs were now called to aſſert and defend their poſition, or to abandon it for ever.

<small>Reſolution to appeal to the People.</small> They were not men to heſitate, and they reſolved upon an Appeal to the People in a more direct form than had ever yet been attempted. Within a week after the Houſe firſt met in November, a committee had been moved for by Lord Digby, in a moſt paſſion‑ <small>Origin of the "Remonſtrance."</small> ate ſpeech, to "draw up ſuch a Remonſtrance " to the King as ſhould be a faithful and " lively repreſentation of the deplorable ſtate " of the kingdom, and ſuch as might diſcover " the pernicious authors of it;" and the pro‑ <small>Firſt moved by Lord Digby.</small> poſal had been adopted in a modified and more moderate form, wherein it will be found on the Journals (ii. 25), of "ſome ſuch way " of Declaration as may be a faithful repre‑ " ſentation *to this Houſe* of the eſtate of the " kingdom;" all the leading men of the houſe being members of the committee, and Lord Digby its chairman. This deſign, ſuper‑ ſeded for the time by matters of more preſſing moment, and whoſe originator had in the <small>The King receives warning:</small> interval become the hotteſt partizan of the King, was revived in the ſummer. Charles received warning of it before he departed for Scotland, on that miſſion which has ſince been ſhown to have had no object ſo eagerly deſired as to gather ſuppoſed proofs on which to build

§ v. Reaction after Strafford's Death.

a charge of treason againſt Pym and Hampden, and ſuch acceſſions from the undiſbanded Scotch army to the conſpirators of the army of the North as to render ſafe the proſecution of ſuch a charge. Biſhop Williams, for purpoſes of his own, had intercourſe with a ſervant of Pym's, and did not ſcruple to tell the King how that he had learned, from this worthy, what had been going on in his maſter's houſe. Some of the Commons were preparing a Declaration to make the actions of his Majeſty's government odious, and he had better try to conciliate them before he went. The King was as ready to accept the ſuggeſtion as the wily prelate to offer it, and negotiations were opened for a revival of the ſcheme of giving office to the leaders of the popular party, ſet on foot a few months before. What had then for its object to ſave Strafford's life was nòw deſigned to ſave the King, by giving him time to ruin the very men he was meanwhile to invite to ſerve him. [side: on eve of journey to Scotland. Biſhop Williams adviſes conciliation. King conſents.]

The continued hoſtility of Pym and Hampden to the Scottiſh viſit, and their calm determination to bring forward the Remonſtrance, baffled the plan. There can be no doubt that for a time the Court party believed their opponents to be on the point of taking office. The rumour firſt went that Hampden was to be Secretary of State. Then it was announced, with more confidence, and by no leſs a perſon than Mr. Nicholas, ſo ſoon himſelf to aſſume that high office and who meanwhile was exerciſing its functions, that the ſeals were to be taken by Denzil Hollis, that Hampden was [side: Scheme baffled. Intended diſtribution of offices.]

The Grand Remonstrance.

[Friday, 30th of July:]

to be Chancellor of the Duchy, that Lord Say and Seale was to be Lord Treasurer, and, as in all the previous proposed arrangements, that Pym was to be Chancellor of the Exchequer. The date of the letter in which such intended distribution of the offices is mentioned by Nicholas is the 29th of July; and on the day following, an Under Secretary in his department writes to a friend that Mr. Treasurer has warned him to be in readiness for the expected change.* Neverthelefs it came to nothing. Within the next feven days, the differences between the King and the leaders of the majority in the Houfe had deepened; in the teeth of all their reprefentations, inftant departure for Scotland was perfifted in, and the propofition for a viceroy during the royal abfence overruled; and on the firft Saturday in Auguft a portion of the King's retinue had already fet forth upon the journey, while the Houfe were ftill in the midft of a confufed debate which lafted till nearly midnight, and in the courfe of which had been brought forward the fubject of "A REMONSTRANCE to be made, how "wee found the Kingdome and the Church, "and how the ftate of it now ftands."†

[New Miniftry expected.]

[Saturday, 7th Aug:]

[Remonftrance formally brought forward.]

* I have printed thefe various letters, from MSS. in the State Paper Office, in my *Arreft of the Five Members,* § v.

† I quote Sir Ralph Verney's *Notes of the Long Parliament* (p. 113): Saturday, 7th Auguft, 1641. It occurs after allufion to the fact of an extraordinary fitting of the Houfe having been appointed for the following (Sunday) morning, and after mention made of an order taken for a "peremptory" call of the Houfe on the next Wednefday "in regard of the great "and weighty affaires that import the faifty of the kingdome." All thefe are indications of the great apprehenfion prevailing at the moment as to the King's obftinate perfiftence in going to Scotland. And on this Saturday, as I remark in the text,

[Excitement as to Scotch journey.]

§ V. *Reaction after Strafford's Death.*

All the pains and labour of the intriguing Bishop, therefore, might clearly have been spared. He needed not to have bribed Mr. Pym's servant, nor was it necessary to have set on his master to bribe Mr. Pym himself. The Declaration, or, as Lord Digby had suggested it should be called, the Remonstrance, appears to have been revived openly, and direction given that it should take its place among the orders of the House, as part of the business of the session remaining to be done. Portions of it certainly came under discussion before the members rose for the recess; and we have evidence that after the King's departure, amid the excitements of the inquiry into the army plot, the committee to whom it had been referred had it under deliberation as "the Remon-
" strance of the state of the Kingdom and the
" Church."* What its promoters prudently concealed, or, to speak perhaps more correctly, had not yet finally settled, was the particular manner in which they proposed to make use of it.

The King quitted London on Monday the 9th August; with what hopes of returning, after his absence, better able to cope with his antagonists in the Houses, an anecdote related by Mr. Hyde may in some degree enable us to judge. He describes† the surprise with which, some little time before, he had received an invitation to wait privately on the King; how he had supposed it was some mistake,

Bishop Williams's labour lost.

Remonstrance openly discussed.

King quits London: 9th August.

Hyde's previous interview.

both Houses sat until after 10 at night, unable to settle upon any satisfactory course.
* So styled in the Commons' Journals (ii. 234).
† In his *Life and Continuation*, i. 92-93.

M

"for that he had not the honour to be known to the King, and that there was another of the same name, of the House;" but how that it proved to be no mistake, and he accordingly saw the King alone in the "square room" at Whitehall. On which occasion his Majesty told him "that he heard from all hands how much he was beholden to him; and that when all his servants in the House of Commons either neglected his service, or could not appear usefully in it, he took all occasions to do him service; for which he thought fit to give him his own thanks, and to assure him that he would remember it to his advantage." For his affection to the Church in particular, Mr. Hyde proceeds to tell us, his Majesty thanked him more than for all the rest; and then he discoursed of what he called the passion of the House, and of the bill lately brought in against Episcopacy, and asked Hyde whether he thought they would be able to carry it, to which the other answered he believed they could not, at least that it would be very long first. "Nay," replied Charles, "If you will look to it that they do not carry it before I go to Scotland, which will be at such a time, when the armies shall be disbanded, *I will undertake for the Church after that time.*"

Plainly one great hope on which Charles built in this expedition to his Northern dominions, was, by means of personal intercourse on his way with the mutinous Northern army, and by similar influences exerted in Edinburgh over the leaders of the yet undis-

[margin notes: Why Charles was grateful to him. His service against Episcopacy Bill. Engagement to defeat it.]

banded Scottish force, to be able to achieve Hopes
some plan for getting certain regiments into from the Scottish
the south with a view to his design against the Journey.
Parliament itself in the persons of its leading
members. Does your Majesty say, then,
exclaimed Hyde, that you can undertake for
the Church *after your return?* " Why, then, Hyde's
" by the Grace of God, it will not be in much promise.
" danger." What Mr. Hyde meant by this
will soon more fully appear.

§ VI. REASSEMBLING OF PARLIAMENT: OCTOBER, 1641.

THE parliamentary recess, during which Pym 20th of
sat as chairman of a committee having absolute October, 1641.
powers to conduct business in the interval, Houses
lasted from the 9th of September, when the meet.
House had not risen until nine o'clock at
night, to the morning of the 20th of October.
On that day the members reassembled ; but
great gaps were seen in their ranks, and it Defaulters
became obvious, as week followed week with- from the Commons.
out supplying these deficiencies, that the
average of attendance had considerably dimin-
ished. Lord Clarendon, though he hesitates
expressly to say so, would have us assume that
the King's party suffered most by this falling
off ; but the assumption is hardly reconcileable
with the strenuous exertions of the patriots to
compel a more full attendance. It appears
from the D'Ewes manuscript that Strode went Strode's
even so far, some two months after the recess, proposition
as to propose to fine a member £50, or expel against the
him, if he persisted in absence without leave ; absent

164   *The Grand Remonſtrance.*

without leave.
Liberal party weakened.
Forebodings coming true.
Report from the Receſs Committee.

and when ſuggeſtion was made on the King's behalf from Edinburgh, for the iſſue of a proclamation requiring full attendance of all the members of the Houſe, the Lord Keeper and Chief Juſtice Bankes were againſt it, as unſeaſonable. The truth ſeems to have been, that the defection compriſed generally the claſs of not very ſettled opinions which had hitherto ſided moſtly with the ſtrongeſt; and that its manifeſtation at this critical time, bringing new proof of influences at work as well within as without the Houſe, to weaken the power of its leaders, furniſhed alſo a more complete juſtification, if that were needed, of the courſe on which they had reſolved.

Nor had they aſſembled many hours before darker warnings gathered in upon them. The Scottiſh journey had borne its fruits. The entire diſbanding of the Northern army at the time appointed had been intercepted by the King's order, under the hand of Vane; there had been communications with it, during the King's progreſs to Edinburgh; and the intrigues in Edinburgh itſelf had been ſo far partially ſucceſſful, that a ſchiſm had been effected among the leaders of the Covenant of a character preciſely ſimilar to that which Hyde had undertaken for England. It was Pym's duty now, as chairman of the committee appointed to ſit during the receſs, after narrating the diſcovery of Goring's plot, to place before the Commons certain evidences exiſting of another widely ſpread army conſpiracy in England, of the weight or importance to be attached to which, and of its poſſible

§ VI. *Reassembling of Parliament: Oct.* 1641.

connection with matters then transpiring in Scotland, the House would judge. Falkland and Hyde attempted to turn the debate into another direction, and the result was still doubtful when Pym, in the midst of the sitting, produced letters which the committee had received from Hampden. Hampden was still in Edinburgh, nominally (with Fiennes and Stapleton) as a commissioner on the Scotch debt, but really to watch the King's proceedings there; and the letters now handed in from the member for Bucks, and which had reached the committee by an express, detailed the scheme just discovered at Edinburgh for the assassination of the leaders of the Covenant.* The entire contents of these letters

Another plot.

Letters produced from Hampden.

The "Incident."

---

* Clarendon says explicitly that Montrose, while professing to be able to satisfy the King of the treason of Argyle and against the Hamiltons, advised the more certain and expeditious mode of disposing of them by assassination, which he "frankly "undertook to do" (*Hist.* ii. 17). The noble historian adds that the King "abhorred that expedient," but unhappily even he is not able to deny that the King continued his regard and confidence to the man who (as at any rate he appears himself to have believed, at the close of his life, when the best opportunities had meanwhile presented themselves for maturing his knowledge and judgment of the facts) had actually suggested assassination. The subject is further pursued in my *Arrest of the Five Members*, § xxviii. From the manuscript records of these proceedings of the Long Parliament which are before me as I write, I find that Pym, as early as ten days after the present date, namely, on the 30th October, appears to have been thoroughly conscious of what had been going on in Edinburgh. In the course of the more elaborate statement he then gave of the circumstances (adverted to in his speech ten days before) of "a new design now lately, "again to make use of the army against us," he has occasion to advert also to the fact that "secret forces were ready in "some places, and secret meetings had been in Hampshire by "sundry great recusants;" and with this he couples a warning "that the Prince" (afterwards Charles II.) "who was "appointed to be at Richmond, was often at Oatlands with

Charge against Montrose.

30th October.

Pym's speech on Army designs.

were not divulged: but, on the further ſtatement then made by Pym, a propoſition by Hyde (which Falkland ſupported) for leaving the buſineſs of Scotland to the Parliament there, and paſſing to conſideration of the pay of the five undiſbanded troops of the Northern army, was ſtrenuouſly refiſted, and at laſt ſucceſſfully. Then, upon the motion of Sir Benjamin Rudyard ſupported by Sir Walter Earle and others, among whom Sir Simonds D'Ewes diſtinguiſhed himſelf by a highly metaphorical and ingenious addreſs in which he enlarged upon a wholeſome barbarous cuſtom prevailing in Africa of hanging up one Lion to ſcare the reſt, reſolutions were paſſed for immediate conference with the Lords on the ſafety of the parliament and kingdom; inſtructions were given for occupation, with a ſtrong force, of all the military poſts of the city; the trained-bands of London were ordered up to guard the two Houſes by night as well as by day; and theſe troops, with the ſimilar force enrolled in Weſtminſter, were ſubſequently turned into a regular parliamentary guard acting under direction of the Earl of Eſſex. All this had paſſed during the day of the 20th of October; and in the evening, Edward Nicholas,* already named as ſo ſoon

Hyde and Falkland outvoted.

Pym's reſolutions carried.

Conſpiracy tracked out.

Character

" the Queen, and away from the Marquis of Hertford his
" Governor, for whom there were no convenient lodgings at
" Oatlands." Then, after a certain break, theſe remarkable
words follow: "*That he feared the conſpiracy went round,*
" *and was in Scotland as well as England.*"
* An able and a moderate man, who ſerved his maſter
faithfully, and (rareſt of qualities in a King's ſervant then)
not unwiſely. Clarendon deſcribes him, in one of the ſuppreſſed paſſages of his Hiſtory, as " one of the Clerks of the

§ VI. *Reassembling of Parliament : Oct.* 1641.

to be knighted and made Secretary of State in place of Windebank, and who now sat for Newton in Hants, keeping the signet during Charles's absence in Edinburgh, wrote to the King that some well-affected parliament men had been with him that day in great trouble, in consequence of news from Scotland, and that he had not been able to calm their anxiety.* As the days passed on, and new light was thrown on the equivocal position of the King with the promoters of the league against Argyle and the Hamiltons, this cause for trouble to the "well-affected" did not diminish. In a second letter, his Majesty is told how much his servants in the House are disheartened to be kept so long in darkness. In a third, he has further notification of the great pain which is caused by his silence. Nevertheless, that most significant silence continued. *Alarm of Secretary Nicholas.*

King's friends disheartened.

Hampden followed soon after his letters, leaving his fellow-commissioners † in Edinburgh, and arrived in London while the newly introduced bill to take away the bishops' votes in the other House was under discussion. *Arrival of Hampden.*

" Council, who had been Secretary to the Duke of Bucking-
" ham for the Maritime Affairs, a man of good experience,
" and of a very good reputation" (ii. 600). The King made
him Secretary of State as soon as he returned from Scotland.
See Clarendon's *Life,* i. 94.
  * " 'The next day after the receipt of the letters," says
Clarendon (ii. 579), " the Earls of Essex and Holland sadly
" told me, that I might clearly discern the indirect way
" the Court, and how odious all honest men grew to them."
  † The Hon. Nathaniel Fiennes, Lord Say and Seale's
second son, member for Banbury ; and Sir Philip Stapleton,
member for Boroughbridge. *of Edward Nicholas.*

Indirect ways of the Court.

Hyde had kept faithfully his promife to the King. Upon this bill being reproduced, Falkland rofe, and, to the general amazement, retracted the views he had formerly been fo deeply pledged to, and declared his determination to vote againft it. D'Ewes, and other ftaunch holders of Puritan opinions, appear to have been completely unprepared for this demonftration; but very fpeedily others joined in it, among whom Sir Edward Dering, the member for Kent, notably diftinguifhed himfelf. Thus Hyde's fcheme was thriving; and the well-affected Parliament-men, as Secretary Nicholas calls them, were now acting as a compact body, and not fcrupling to avow the new tactics that governed them. "I am forry," faid Hampden, "to find a noble lord has "changed his opinion fince the time the laft "bill to this purpofe paffed the Houfe; for "he then thought it a good bill, but now he "thinketh this an ill one." "Truly," replied Lord Falkland, "I was perfuaded at that time, "by the worthy gentleman who hath fpoken, "to believe many things which I have fince "found to be untrue; and, therefore, I have "changed my opinion in many particulars, as "well as to things as perfons." It was the firft frank bold announcement of the rupture in the Parliamentary party, and it may be interefting to paufe and confider the character of the man from whom it came.

§ VII. Lord Falkland.

THE sudden and impetuous break-off from the party with whom he had acted so zealously in matters requiring no common nerve and resolution, characteristic as it was of the real Falkland, jars with the popular impressions that arise at mention of his name. But merely to compare it with the course we have seen him adopt upon such questions as Strafford's Attainder, may well suggest some doubt as to the entire correctness of the estimates ordinarily formed of the political character and opinions of this celebrated man. He is generally assumed to have been the incarnation of moderate and temperate counsels. It is but a few years since his example was publicly pleaded by a first minister of the Crown to justify the sincerity with which he might be prosecuting a war in the midst of continual protestations of a desire for peace. We were asked to remember that the most virtuous and self-restrained character in our great rebellion, and the man most devoted to the Royalist cause, still murmured and "ingeminated" *peace, peace,* even whilst arming for the combat. But the allusion was unfortunate in turning wholly on that alleged circumstance in Falkland's career which is most capable of clear disproof. He was by no means devoted to the cause he fought for; and he cried out *peace, peace,* solely because he detested the war.

No doubt, however, he is the man of all others of our civil conflict who is most generally supposed to have represented therein the

[marginalia:]
Beliefs as to Falkland's character.

Supposed type of moderation.

Errors and misjudgments.

monarchical principle; and upon this ground his ſtatue was among thoſe voted earlieſt for the hiſtorical adornment of the new Palace at Weſtminſter. But the real truth is, that Falkland was far more of an apoſtate than Strafford, for his heart was really with the Parliament from the firſt, which Strafford's never was; and never, to the very end, did he ſincerely embrace the cauſe with which his gallant and mournful death at the age of thirty-four * has eternally connected him. I have no wiſh to ſay anything to unſettle the admiring thoughts which muſt always cluſter round the memory of one whom Lord Clarendon has celebrated not ſimply as a ſtateſman and ſoldier, but as a patriot, poet,† and philoſo-

<small>Never zealous for the King.</small>

<small>Tribute by Hyde.</small>   * " Thus fell that incomparable young man, in the four-
"and-thirtieth year of his age, having ſo much diſpatched
" the buſineſs of life, that the oldeſt rarely attain to that
" immenſe knowledge, and the youngeſt enter not into the
" world with more innocence. Whoſoever leads ſuch a life,
" need not care upon how ſhort a warning it be taken from
" him." *Hiſt.* iv. 257. For " need not care" the firſt
editors had ſubſtituted " needs be the leſs anxious."

<small>Gratitude of the Poets to Falkland.</small>   † To the gratitude of the poets themſelves,—to the eternal
remembrance with which ſuch men as Ben Jonſon, Suckling,
Waller, and Cowley, can pay richly back in their loving verſe
all kinds and degrees of loving ſervice,—Falkland rather owes
his title than to any achievements of his own. But there are
yet a ſufficient number of good lines in his occaſional poetical
pieces to juſtify Suckling's having placed him in his ' Seſſion
' of the Poets.' There are many manly verſes in his Eclogue
on Jonſon's death.

<small>His Eclogue on Jonſon's death.</small>

"Alas! that bard, that glorious bard is dead,
Who, when I whilome cities viſited,
Hath made them ſeem but hours which were full days,
Whilſt he vouchſaft me his harmonious lays;
And when I lived, I thought the country then
A torture; and no manſion, but a den."

Falkland puts this into the mouth of Hylas, and it may

§ VII. *Lord Falkland.*

pher, in sentences that will be immortal. But it is impossible to become familiar with the details of this period of our history, and with

remind us of what Clarendon says of the writer's own passionate fondness for London. Melybœus rejoins:

" Jonson you mean, unless I much do err
I know the person by the character."

The same speaker continues:

" His learning such, no author, old or new,
Escaped his reading that deserv'd his view,
And such his judgment, so exact his test
Of what was best in books, as what books best,
That, had he joined those notes his labours took
From each most praised and praise-deserving book,
And could the world of that choice treasure boast,
It need not care though all the rest were lost."

On Jonson's learning.

Of his great art he then speaks, so that what he pleased to write—

" Gave the wise wonder and the crowd delight.
Each sort as well as sex admir'd his wit,
The hes and shes, the boxes and the pit;
And who less liked, within did rather chuse
To tax their judgments than suspect his muse.
Nor no spectator his chaste stage could call
The cause of any crime of his, but all
With thoughts and wills purg'd and amended rise
From the ethick lectures of his Comedies:
Where the spectators act, and the sham'd Age
Blushes to meet her follies on the stage;
Where each man finds some light he never sought,
And leaves behind some vanity he brought.
Whose Politicks no less the mind direct
Than those the Manners, nor with less effect,
When his majestic Tragedies relate
All the disorders of a tottering state." . . .

His vogue in theatres.

It was to be remembered also, Melybœus adds, that of all this old Ben was himself " sole workman and sole architect," as to which he concludes:

His self-raised fortune.

" And surely what my friend did daily tell,
If he but acted his own part as well
As he writ those of others, he may boast
The happy fields hold not a happier ghost!"

These are not only good lines, but very valuable personal notices of rare old Jonson.

Opinions held by Falkland;
Falkland's fhare in what preceded the Debates on the Remonftrance, and to doubt in what fpirit alone he could have taken the part which he fubfequently played. Over and over again does Clarendon himfelf find it neceffary to remark of him, that he never had any veneration for the Court, but only fuch a loyalty to the King as the law required from him; and as often is he conftrained to admit, on the other hand, that he had naturally a wonderful reverence for Parliaments, as believing them moft folicitous for juftice, the violation whereof, in the leaft degree, he could not forgive *any mortal power.**

as to Court and Parliament.

But the friend who has done fo much to preferve and endear his fame fince his death, had unhappily influence enough, while he lived, to lead him into a pofition which made the exact reverfe of thofe opinions an official neceffity; and Falkland was eminently a man who, finding himfelf fo placed, however unexpectedly, was ready to facrifice everything to the punctilio of honour. In his opinions, if not in his perfonal antecedents, he was like the old cavalier Sir Edmund Verney, whofe doubts were expreffed to Hyde, the tempter of all thefe men. " I have eaten the King's bread, " and ferved him near thirty years, and I will " not do fo bafe a thing as to forfake him. I " choofe rather to lofe my life (which I am " fure I fhall do) to preferve and defend thofe

Influence of Hyde.

Faith of the old Cavalier.

---

* This paffage is of courfe meant to convey, as Bifhop Warburton has remarked, that Falkland thought refiftance lawful, which Hyde himfelf did not. And the fame feeling is expreffed in other paffages, as ii. 94; iv. 244, &c.

"things which are againſt my conſcience to preſerve and defend; for, I will deal freely with you, I have no reverence for the biſhops for whom this quarrel ſubſiſts." There was only this important difference in Falkland, that the bread which he had eaten, and the ſervice to which he was vowed, before he made his final election, was that of the Parliament and not of the King. And it is not difficult to diſcern that his ſtrongeſt feeling remained in this direction throughout: even when he ſeemed, as it will be my duty to ſhow him in this party ſtruggle of the Remonſtrance, moſt deeply to have committed himſelf againſt its leaders. His convictions never ceaſed to be with the opinions which the Parliament repreſented, though his perſonal habits, his elegant purſuits, his faſtidious taſtes, his thorough-going ſenſe of friendſhip, and even his ſhyneſs of manner and impatient impulſiveneſs of temper, made him an eaſy prey to the perſuaſive arts that ſeduced him to the ſervice of the King. Nor will it be unjuſt to add that it is the admiration thus attracted to his perſonal character and habits, rather than any ſenſe of his public ſervices, which conſtitutes the intereſt of his name. It is not therefore in parliament, nor on the field of battle, that they ſhould ſeek for Falkland who would cheriſh him moſt, but rather in that private home to which his love and patronage of letters lent infinite graces and enjoyments, and where the man of wit and learning found himſelf invariably welcomed as to "a college ſituated in a purer air."

Sentiment not judgment.

Eaſy prey to Hyde's perſuaſion.

Falkland's ſtronghold.

The Grand Remonstrance.

View taken by Macaulay.

Lord Macaulay has remarked that he was too faftidious for public life, and never embarked in a caufe that he did not fpeedily difcover fome reafon for growing indifferent or hoftile to.* There is fomething in that; but we fhould prefer to fay that his fpirit in all things was too much on the furface—too quick, impetuous, and impatient; and hence both his ftrength in impulfe, and his weaknefs in aftion. He carried about with him a painful fenfe of perfonal difadvantages which he was

Macaulay's Effays i. 160.

* The subjoined paffage is fo happy a fpecimen of the manner of the writer, that I cannot refift appending it. "He did not "perceive that in fuch times as thofe on which his lot had "fallen, the duty of a ftatefman is to choofe the better caufe "and to ftand by it, in fpite of thofe exceffes by which every "caufe, however good in itfelf, will be difgraced. The "prefent evil always feemed to him the worft. He was always "going backward and forward; but it fhould be remembered "to his honour that it was always from the ftronger to the "weaker fide that he deferted. While Charles was oppreffing "the people, Falkland was a refolute champion of liberty. He "attacked Strafford. He even concurred in ftrong meafures "againft Epifcopacy. But the violence of his party annoyed

A public man unfit for public life.

"him, and drove him to the other party, to be equally "annoyed there. Dreading the fuccefs of the caufe which he "had efpoufed, difgufted by the courtiers of Oxford, as he "had been difgufted by the patriots of Weftminfter, yet "bound by honour not to abandon the caufe for which he "was in arms, he pined away, neglefted his perfon, went "about moaning for peace, and at laft rufhed defperately on "death, as the beft refuge in fuch miferable times. If he had "lived through the fcenes that followed, we have little doubt "that he would have condemned himfelf to fhare the exile "and beggary of the royal family; that he would then have "returned to oppofe all their meafures; that he would have "been fent to the Tower by the Commons as a ftifler of the "Popifh Plot, and by the King as an accomplice in the Rye "Houfe Plot; and that if he had efcaped being hanged, firft

What if he had lived to Revolution?

"by Scroggs, and then by Jefferies, he would, after manfully "oppofing James the Second through years of tyranny, have "been feized with a fit of compaffion at the very moment of "the Revolution, have voted for a Regency, and died a Non- "juror." (Ed. 1843.)

§ VII. *Lord Falkland.*

eager to overcome, and his very impetuofity was often but another form of fhynefs. But to whatever caufe attributable, it is certain that what he would do in public life, he was apt to overdo; and there cannot be a greater miftake than that which fo often reprefents him, and which voted him the firft ftatue among Englifh worthies in the palace at Weftminfter, as the incarnate fpirit of the moderation of our ftruggle in the feventeenth century. His temperament had in it as little as poffible of calmnefs or moderation. He fought a duel before he was nineteen; and while yet in his minority, he had defied his father's authority and made a runaway match. What his friend Hyde calls a "notable vivacity" was always expreffing itfelf in him, by words or deeds; whether the matter was great enough to impel him fuddenly into the allegiance for which he died, or only fmall enough to bring down " his clafped hands tightly on the crown of his " hat" where another man would have thought it enough quietly to fit covered. Mentioning a vote of the Commons for fome certain fpecial fervice, by which the Speaker was inftructed in the name of the whole Houfe to give thanks to him who had rendered it, and every member was alfo defired as a teftimony of his particular acknowledgment "to ftir or move his hat," Hyde tells us that, believing the fervice itfelf not to be of that moment, and that an honourable and generous perfon would not have ftooped to it for any recompenfe, "in-
" ftead of moving his hat, *he ftretched both*
" *his arms out and clafped his hands together*

Objections thereto.

Excitability of temper.

Anecdote by Clarendon.

Emphafis overdone.

"*upon the crown of his hat, and held it clofe down to his head,* that all men might fee how odious that flattery was to him, and the very approbation of the perfon though at that time moft popular." The action might for once have excufed the ftrange defire of the privy councillor before named, to compare his countrymen in thefe wars to very different actors in a very different revolution. "Firm as the hat of Servandony!" fhouted Danton, with happy allufion to one of the towers of St. Sulpice fo named, as he crufhed down and held his hat immovably over his great broad face, when threatened with chaftifement if he would not uncover while he fat in the pit of the Français on the eve of the Convocation of the States-General. And certainly, however unlike the men, a fudden, indignant, too impatient fpirit, was common to both. It largely contributed to what was right as well as to what was wrong in Falkland, and might equally have juftified his felection as the reprefentative, not of the moderation of the ftruggle, but of either of its extremes. The artift who received the commiffion for his ftatue might have fculptured him as on the 8th of February (1640-1), the vehement affailant of the Bifhops, or as on the 25th of October (1641), the vehement fupporter of the Church. He might have been taken in 1640 as eager for Strafford's life, as in 1643 he had become reckles of his own in the fame ill-fated fervice as Strafford's.

Very certain it is, at any rate, that he is the laft perfon to take for a model of devotion to

Similar trait of Danton.

Strange refemblances.

Stranger contrafts.

§ VII. *Lord Falkland.*

the caufe he was laft engaged in. Hyde exprefsly tells us that "from the entrance into this unnatural war his natural cheerfulnefs and vivacity grew clouded;" that only "when there was any overture or hope of peace, he would be more erect and vigorous;" and that fuch, in fhort, was his friend's diflike of the war that he invited and fought death merely to get himfelf fairly out of it. Before war was actually entered on, indeed, we have proof that this dejection and fadnefs of fpirit had ftolen upon him. When, for inftance, on the 5th of September, 1642, he delivered to the Houfe of Commons, as minifter to the King, the laft meffage fent by Charles to the reprefentatives of his people, he is defcribed in the Manufcript Journal of D'Ewes, who witneffed the fcene, to have ftood bareheaded at the bar, even as Culpeper had ftood but ten days before, looking fo dejectedly as if he had been a delinquent rather than a member of the parliament, a privy councillor, and meffenger from the King. Was he thinking, then, of that old reverence he bore to Parliaments, infomuch that he thought it really impoffible they could ever produce mifchief or inconvenience to the kingdom, or that the kingdom could be tolerably happy in the intermiffion of them?* As he furveyed the old familiar benches, was he forrowful with the fad mifgiving that he had elfewhere now transferred his allegiance, and that it was no longer permitted him to hold the exalted opinion he once held

marginalia: Diflike of the war. Laft appearance in Houfe of Commons. More like delinquent than Minifter. Regret or felt-reproach?

* Clarendon, *Hift.* iv. 244.

of the uprightnefs and integrity of the leading men who fat there, efpecially of Mr. Hampden ? *

But whatever fuch doubts or felf-queftionings may have been, they need not now overfhadow or cloud a memory that Englifhmen of all opinions may well be proud to cherifh. If we defire to reclaim Falkland to the Parliament, it is that we would gladly, for ourfelves, affociate with that fide in the ftruggle thofe *Falkland's nobler qualities.* prodigious parts of learning and knowledge, that inimitable fweetnefs and delight in converfation, that flowing and obliging humanity and goodnefs to mankind, that primitive fimplicity and integrity of life. But it is doubtlefs the wifer courfe to feparate from all mere party affociations fuch qualities as thefe, and rather to think of them as vouchfafed to fuftain and fweeten our common nature under all its conditions of conteft and trial. *Services to men of wit.* He afked no man's opinion, fays Clarendon, whom he defired to ferve; it was enough that he found a man of wit, family, or good parts, clouded with poverty or want; and fuch was his generofity and bounty for all worthy perfons of that kind needing fupplies and encouragement (whofe fortunes required, and whofe fpirits made them fuperior to, ordinary obligations),†

* *Hift.* iv. 245.

Hyde's happy eulogy. † " As," Clarendon takes occafion to fay (*Life*, i. 46), " Ben Jonfon, and many others of that time." " Which " yet," he adds, " they were contented to receive from him, " becaufe his bounties were fo generoufly diftributed, and fo " much without vanity and oftentation, that, except from " thofe few perfons from whom he fometimes received the " character of fit object for his benefits, or whom he intrufted " for the more fecret deriving them to them, he did all he

§ VII. Lord Falkland.

that he seemed to have his estate in trust for such alone. To that generous home which he kept open to his friends near Oxford, no man had to pay toll or tax of opinion at entering.* There, without question asked, men of all opinions in Church and State assembled; finding in their host such an immenseness of wit and such a solidity of judgment, so infinite a fancy bound in by a most logical ratiocination, such a vast knowledge that he was not ignorant in anything, with such an excessive humility as if he had known nothing, that the place was

marginalia: Open house at Oxford: to men of all opinions.

" could that the persons themselves who received them should
" not know from what fountain they flowed; and when that
" could not be concealed, he sustained any acknowledgment
" from the persons obliged with so much trouble and bashful-
" ness, that they might well perceive, that he was even
" ashamed of the little he had given, and to receive so large
" a recompense for it."

marginalia: Exquisite delicacy.

* " Who all found their lodgings there," says Clarendon,
" as ready as in the colleges; nor did the lord of the house
" know of their coming or going, nor who were in his house,
" till he came to dinner, or supper, where all still met : other-
" wise there was no troublesome ceremony or constraint, to
" forbid men to come to the house, or to make them weary of
" staying there; so that many came thither to study in a better
" air, finding all the books they could desire in his library,
" and all the persons together whose company they could
" wish, and not find in any other society." *Life,* i. 48. In
his history Clarendon adds that upon one subject only was
Falkland intolerant in respect of those whom he received, and
he attributes it to the fact that the Papists had corrupted his
two younger brothers (his mother was a Catholic) "being
" both children, and stolen them from his house, and transported
" beyond seas;" and that they had also "perverted his
" sisters:" upon which occasion, Clarendon mentions, " he
" writ two large discourses against the principal positions of
" that religion, with that sharpness and style, and full weight
" of reason, that the Church is deprived of great jewels in the
" concealment of them, and that they are not published to the
" world." *Hist.* iv. 244. Some curious letters having
reference to these incidents in Falkland's family will be found
in the *Clarendon State Papers,* ii. 535—538.

marginalia: Picture of Falkland's house. Intolerant only of intolerance. Discourses against Popery.

179

to them as a college situated in a purer air.*

A college in purer air.

Were it possible that a time might come when all recollection should have passed away of the momentous quarrel in which Falkland threw down his life, those things might yet continue his name and memory with profit and advantage to all men. And even above them we would place the three particular characteristics which the affection of his friend cannot help recording, while he qualifies them as niceties with which he was reproached during life as unsuited to "the necessity and "iniquity of the time." Holding, on the other hand, that were it only possible to find men pure enough to practise them, they would abate the necessity and iniquity of every time, I shall close the section by placing them on record here as the highest human eulogy to be pronounced on Falkland. The first was, that so severely did he adore truth that he could as easily have given himself leave to steal as to dissemble. In other words, to suffer any man to think that he would do anything which he was resolved not to do, he thought a far more mischievous kind of lying than any positive averring of what could easily be contradicted. The second was, that he would never give the remotest countenance or entertainment to the employing of spies. Such instruments, he held, must be so void of all ingenuousness and common honesty before they could be of use, that afterwards they

Three special characteristics:

love of truth;

hatred of spies;

---

* Clarendon, *Hist.* iv. 243.

could never be fit to be credited; and he could account no single preservation to be worth so general a wound and corruption of human society as the cherishing such persons would carry with it. The third was, that he de- *reverence* nounced ever with vehement indignation the *for pri-* liberty of opening private letters, upon suspi- *vate letters.* cion that they might contain matter of dangerous consequence; thinking it such a violation of the law of nature that no qualification by office could justify a single person in the trespass.

Such and so great that last particular trespass, indeed, that it may in some cases be a moot question whether any lapse of time absolves the responsibility of keeping private letters, which the writers of them never meant to be laid open, ever strictly and sacredly closed.

§ VIII. THE SECESSION AND ITS DANGERS.

THERE was certainly no kind of conceal- *Falk-* ment or reserve, and no dissembling, in what *land's* Falkland told the House upon Hampden's *leader:* return from Scotland. So far he showed the strength of his character even in a confession of the weakness of his conduct. He was no longer disposed to accept or act upon the counsels of the member for Buckinghamshire, and he avowed at once that, upon the question where they most widely diverged, he meant to follow Hyde's counsels. He had changed his *not* opinion in many particulars, as well as to *Hampden but* things as persons, and he chose frankly to say *Hyde.* so. This was at least fair warning. On whichever side might be found to lie ultimately the right or the wrong, here was at any rate an end to that phalanx which had brought Strafford to the scaffold, lodged Laud in the Tower, and driven Finch and Windebank into exile; which had condemned ship-money, impeached the judges who gave it their sanction, and dragged one of them in open court from the seat his injustice had polluted;* which had passed the triennial bill, and voted as unlawful every tax upon the subject imposed without consent of the House of Commons; which had abolished all jurisdictions that reared themselves above the law; and before whose unshrinking, compact array, alike the petty and the mighty instrument of wrong had fallen, the Stannary Courts and the Court of York, the Star Chamber and the High Commission. In not one of these retributive or reformatory acts, had the party of Hyde and Falkland wavered in the least: in many, they had outstripped even Denzil Hollis, Cromwell, Hampden, and Pym. But they now did not hesitate to give out, as in Falkland's reproach to Hampden, that unfounded inducements had been addressed to them; and that this justified their instant

Liberal phalanx broken up.

Its achievements.

Desertion by seceders:

A Judge arrested on the Bench.

---

* I quote from Whitelocke's *Memorials* (p. 40, Ed. 1732). "February 13, 1640. Sir Robert Berkley, one of the Judges "of the King's Bench, who gave his opinion for Ship money, "was impeached by the Commons of High Treason, in the "Lords' House, and, by their command, Maxwell, the Usher "of the Black Rod, came to the King's Bench when the "Judges were sitting, took Judge Berkley from off the Bench, "and carried him away to prison, which struck a great terrour "in the rest of his brethren then sitting in Westminster Hall, "and in all his profession."

§ VIII. *The Seceſſion and its Dangers.* 183

deſertion, as well of the principles they had acted on, as of the men they ſo long had acted with. What the alleged miſrepreſentations were, has never been explained. But it is certain that not an attempt was made by them, before they paſſed into oppoſition againſt their old aſſociates, to obtain a ſingle ſecurity for the King's better faith as to any one tranſaction of the year during which they had ranked as his opponents. Still in all reſpects unaltered, ſave that Strafford ſtood no longer by his ſide, at leaſt Charles the Firſt cannot be accuſed of having tempted theſe men. Their names, and their exertions in debate, are ſubmitted by Secretary Nicholas to his maſter, with a requeſt for due encouragement to ſuch ſervice, in the very letters which bear evidence of Charles's continued hatred of the Cauſe of which they had been the defenders, and were now the betrayers. There is hardly an interchange of confidence at this date between Edinburgh and Whitehall, in which there is not either news of ſome freſh ſuppoſed danger to the parliamentary leaders, received with unconcealed ſatisfaction; or the ſuggeſtion of ſome plot or intrigue againſt them, thrown out with eager hope. If they had flinched or wavered for a moment, all that they had gained muſt at once have paſſed from their keeping. Happily for their own fame, more happily for our peaceful enjoyment of the fruits of their deſperate ſtruggle, they ſtood quiet and undiſmayed under every danger and every form of temptation.

Some days before the reaſſembling of the

never accounted for.

The King unaltered.

Old cauſe ſtill hateful to him.

Danger of loſing all.

Reappear-

Houſe, great ſickneſs had broken out in London; the plague had reappeared in ſome quarters; and the occaſion had been ſeized for an intrigue to ſtay the reaſſembling, or to procure at leaſt an adjournment of place if not of time. It is a leading topic in ſeveral letters from Secretary Nicholas to the King. At firſt he is full of hope, deſcribing the ſpread of the plague and the ſhutting up of infected houſes around Weſtminſter, and confidently anticipating that adjournment in ſome form muſt be reſorted to, ſo rife and dangerous the ſickneſs grows. But after three days he has to change his tone, and to tell the King that "Mr. Pym" and thoſe of his party will not hear that parliament ſhall not be held, or ſhall meet anywhere but in London or Weſtminſter. It met, as we have ſeen; and Mr. Pym, five days after the meeting, received very deciſive intimation of the temper with which the King's partizans out of doors now regarded him.

He was ſitting in his uſual place, on the right hand beyond the members' gallery, near the bar, on the 25th of October, when, in the midſt of debate on a propoſition he had ſubmitted for allowance of "powder and bullet" to the City Guard, a letter was brought to him. The Serjeant of the Houſe had received it from a meſſenger at the door, to whom a gentleman on horſeback in a grey coat had given it that morning on Fiſh-ſtreet-hill; with a gift of a ſhilling, and injunction to deliver it with great care and ſpeed. As Pym opened the letter, ſomething dropped out of it on the

§ VIII. *The Secession and its Dangers.* 185

floor; but without giving heed to this he read *by the Serjeant.* to himself a few words, and then, holding up the paper, called out that it was a scandalous libel. Hereupon it was carried up to the lately-appointed Clerk's Assistant, Mr. John Rush- *Handed to Mr. Rushworth.* worth, who, in his unmoved way, read aloud its abuse of the great leader of the House, and its asseveration that if he should escape the present attempt, the writer had a dagger prepared for him. At this point, however, young Mr. Rushworth would seem to have lost his coolness, for he read the next few lines in an agitated way. They explained what had dropped from the letter. It was a rag that had covered a plague- *Its contents.* wound, sent in the hope that infection might by such means be borne to him who opened it. "Whereupon," says the eye-witness, from whose report the incident is now first related as it really happened, "the said clerk's assistant *Mr. Rushworth's alarm.* " having read so far, threw down the letter " into the house; and so it was spurned away " out of the door." Its threats, however, could not so be spurned away, and were not mere empty brutalities. Nicholas's report of it to the King was dated but a few days after the occurrence, yet, in the brief interval, not only had another attempt upon Pym's life *Further attempts against Pym.* been discovered, but a person mistaken for him had been stabbed in Westminster Hall. Charles made no comment on the particular subject reported upon by his correspondent. But, if so minded, his Majesty might have told him that he and his Queen had their plots also, against the foremost man of the parliament; and that Pym's name, for purposes of

their own, was become a word of familiar
found in their letters to each other.*

His aſſailants in the Houſe.
Pym had aſſailants in the Houſe itſelf, too,
more open, but hardly more honourable.
The firſt direct reſult of the dark rumours
from Scotland inculpating the King, was a
propoſition moved in the Commons for a
vote affirming the King's right to nominate
all officers, councillors, ambaſſadors, and
Reſolution moved:
miniſters; but demanding that the power of
approving them ſhould in future reſt with the
parliament. It was brought forward by Mr.

Alluſions to Pym in Queen's letters.

* "I received yeſterday a letter from Pym, by which he "ſends me word that he fears I am offended with him, becauſe "he has not had a letter from me for a long time. I beg you "tell him that that is not the caſe, and that I am as much "his friend as ever, but I have ſo much buſineſs, that I have "not been able to write by expreſſes, and by the poſt it is not "ſafe." So wrote Henrietta Maria to her huſband the King; and the intention of courſe was to damage Pym, if poſſible, by letting ſuch expreſſions, in themſelves a pure

Attempts to bring him into ſuſpicion.
invention, caſually be ſeen. Again ſhe ſays, in another letter: "As to the thirty thouſand pieces which Pym ſends "me word have been promiſed a long time ago, and not ſent, "you will alſo be ſhown how they have been employed moſt "uſefully for your ſervice." Again, artfully naming him with a known agent and miniſter of Charles: "I have ſo "much buſineſs that I have not leiſure to write to Pym nor "to Culpeper. Remember me to them, and tell them I am "returned to England as much their friend as when I "left, &c." The ſubject of Pym's extraordinary popularity,

Cauſes of his popularity.
and its cauſes, is treated in more detail in my *Arreſt of the Five Members*, § v, but I will here ſubjoin the ſtriking teſtimony borne by Covenanter Baillie to the qualities which had ſingled out this great man for thoſe onerous duties of leaderſhip under which he ſank exhauſted in the ſecond year of the war. Baillie is writing to his friend Spang on the 10th

Tribute by Covenanter Baillie.
Auguſt, 1644: "Since Pym died, not a State Head amongſt "them: many very good and able ſpirits, but not any of ſo "great and comprehenſive a braine, as to manage the multi-"tude of ſo weightie affaires as lyes on them. If God did "not fit at their helme, for any good guiding of theirs long "ere this they had been gone." *Journals*, ii. 216.

§ VIII. *The Seceſſion and its Dangers.*

Robert Goodwin, the member for Eaſt Grinſtead, in a ſpeech levelled at the new party in the Houſe. He dilated on the diſaſters undergone from former adviſers and miniſters of the Sovereign; and argued that all they had gained would now be loſt, if they could not guard againſt poſſible dangers from new counſellors as unworthy, and who might perhaps become as powerful, as the old. The matter was debated on both ſides with vehemence, and Mr. William Strode,* who ſat for Beer-

againſt King's appointments to office.

* What Clarendon ſays of Strode, that he was " one of " thoſe ephori who moſt avowed the curbing and ſuppreſſing " of Majeſty " (i. 253), and further (ii. 23), that he was " one of the fierceſt men of the party, and of the party only " for his fierceneſs," is coloured always by ſtrong perſonal diſlike, but it had probably ſome foundation. Only he forgets to ſtate that Strode had preciſely the ſame claims to popular ſympathy and confidence of which he does not withhold the credit from other leading men, in ſo far as ſuch might fairly reſt on former ſufferings, and long impriſonments, for independent conduct in preceding parliaments. And indeed, conſidering the ſtrong claim which, in every other caſe, ſuch ſufferings conſtituted—the title which the mere fact of having ſo ſuffered gave, to popularity out of the Houſe, to authority within it, and to continued diſlike and jealouſy from the Court—it is perfectly inexplicable to me that Clarendon, in remarking on the arreſt of the five members, ſhould bring himſelf to talk of a man who had ſat in the laſt two Parliaments of James and in all the Parliaments of Charles, who had been a foremoſt actor in the great ſcene of the diſſolution of the Third Parliament, and who for his ſpirited and manly conduct that day had ſuffered perſecution and long impriſonment, as he ſpeaks of Strode. After obſerving that three of the five members impeached were really diſtinguiſhed men, he adds (vol. ii. 161), " Sir Arthur Haſelrig and Mr. Strode were " perſons of too low an account and eſteem; and though " their virulence and malice was as conſpicuous and tranſcen- " dent as any man's, yet their reputation, and intereſt to do " any miſchief, otherwiſe than in concurring in it, was ſo " ſmall, that they gained credit and authority by being " joined with the reſt, who had indeed a great influence."

Clarendon's attack on Strode: James's reign.

Probable confuſion

I had written thus far when it occurred to me to make further inquiry, and the reſult is a conviction to my mind

The Grand Remonstrance.

alston, appears to have given the member for

between two Strodes.
that the Strode of the Parliaments of James and the early Parliaments of Charles, and the Strode of the Long Parliament, in whose identity every historian and writer upon these times, so far as I am aware, has hitherto implicitly believed, and by whom, as one and the same speaker, a large place is filled in both Editions of the Parliamentary History, were two distinct persons. That so extraordinary a mistake should have been made as to a person whom the King's fatal attempt was calculated to render notorious, may serve to show, among other things, how much has yet to be learned respecting the incidents and actors in these momentous times. The proof as to Strode

The later Strode a young man.
consists in the fact of repeated references to him as a young man, in the manuscript reports of the proceedings of the house which I have had before me while writing. Rushworth had already drily noticed (*Collections*, Part iii. Vol. I. 477) his obstinacy in refusing, when the King's intention was made known, to leave the house with the other members, until his ancient acquaintance Sir Walter Earle forced him out: but I subjoin an ampler account of the scene, until now unpublished, which is interesting in itself, and appears decisive

Evidence of D'Ewes's Journal.
as to the mistake hitherto made. " But Mr. William Strode,
" the last of the five, being a young man and unmarried,
" could not be persuaded by his friends for a pretty while to
" go out ; but said that knowing himself to be innocent, he
" would stay in the house, though he sealed his innocency
" with his blood at the door: nor had he been at last over-
" come by the importunate advice and entreaties of his friends,
" when the van or fore-front of those ruffians marched into
" Westminster Hall. Nay, when no persuasions could prevail
" with the said Mr. Strode, Sir Walter Earle, his entire

Scene at Arrest of Five Members.
" friend, was fain to take him by the cloak, and pull him
" out of his place, and so get him out of the house." From
the fact of his representing Beeralston, and of the connection
between the family of the elder Strode and Sir Walter Earle,
young Strode was in all probability the son ; but both the Editions of the Parliamentary History, and all other biographies and histories relating to him, beginning with the very positive account in the Second Impression of the *Athenæ Oxonienses* (iii. 176-8, Edit. 1817), must now be altered, if what I have here advanced be correct.

[The dispute of Strode's identity was restated, and the view here expressed further enforced, in my *Arrest of the Five Members*, § xxi, in reply to some remarks which the present note had elicited in a very able book (*Illustrations of the Great Rebellion*, by Mr. Langton Sanford) published after my

Counter testimony in
Essays. But, in now leaving as it stands this curious historic doubt, I am bound frankly to say that the counter testimony

§ VIII. *The Secession and its Dangers.*

Saltaſh, Mr. Edward Hyde*, ſome advantage, by the unuſual violence of tone with which he broadly inſiſted on the right of the Houſe to a negative voice in placing great officers of ſtate. " I think moſt he ſaid was premedi- " tated," ſays a member who was preſent ; " but it was ſo extreme in ſtrain, as Mr. " Hyde did, upon the ſudden, confute moſt

[margin: Strode's violence.]

in favour of identity, though far from deciſive, is ſtronger than I ſuppoſed. A Reſolution of the Houſe is reported, vot- ing a tribute after the death of Strode of the Long Parlia- ment, which would ſeem to recogniſe, not only his attempted arreſt by Charles, but his former ſufferings under James. On the other hand, this vote belongs to a period when a con- fuſion between perſons of the ſame family was quite poſſible in a reſolution having for its object to expreſs the public grati- tude. And I ſubjoin, in further corroboration of doubts which I ſtill hold to predominate, an extract from a private letter of D'Ewes to his wife deſcribing the introduction of the Triennial Bill, unqueſtionably the act of the man aſſociated afterwards with Hampden and Pym in the King's attempted Arreſt. " My dear Love," writes D'Ewes, "I had thought " to have written at large unto you this weeke, but multitude " of buſineſs hinders mee. I heere encloſed ſend you a copie " of an Act of Parliament which was firſt brought into the " Houſe by *one Mr. William Stroud, a young man.*" Is it conceivable that D'Ewes, one of the moſt punctiliouſly accurate of writers, would thus have deſcribed a man who had obtained diſtinction as a repreſentative of the people before the cloſe of the preceding reign, when D'Ewes himſelf was little more than a lad from college? And as he thus firſt deſcribed the Strode of the Long Parliament, ſo, after nearly twelve months had paſſed, we have ſeen that he continued to deſcribe him. 1860.]

[margin: favour of identity. The other view ſtrength- ened: in a letter to Lady D'Ewes. Another Hyde: more decidedly Royaliſt than Edward.]

* I call him by either name indiſcriminately, Hyde or Lord Clarendon, in the courſe of this work ; but he was not the only Hyde who ſat in the Long Parliament. There was a Robert Hyde, alſo a lawyer and a royaliſt, who ſat for Saliſ- bury ; commonly called Serjeant Hyde. Robert voted againſt Strafford's attainder, and has occaſionally been miſtaken for Edward in the liſt of " Straffordians." When Edward firſt received the King's meſſage for an interview before he ſet forth to Scotland, he affected to believe the meſſenger had committed a miſtake, and that his royaliſt nameſake was intended. Much more likely he, than one who had taken ſuch part on the other ſide ! See *Life,* i. 92.

"of it." Eagerly was Mr. Hyde now plying his chosen office of King's defender; but he doubtless found his task more difficult after the interval of a week, during which the startling news had arrived (received in the House, says Clarendon, with deep silence and a kind of consternation) of that rebellion and most appalling massacre by the Irish papists, from some connivance with whose abettors the memory of Charles the First has never yet been cleared. Pym then saw *his* advantage. He put the matter of evil counsellors in a more practical form, and brought suddenly into open clash and collision the two parties into which the House had become divided. And the same great name of Strafford which had formerly united them, re-appeared now but as the signal to show how completely they were riven asunder.

§ IX. THE NEW PARTY AND THE OLD.

ON Friday, the 5th of November, upon the question of the supply necessary for the forces to be sent into Ireland, and whether or not assistance should be asked from the Scotch, Pym arose, and after remarking that no man should be readier or more forward than himself to engage his estate, his person, his life, for the suppression of this rebellion in Ireland, there was yet another question also to be considered. All that they there did would be vain, as long as the King gave ear to the counsellors about him. His Majesty must be told, said the member for Tavistock, that Parliament

§ IX. *The New Party and the Old.*

here finds evil counsels to have been the cause of all these troubles in Ireland; and that unless the Sovereign will be pleased to free himself from such, and take only counsellors whom the kingdom can confide in, Parliament will hold itself absolved from giving assistance in the matter. "Well moved! Well moved!" cried many members; and "divers," says D'Ewes, "would have had it speedily assented "unto, but Mr. Hyde stood up, and first "opposed it, and said, amongst other things, "that by such an addition we should as it "were menace the King." Upon this hint up sprang suddenly the member for St. Ives, Mr. Edmund Waller, cousin to Hampden and to Cromwell, yet one of Hyde's most eager recruits, nor more despised for his abject, veering, vacillating spirit, than he was popular for his wit, vivacity, and genius.* These he had now placed entirely at the King's disposal. He begged the House to observe what Mr. Pym had just said, and to remember what formerly had been said by the Earl of Strafford. Where in effect was the difference between such counsel to a King, as that he was absolved from all laws of government, on Parliament

margins: Excitement in House. Edmund Waller's reply. Compares Pym to Strafford.

---

* "He had a graceful way of speaking; and by thinking "much upon several arguments, he seemed often to speak "upon the sudden, when the occasion had only administered "the opportunity of saying what he had thoroughly con- "sidered, which gave a great lustre to all he said; which yet "was rather of delight than weight. There needs no more "be said to extol the excellence and power of his wit, and "pleasantness of his conversation, than that it was of magni- "tude enough to cover a world of very great faults; that is, "so to cover them, that they were not taken notice of to his "reproach." Clarendon, *Life*, i. 54.

margin: Value of preparation in oratory.

refufing his unjuft demands; and fuch advice to a Parliament, as that it fhould hold itfelf abfolved from affifting the State, on the King's non-compliance with demands perhaps not more juft? The too ingenious fpeaker was not permitted to fay more. Pym rofe immediately and fpoke to order. If the advice he had given were indeed of the fame nature as Lord Strafford's, then he deferved the like punifhment; and he craved, therefore, the juftice of the Houfe, either to be fubmitted to its cenfure, or that the gentleman who fpoke laft be compelled to make reparation. Many and loud were the cries for Waller which followed this grave and dignified rebuke; but a ftrong party fupported him in his refufal to give other than fuch modified explanation as he at firft tendered, and it was not until after long debate that he was ordered into the committee chamber, and had to make fubmiffion in the required terms. It was near five o'clock on that November evening, when Mr. Waller " pub-" lickly afked pardon of the Houfe and Mr. " Pym." *

Pym rifes to order.

Cries for Waller.

Reparation made.

* All, until now, revealed of this affair, is contained in the fubjoined entry from the Commons' Journals (ii. 306), under head of Friday, 5th Nov. 1641:

Commons' Journals: 5th Nov.

" Exceptions were taken at words fpoken by Mr. Waller,
" which reflected upon Mr. Pym in a high way: for which
" he was commanded to withdraw.
" And he being withdrawn, the Bufinefs was a while de-
" bated: And then he was commanded to return to his place.
" And then the Speaker told him, that the Houfe held it
" fit, that, in his place, he fhould acknowledge his offence
" given by his words, both to the Houfe in general, and Mr.
" Pym in particular.
" Which he did ingenuoufly, and expreffed his forrow
" for it."
The fpecial caufe of offence is now firft made known.

Waller's apology.

§ IX. *The New Party and the Old.*

But the Houfe, or Mr. Pym, was little now to Mr. Waller and his friends, in comparifon with their new and late-found allegiance to the other mafter whom till now they had determinedly oppofed. So quick and complete the change, it was as the fhifting of a fcene upon the ftage. The men who had always been courtiers were feen fuddenly depofed from what importance they had, and an entirely new fet of characters promptly filled their place. " I may not forbear to let your Majefty " know," writes Nicholas immediately before the fcene juft named, and defcribing the debates which led to it, " that the Lord Falkland, " Sir John Strangways, Mr. Waller, Mr. " Edward Hyde, and Mr. Holborne, and " divers others, ftood as champions in mainte- " nance of your prerogative, and fhowed for " it unanfwerable reafon and undeniable prece- " dents, whereof your Majefty fhall do well " to take fome notice, as your Majefty fhall " think beft, for their encouragement." Eagerly did the King refpond, that his good Nicholas was commanded to do fo much at once in his name, and to tell thofe worthy gentlemen that he would do it himfelf at his return. The Secretary was ill when that meffage reached him, but it was not a matter that admitted of delay. Hyde was fent for to King Street, where Nicholas lived; was fhown up to his bed-room, in which he lay very fick; and the bufinefs was wholly, Mr. Hyde informs us with a modeft fatisfaction, " to fhow Mr. " Hyde a letter from the King to Mr. Nicholas, " in which he writ to him, that he underftood,

Dramatic changes:

reported to the King:

Royal thanks to managers.

Hyde fent for by Nicholas.

The Grand Remonstrance.

"by several hands, that he was very much
"beholden to Mr. Hyde for the great zeal
"he showed to his service; and therefore
"commanded him to speak with him, and to
"let him know the sense he had of it; and
"that when he returned, he would let him
"know it himself."* Through Mr. Hyde
passed doubtless several similar messages, and
thereupon closely had followed Mr. Waller's
assault on Mr. Pym, and the rebuke at
Westminster winning him fresh favour at
Whitehall.

Is shown a letter from the King.

Each incident that had manifested thus, however, the spirit and purpose of the new opposition, served only to knit more closely what was left of the old liberal phalanx. No word was breathed of any kind of concession. Their speech had not been more decisive, or their action more vigorous, while Strafford stood at bay. Broken as were their ranks, their majority was sufficient and decisive; and they had a supreme force in reserve to which they were about to appeal. Wherever Hyde and his friends, therefore, might be expected to muster strongest, there they struck ever themselves the first, and still the heaviest.

Old leaders unmoved.

Majority still sufficient.

Before the recess, thirteen bishops had been impeached for an attempt to override the law by asserting a legislative authority in new Canons which they claimed to impose; after the House again met, as we have seen, a bill had been introduced for taking away their votes in the upper House; subsequently there

Measures against Bishops:

---

* *Life and Continuation*, i. 94 (Ed. 1827).

§ IX. *The New Party and the Old.*

had been several sharp debates on a proposal to sequester them from giving votes on the disabling bill, because they should not thereby be at once parties and judges: yet this was the time selected by Charles for pressing with characteristic vehemence the investiture of five new bishops, of whom four had sat in the Convocation which imposed the disputed Canons! In writing to Edinburgh, Nicholas had been careful to recount the surprise he heard expressed that any man should move his Majesty for making of bishops in those times, to which his Majesty wrote instantly back that on no account was there to be any delay; and at the very moment these letters were thus interchanged, Mr. Oliver Cromwell had carried in the Commons, by a majority of eighteen, a motion for a conference with the Lords to stay the investiture. "This busi- "ness," says D'Ewes, "was debated with as "great earnestness almost as I ever saw in the "House." *proposal to make five new ones. Cromwell's counter motion.*

The earnestness had certainly not abated a few days later, when, the time limited for pleading to the impeachment having arrived, the impeached bishops were to put in their answer; and a demurrer was entered on their behalf so skilfully drawn up, that the curiosity was great to ascertain its author. It came on for discussion in the House; and the one of Hampden's counsel who had argued with most consummate ability against ship-money, and who had not heretofore been very friendly to bishops, Mr. Holborne, member for St. Michael's, and of late entirely leagued with *Bishops' demurrer Holborne supports bishops.*

Hyde, got up to fupport it. Hereupon Sir Simonds D'Ewes, that wealthy and refpected country gentleman and collector of precedents and records, who now fat for Sudbury, ex-high-fheriff of Suffolk but formerly ftudent and barrifter of the Middle Temple, made a lucky hit. He complimented his learned friend; recalled the days when they ufed to meet at mootes in Lincoln's Inn, and admitted that, of all men, he was wont to get deepeft into the points of a cafe; but, truly, he had this day fo ftrongly maintained the plea and demurrer of the bifhops, that he could not have performed it more exactly if he himfelf had drawn the fame. Something here perhaps in Holborne's manner betrayed him, but a loud laugh burft forth which was kept up fome time. "All the Houfe laughed "fo long," fays D'Ewes, "as I was fain to "remain filent a good while; for I believe "many in the Houfe did fufpect, as well as "myfelf, that either the faid Mr. Holborne "had wholly drawn them, or at leaft had "given his affiftance therein." It was quite true; but the great fhip-money lawyer took little for his pains in having thus come to the refcue. Upon the fuccefs of the demurrer, Pym headed a conference with the Lords; demanded, in the name of the Commons, that the votes of the bifhops fhould be fufpended until the fate of the bill under difcuffion was decided; and fo began the conflict with the Right Reverend Bench which ended in their committal to the Tower.

In like manner it fared with the two other

§ IX. *The New Party and the Old.*

questions, control of his Army and choice of his Counsellors, on which the King was himself most sensitive, and his friends in the House most busy and eager. Every move they made was outmoved. Vehement as were the excitements, and grave the dangers, of the Irish Rebellion, of the doubtful allegiance of the force under arms in England, and of the attempts in Scotland against Argyle and the Hamiltons, Pym seized and turned to instant advantage, as already we have seen on one subject, the equivocal position regarding all in which ill counsels had placed the King. *Moves and counter moves.*

At the same time, being far the most practical man in the House, he never insisted upon any proposition, however in itself desirable, which carried with it the danger of dividing his party;* setting himself to discover, in all such cases, a less objectionable mode of effecting the same object; and Oliver St. John, who continued to hold the office of Solicitor-General, having pointed out the ill consequence, to many members, of such a resolution as that objected to by Waller, absolving the House under any conditions from its necessary engagement to assist in reducing the Irish Rebellion, Pym at once recast his resolution, and brought it forward in its new form on the 8th of November. Substantially it was the same as at first; but so expressed, that while it met the objection of St. John, it also met with greater directness what was known to be the purpose of the King. Assuming that his Majesty should not *Prudence and sagacity of Pym.* *Gives effect to suggestion of St. John.* *Position*

---

* See other illustrations of this in my *Arrest of the Five Members*, § xxiii.

be gracioufly pleafed to difmifs his evil counfellors, it declared that, while the Houfe would neverthelefs continue in the obedience and loyalty due by the laws of God and the kingdom, yet they would take fuch a courfe for the fecuring of Ireland *as might likewife fecure themfelves*. "I hope this ill news of Ireland," Charles had curtly written to Nicholas, in the midft of the fudden public horror at that appalling news, "I hope this ill news of Ireland may "hinder fome of thefe follies in England!" Small chance of fuch hope finding realization if a refolution worded like Pym's might pafs the Houfe! Charles would have ufed the neceffity for an armed force fo as to direct it againft Englifh as well as Irifh "follies." Pym faw what was meant, and rendered the fcheme impoffible.

Orlando Bridgman led the oppofition, and after a long and fierce debate Pym's refolution paffed by a majority of 151 to 110. Then, at a conference with the Lords the following day, every ftep to which had been hotly contefted in the Commons, he obtained their confent to the introduction of a fimilar claufe againft evil counfellors into the inftructions for requefting help from the Scotch Parliament for fuppreffion of the Irifh Rebellion; and this after a fpeech confummate in its power and effect, and remarkable for the fubtlety of its argument againft the Roman Catholic religion as in its full indulgence incompatible with the exiftence in a State, not only of any other form of religion, but of any form whatever of political government and freedom. It is alfo a fact full of fignificance that on the

§ IX. *The New Party and the Old.*

fame day when the refolution embodied in this clause had paffed the lower Houfe by a majority of forty-one, and the conference with the Lords was obtained, which was only two days later than that of the fierce refiftance of Hyde, Culpeper, and Falkland, and of Waller's high-flying parallel between Strafford and Pym, I difcover that "Mr. Cromwell" moved and carried an addition to the fubjects for conference: "'that we fhould defire the Lords that "an Ordinance of Parliament might pafs to "give the Earl of Effex power to affemble, at "all times, the trained bands of the kingdom on "this fide Trent, for the defence thereof, till "further orders therein taken by the Houfes." *Refolution paffed.*

A motion by Oliver Cromwell.

Therein lay the ominous germ and beginning of the victorious army of the parliament! Such power as Cromwell thus obtained for Effex, during the pleafure and under the authority of Parliament, the King had given him before his departure, with a limit of its duration to the period of his abfence in Scotland. But even more pregnant of difafter to the King's defigns than the power thus invefted in the moft popular member of the Houfe of Lords, was the character of the authority by which the right fo to give or to withhold fuch power was affumed. *Germ of the Parliamentary Army.*

Then for the firft time had appeared the ill-boding claim of authority for an Ordinance of both Houfes in the abfence of the King. Nicholas haftened to inform the King of the portent. A great lord had objected, he faid, and expreffed doubts whether men might be raifed without warrant under the Great Seal; whereupon, this doubt being made known in *Ominous claim put forth.*

the Commons' Houfe, it had been declared that an Ordinance of both Houfes was a fufficient warrant for levying of volunteers by beating of the drum, " and an entry of fuch their " declaration was accordingly made in the " Regifter of that houfe." The letter of Nicholas is dated the 10th November, only two days later than Cromwell's refolution. Meanwhile, however, the Queen appears to have fent, upon this all important point, even earlier tidings to the King; for, in a letter dated the 12th November, only two days later than the communication to Nicholas, fhe thus writes to him : " I fend you a letter for Milord " Keeper, that the King did fend to me to " deliver if I thought it fit. *The fubject of it is* " *to make a Declaration againft the Orders of* " *Parliament which are made without the King.* " If you believe a fit time give it him, if not " you may keep it till I fee you." In the fame letter fhe tells Nicholas that the King will certainly be in London by the 20th of the month, and that he is therefore to advertife the Lord Mayor of London of the fact. The chief magiftrate was duly informed, and haftened to make good ufe of the time fo given him : but the leaders of the Commons had already made provifion for turning to ftill better ufe the opportunity afforded by the time.

Ordinances minus the King.

Alarm thereat.

Preparations for conflict.

§ X. CONFLICT BEGUN.

8th Nov. 1641.

IN the afternoon of the fame Monday the 8th of November when Pym's modified

§ x. *Conflict Begun.*

resolution against evil counsels passed, the "Declaration and Remonstrance" was submitted in its first rough draft for discussion by the House. Never before was presented to it, never since has it received, such a State Paper as that!—Immediately upon its production, it was read at the clerk's table; whereupon several notices of motions for additions and amendments were given, and order was taken for commencing the discussion upon its several clauses, *seriatim*, on the following morning at nine o'clock. *Rough draft of Remonstrance submitted.*

The character of the impression at once made by it will be inferred from the instant communication of Secretary Nicholas to the King. On the evening of the same day, he wrote off to Scotland that there had been that afternoon brought into the Commons' house, and there read, a Declaration of the State of Affairs of the kingdom, which related all the misgovernment and all the unpleasing things that had been done by ill counsels ("as they "call it") since the third year of the reign until now. The further consideration of it was to be had the next day in the House; and so much was it likely to reflect to the prejudice of his Majesty's Government, that Mr. Secretary "troubled" to think what might be the issue if his Majesty came not instantly away from Edinburgh. Every line in the letter showed the sore perplexity the writer was in. He could not possibly account for this Remonstrance satisfactorily as a party demonstration. " Surely if there had been in this," he says, " nothing but an intention to have justified *Nicholas writes to the King.*

Mr. Secretary's trouble.

Urges King's

inftant return:

"the proceedings of this Parliament, they would not have begun fo high." He entreated the King to burn his letter, or he, Nicholas, might be loft; and at its clofe he again made urgent and anxious reprefentation to his Majefty, that he could not poffibly fo much prejudice himfelf by at once leaving Edinburgh and all things there unfinifhed, as by delaying his return to London even one day. The King's anfwer, avoiding the queftion of the immediate return, as to which he had already communicated with the Queen, was not lefs urgent. "You muft needs fpeak with fuch of my fervants that you may beft truft, in my name, *that by all means poffible this Declaration may be ftopped.*"

King's anfwer:

Stop the Remonftrance!

Alas! this was not by any means poffible. All that could now be done, by earneft recruiting for the royal fervice, was to aroufe and league firmly together, in defperate oppofition to the Remonftrance and its authors, a band of members of the lower Houfe, even more fierce and only lefs determined than the other indiffoluble league already pledged to fupport it, and bent upon carrying it to the people. And fo the ftruggle began.

Forces organifed for the ftruggle.

§ XI. THE OPENING DEBATES: 9TH, 10TH, 12TH, 15TH, AND 16TH NOVEMBER.

Firft Debate: 9th Nov.

ON Tuefday, the 9th of November, the firft debate was taken. The hour appointed for it was nine o'clock, but it did not begin till about twelve o'clock, and it continued until a

§ XI. *The Opening Debates: 9th Nov.* 203

late hour. The order of procedure was firſt ſettled. The Declaration was to be read clauſe by clauſe; every member was to ſpeak to each clauſe, if he would; and if any ſpoke to have the clauſe amended, and that the Houſe gave leave, then it was to be amended, and the clauſe with the amendments put to the queſtion. Cromwell and Strode were among thoſe who moved the firſt amendments. At this firſt ſitting alſo, Bulſtrode Whitelocke, who ſat for Marlow, Serjeant Wylde, the member for Worceſterſhire, Mr. Henry Smith, the member for Leiceſterſhire and afterwards one of the King's judges, Sir John Clotworthy, who ſat for Malden; Mr. Wingate, the member for St. Albans, and Mr. Geoffrey Palmer, the member for Stamford, and formerly one of the managers of Strafford's impeachment, moved and carried inſertions and additions; all of them, with exception of the laſt, deſigned to make it more ſtringent and ſevere in tone. On the following day, Nicholas reported as uſual to the King. A fourth part had been gone through, compriſing nearly fifty clauſes; and the reſt of it, Mr. Secretary had learnt, was to be voted in the ſame way, as faſt as might be; after which it was to be tranſmitted ſtraightway to the Lords. The latter information was inaccurate; but the King's inſtant order to act upon it, though deſtined to be of no avail as to the upper Houſe, was a new incentive to activity in the lower. "Com-
"mand the Lord Keeper in my name," he wrote, "that he warn all my ſervants to oppoſe
"it in the Lords' houſe."

Procedure ſettled.

Movers of Amendments.

Report of Nicholas to King.

King's order thereon.

On Wednefday, the 10th of November, fays a member who took part in the debate, "we proceeded with the Remonftrance where "we left off yefterday." Infertions and additions were again made, among them one having reference to flavifh doctrines againft the fubject's property in his eftate, very generally preached from pulpits before the King; and a peremptory order, iffued at this fitting, to the effect that the clerk fhould on no account give out copies of the Declaration until the Houfe had fully perfected it, may ferve to fhow how intereft was gathering around it from day to day.

Second Debate: 10th Nov.

No copies to be given out.

The Irifh Rebellion, and provifion for the levies and expenditure it had fuddenly rendered neceffary, occupied the Houfe fo inceffantly during the fitting of the 11th of November, that the order for refuming the Remonftrance had to be laid afide; but a remarkable allufion was thrown out in reference to it, by Strode, in the courfe of the debate on the raifing money for fupply of his Majefty's wants in Ireland. He fpoke of the diffatisfaction of the people, and of the injuftice of laying further burdens on them, until fomething were done to reaffure them under their prefent fears and mifgivings, and to give them hope that what with fo much toil and facrifice had been lately gained was not again to be completely loft. "Sir," faid the member for Beeralfton, "I move againft "the order of the committee that we fhould "not admit of the giving of money till the "Remonftrance be paffed this Houfe, and gone "into the country to fatisfy them." This at

11th Nov. Speech by Strode.

Deftination of Remonftrance avowed: to go to the people.

§ XI. *The Opening Debates: 12th Nov.*   205

any rate was plain speaking.* Thus early in
the debates, the desire and the design of the
promoters of the Remonstrance were frankly
avowed. It was to be to them some guarantee that the army about to be raised for the To be
suppression of Irish rebellion, should not here- printed
after be used for the suppression of English and circulated.
liberty. It was to be printed and circulated
among the people.

That was on Thursday, the 11th of Novem- Third
ber. On the day following, the Remonstrance Debate:
12th Nov.
was proceeded with, and every part so obsti-
nately disputed, that the House sat far into
that November afternoon. A motion for
rising having been resisted successfully, another
member moved that candles should be brought. Motion
This was a proceeding as yet very rarely for candles.
resorted to; it having been only during the
proceedings on the Attainder of Strafford that
the order of the House had been so far relaxed
as to admit of new motions made, except with
special permission, after noon.† "Sir," said

---

* Strode seems to have had the habit of blurting out in Strode's
words, in a sudden impulsive way, what the more reserved of manner of
the party more prudently were content to leave as matter of speech.
inference from their acts. As to the question of disbanding
the Scotch army, for instance, he frankly avowed: "We
" cannot yet spare the Scotch. The sons of Zeruiah are too
" strong for us;" for which, being called to order, the House
refused to exact any apology. (*Journals*, Feb. 6, 1640-1.)
What he thus openly declared had till then (according to
May, lib. i. cap. viii.) been asserted principally by the ill- Avowal
affected, who not only in discourse but written libels taxed the as to
Parliament with it, imputing it to them as a crime of too Scotch
much distrust of the King, and accusing them of having kept army.
up a foreign army to overawe their own Prince.

† I find, from the D'Ewes manuscript before me, that on the
4th December 1640, on the motion of Strode, an order was
made that " every one upon coming into the House who did

the advocate for candles, who was no other than D'Ewes himfelf, "we have now been " fitting in the houfe near upon feven hours " (the ordinary hour of meeting was eight o'clock in the morning, but of late, in confequence of the prolonged fittings, the hour had been generally nine, fometimes even ten o'clock), " and we do not now think fit to rife, but " we will ftill fit. I defire that we may fit " according to the ancient ufe of parliaments, " having the ufe as well of our eyes as of our " ears ; and that lights may be brought in."

On this very day, Nicholas had written fomewhat more hopefully to the King that the Houfe had been the day before fo employed about Irifh affairs, that they meddled not with their Declaration : but after a very few days he has, lefs eagerly, to report that they have been making up for loft time. " The Houfe " of Commons," he wrote, " haftens by all " means the finifhing of the Declaration or " Remonftrance ; and for the more fpeedy " expediting of it, they have at the committee

Shilling fines. " not take his place, or did, after taking his place, talk fo " loud as to interrupt the bufinefs of the Houfe from being " heard, fhould pay a fhilling fine, to be divided between the " ferjeant and the poor." And to this order, on the motion of Sir John Strangways, the member for Weymouth, it was added " that after twelve o'clock no new bufinefs be entered *Orders as to bufinefs:* " into, or moved, without the leave of the Houfe." More formally it was refolved a few days later, upon the motion of Sir Walter Earle, the other member for Weymouth, " that " the ancient order of the Houfe be obferved : namely, that " no bills be read the fecond time but between the hours of " nine and twelve." To which it was added, at the fuggeftion *as to reading of Bills.* of Mr. Speaker (Lenthal), that all bills might be read a firft time, early in the morning. For further notices of fuch orders and modes of proceeding in the Houfe, fee *Arreft of Five Members*, § xxiii.

§ XI. *The Opening Debates: 15th Nov.*

" paſſed by many particulars to avoid the
" delay of long debates."

In thoſe few words were alſo expreſſed the ſteady perſeverance and tenacity of what was truly to be called His Majeſty's Oppoſition. Every inch of the ground was ſo conteſted, indeed, that only the moſt watchful and reſolute determination could avail to maintain any part of it unimpaired; and all the forms of the Houſe were exhauſted in pretences for delay. The whole of the ſitting of Monday, the 15th of November, was taken up with the diſcuſſion of the ſingle clauſe which ultimately ſtood as the hundred and ninetieth. In this, adverting to the charges brought by the ill-affected party againſt the leaders of the Houſe of Commons, it was affirmed, in contradiction of thoſe charges, that not the meddling of the Commons with the power of epiſcopacy, but the idolatry and popiſh ceremonies introduced into the Church by command of the biſhops themſelves, were the cauſes why ſectaries and conventicles abounded in England, and why Engliſhmen, ſeeking liberty of worſhip, had been driven into exile. A debate of extraordinary vehemence aroſe upon this word *command*. It was led by Sir Edward Dering, the member for Kent,* who but a

Tenacity of His Majeſty's oppoſition.

Fourth Debate: 15th Nov.

As to biſhops' favouring idolatry.

Speech by Dering.

---

* Poor Sir Edward Dering got himſelf only laughed at for his pains in going ſuddenly over to Hyde's party on this and the other queſtion of the Biſhops. He loſt his ſeat in the Houſe ſhortly after, and failed to obtain any ſtanding with the Royaliſts. Yet he ſeems to have been an eloquent and on the whole a well-meaning man, and hardly to have deſerved the ſneers of Clarendon; who in his *Hiſtory* (i. 416) characteriſes him as a man of levity and vanity, eaſily flattered by being commended; and goes ſo far as to aſſert that his "greateſt motive" in moving the

Dering ſneered at by Clarendon.

little while before had moved the reading of a bill for extirpating bifhops, deans, and chapters; and it was fupported by Lord Falkland, who, on the 8th of the preceding February, had diftinctly charged the bifhops with having deftroyed unity under pretence of uniformity, with having brought in fuperftition and fcandal under the titles of reverence and decency, with having defiled the Church by adorning the churches, and deftroyed of the gofpel as much as they could without bringing themfelves into danger of being deftroyed by the law. With a pettifogging worthier of Hyde than of himfelf, Falkland now joined Dering in afking where proof was to be found that the bifhops had iffued any "command" for the introduction of idolatry. Who hath read this command? they afked. "Who hath "heard it? Who hath feen this commanded "idolatry?" The day clofed while yet the debate had not; an order being made that the Remonftrance fhould be refumed the next day at ten o'clock, and that meanwhile the claufe which had then been debated fo much, fhould be recommitted to the committee that originally drafted it, to prepare it in fuch a manner as might be agreeable to the fenfe of the Houfe.

Falkland's former attack on Bifhops.

Prefent vehement defence.

Fifth Debate: 16th Nov. On Tuefday, the 16th, the debate was refumed accordingly; but the obnoxious word remained in the claufe as again introduced,

trenchant bill againft the Bifhops, was that he might have the opportunity of applying the two lines from Ovid,

Cuncta prius tentanda, fed immedicabile vulnus
Enfe recidendum eft, ne pars fincera trahatur!

§ XI. *The Opening Debates: 16th Nov.*

and after further hot debate, the queſtion of whether it ſhould ſtand paſſed to a diviſion. It was carried in the affirmative by a majority of 25, Sir Thomas Barrington, the member for Colcheſter, and Sir Martin Lumley, the member for Eſſex, being tellers for the 124 ayes, and Sir Edward Dering, with Sir Hugh Cholmley, the member for Scarborough, for the 99 noes. The diſcuſſion on this day again occupied nearly all the ſitting, and was only at laſt cloſed by the compromiſe of laying aſide ſome clauſes in which exception had been taken to parts of the Liturgy as favouring of ſuperſtition. Other changes, compriſing ſome additions, were alſo aſſented to; and theſe, with the Declaration as amended thus far, were referred to " the ſame committee that was " appointed for penning of it, and they are to " bring it back to the Houſe with all convenient " ſpeed." A further conceſſion to the Oppoſition was at the ſame time made, in the addition to that committee of the names of Culpeper and Falkland.

The two following days, Wedneſday and Thurſday, the 17th and 18th of November, were ſilent as to the Remonſtrance, but filled with matters of grave import having a direct bearing upon it. Complaints had been made of unauthoriſed and exaggerated accounts ſent abroad of the recent proceedings of the Houſe, and after debate an order was iſſued for peremptory ſuppreſſion of all preſent printing, " or " venting in manuſcript," of the Diurnal Occurrences of parliament. The examinations as to the new army plot were alſo completed, the

Clauſe againſt Biſhops carried.

Compromiſe as to Liturgy.

Conceſſions to Oppoſition.

Unauthoriſed reports.

Suppreſſion of Printed and MS. Diurnals.

r

evidence leaving little doubt as to the defign having been known to the King; and Pym moved and carried a refolution, "that, in the "examinations now read unto us, we did con- "ceive there was fufficient evidence for us to "believe that there was a fecond defign to "bring up the army to overawe the delibera- "tions of this Houfe." That was the moft direct avowal yet made of a confcioufnefs on the part of the Commons, not merely of what had taken the King to Scotland, but of what ftill kept him there. The alarm and difmay it carried with it, fhowed how unerringly the mark had been hit.

Refolution as to fecond Army Plot.

§ XII. PREPARATIONS FOR THE FINAL VOTE. 19TH NOV. AND 20TH NOV.

ON the day after Pym's refolution had been paffed, Friday the 19th, Secretary Nicholas wrote with unconcealed alarm and mifgiving to his mafter. "The worft in all that bufinefs "is, that it reflects on your Majefty, as if "you had given fome inftructions concerning "the ftirring up the army to petition the "Parliament. I hope it will appear that your "Majefty's intentions were only to retain the "army in their duty and dependance on your "Majefty." After which, in the fame letter, Mr. Secretary went on to fay, that there had been nothing done thefe two days by the Commons touching the Declaration remonftrating the bad effects of ill counfels; but it was thought that the fame would be finifhed that week. There were, he added, divers well affected

Nicholas's fear for the King.

Progrefs of Remon- ftrance reported.

§ XII. *Preparations for Final Vote.*

servants of his Majesty in the House who had continued to oppose the Remonstrance with unanswerable arguments; but it was verily thought that it would pass notwithstanding, and that it would be "ordered to be printed" without transmission to the Lords. Upon which it is to be observed as beyond question, that manifestly there was no longer any concealment of the ultimate design of the leaders of the House of Commons. Thus early, the destination of the Remonstrance was known. Strode had already, indeed, argued upon the assumption of its being printed and diffused among the people, as a thing to be admitted; and any subsequent complaint, therefore, of being taken by surprise when the proposition for the printing was formally made, could have been but a sheer pretence on the part of its opponents. Nicholas as to printing: the design avowed.

While Nicholas was writing to the King, it had been brought back to the House from the committee, pursuant to the last order; certain amendments to it had been violently debated, having reference to portions of the service-book;* these ultimately, upon concession by the majority, had been read and assented to, and certain other verbal alterations made; and another lengthened debate had given further Sixth Debate: 19th Nov. Amendments and

---

* I subjoin a characteristic passage from a speech of Dering's delivered in this debate, as reported and preserved by himself.
" Why, Sir, at one of your committees I heard it publicly
" asserted by one of the committee that some of our Articles
" do contain some things contrary to Holy Scripture ... I
" started with wonder and anger to hear a bold mechanick A bold
" tell me that my creed is not my creed. He wondered at mecha-
" my wonder, and said, *I hope your worship is too wise to* nick.
" *believe that which you call your creed.*"

opportunity for the "unanswerable" arguments on the one side, and the quiet and resolved answers on the other, which had now occupied the House, with small intermission, since the 9th of November. Why should you pass this unnecessary and unseasonable Declaration? urged Hyde and his friends once more. It is unnecessary to detail grievances, most of which are already fully redressed; and it is unseasonable to welcome home from Scotland, with such a volume of reproaches, the very author of that redress, and to assail his Majesty the King for what others have done amiss, and for what he himself hath reformed. We propose to pass it, was the determined answer of Pym and his associates, because we hold it to be necessary for the preservation and maintenance of the concessions which have so been made. We believe ourselves in danger of being deprived of all the good acts we have gained, if great care and vigilance be not still used to disappoint malignant counsels. They who most exalt the grace and bounty of the King in regard to those good acts, have been most busy to pervert the affections of the people from ourselves in regard to the same matter. For our own acquittal, therefore, we would let the kingdom know in what state we found it at our first convention, what fruit it hath received by our counsels, wherein we think the securities obtained are not yet sufficient, and such further measures as in our consciences we believe to be called for. Because, though the prime evil counsellors have been removed, there are others growing up in

§ XII. *Preparations for Final Vote.*

their places like to do quite as much mifchief. —To which laft home thruft, reply could not have been very eafy!—It was late in the afternoon, when at the clofe of this debate, the order was moved and carried that the Declaration fhould be duly engroffed, and again brought in at two o'clock the next day. All which having been accomplifhed, the Houfe was about to pafs to other bufinefs, when D'Ewes informs us that Mr. Speaker Lenthal made an appeal *ad mifericordiam* for himfelf. He fhowed that he had been fitting very late yefterday (Thurfday 18th), that it was now paft four o'clock, and that he really could not hold out daily to fit feven or eight hours. Whereon the indefatigable Mr. Pym, admitting the appeal, fuggefted that the Houfe fhould rife, and that a grand committee fhould prefently fit.

Order for engroff- ment.

Complaint of Mr. Speaker.

Lenthal relieved.

On Saturday, the 20th of November, at two o'clock, the Remonftrance, engroffed and finifhed, was laid upon the table. Doubtlefs it was then expected by its fupporters, and with fome fhow of reafon, that after having ftood the brunt of fo many prolonged debates, it might be voted without further refiftance. A refolution was accordingly moved upon its introduction, "that it be read and finifhed to-night;" which was met, however, by fuch determined oppofition, that Pym was obliged to yield, and the final debate was fixed for ten o'clock on the morning of Monday the 22nd. "Why would you have it ftill put "off," afked Cromwell of Falkland, as they left the Houfe; "for this day would quickly

Seventh debate: 20th Nov.

Final debate fixed.

Cromwell and Falkland.

"have determined it." To which Falkland made reply that there would not have been time enough, for sure it would take some further debate. Oliver rejoined, "A very "sorry one."*

Preparations for Last Debate.
Cromwell was mistaken, no doubt. He was not in Hyde's confidence, and could not know of the desperate party-move to be attempted on the occasion of the last debate. But before this is described, and while the Remonstrance, ready engrossed, is lying on the table of the house, the time would seem to have arrived for the endeavour to present it to the reader,

Remonstrance lying on table.
at once with sufficient fulness for accurate reflection of all its statements and in such form as to render justice to the striking narrative they embody, yet at the same time so compressed as to bring it within the limits of ordinary histories. There, it should long ago have had the place, from which it may hardly be too much to believe now, with some degree of

Statement by Clarendon:

* *Hist.* ii., 42. Clarendon tells the anecdote, however, in a sense quite different from that which it derives from an authentic statement of the circumstances. It was in the ordinary course of the business of the House that Pym had proposed at once to bring the matter to a conclusion, but Clarendon (ii. 41) would have us believe that he made that proposition in direct forfeiture of a previous engagement.

charge against Pym:
" And by these and the like arts, they promised themselves " that they should easily carry it; so that, *the day it was to be* " *resumed,* they entertained the House all the morning with " other debates, and towards noon called for the Remon- " strance," &c, upon which they were forced to go back to the first understanding of giving an entire day to the debate.

a misrepresentation.
Accordingly, he continues, " the next morning, the debate " being entered upon about nine of the clock," &c. Now, no such incidents occurred. On the day fixed for the resumption of the debate, it *was* resumed, and at the hour precisely which before had been arranged; namely, twelve o'clock. Clarendon's statement is an entire misrepresentation.

Abstract: The Preamble. 215

confidence, that it never more can be excluded. In which expectation are here appended to it some notes of matters not lying on the surface of ordinary books, which will be found to illustrate and completely corroborate the most startling of its averments. _{Proposed historical illustrations.}

And so to modern readers is committed that Great Vindication of the rising of their ancestors against the Sovereign in the seventeenth century, as to which one who opposed it eloquently through all its stages thus frankly confessed the secret of his opposition: " *Sir,* " *this Remonstrance, whensoever it passeth, will* " *make such an impression, and leave such a cha-* " *racter behind, both of his Majesty, the People,* " *and the Parliament, and of this present Church* " *and State, as no time shall ever eat it out,* " *while histories are written, and men have eyes* " *to read them!*" _{Dering on the Remonstrance.}

ABSTRACT OF THE GRAND REMONSTRANCE.

1. *The Preamble: Purpose aimed at.*

THE Preamble, consisting of twenty not numbered clauses, and opening in the name of " the Commons in the present Parliament " assembled," begins by declaring that for the past twelve months they had been carrying on a struggle of which the object was to restore and establish the ancient honour, greatness, and security, of the Nation and the Crown. That during this time they had been called to wrestle _{Struggle of past twelve months.}

with dangers and fears, with miseries and calamities, with distempers and disorders so various, great, and pressing, that for the time the entire liberty and prosperity of the kingdom had been extinguished by them, and the foundations of the throne undermined. And that now, finding great aspersions cast on what had been done, many difficulties raised for the hindrance of what remained to do, and jealousies everywhere busily fomented betwixt the King and Parliament, they had thought it good in this manner to declare the root and growth of the designs by which so much mischief had been caused; the heighth to which these had reached before the beginning of the present Parliament; the means that had been used for extirpating those mischievous designs; and, together with the progress made therein, the ways of obstruction by which such progress had been interrupted, and the steps still remaining to be taken as the only course whereby the obstacles at present intervening could be finally removed.

Why Remonstrance introduced.

Necessary to completion of Reforms.

Then, in express terms, they state the general plan or scheme of the authors of those evils, as a conspiracy to subvert the fundamental laws and principles of government on which alone the religion and justice of the kingdom can firmly rest; and they denounce the conspirators as threefold, (1) the jesuited papists, (2) the bishops and ill-affected clergy, and (3) such counsellors, courtiers, and officers of state, as had preferred their private ends to those of his Majesty and the Commonwealth. All three classes of conspirators, they continued,

Court conspiracy:

to subvert Laws:

Abstract: The Preamble.

had principles and counsels in common; and these were to keep up continual differences betwixt the King and People, and to lower and degrade the Protestant religion through the sides of those best affected to it. To the end that so, on the one hand, setting up the prerogative whenever a question of liberty was mooted, discrediting the claims and authority of Parliament, and ever pretending to be *siding* with the King, they might get to themselves the places of greatest trust and power, putting him upon other than the ancient and only legitimate ways of supply; and, on the other hand, by cherishing to the utmost such views of church doctrine and discipline as would establish ecclesiastical tyranny, by sowing dissensions between the common Protestants and those whom they called Puritans, and by including under the name of Puritans all who desired to preserve unimpaired the public laws and liberties and the purity and power of the true religion, they might be able ultimately to introduce such opinions and ceremonies as would necessarily end in accommodation with Popery.* For, of the three elements of the

to degrade Protest-antism:

to discredit Parliament.

Upholders of right nick-named Puritans.

---

* " It seemed that their work," said Falkland, in one of his admirable speeches against Laud and his associates (already spoken of, *ante*, 208), " was to try how much of a Papist " might be brought in without Popery; and to destroy as " much as they could of the Gospel without bringing them- " selves into danger of being destroyed by the Law. . . . " The design has been to bring in an English though not a " Roman Popery : I mean, not only the outside and dress of " it, but an equally absolute and blind dependence of the " people upon the clergy, and of the clergy upon themselves. " They have opposed the papacy beyond the seas that they " might settle one beyond the water." [He means at Lambeth.] " Nay, common fame is more than ordinarily false, if

Falkland against Laud.

Proposed Pope at Lambeth.

Popery the chief conspiracy, that was the strongest. And as in all compounded bodies, so in this, the operations had been qualified and governed throughout by the predominating element.

Such in substance was the preamble to the Great Remonstrance; of which all that followed was in the form of practical proofs and illustrations. These were contained in two hundred and six numbered clauses; each clause, as we have seen, having been put separately to the House, and so voted.

2. *First, Second, and Third Parliaments of Charles.*

Clauses 1—6.

THE first six had relation to the First Parliament of the reign, and to the recovery of strength by the Popish party after their discomfiture by the breach with Spain at the close of the reign of James. Two subsidies had been given by that parliament, yet it was dissolved without the relief of a single grievance; Incidents of first Parliament. and then followed the disasters of Rochelle, the desertion of the Protestant party in France, the discreditable attempt on Cadiz, the abandonment of the Palatinate and of the Protestant struggle in Germany, the wrongs inflicted on merchants and traders, the pressing and billeting of soldiers * in all parts of the king-

English livings and Romish opinions.
" none of them have found a way to reconcile the opinions of
" Rome to the preferments of England; and to be so abso-
" lutely, directly, and cordially papists, that it is all that
" fifteen hundred pounds a year can do to keep them from
" confessing it."

* The intolerable wrong and misery implied in this grievance will be better understood by reminding the reader of the passionate speech of Wentworth (afterwards Earl of Strafford)

Abstract: First and Second Parliam^ts. of Charles.

dom, and the endeavour, happily frustrated, to introduce therein large bodies of mercenary troops.

The next four clauses described the Second Parliament, its dissolution after a declared intention to grant five subsidies, and the subsequent levy of those subsidies, not by parliamentary authority, but by the sole order of the King. Commissions of loan were issued, and all who refused were imprisoned; many contracting sicknesses in prison from which they never recovered. Privy seals went forth, raising enormous sums. Court waste and profusion were spoken of on all sides, while the people were unlawfully impoverished.* And a com-

Clauses 7—10.

Incidents of second Parliament.

---

in the debates on the Petition of Right, in which, referring to the billeting of soldiers, he exclaims, "They have rent "from us the light of our eyes! enforced companies of "guests worse than the ordinances of France! vitiated our "wives and daughters before our faces!" In the Verney Papers, Mr. Bruce prints the subjoined very curious return of recusant parishes in the three hundreds of Ashindon.

Billeting grievances.

"A retorne of those parishes that doe refuse to paye for "the billiting of soldiers in my diuision with in the three "hundreds of Ashindon.

	li.	s.	d.
"Chersly. Mr. Thomas Britwell, John Winter, with the rest	1	13	3
"Brill. George Carter, Mr. John Pim, Mr. William Pim, Mr. John Caswell, with the rest	2	4	0
"Ilmor. Thomas Lyeborn, Edmon Brooks, with the rest	1	6	0
"Lurgefall. The whole parish	1	18	3
"Borstall. The whole parish	1	13	6

Lists of recusants.

"*Per me*, Edward Bulstrod."

The two Pyms named in this return, if not connections or relatives of the great statesman, at least were worthy of the name they bore.

* In the *Diary of Walter Yonge, from 1604 to 1628*, edited by Mr. Roberts for the Camden Society (1848) with an interesting and well-informed introduction about the leading

Yonge's Diary.

220   *The Grand Remonstrance.*

miſſion under the great ſeal exacted payments from the ſubject by way of excife, to an extent and in a manner before unheard of.*

Clauſes 11—16.
Incidents of third Parliament.

The Third Parliament; the attempt, by a ſurreptitious declaration, to evade its enactment of the Petition of Right; its forcible diſſolution; the impriſonment and perſecution of its moſt diſtinguiſhed members; and the Royal Declaration printed and diſperſed among the people to diſcredit and diſavow its pro-

weſtern families (Yonge was a Devonſhire magiſtrate and member for Honiton), the two following notices occur in cloſe juxtapoſition (p. 98):

Proceedings to get money.

(1) "December, 1626. The King having determined heretofore to demand of all his ſubjects ſo much money by way of loan as they are ſet in ſubſidy, viz.: he that's ſet at 20l. in ſubſidy to lend unto the King 20l., the judges were urged to ſubſcribe. They paid their money, but refuſed to ſubſcribe the ſame as a legal courſe: for which Sir Randall Crewe, Chief Juſtice of England, had his patent taken from him, and he was diſplaced *Ter. Michael.* 1626, *anno* 2 *Caroli.* The privy council ſubſcribed; the lords and peers ſubſcribed, all except fourteen, whereof ſix were Earls: viz. Earl of Eſſex, Earl of Warwick, Earl of Clare, Earl of Huntington, Earl of Lincoln, and the Earl of Bolingbroke, being Lord St. John."

How ſpent.

(2) "The Duke of Buckingham feaſted the King, Queen, and French Ambaſſador, and beſtowed 4000l. in a banquet. The ſweet water which coſt him 200l. came down the room as a ſhower from heaven; the banquet let down in a ſheet upon the table, no man ſeeing how it came; with other pompous vanities to waſte away and conſume money, the country being in poverty, and more neceſſary occaſions for it."

Any one who cares to purſue this ſubject will find many important illuſtrations of it among the Clarendon *State Papers.*

Amendments by J. C.

* Among the notices for additions to the original draft of the Remonſtrance, entered on the Journals, the ſubjoined appear with the initials J. C. and may doubtleſs be aſſigned to Sir John Clotworthy.
  "The laſt expedition into Germany.
  "The loans upon Privy Seal.
  "The Commiſſion of Excife."

Abstract: *Third Parliament of Charles.*

ceedings,* and give colour or excuse for the
violence used to its chiefs; form the subject

> * It was on the motion of Strode, member for Beeralston, when the Remonstrance was before the House, that there was ordered to be inserted therein a mention of "The Declaration set forth upon the breach of both "Parliaments." [Addition by Strode.]

Some remarkable illustrations of the exciting incidents which immediately preceded and very shortly followed the ill-fated dissolution of this great Parliament, have been found among the family papers of the Moundefords of Norfolk. I select one or two out of many passages which furnish traits and characteristics of the lawless time, and throw a surprisingly vivid light upon the allusions in the Great Remonstrance. From London, the 14th April, 1628, Sir Edmund Moundeford, member for Thetford in the Third Parliament then sitting, and who sat for Norfolk in the Long Parliament, writes: "We "went this afternoon with our Speaker to the King to deliver "him a petition for the billeted souldiers, what answer we "shall have is not known. Our house proceeds not with that "calm it did. God grant a good end." On the 5th of the following month he writes: "Sorrye am I to be a messenger "of sadd tidings. The feares of an ill ending of this Parlia- "ment are now growne so great as they command beliefe. "Our last day is appointed to-morrow seven-night, and we "are as farre from ending our worke as when wee began." In the interval between the Third and the Long Parliament, he writes: "We have no new sheriffs pricked, nor shall not "(it is said) untill the now sheriffs have accounted for this "ship-money: in some counties they pay, in others not, *and* "*many make the sheriffs take distress.* New impositions are "set upon fruit, silver, pewter, pines, and divers other things "to the value 80,000 li. p^r ann. *There is a patent to be* "*granted for making Salt, which will make us all smarte.*" [Moundeford MSS. Billeting soldiers. Sheriffs and ship-money.]

From Drury Lane, on the 13th of November 1632, he writes: "On Wednesday last, one Mr. Palmer was censured 1,000 li. "in the Star Chamber for living in London contrary to the "Proclamation, *and yet he was a Batchelor, and never had* "*family, and lately had his mansion house burnt in the countrie.* "*There is diligent search made by the constables of everie* "*ward, and the names taken of all such lodgers as lay in towne* "*the last vacation.*" The allusion in this last letter is to one of the most scandalous of all the projects for the plunder of the subject set on foot by this reckless government to enrich the exhausted treasury of the King. A Proclamation came forth from the Council Table commanding all who could not show their stay in London to be absolutely necessary, to go within forty days and reside in their respective counties and at [Projects for plundering the subject.]

of the fix following claufes.* Strenuous as had been the ftruggle to pafs the Great Petition, its only ufe had been to fhow with what recklefs prefumption, by wicked and daring minifters, the laws had been broken and the liberties fuppreffed which therein were fo folemnly and recently declared. And what, meanwhile, had been their fufferings, whofe only crime was to affert the laws, and who could be punifhed only by their entire fubverfion? The reprefentatives of the people had been flung into prifon, and there treated like felons for words fpoken in parliament. All the comforts of life, all means of prefervation of health, all more neceffary means of fpiritual confolation, were denied to them. Not fuffered to go abroad to enjoy God's ordinances in God's houfe, His minifters not permitted to minifter comfort in their prifons, the liberty of reading

<small>Violation of Petition of Right.</small>

<small>Imprifonment of Members.</small>

their manfion houfes, " in order to hinder them from wafting " their eftates" (!); and by the example which Sir Edward Moundeford here furnifhes, fome idea may be formed of the atrocities perpetrated under cover of this Proclamation. How truly fays Bifhop Warburton (Notes on *Hift. of Reb.* vii. 579) that every now and then a ftory comes out which fhows the Court to have been fo exceedingly tyrannical as to abate all our wonder at the rage of thofe who had been oppreffed by it.

<small>Atrocities of the Court.</small>

* Several of thefe claufes appear to have received additions in the Houfe ; and to feveral notices of motions in the Journals that the confideration of fuch and fuch particulars fhould be added, are appended fometimes initials, fometimes the abbreviated name, more rarely the name in full. One name is thus given:

"*Pal.* The additional explanation to the Petition of "Right."

Which may ftand for Geoffrey Palmer, the Member for Stamford, who took a leading part in the debates; or it may be intended for Sir Guy Palmes, member for Rutlandfhire: the former is the more probable.

<small>Authors of Amendments.</small>

and of writing taken from them; in such miserable durance, years upon years had passed. Towards the close of the second year, indeed, some had been released, yet not without heavy fines, and the shame of being enforced to give security for good behaviour: but others might have wearied out their lives in imprisonment, if, eighteen months ago, a parliament had not come; and to one, the most distinguished of them all, after four years' tedious misery, there had come a mightier friend. In the last days of November, 1632, the brave and dauntless Eliot died in the Tower. Petition after petition had been sent up for his release; application had been made for but a few months' freedom, even to give him strength to bear further imprisonment; without such temporary change, his physician had testified that he must perish; but a cold and stern refusal was the only answer vouchsafed, and the end came which was past remedy, and never to be redressed. His blood cried for vengeance still;* or for repentance of those Ministers of State who had so obstructed the course alike of his Majesty's justice and his Majesty's mercy.

Heavy fines.

Sufferings and death of Eliot.

His blood crying for vengeance.

---

* There was no wrong which Pym appears more deeply to have resented than this murder (for such it really amounted to) of his great associate in the former parliaments of the reign. The little parliament (which met in April, 1640) had not assembled many days when Pym moved "that it be "referred to the committee of the Tower to examine after "what manner Sir John Eliot came to his death, his usage in "the Tower, and to view the rooms and places where he was "imprisoned and where he died, and to report the same to "the House."

Eliot's usage in Tower.

3. *Government by Prerogative: from Third Parliament to Pacification of Berwick.*

Clauſes
17—60.

Government by Prerogative.

THE long and terrible interval which ſucceeded, and which only Laud's mad reſolve to impoſe the ſervice-book on Scotland at laſt abruptly cloſed, during which no parliament met, and the people were forbidden even to ſpeak of parliaments,*—forbidden merely to look back to their ancient liberty,—fills forty-four clauſes, up to the ſixtieth incluſive. Then paſſed over the land a net-work of tyranny ſo elaborate and comprehenſive, that, excepting only its agents and projectors, not a ſingle claſs of the community eſcaped it. Nearly all men ſuffered alike, in lands, goods, or perſon; nor was there left to any one that which ſafely he could call his, except the wrong, and the too patient endurance.

Clauſes 17, 21, 22, 31, 44, 45, and 49.

Revival of feudal ſtatutes.

Obſolete laws and ſervices which it was hoped had been extinguiſhed for ever, confronted ſuddenly all families of reaſonable condition. Old laws of knighthood were revived; and ſuch ſums exacted for default, as, whether in reſpect of the perſons charged, the fines demanded, or the modes of exaction, were entirely monſtrous. By fines and compoſitions for wardſhips alone,† eſtates were

---

* During the firſt diſcuſſion of the Remonſtrance, Mr. Wingate, member for St. Alban's, moved that there ſhould be named therein
 "The Proclamation ſet forth, forbidding people ſo much
 " as to talk of a parliament."
 † Some notion of the advantage taken, for purpoſes of extortion, of thoſe obſolete feudal ſtatutes, may be derived

Abstract: Government by Prerogative.

weakened past help. Coat and conduct money,* and other military charges, were either pressed as due, or, failing that claim of right, were required as loans. Without a shadow of pretence, either in fact or law, the ancient securities and charters of real property were everywhere violated; and from forests where never any deer fed, from depopulations where never any farm was decayed, and from enclosures where never any hedges were set, charges unceasing and insatiable were drawn against the land.† When flaws in title were

Ancient charters broken.

from the documents in the Verney Papers relating to Mrs. Mary Blacknall, who had the misfortune, on her father's death, to become a ward of the Crown, and four of whose maternal relations, " Anthony Blagrove the elder, Anthony " Blagrove the younger, both of Bulmarsh, Richard Libb " esquire of Hardwick in the county of Oxford, and Charles " Wiseman esquire of Steventon in Berks," are obliged to purchase from the Court of Wards (that is, the Government) freedom from oppression, and mere ordinary rights of citizenship, by payment to the Crown of a fine of 2000*l*, half of which is paid down, and a bond given for the remainder.

Wardship extortions.

* This oppressive tax was assessed on the several hundreds separately, each being obliged to supply its quota of men by pressing or enlistment, in proportion to its size and the number demanded; one shilling being paid to each man, fourteen shillings levied for the cost of his " coat," and two other payments made severally, as remuneration to the constable who took him to the place of embarkation, and as fine or charge for his " conduct," or expenses on the way.

Coat and conduct money.

† From a Schedule of Grievances largely circulated through the country before April 1640, I select one or two items:

" The new taxe of Coate and Conduct Mony, with undue " meanes used to inforce the payment of it, by messengers " from the counsell table."

" The infinite number of Monopolies upon everything the " countryman must buy."

" The rigid execution of the Forrest laws in theire extremity."

" The exaction of immoderate fees by some officers under " the Lord Chief Justice in Eyre."

Schedule of Grievances. April, 1640.

Q

alleged, they were judged by packed juries; and when commiffions of inquiry into exceffes of fees or fines were iffued, they were made but additional means of increafing and confirming the grievance. They ended, for the moft part, in compofitions with the delinquents themfelves; fo that offences to come were compromifed as well as the offences paft, and a complete impunity eftablifhed for future wrongs. To thefe matters were devoted the 17th, 21ft, 22nd, 31ft, 44th, 45th, and 49th claufes.

Nor was the lot of the merchant and trader, in this difaftrous interval, more to be envied than that of any owner of a moderate eftate. In the very teeth of the Petition of Right, tonnage and poundage were again levied, with many other fimilar impofitions, of which fome were in a difproportion fo monftrous, that the amount of the charge exceeded the entire value of the goods. The book of rates generally was alfo enhanced to fuch an extent that the ordinary tranfactions of commerce became impoffible. And though, for thefe violent affeffments, there was fet up the notable pretence of duly guarding the feas; and though there was fuddenly added thereto that new and unheard of tax of fhip-money,* by which, for

Side notes: Packed juries and robberies by law. Claufes 18, 19, 20, and 24. Monftrous taxation of commerce. Pretence of guarding feas.

Finch was at this time Chief Juftice of the Common Pleas, and no part of his conduct in the circuit in Eyre more exafperated the people than his extending the boundaries of the forefts in Effex, and annihilating the ancient perambulations.

The tax leaft fupportable.

* In the above-named "Schedule of fuch Grievances as "moft oppreffe this country," largely circulated in the early part of 1640, ftands firft "The illegall and infupportable "charge of fhip-money, now the fifth yeere impofed as high "as ever, though the fubject was not able to pay the laft

Abſtract: Government by Prerogative.

many years, with the help of the book of rates, near upon 700,000*l*. was yearly taken by the Crown; the ſeas meanwhile were left   *Ship-money.*

" yeer, beeing a third." The Lord Deputy Wentworth's
newſwriter gives us curious notices of this memorable tax,
" word of laſting found in the memory of this kingdom;"
but even his goſſiping letters loſe ſomething of their careleſs
tone in talking of it, and ſhow that he alſo winces and ſmarts   *Hardſhips*
under the preſſure no one can eſcape.   In one year, Mr.   *of ſhip-*
Garrard ſays, "it will coſt the city at leaſt 35,000*l*." He   *money*
names particular aſſeſſments to the amount of 360*l*. and 300*l*:   *aſſeſſment.*
" great ſums to pay at one tax, and we know not how often
" it may come. It reaches us in the Strand, being within
" liberties of Weſtminſter, which furniſheth out one ſhip—
" *nay lodgers*, for I am ſet at 40*s*; but I had rather give and
" pay ten ſubſidies in parliament than 10*s*. this new-old way
" of dead Noy's." And as in the cities, ſo in the country.
" Mr. Speaker," ſaid Sir John Culpeper, " this tax of ſhip-
" money is the grievance which makes the farmers faint, and   *Priſons*
" the plough to go heavy." So intolerable was it everywhere,   *filled.*
indeed, that the priſons were literally filled with thoſe who
had refuſed and reſiſted payment, before the Crown (which,
through the judges on circuit, had reſiſted every former
attempt to bring the queſtion into the courts as refuſing even
to admit a doubt of its legality) conſented to appear to
Hampden's plea.   The Court lawyers had ſelected Hampden   *Hampden*
as a better man to fight it out with, than the leſs affable and   *one of*
apparently more obdurate Lord Saye; but here, as everywhere,   *many re-*
they were fated to diſcover their miſtake. I give a curious   *cuſants.*
note (not otherwiſe reported) as to Lord Saye's ſubſequent
proceedings :
   " March 19, 1638-9.   Shipmoney, determined for the
" king by his prerogative, argued Eaſter and Trinity Term.
" In Michaelmas term, the lord Saye brought his action   *Lord*
" about it to the King's Bench barre. Mr. Holborne, plead-   *Saye's*
" ing ſtrongly for him, was rebuked by Judge Bartlet   *reſiſtance:*
" [Berkeley], becauſe it was determined as before.   He
" alleged a preſident when ſuch determinings have been
" againe queſtioned.   Judge Crooke alledged preſidents.
" Judge Joanes ſaid they were not like.   Sir Jo. Brampton
" [Bramſton] alledged that they had no preſident like this,
" viz. to call the thing in queſtion the next terme, and before
" the judges' faces that did determine it. The lord Saye
" affirmed, that if their Lordſhips wold ſay it were lawe, then   *deciſion*
" he wold yeeld; but otherwiſe not, to the wronging of his   *in his*
" country.   He hath time to conſider until the next terme."   *caſe.*
   Pym, in his great ſpeech in the little parliament, ſtruck at

The Grand Remonſtrance.

<small>Seas wholly unguarded.</small> ſo utterly unguarded that the Turkiſh pirates ranged through them uncontrolled, repeatedly taking great ſhips of value, and conſigning to ſlavery many thouſands of Engliſh ſubjects.*

<small>Pym on ſhip-money.</small> the root of the extraordinary and univerſal reſiſtance provoked by this tax when he pointed out, that it extended to all perſons and to all times, that it ſubjected goods to diſtreſs and the perſon to impriſonment, that, the King being ſole judge of the occaſion, there was no poſſibility of exception or relief, and that there were no rules or limits for the proportion, ſo that no man, under it, knew what eſtate he had, or how to order his courſe or expenſes. It is quite a miſtake to ſuppoſe, as ſome have repreſented, that it was a light tax; and that Hampden, well able to afford it, oppoſed it only on principle. <small>Not a light tax.</small> No man, not the wealthieſt in that day, was able to afford it. It muſt, ſooner or later, have broken him down.

* " About the end of March, 1627, Sir William Courtenay
" his houſe of Ilton, near Salcomb, in Devon, was robbed;
" and much of his pewter plate and houſehold ſtuff carried
" away. It was done by certain pirates, which came up in
" boats from Salcomb, and fled the ſame way they came
" without apprehenſion "—*Diary of Walter Yonge*: to which
paſſage a valuable note is appended by the editor. The
ſovereignty of the ſea was as yet but the emptieſt of claims.
Pirates of all lands ſwept our coaſts during the whole of this
<small>Piracies in the Channel.</small> period of government by the ſole will of the King. Piracy had become indeed ſo much more profitable than honeſt trading that many Engliſhmen turned Turks and lived at Tunis. Sir Francis Verney is ſuppoſed to have been among them; and Mr. Bruce (in his moſt intereſting collection of Verney Papers, printed for the Camden Society, 95-102) does not effectually rebut the ſuppoſition. " Aſſiſted by Engliſh-
" men," ſays the editor of Yonge's *Diary*, "the Barbary
" corſairs not only ſcoured the Engliſh and St. George's
" Channels, but even diſembarked, pillaged the villages, and
" carried the inhabitants into ſlavery, to the number of ſeveral
" thouſands.... One veſſel the Algerines captured was worth
" 260,000*l*. The Dutch reſumed their fiſhing without a
" licence, and captured two rich Eaſt Indiamen. France,
" Spain, and Holland violated the neutrality, and inſulted
<small>Inſults to Engliſh flag.</small> " the Engliſh flag. The French ſcoured the Severn in
" 1628 ... So late as the year 1633, Lord Wentworth, ap-
" pointed lord-deputy of Ireland, names noted pirate veſſels
" off the coaſt of Ireland, and their captures. The Turks
" carried off a hundred captives from Baltimore in Ireland,
" in 1631. They landed their poor captives at Rochelle and
" marched them in chains to Marſeilles. And in 1645, the

Abstract: Government by Prerogative. 229

It was in vain that the leading merchants would have appealed to the law. The ordinary courſe of juſtice, the common birthright of the ſubject of England, was cloſed to them. The moſt diſtinguiſhed of their number who made the trial was dragged into the Star Chamber, fined 2000*l*, kept twelve years in priſon, and releaſed a beggar.* Theſe things are the ſubject of clauſes 18th, 19th, 20th and part of the 34th.

Other wrongs, too, equally grave, the mer-

<small>No laws to appeal to.</small>

<small>Caſe of Richard Chambers.</small>

"Turks carried off twenty-ſix children at one time from
"Cornwall. The editor has a curious bill of expenſes for
"ſending pirates with their hands tied behind them on horſe-
"back to Dorcheſter gaol."

* A man had but to queſtion the moſt profligate deciſions of the Courts to be dragged into the Star Chamber. One inſtance of a different kind, ſhowing the deep reſentment of the people at ſuch proceedings, is well worthy of preſervation. Of the twelve judges who pronounced on ſhip money, three diſſented, of whom Hutton was one; and a clergyman named Harriſon was brought before a jury for having charged Judge Hutton with treaſon, in having denied the King's prerogative in the matter of ſhip money. The jury gave 10,000*l*. damages againſt him; a judgment diſallowed, but evincing unmiſtakeably the feeling of the people. That was in 1638-9. I may add, not leſs as a valuable illuſtration of this part of the ſubject, than as a good ſpecimen of Hyde's tone in the Houſe at this time, a few ſentences from his ſpeech upon the miſ-doings of the Bench of Judges. "The great reſolution in
"ſhip money was a crime of ſo prodigious a nature, that it
"could not be eaſily ſwallowed and digeſted by the con-
"ſciences even of theſe men; but as they who are to wreſtle,
"or run a race, by degrees prepare themſelves by diet and
"leſſer eſſays for the main exerciſe, ſo theſe judges enter
"themſelves, and harden their hearts, by more particular
"treſpaſſes upon the law—by impoſition and taxes upon the
"merchant in trade, by burdens and preſſure upon the gentry
"by knighthood—before they could arrive at that univerſal
"deſtruction of the kingdom by ſhip money; which promiſed
"them reward and ſecurity for all their former ſervices, by
"doing the work of a parliament to his Majeſty in ſupplies;
"and ſeemed to elude juſtice in leaving none to judge them,
"by making the whole kingdom party to their oppreſſion."

<small>Captures by Turks.</small>

<small>Popular ſympathy for Judge Hutton.</small>

<small>Hyde's ſpeech againſt the Judges.</small>

chant shared with the mass of his countrymen. As with the Petition of Right, which had been solemnly enacted only eight months before, so it fared with the statutes against monopolies and projectors, won by as hard a struggle in the fourth parliament of James, and which now had been the law for many years. Again had monopolies and protections of every kind sprung up into existence, and the whole community smarted and groaned under them. There were monopolies of soap, of salt and saltpetre, of wine, of leather, of coals; literally, of everything in most common and necessary use; and, as the immediate and universal consequence, not merely were the most extravagant prices required to be paid for everything so protected, but articles of the worst quality, and subject to the basest adulterations, were sure to be supplied. Purveyors, clerks of the markets, saltpetre men,* became bye-words of petty oppression. Not only a man's unavoidable daily wants, but his trade, his employment, his habitation, anything, served as the pretext for some vexatious restraint to his liberty. If he would build near London, he found such building was adjudged a nuisance, and had to pay some projector for permission to inflict the nuisance on his neighbours. If he would trade at sea, he was surprised, even there, by the projector, as by a foreign enemy. Merchants commonly were prohibited from unlading their goods in ports for their own advantage, and

<small>Clauses 27, 28, 29, 30, 33, 34, and 35.</small>

<small>Monopolies revived:</small>

<small>all necessaries of life protected and debased.</small>

<small>Restraints on enterprise.</small>

---

* Bulstrode Whitelocke moved and carried, in the House itself, this addition of " the abuses of Purveyors and Salt- " petre men."

compelled to unlade in places for the advantage of monopolifers and projectors. There was alfo a fcheme of brafs money fet on foot* which would have had the effect of beggaring the whole kingdom at a ftroke, by fummary and fimultaneous procefs. And when fome folitary citizen was occafionally moved to refiftance, it was but to difcover that what he had imagined to be courts of law for the determination of the fubjects' rights, were now become courts of revenue to fupply the treafury of the King. The common refult of fuch refiftance was long and hard imprifonment; lofs of health to many, lofs of life to fome; and theirs was an enviable lot, who efcaped with the mere breaking up of their eftablifhments and the feizure of their goods.† The points fo dwelt

Debafement of currency.

Courts of law become courts of royal revenue.

* " About the month of July, 1638, there was a project
" on foot for braffe money. It was folemnly debated whether
" it be for his Majefty's fervice to coine braffe money, and to
" make the fame currant within his dominions."—*Diary of*
Rous, p. 95. Of the confequences that muft immediately
have enfued upon this wicked propofal to debafe the coin of
the realm, it is needlefs to fpeak; but fome of them are detailed in a paper printed by Rous, pp. 95—98. Lord Falkland made a happy allufion to the brafs project in one of his
refolute fpeeches againft the bifhops, while yet he acted on
that queftion with Hampden and Pym. " As fome ill
" minifters in our State firft took away our money from us,
" and after endeavoured to make our money not worth the
" taking by turning it into Brafs by a kind of anti-philofo-
" pher's ftone—fo thefe men ufed us in this point of preach-
" ing: firft depreffing it to their power, and next labouring
" to make it fuch as the harm had not been much if it had
" been depreffed."

Project for brafs money, Falkland's reference thereto.

† The ftate to which in this refpect the kingdom had been
brought was briefly and forcibly expreffed by Mr. Harbottle
Grimfton, the member for Colchefter, fubfequently Mafter of
the Rolls and Speaker of the Parliament that welcomed back
Charles the Second, in one of the great debates on grievances.
" Sir," he faid, " by fome judgments lately obtained in

Grimfton on denials of juftice.

upon were in the 27th, 28th, 29th, 30th, 33rd, part of the 34th, and the 35th clauses.

<small>Clauses 23, 24, 25, 26, and 32.</small> From the private wrong the public grievance is of course rarely separable; but here it happened frequently that the one received peculiar exasperation from the other, and a striking instance was alleged in the monopoly of gunpowder. So high was the rate set upon gunpowder, that the poorer sort of people were unable to buy it; so strict was the protection, that without a licence it was not procurable at all; and, besides the unlawful advantages thus permitted to individuals, many parts of the kingdom were left in consequence utterly without defence.* It resulted, in fact, in one of the heaviest wrongs inflicted on the commonwealth. The Trained Bands were generally discouraged in their exercises, the country began to lose its martial spirit, and several bodies of militia in the counties had their arms taken away. Belonging also to the same class of

<small>Gunpowder monopoly:</small>

<small>Trained bands discouraged thereby.</small>

"courts of justice, and by some new ways of government
"lately started up amongst us, the law of property is so much
"shaken that no man can say he is master of anything. All
"that we have, we hold but as tenants by courtesy and at
"will, and may be stripped of at pleasure."
* It was moved by J. C. (Sir John Clotworthy) in the House that the gunpowder monopoly should be specially entered "as it was a project for disarming of the kingdom."

<small>Culpeper on protection of gunpowder.</small> Another J. C. (Sir John Culpeper), unhappily now the fiercest opponent of the Remonstrance, had strongly pressed this as a grievance at the opening of the Long Parliament. "However little it may seem *primâ facie*, sir," he said, with admirable sense and shrewdness, "upon due examination it "will appear a great grievance, that enhancing of the price "of gunpowder whereby the Trained Bands are much dis- "couraged in their exercising . . . Mr. Speaker, the Trained "Band is a Militia of great strength and honour, without "charges to the King, and deserves all due encouragement."

grievances, were such incidents as the breaking up of the forest of Dean, and the assignment to projectors, for supply of temporary needs, of the royal timber therein. One of the best *[Favours to papist projectors.]* store-houses of the kingdom for maintenance of its shipping was thus lost; nor was the grief of good subjects abated, when they saw it leased and sold to papists. And as public possessions were seized by private projectors, so was private land appropriated under pretences of public or royal title. The Crown lawyers *[Seizures under Crown Commissions.]* put in claims incessantly to portions of estates between high and low water marks, against which the owners had no remedy;* and commissions were granted under vexatious and all but obsolete statutes, by which, for the sole benefit of the rich, the poor were most heavily burthened.† Large quantities of Common, *[Commons taken from people.]* also, and several public grounds, were taken from the subject under colour of the statute of improvement, and by abuse of the commission of sewers. The 23rd, 24th, 25th, 26th, and 32nd clauses were thus occupied, the last having

* Mr. Serjeant Wilde had moved in the House as to "the *[Wilde and Clotworthy.]* " Destruction of Timber, especially in the Forest of Deane, " by Recusants;" and consideration was moved to be added by J. C. (Sir John Clotworthy) of " the Entitling the King " to the lands between the high-water and low-water mark."

† " Here is at this present," writes Garrard to the Lord Deputy Wentworth, " a Commission in execution against " cottagers who have not four acres of ground laid to their " houses, upon a statute made the 31 Eliz. which vexeth the " poor people mightily, all for the benefit of the Lord Mor- " ton, and the Secretary of Scotland, the Lord Sterling; *[Plunder of the poor.]* " much crying out there is against it, especially because mean, " needy, and men of no good fame, prisoners in the Fleet, " are used as principal Commissioners to call the people before " them, to fine and compound with them."

been specially inserted at the urgent representation of Cromwell.*

<small>Clauses 38, 39, 40, 41, 42, 43, 46, and 47.</small> The steps by which the ordinary courts of judicature had become meanwhile so degraded, as to render possible the prolongation of this lawless time, are succinctly detailed in the 38th, <small>Patents of the Judges altered.</small> 39th, 40th, 41st, 42nd, 43rd, 46th, and 47th clauses. The patents of the judges were altered; and the condition of absolute servility, *durante bene placito*, took the place of that which might imply at least moderate independence, the *quamdiu se bene gesserit*. Some few judges were displaced for refusing to betray their oaths and their consciences;† nearly all the rest were <small>Justice intercepted.</small> overawed into treachery to both; the ordinary approaches to justice were interrupted or foreclosed;‡ and they who should have been as dogs to defend the sheep, became the very

<small>Commissions.</small> * "The Commission of Sewers to be farther explained" are the terms of a notice given in the House by Cromwell. This, and the Commission for Depopulations, were often indignantly recurred to, both by Pym and Cromwell.

† The opportunities for violating both were unceasing. Under the pretext of curing defects in titles of land, a proclamation was issued proposing to grant new titles on payment of a reasonable composition; the alleged flaws to be <small>Alleged defects in title deeds.</small> tried by judges empowered, without appeal, to establish the objections; and whoever declined to avail himself of this facility for being plundered, was threatened in no measured terms with the seizure and utter loss of all belonging to him.

‡ "Sir," said Mr. Harbottle Grimston, in one of his able speeches on grievances at the opening of this parliament, "I "will tell you a passage I heard from a judge in the King's "Bench. There was a poor man committed by the Lords, "for refusing to submit to a project; and having attended a <small>Anecdote of a Judge.</small> "long time at the King's Bench bar upon his habeas corpus, "and at last pressing very earnestly to be bailed, the judge "said to the rest of his brethren, 'Come, brothers,' said he, "' let us bail him; for they begin to say in the town, that "' the judges have overthrown the Law, and the bishops the "' Gospel.'"

Abstract: Government by Prerogative.

wolves to worry them. If a lawyer fhowed fidelity to his client in any queftion affecting the Crown, he was marked by the court diffavour. Solicitors and attornies were repeatedly threatened, and not feldom were punifhed, for profecuting the moft lawful fuits. New oaths were forced upon the fubject. Undue influences were employed to make juries find for the King. Men found themfelves fuddenly, in their freeholds and eftates, their fuits and actions, bound and overruled by orders from the Council Table.* Old judicatories, as the Chancery, the Exchequer Chamber, the Courts of the Houfehold,† the Court of Wards, and

Law and lawyers degraded.

Old jurifdictions abufed.

* "The Council Table bit like a ferpent; the Star
" Chamber like fcorpions. Two or three gentlemen could
" not ftir out, for fear of being committed for a riot. Our
" fouls and confciences were put on the rack by the Arch-
" bifhop. We might not fpeak of Scripture or repeat a
" fermon at our tables. Many godly minifters were fent to
" find their bed in the wildernefs. The oppreffion was little
" lefs in the lower courts and in the fpecial courts."—Speech
by Sir Arthur Hafelrig in Richard Cromwell's parliament,
Feb. 1658-9. Clarendon reports it as not merely an ordinary
faying but a regular principle of conduct with Finch, fworn
in to the high office of Lord Keeper in January, 1639-40,
that while he was Keeper, no man fhould be fo faucy as to
difpute orders of the Council Board; but that the wifdom of
that Board fhould be always ground enough for him to make
a decree in Chancery. *Hift.* i. 131.

Council Board tyranny.

Policy of Keeper Finch.

† Of the kind of courts thus recklefsly allowed to override
or fuperfede the ordinary courts of judicature, a remarkable
inftance occurs in the *Verney Papers*, where a reprieve appears figned by Secretary Windebank for " one Elizabeth
" Cottrell, condemned to death at the Verge holden on
" Thurfday laft for ftealing one of his Majefty's difhes," and
ferving notice to the Treafurer and Comptroller of the Houfehold to ftay the execution. But moft undoubtedly no authority exifted, even in the two infamous Tudor ftatutes creating
criminal courts within the royal precincts, by which Charles
the Firft's Treafurer or Comptroller was empowered to try,
convict, and capitally fentence any Englifh fubject. Mr.
Bruce has properly pointed out that the only criminal cafes

Courts of the Houfehold.

Verney Papers, p. 182.

the Star Chamber, were enlarged fo as grievoufly to exceed their proper jurifdiction; and new judicatories, fuch as the Court of the Earl Marfhal, were created without a pretence of legality. No man who was in favour at Whitehall, any longer cared or needed to feek juftice except where juftice might be fitted to his own defire; and the rules of common law, which had furvived through centuries of comparative barbarifm, began to lofe their certainty and efficacy in this brief term of twelve miferable years.*

The 37th claufe dealt with the Star Chamber, and recited the fines, imprifonments, banifhments, ftigmatifings, whippings, gags, pillories, and mutilations,† which it adminif-

<small>New Courts created.</small>

<small>Rules of law unfettled.</small>

<small>Claufes 37, 51, 52, 53, 54, and 55.</small>

<small>Death for ftealing royal difh.</small>

to which the limited jurifdiction of the Tudor Courts could poffibly apply, were thofe of members of the royal houfehold confpiring to kill the King or any great officer of the ftate, or fhedding blood within the limits of the palace. To punifh capitally the theft of one of his Majefty's difhes, even though committed by a fervant of the royal houfehold (which Elizabeth Cottrell prefumably was), is a notion that could only have entered into the projects and arrangements of the moft lawlefs government that England had ever known.

<small>Notices for infertions in Remonftrance.</small>

* Several notices of motion for additions to the Remonftrance, given after its introduction into the Houfe, had reference to thefe fubjects. I fubjoin a few fuch notices:

"The Courts of Wards."

"The Jurifdiction of the Council of the Marches."

"The Council Table, as they take cognizance of *me* " and *te*."

"The Buying and Selling of Honours and Dignities."

Smyth, the fignature attached to the firft, was doubtlefs Henry Smyth, the member for Leicefterfhire, who furvived the viciffitudes of the eight following years, and fat on the trial of the King.

<small>Tragedies of Baftwick,</small>

† The bloody tragedies of Baftwick, of Burton, and of Prynne,—men of fpotlefs reputation in their feveral learned callings, and whofe offence was fimply to have claimed the commoneft right of freemen,—are well known, and cannot to

Abstract: Government by Prerogative.

tered to cafes of confcience. Nothing was too trivial, nor anything too grave, to efcape its tyranny;* and they were fortunate who, once within its clutches, were again reftored fafely *[Ecclefiaftical tyranny.]* this day be read without a burning fenfe of irritation and amazement that even the much-enduring Englifh people could have poffeffed their fouls in patience, under fo many years of fuch a government. Thomas May, the hiftorian of the Parliament, has a pregnant remark upon the fubject. " It " feemed, I 'remember, to many gentlemen (and was accord- " ingly difcourfed of), a fpectacle no lefs ftrange than fad, " to fee three of feveral profeffions, the nobleft in the king- " dom, Divinity, Law and Phyfick, expofed at one time to " fuch an ignominious punifhment, and condemned to it by " proteftant magiftrates, for fuch tenets in religion as the " greateft part of proteftants in England held, and all the " reformed churches in Europe maintained." (Lib. 1. cap. 7.) *[Burton, and Prynne. Mutilations for confcience fake.]* And this feeling it was, ftored up in the minds and hearts of the people, that found afterwards fuch terrible vent. Yet the few leading names, fuch as Leighton's and theirs, which live in the hiftory of fuch perfecutions, are of courfe but the type of countlefs others, the record of whofe fufferings has perifhed. Here is a marginal notice from Rous's *Diary* as of one of the commoneft incidents of the time. " Many great " cenfures in the Starre Chamber. Tubbing's cafe. Tubbing " loft one eare at Weftminfter, and, ere he loft the other in " Norfolk, he died in prifon in London." Rous was a clergyman of Suffolk; a man apparently of fupreme fillinefs and dulnefs, and who had no opinions worth mention on any fubject, to trouble either himfelf or his neighbours with. The only merit of his Diary (and this but fcant) is to collect pieces of goffip, and fo preferve evidences of popular facts or feelings, quite above the colour of fufpicion on the ground of any popular fympathies in the goffiper himfelf. *[Rous's Diary, p. 86.]*

* " When," faid Mr. Bagfhaw, member for Southwark, in his fpeech at the meeting of the Long Parliament, " I " caft my eyes upon the High Commiffion and other Eccle- " fiaftical Courts, my foul hath bled for the wrong and " preffure which I have obferved to have been done and com- " mitted in thefe Courts againft the King's good people. I " have fome reafon to know this, that have been an attendant " to the Court thefe five years, for myfelf and a dear friend of " mine, fometime knight of our fhire, for a mere trivial bufi- " nefs. The moft that could be proved againft him was the " putting on his hat in the time of fermon." But, alas! Mr. Bagfhaw yielded afterwards to Hyde's temptations, and joined the party of the King. *[Cafe of a hat.]*

to their friends and to their callings; thrice happy, if not feparated for ever from the ftudies they cherifhed and the affociates they loved. Yet, even fo adminiftered, the Star Chamber ftill fell fhort of the perfect tyranny which the Primate fought to eftablifh over opinion and confcience throughout England. It was not until the feverity of the High Commiffion, yet further fharpened by the rigour of the Council Table, had brought the Star Chamber at laft into the form and ufes of a Romifh Inquifition, that Archbifhop Laud at length feemed fatisfied (51, 52, 53, 54, and 55). And while its fufpenfions, excommunications, deprivations, and degradations, fell daily upon learned and pious minifters, whofe zeal marked them out in its metropolitan jurifdiction, Bifhops' Courts were eftablifhed throughout the country on a fimilar model, which, though not reaching fo high in extremity of punifhment, made themfelves more generally grievous by the multiplicity of their vile perfecutions. No man was now fo poor as not to know what ecclefiaftical domination meant. It lighted upon the meaner fort of tradefmen. It ftruck the induftrious artificer. It impoverifhed by thoufands large claffes of the people. And thofe whom in that refpect it fpared, it yet fo afflicted and troubled, that great numbers departed, with all that they poffeffed, into Holland, into New England, into whatfoever land or wafte beyond the fea the oppreffed confcience might hope for freedom. Such was the extent of this emigration, that it was felt in that fpring and fountain of Englifh wealth, the

Abstract: Government by Prerogative. 239

woollen-cloth manufacture, as well by the transport abroad as by diminution of the stock at home.

The clauses remaining to be enumerated in this section of the Remonstrance, the 48th, 50th, 56th, 57th, 58th, 59th, and 60th, spoke of appointments to offices; of distributions of preferments; of tamperings with the magistracy; and of the predominance at the Council Table of one or two favoured Ministers, by whose counsels all others were negatived or overruled. The divines selected for promotion in the Church were those in whose pulpits the prerogative had been preached above the law, superstitious formalities elevated above religion, and the property and rights of the subject most decried;* and it became quite the fashion to put forth these doctrines in public and solemn sermons before the King.† The sheriffs in the several counties were no longer named in the usual course; but, when they escaped being the victims of oppression, were made its instruments. They were either pricked for sheriffs as a punishment and charge, or as mere agents or commissioners ‡ to execute

Clauses 48, 50, 56, 57, 58, 59, and 60.

Church preferments.

Pulpit doctrines.

Use and abuse of Sheriffs.

---

* " Ministers in their pulpits," said Wentworth, talking, in his days of patriotism, of the sovereign's monstrous claim to the subject's estate, " have preached it as gospel, and damned " the refusers of it."

† I find in the Journals of the 10th of November, a notice of motion for insertion in the Remonstrance, to which no name is attached, of " The sermons preached in divers places " before the King that the subject had no property in his " estate."

‡ Adverting to the common and ordinary instructions of the Council to the various Commissions they issued against the subject, that they should " proceed according to their discre- " tion" it had been well said in the House by Hyde himself:

Royalist preachers.

Hyde on the Coun-

	what the Council would have to be done. So, no less, it fared with the magistracies and places of great trust in the counties. Whosoever had shown the wish to maintain religion, liberty,
Treatment of patriots:	

	"Such a confusion hath this 'discretion' produced, as if discretion were only one remove from rage and fury. No inconvenience, no mischief, no disgrace, that the malice, or insolence, or animosity of these commissioners had a mind to bring upon that people [he is speaking of the assumed jurisdiction of the Court of York], but, thro' the latitude and power of this 'discretion,' the poor people have felt. This 'discretion' hath been the quicksand which hath swallowed up their property, their liberty. I beseech you, rescue them from this 'discretion.'" Mr. Hyde took great pride to himself in after years for his patriotic exertions in this matter, and with infinite self-complacency tells us how, on his joining the King at York on the eve of the war, he became curiously aware of the impression which his exposure of the "Council of the North" had made in that ancient city. One of the King's servants had taken a lodging for him before his arrival, which he found to be an excellent lodging; and, in the greatest good humour therewith, he was undressing for bed, when his own servant came up to him from a lower room in much alarm, protested that the people of the house must be mad, and entreated him to leave the place at once. By no means disposed to quit hastily such comfortable quarters, he insisted upon the why and wherefore, to which the man replied that nothing could be more civil than the conduct of the people at first; and that he was himself made welcome in the room below, occupied by the mistress of the house; and that, sitting together there quite pleasantly, "she asked him what his master's name was, which he told her. *What!* said she: *That Hyde that is of the House of Commons!* And he answering Yes, she gave a great shriek, and cried out that he should not lodge in her house: cursing him with many bitter execrations. Upon the noise, her husband came in; and when she told him who it was that was to lodge in the chamber above, he swore a great oath that he should not; and that he would rather set his house on fire than entertain him in it. . . . He knew him well enough: he had undone him, and his wife, and his children!" Such was the servant's account, with more oaths, and flamming of doors, than may here be dwelt on; and for which, on Mr. Hyde's resolving nevertheless to wait till morning to try and find out some rational explanation, the next day brought reason enough. "The man of the house had been an Attorney in the Court of the President and Council of the North, in great reputation and practice
Council of the North.	
Anecdote of Hyde at York.	
Trouble at his lodgings.	
Landlady curses and abuses him.	
The mystery explained.	

Abstract: Government by Prerogative.

and the laws, were weeded out of the commission of peace, and all employments of influence in their districts; which afterwards passed, by secret bribery or open purchase, into the least worthy hands. Titles of honour, serjeantships of law, and places affecting the common justice of the kingdom, were made matters of open bargain in this way, passing to men of the weakest parts; and of course what were ill gotten were ill administered and ill used. Nor did the course of terrorism and corruption, thus taking in the middle and higher grades, and already stretching down, as we have seen, to the lowest, stop upward until the highest were reached. It had its consummation only at the very council-table of the King. There sat councillors, who were councillors only in name; and whose sole use was to confirm, in a few, the real power and authority. Though otherwise persons of never so great abilities and honour, whosoever opposed those few were

excluded from offices and honours.

Terrorism and corruption.

Strafford's and Laud's

" there; and thereby got a very good livelihood, with which
" he had lived in splendour; and Mr. Hyde had sat in the chair
" of that Committee, and had carried up the votes of the Com-
" mons against that Court, to the House of Peers, upon which
" it was dissolved." (*Life*, i. 149-152.) Another trait of
the time worth preserving may be taken from the same part
of Clarendon's recollections. Rapidity of communication
had then become of vital necessity to the king's service, and
he takes occasion to mention the marvellous speed wherewith
it had become possible to accomplish the journey between
London and York. It *is* (even to us in these days) remarkable.
" It was a wonderful expedition that was then used between
" York and London, when gentlemen undertook the service,
" as enough were willing to do; insomuch as when they
" despatched a letter on Saturday night, at that time of the
" year (end of April), about twelve at night, they received
" always the King's answer, Monday by ten of the clock
" in the morning." *Life* i. 135.

Travelling between London and York.

R

marked out for difcountenance and neglect; and the refolutions of ftate which were brought to the table, were not offered for debate and deliberation, but merely for countenance and execution.

Such being the ftate of the kingdom in the clofing months of 1639 (I now proceed to ftate the fubftance of the next 15 claufes, from the 61ft to the 75th inclufive), all things appeared ripe for putting the finifhing touches to the great defign of the leading men, the few juft named, which, as was now made fufficiently obvious, had three diftinct parts. A folemn adjudication of fhip-money had been lately obtained; and the Government was to be fet free from all reftraint of laws in regard to perfons and eftates. There muft be an identification (only not as yet to be called Popery) betwixt Papifts and Proteftants, in doctrine, difcipline, and ceremonies. And the Puritans,* who remained ftill as the Englifh wall or partition flung up againft Rome, muft be either rooted out of the kingdom with force, or driven out by fear (61, 62, 63, 64). The main ftumbling-block to the entirenefs of the plan was Scotland; and Laud, bent on doing the work thoroughly, now ftruck in there with his fervice book, his new canons, and his liturgy. The Scots refifted; the Archbifhop

Sidenotes: predominance at council. Claufes 61-67. Defign of the Court. Puritans the partition againft Rome: to be flung down. Who were called Puritans.

---

* "Whofoever fquares his actions by any rule, either divine "or human, he is a Puritan; whofoever would be governed "by the King's laws, he is a Puritan; he that will not do "whatfoever other men would have him do, he is a Puritan. "Their great work, their mafterpiece, now is, to make all "thofe of the true religion to be the fufpected party of the "kingdom."—*Sir Benjamin Rudyard*, Nov. 7, 1640.

Abstract: Government by Prerogative.

would not recede; and, occupying filently either fide of the Tweed, two armies gradually arofe (65, 66, 67). Scotch Rebellion.

But, when they were ready to encounter, counfels of fear, if not of prudence, led to the pacification of Berwick; which had however hardly been completed, when Strafford refumed his place at the council board, condemned the courfe that had been taken, and advifed what he declared to be the Crown's laft and beft refource, the fummoning of a parliament.* Not indeed to give counfel and advice, but to reftrict itfelf to the giving of countenance and fupply; for, to men who had corrupted and diftempered the whole frame and government of the kingdom, the attempt alfo to corrupt what alone could reftore all to a right frame again, was become matter of fafety and neceffity. If the plan fhould fucceed, and parliament be pliant, the feffion would be continued, and mifchief eftablifhed by a law. If it fhould fail, and parliament be ftubborn, the feffion would at once be broken, and the Crown abfolved for ufing foul means by the

Claufes 68-75. Strafford at the Council Board. His reafons for a parliament.

---

* The fubjoined is characteriftic of the feeling of the time.

"The 27 of March, 15 Car. 1639, his Majeftie rode
" through Roifton to Yorkeward, there to meete his army,
" &c. It was told me, April 1, that whereas it is an ufe to
" deliver billes to the ficke to be praid for in this manner;
" one from the church dore, perhaps in the throng, pulles
" another by the fhoulder, and gives him the note or bill, he
" another &c. untill it come to [the] clerke; the clerke, at
" the preacher's comming into the pulpit, delivers them to
" him, &c. Some one had put up a bill which the preacher
" wold not reade, but let it fall. The bill was thus: *John*
" *Commonwealth's-man of Great Britaine, being ficke of the*
" *Scottifh difeafe, defires the prayers of this congregation for a*
" *parliament.*"—*Diary of Rous*, 88.

Diary of Rous, March, 1639. Prayers for a parliament.

pretence of having endeavoured to ufe fair (68, 69, 70, 71, 72). Simultaneoufly with the iffue of writs, went forth levies for a new army, with frefh acts of violence againft the Scots. At the fame time, Strafford, paffing over into Ireland, called together a parliament in Dublin; wrefted from it four fubfidies; and, without concealing the purpofe for which they were defigned, fummoned levies of eight thoufand foot and one thoufand horfe from the well-appointed army, chiefly of Papifts, which he had been able to raife in that kingdom (73, 74, 75).

His Irifh levies againft the Scots.

4. *The Short Parliament and the Scottifh Invafion.*

Claufes 76-78.

THE meeting of the Houfes at Weftminfter on the 13th April, 1640; the demand of twelve fubfidies for the releafe of fhip-money alone; the temperate tone of both the Commons and the Lords, and the fudden and intemperate diffolution; occupy claufes 76, 77, and 78. The next twenty-fix, from the 79th to the 104th inclufive, defcribe the momentous interval before the affembling of the Long Parliament.

Claufes 79—84.

On the very day of the diffolution of the Parliament of April, the King's moft powerful Counfellor advifed that he was now abfolved from all rule of government, and entitled to fupply himfelf out of his fubjects' eftates without their confent.* A vigorous levy of

Strafford's fatal counfel:

---

* This memorable advice, which coft Strafford his head, was given on the 5th May 1640; and it was from the notes

Abstract: Short Parliament & Scottish Invasion. 245

ship-money was accordingly ordered; a forced loan was set on foot in the city of London; a false and scandalous Declaration against the House of Commons was issued in the King's name; on the day following the dissolution, some members of both houses had their studies and cabinets, " yea, their pockets," searched;* and soon after, for having maintained the privilege of parliament, one of the members of the lower House was committed from the Council Table. Harsher courses were contemplated, and the report of them went abroad; but the sickness of the Earl of Strafford, and a tumultuous rising in Southwark and about Lambeth,† were supposed to have intercepted

Its results.

Dissolution of Short Parliament.

Arrests of Parliament men.

Riots at Southwark and Lambeth.

Allusions by Clarendon.

of the elder Vane, taken that day at the Council Table, and subsequently found by his son and handed to Pym, that the evidence was obtained against him.
    * " Sir William Beecher was committed to the usher of
" the blacke rod for not disclosing his warrant to serche the
" pockets of Erle of Warwicke, Lord Say, Lord Brooke,
" presently after the last parliament broken up. It was done
" the next morne to the Lord Say and Lord Brooke in bedde;
" the Lord Brooke's lady being in bedde with him. The
" King at length affirming that he commanded it, he was
" released."—*Diary of John Rous,* p. 101.
    † " Upon the dissolution of the parliament (5th May, 1640)
" presently were two insurrections in one weeke, at South-
" wark and Lambeth; in the first the White Lion pryson
" was broken and prisoners set free, &c.; in the second, Lam-
" beth House in hazard, &c. One man was taken, and
" hanged and quartered."—*Diary of John Rous,* p. 90. Clarendon tells us, (*Hist.* i. 253) that the reference to the Lambeth riots in the Remonstrance received modification during the debates. What he says is characteristic, as well for its dishonest reference to those riots (for which one man suffered execution), as for its allusion to Mr. Strode. " This infa-
" mous, scandalous, headless insurrection, quashed by the
" deserved death of that one varlet, was not thought to be
" contrived or fomented by any persons of quality, yet it was
" discovered after in the House of Commons by Mr. Strode
" (one of those Ephori who most avowed the curbing and

the execution of them. (79, 80, 81, 82, 83, 84.)

Clauſes 85-87.

Laud ſtill moving to Rome.

Crown above the Laws:

Nevertheleſs they failed to turn aſide the Archbiſhop from his eager and unſwerving advance to Rome. Undaunted and undeterred by diſcontents and tumults, never did he and the other biſhops follow up that purpoſe more actively than in thoſe ſix memorable months. If any before could have doubted what they aimed at, now it was made plain to all. For now it was that, with the authority of a ſo-called provincial ſynod, canons were put forth declaring things lawful which had no warrant of law; juſtifying altar-worſhip, and other ſuperſtitious innovations;* ſetting at defiance the uſages and the ſtatutes of the realm; trampling alike on the property and liberty of the ſubject, the rights of Parliament, and the prerogative of the King; and ſhowing that they who would ſet the Crown above the

"ſuppreſſing of Majeſty) with much pleaſure and content;
"and it was mentioned in the firſt draught of the firſt Re-
"monſtrance (when the ſame was brought in by Mr. Pym)
"not without a touch of approbation, which was for that
"reaſon ſomewhat altered, though it ſtill carried nothing of
"cenſure [judgment] upon it in that piece." It is quite true, as Clarendon alleges, that only one man ſuffered death for this diſturbance, but it was not the clemency of the Government, but of one of the few upright judges of the day, which

An honeſt judge.

had prevented other capital proſecutions. "Judge Reeve," ſays Rous, November, 1640, "this ſummer aſſizes did in
"Southwarke refuſe to proceede upon the inditement of one
"of the Lambeth tumult, ſaying he wold have no hand in
"any man's bloud; but, becauſe the fellow had been buſie,
"&c. remitted him to priſon againe." *Diary*, 101.

Sir Ben. Rudyard.

* "They would evaporate and diſpirit the power and
"vigour of religion by drawing it out into ſolemn ſpecious
"formalities, into obſolete antiquated ceremonies new fur-
"biſhed up."—*Sir Benjamin Rudyard*, 7th Nov. 1640.

Abstract: Short Parliament & Scottish Invasion.

laws, would also set themselves above the Crown. They imposed new oaths; they taxed the great mass of the clergy for the King's supply;* they fomented the quarrel with Scotland, which they fondly styled *Bellum Episcopale*;† they composed, and enjoined to be read in the churches, a prayer against the Scots as rebels, of which the object was to drive the two nations to irreconcileable bloodshed; and, above all, upon authority of their pretended canons and constitutions, they proceeded to such extremities of suspension, excommunication, and deprivation against good ministers and well-affected people, as left the passage easier than it yet had seemed to their design of reconciliation with Rome. (85, 86, 87.)

For it was part of the design that the Papists at this time should receive peculiar exemptions from the penal laws, besides many other encouragements and court favours.‡ They

Mitre above Crown.

Church oppression.

Clauses 88-94.

---

* "Sir, imagine it!" exclaimed Mr. Harbottle Grimston. "See what a pitch they have flown! A synod called together upon pretence of reconciling and settling controversies in religion, take upon themselves the boldness, out of parliament, to grant subsidies and to meddle with men's freeholds! I say, the like was never heard of before; and they that durst do this will do worse, if the current of their raging tyranny be not stopped in time."

† In the last great debate on the Remonstrance, Falkland (of all men in the world) took objection specially to this passage; feeble and faint transcription as it is, of what, some few months earlier, he was never himself wearied of urging and repeating in fiery and passionate speeches.

‡ The celebration of mass, though illegal, was openly connived at; but woe to the Protestant who declined attendance at his parish church because he would not bow to the altar! He was punished first by fine, and, on a repetition of his refusal, by transportation. "It hath been more dangerous,"

Grimston.

Falkland.

Mass connived at:

Defigns and power of Papifts.

Secret meetings.

poffeffed, in the King's fecretary of ftate, Sir Francis Windebank, a powerful agent for fpeeding all their defires.* They had a refident Pope's Nuncio, by whofe authority, under direct inftructions and influences from Rome itfelf, all the moft influential of the nobility, gentry, and clergy of that perfuafion held fecret convocations after the manner of a parliament. So led and ftrengthened, they erected

conventicles made criminal.

Favour to Papifts.

Matters fubject to monopoly.

exclaimed Falkland, in his fpeech upon grievances in the Short Parliament, " for men to go to fome neighbour's parifh " when they had no fermon in their own, than to be obftinate " and perpetual recufants. While maffes have been faid in " fecurity, a conventicle hath been a crime; and, which is " yet more, the conforming to Ceremonies hath been more " exacted than the conforming to Chriftianity." In like manner the Roman Catholics were fingled out for fpecial conceffions of monopolies. " They grew," fays Clarendon, " not only fecret contrivers but public profeffed promoters " of, and minifters in, the moft grievous projects; as that of " foap, formed, framed, and executed by almoft a corporation " of that religion, which, under that licenfe and notion, " might be, and were fufpected to be, qualified for other " agitations" (i. 262). Fancy the monopoly of fuch a neceffity as foap in the hands of a corporation of Roman Catholics, ufing it to impofe the worft articles at the higheft price upon all claffes of the people ! " Continual complaints rife up," writes Garrard to Lord Deputy Wentworth, " that it burns " linen, fcalds the laundrefs's fingers, and waftes infinitely in " keeping, being full of lime and tallow." And fancy the fame fort of thing going on with refpect to every conceivable thing on which a tax could be laid, or out of which a monopoly could be formed ! Salt, ftarch, coals, iron, wine, pens, cards, dice, beavers, belts, bone-lace, meat dreffed in taverns (the vintners of London gave the King 6000*l.* for freedom from this horrible impofition), tobacco, wine cafks, game, lamprons, brewing and diftilling, weighing of hay and ftraw in London, guaging of red herrings, butter-cafks, kelp and feaweed, linen cloth, rags, hops, buttons, hats, gut-ftring, fpectacles, combs, tobacco-pipes, fedan chairs, and hackney coaches (now firft invented), faltpetre, gunpowder, down to the privilege of gathering rags exclufively—all thefe things were fubject to monopolies, and all heavily taxed!

* For proof in all refpects confirmatory of this ftatement, fee Clarendon's *Hiftory*, i. 311-12.

Abstract: Short Parliament & Scottish Invasion.

new jurisdictions of Romish Archbishops;
levied taxes; secretly stored up arms and
munition; and were able to set in motion
such powerful agencies, at the Court and in Agencies
the Council, that it actually there became   at Court
matter of debate whether or not to issue to and in
some great men of the party, under private   Council.
conditions and instructions, a commission for
the raising of soldiers. And thus there was *Imperium*
moulded within the English State another State *in imperio.*
independent in Government, opposed in affec-
tion and interest, secretly corrupting the careless,
actively combining against the vigilant, and in
this posture waiting the opportunity to destroy
those whom it could not hope to seduce.*
(88 to 94 inclusive.)

* Let me illustrate what is said in the text by one of the Speech by
most masterly expositions ever made of the true state of the Rudyard.
case, and of the real issue that was then to be determined.
" Sir," said Sir Benjamin Rudyard, in perhaps the most
eloquent of all the speeches delivered in the great debates
of November 1640, " if we secure our Religion, we shall
" cut off and defeat many plots that are now on foot by
" them and others. Believe it, Sir, Religion hath been for a
" long time, and still is, the great design upon this kingdom.
" It is a known and practised principle, that they who would
" introduce another religion into the Church, must first trouble State and
" and disorder the government of the State, that so they may Church
" work their ends in a confusion: which now lies at the   grievances
" door. . . . . . . I have often thought and said, that it must insepara-
" be some great extremity that would recover and rectify this ble.
" State; and when that extremity did come, it would be a
" great hazard whether it might prove a Remedy or Ruin.
" We are now, Mr. Speaker, upon that vertical turning
" point, and therefore it is no time to palliate, to foment our
" own undoing. . . . . To discover the diseases of the State is
" (according to some) to traduce the Government; yet others
" are of opinion that this is the half-way to the cure. . . . . .
" Men that talk loudly of the King's service and yet have
" done none but their own, that speak highly of the King's
" power yet have made it a miserable power producing nothing
" but weakness, these are they who have always peremptorily

Clauses 95-104.

Prisons full.

Non-parliamentary supply exhausted.

Discontent of Lords:

But a crisis came unexpectedly. At the moment when any further illegal pressure on the subject seemed hopeless, his Majesty's treasure was found to be consumed, and his entire revenue to be anticipated. Though the prisons were filled with commitments from the Council Table,* yet "multitudes" who had refused illegal payments still hung in attendance at its doors. Several of the sheriffs had been dragged up into the Star Chamber from their respective counties, and some had been imprisoned for not having levied ship-money with sufficient vigour. In a word, the source of non-parliamentary supply was exhausted. The people, with no visible hope left but in desperation, languished, beginning to seem passive under grief and fear; and the King's chief advisers suggested a subscription to supply his wants, to which they made very large personal contribution. But the example was lost on the class to which alone, with any effect, the appeal could be made. For now the Nobility themselves, weary of their silence and patience, began to be sensible of the duty and trust which belonged to them as hereditary counsel-

---

Ruin of old monarchy.

"pursued one obstinate pernicious course. First, they bring things to an extremity; then they make that extremity, of their own making, the reason of their next action, seven times worse than the former. And there, Sir, we are at this instant. They have almost spoiled the best instituted Government in the world, for sovereignty in a king, for liberty to the subject; the proportionable temper of both which, makes the happiest State for power, for riches, for duration."

Yonge's Diary.

* "Many are daily imprisoned for refusing to lend the King, so that the prisons in London are full; and it's thought they shall be sent and imprisoned in divers gaols in the country, remote from their own dwellings."— *Walter Yonge's Diary,* p. 105.

Abstract: Short Parliament & Scottish Invasion.

lors of the Crown; and some of the most ancient of them petitioned his Majesty for the redress to which his subjects were entitled.*

petition for Parliament.

* This memorable Petition, which was afterwards the subject of special thanks in both Houses, which bore attached to it the names of the Earls of Bedford, Bristol, Hertford, Essex, Mulgrave, Paget, Warwick, and Bolingbroke, of the Viscounts Say and Seale, and Mandeville, and of the Lords Brook, and Howard of Escrick, has never been so correctly printed as in the copy now subjoined. Every word has its weight and value.

The York Declaration.

" The humble Petition of your Majesty's most loyal sub-
" jects, whose names are here underwritten, in behalfe of
" themselves and many others.

' Most Gracious Sovereign:
' The sense of that duty and service which we owe unto
' your Majesty, and our earnest affection to the good and
' welfare of this your realm of England, have moved us, in
' all humility, to beseech your Majesty to give us leave to
' offer unto your most princely wisdom, the apprehension
' which we, and other your faithful subjects, have conceived,
' of the great distempers and dangers now threatening the
' Church and State, and your Royal Person, and of the fittest
' means by which they may be removed and prevented.
' The Evils and Dangers whereof your Majesty may be
' pleased to take notice are these:
' 1. That your Majesty's sacred person is exposed to hazard
' and danger in the present expedition against the Scotish
' armie: and by the occasion of this war, your revenues much
' wasted; your subjects burthened with Coat and Conduct
' money, with Billeting of Souldiers and other Military
' Charges, with divers rapines and disorders committed in
' several parts in this your realm by the souldiers raised for
' that service; and your whole kingdom become full of care
' and discontent.
' 2. The sundry innovations in matters of Religion, the
' Oath and Canons lately imposed upon the clergy, and other
' your Majesty's subjects.
' 3. The great Increase of Popery; and Employing of
' Popish Recusants, and others ill-affected to the Religion by
' Law established, in places of power and trust, especially in
' commanding of Men and Armes both in the Field and in
' sundry Counties of this your realm: whereas, by the Laws,
' they are not permitted to have Armes in their own houses.
' 4. The great mischief which may fall upon this king-
' dom, if the Intention, which hath been credibly reported,

Dangers to State and Church.

Grievances of subject.

Innovations in religion.

Which Petition had yet borne no fruit, when the Scots, oppreſſed in their conſciences, reſtrained in their trades, impoveriſhed by the

> 'of bringing in of Iriſh and foreign forces ſhould take
> 'effect.

Taxation without repreſentation.
> '5. The urging of Ship-money, and proſecution of ſome
> 'ſheriffs in the Star-chamber for not Levying of it.
> '6. The heavy charges upon Merchandize, to the diſ-
> 'couraging of Trade. The multitude of Monopolies, and
> 'other Patents, whereby the Commodities and Manufactures
> 'of the Kingdom are much burthened, to the great and
> 'univerſal Grievance of your people.
> '7. The great grief of your ſubjects by the long Intermiſ-
> 'ſion of Parliaments, and the late and former Diſſolving of
> 'ſuch as have been called, without the happy effects which
> 'otherwiſe they might have produced.
> 'For remedy whereof, and prevention of the danger that
> 'may enſue to your Royal perſon, and to the whole State,

Parliament the only remedy.
> 'We do, in all humility and faithfulneſs, beſeech your
> 'moſt excellent Majeſty, that you will be pleaſed to ſummon
> 'a Parliament within ſome ſhort and convenient time, where-
> 'by the cauſe of theſe and other great greivances which your
> 'people and your poor Petitioners now lye under, may be
> 'taken away, and the Authours and Councellours of them
> 'may be there brought to ſuch Legal Tryal and condign
> 'puniſhment as the nature of their ſeveral offences ſhall require;
> 'and that the preſent War may be compoſed by your Ma-
> 'jeſties wiſdom without effuſion of blood, in ſuch manner as
> 'may conduce to the honour and ſafety of your Majeſties
> 'perſon, the content of your people, and the unity of both of
> 'your realms againſt common enemies of the Reformed
> 'Religion.'
> "And your Majeſty's Petitioners ſhall always pray, &c."

Story by Shafteſbury.
A ſingular anecdote is told of this petition on no leſs authority than that of the firſt Lord Shafteſbury. It occurs with his ſignature in Locke's Common Place Book (King's *Life*, i. 222), and other undoubted references by Shafteſbury to the ſame ſtory (Martyn's *Life*, i. 115, 119), eſtabliſh the authorſhip: "This petition," he ſays, "was preſented to the King "at York by the hands of the Lord Mandeville and the Lord "Howard. The King immediately called a Cabinet Council, "wherein it was concluded to cut off both the lords' heads

Firſt reſolve of the Court:
"the next day; when the Council was up, and the King "gone, Duke Hamilton and the Earl of Strafford, general of "the army, remaining behind, when Duke Hamilton, aſking "the Earl of Strafford whether the army would ſtand to them, "the Earl of Strafford anſwered he feared not, and proteſted

Abstract: Acts of the Long Parliament.

seizure of their ships in English and Irish
ports, and hopeless of satisfying the King by
any naked unsupported supplication, forced The
the passage of the Tyne at Newburn with a Scotch
powerful army; and having possessed themselves invasion.
of Newcastle, there, out of brotherly love to
the English nation, stayed their march, and
gave the King leisure to entertain better counsels. A cessation of arms was determined
upon for a certain fixed period, and all differences were referred in the interval to the wis- Parlia-
dom and care of the Ancient Council of the ment sum-
nation. A Parliament was summoned to meet 3d Nov.
on the 3rd November, 1640. (95 to 104 1640.
inclusive.)

5. Acts of the Long Parliament.

THE great deeds done by this memorable Clauses
assembly during the first twelve months of 105&110.
its existence, are then, in no boastful or vain-
glorious spirit, detailed by their authors. History speaks to us, here, while yet in the very
process of creation; and, by a rare privilege, Heroes of
records the actions of her heroes in language the Long

" he did not think of that before then. Hamilton replied, if
" we are not sure of the army, it may be our heads instead of
" theirs; whereupon they both agreed to go to the King and second
" alter the Council, which accordingly they did." There are thoughts.
some probabilities against the story, but at least it vividly reflects
the popular belief of the singularly dangerous and critical
turning point to which public affairs, and all actors in them,
had then unquestionably come. I take the opportunity of Shaftes-
referring to the Papers respecting the first Lord Shaftesbury's bury
life, of which a portion has been lately published by Mr. Papers.
Christie, as extremely interesting in themselves, and not un-
likely to clear off some mists of exaggeration and prejudice
from a famous historic name.

The Grand Remonſtrance.

Parliament. they have themſelves left to us. They do not underſtate the work they had to do; nor do they exaggerate their own power in doing it. All oppoſition, they remark, ſeemed to have vaniſhed when firſt they met. So evident were the miſchiefs, ſo manifeſt the evil of the counſellors reſponſible for them, that no man Their taſk. ſtood up to defend either. Yet very arduous was the work of reformation. The difficulties ſeemed to be inſuperable, which by the Divine Providence they overcame: the contrarieties incompatible, which yet in a great meaſure they reconciled. (105 and 110.)

Clauſes 106-109, and 111-124. It was not only that the multiplied evils and corruption of ſixteen years ſtrengthened by authority and cuſtom, and that the powerful delinquents whoſe intereſts were identified with their continuance, were together to be brought to judgment; but that two armies were to be Two armies paid. paid, at a coſt of near 80,000*l*. a month; that the King's houſehold was to be ſupplied, in even its ordinary and neceſſary expenſes; and that the people were yet to be tenderly charged, as already exhauſted by unjuſt and groſs exactions (106, 107, 108, and 109). And all this was Twelve ſubſidies raiſed. done. During the year, twelve ſubſidies had been raiſed, to the amount of 600,000*l*.; yet had the kingdom been ſubſtantially no loſer by thoſe charges. Ship-money, which drew ſupplies almoſt without limit from the ſubject, Grievances redreſſed. was aboliſhed. Coat and conduct-money, and other military aſſeſſments, in many counties amounting to little leſs than ſhip-money, were declared illegal and removed. Monopolies, of which but the leading few, ſuch as ſoap, wine, leather, and falt, prejudiced the common people to the amount of nearly a million and a half yearly, were univerfally fuppreffed.* And, what was more beneficial than all, the root of thefe intolerable evils had been extirpated.

Monopolies abolifhed.

* No one was more eager againft the Remonftrance, or fought every ftage of it with a more impaffioned refiftance, than Sir John Culpeper, fo foon to be appointed "for life" Chancellor of the Exchequer (until Hyde was ready to affume that office, when Culpeper became a lord and Mafter of the Rolls); yet it was he who, at the meeting of the Long Parliament, had fpoken that memorable fpeech againft monopolies and projectors which might have fupplied Sydney Smith with his famous diatribe on the univerfality of Britifh taxation two hundred years later. "It is a neft of wafps, or fwarm of vermin, which "have overcrept the land; I mean the monopolers and polers "of the people. Like the frogs of Egypt, they have gotten "the poffeffion of our dwellings, and we have fcarce a room "free from them. They fup in our cup, they dip in our "difh, they fit by our fire. We find them in the dye-fat, the "wafh-bowl, and the powdering-tub. They fhare with the "butler in his box. They have marked and fealed us from "head to foot. Mr. Speaker, they will not bait us a pin. We "may not buy our own clothes without their brokage." To illuftrate the operation of fome of thefe monopolies, a ftriking paffage may alfo be taken from a fpeech of Pym's, in which he undertook to fhow that the gain of the King was wonderfully difproportioned to the lofs of the Subject. "In France, "not long fince, upon a furvey of the King's revenue, it was "found that two parts in three never came to the King's "purfe, but were diverted to the profit of the officers and "minifters of the Crown; and it was thought a very good "fervice and reformation to reduce two parts to the King, "leaving ftill a third part to the inftruments that were em-
"ployed about getting it in. It may well be doubted if the "King have the like or worfe fuccefs in England. For "inftance, he hath referved upon the monopoly of wines "thirty thoufand pound rent a year; the vintner pays forty "fhillings a tun, which comes to ninety thoufand pounds; "the price upon the fubject by retail is increafed twopence a "quart, which comes to eight pounds a tun, and for forty-"five thoufand tun brought in yearly amounts to three "hundred and fixty thoufand pounds; which is three hundred "and thirty thoufand pounds lofs to the kingdom, above the "King's rent!"

Culpepper againft projectors.

Swarm of monopolift vermin.

Speech by Pym:

fmall gain to King from large lofs to Subject.

256   *The Grand Remonstrance.*

<small>Taxation restored to Commons.</small> The judgment of both Houses, subsequently embodied in a statute, had put an end for ever to the arbitrary power pretended to be in the King, of taxing the subject, or charging their estates, without consent of their representatives in parliament. Judgment had been dealt, also, upon the living grievances; upon the evil counsellors, and actors, of treason to the commonwealth. <small>Delinquents punished.</small> The Earl of Strafford had perished on the scaffold. Lord Finch, the Lord Keeper, and Sir Francis Windebank, the Secretary of State, had taken flight into ignominious exile. Archbishop Laud and Judge Berkeley were lodged in the Tower. And such was the report gone forth of these memorable acts of retribution, that not the present only, but all future times, were like to find safety and preservation therein. (111 to 124 inclusive.)

<small>Clauses 127-136, 125 and 126, and 137-142.</small> Through ten succeeding clauses the great recital continued. The abolition of the Star Chamber, of the High Commission, and of the Courts of the President and Council in the North, as of so many forges of oppression, misery, and violence,* was exultingly detailed.

<small>Ralph Verney to James Dillon: 1634.</small>   * To what extent these courts might be, and were, made to minister to oppression, could only be shown by a relation too particular for this place; but there is a letter from Ralph Verney to his friend James Dillon, describing Prynne's fine and punishment, which remarkably illustrates the reckless liberty of indulgence to private spleen and passion, on which they were all based, and by which all were governed. The judgment for a fine, as will be observed, was taken on the average of the various sums suggested.
   1633—4. *February* 26*th.* " I did but even now receave a " letter from you, wherein you desire an account of Mr. " Prinn's censure. To satisfie you therein. He is to be " degraded in the Universitie, disbarred at the Innes of Court;

Abstract: Acts of the Long Parliament.

And thofe votes of both Houfes were recounted, which had taken away the immoderate power of the Council Table; had blafted for ever the defign of overriding gofpel and law by canons of the Church; had ftruck down the exorbitancies of Bifhops and their courts; had punifhed fcandalous minifters; had reformed the foreft laws; had put an end to the encroachments and oppreffions of the Stannary Courts; had abolifhed the extortions of the Clerk of the Market; had relieved the fubject of the vexations of the old laws of knighthood; and, of all thefe and other as grievous public wrongs, left no more trace or veftige than might fuffice to tell to future generations the ftory of the miferies they had occafioned.* (127 to 136 inclufive.) In the fame recital, but ftanding apart from the general ftatement of redrefs, was the mention made (125 and

Overthrow of tyranny:
Ecclefiaftical and Civil.
How accomplifhed.

" he was fined in foure thoufand pounds by fome, by others
" in 5,000li., in 6,000li., in 10,000li; but which of thefe does
" now ftand I cannot refolve you, becaufe I counted not in
" which of thefe fummes moft of the Lords did agree; but I
" believe it was in 4000li. He was withall condemned to the
" loffe of his ears, whereof he is to part with one at Weftmin-
" fter, with the other at Cheapfide, where, whileft an officer
" doeth execution on him felf, the hangman is to doe execu-
" tion on his booke, and burne it before his face. He is
" withall to fuffer perpetuall imprifonment by the decree of
" the Starr Chamber. *There were of the lords, that counted*
" *this not enough; they would have his nofe flitt, his arme*
" *cutt off, and penn and inke for ever withheld from him; but*
" *thefe were but fewe, and their cenfure ftood not."*

Prynne's punifhment defcribed.

* A claufe introduced in the courfe of this fummary, having reference to the Court of Requefts, was fubfequently objected to by the liberal leaders, and on a divifion was rejected by 187 to 123 (this was the firft divifion on the great day when the final vote was taken), Sir John Clotworthy and Sir Thomas Barrington being tellers for the majority, and for the minority, Mr. Stanhope and Sir F. Cornwallis.

Court of Requefts divifion.

s

126) of the two memorable ſtatutes, for triennial parliaments, and for prevention of any abrupt diſſolution of the exiſting parliament, as conſtituting not only a remedy for the preſent, but a perpetual ſpring of remedies for the future; and, cloſing the ſtatement (137 to 142 incluſive), was a brief ſketch or intimation of other contemplated meaſures, which the exiſtence of thoſe two ſafeguards had enabled them to prepare with ſome reaſonable certainty of enactment even before the cloſe of the ſeſſion. Among them were laws and proviſions for defining and ſettling the powers of the biſhops; for abating pride and idleneſs in the clergy; for eaſing the people of needleſs and ſuperſtitious ceremonies; for removing unworthy, and maintaining godly, preachers; for ſo eſtabliſhing the King's revenue, as both to cut off ſuperfluities, and make more certain all neceſſary payments; for ſo regulating courts of juſtice as to abridge both the delays and the coſts of law; for better ſettling of the currency, and equality of exchanges; for increaſing manufactures and facilitating trade; for putting an end to the iniquities of preſs-money;* and for ſo improving the herring fiſhery on their own coaſts, as not only to give large employment to the poor, but to create and cheriſh a plentiful nurſery of ſeamen.

Marginalia: Two famous Statutes. Other acts prepared: titles and object thereof. Horror of impreſſment.

* In the Schedule of Grievances, before referred to, appears " the compelling ſome free-men, by impriſonment and threat-
" ening, to take preſſe-money; and others, for feare of the
" like impriſonment, to forſake their place of habitation, hid-
" ing themſelves in woods, whereby their families are left to
" ye charge of the pariſh, and harveſt worke undone for want
" of labourers." *Diary of John Rous*, p. 92.

Abstract : Practices of the Court Party.

6. *Practices of the Court Party.*

THEN arose, in connection with this mention of laws so desirable to be passed, the consideration of such and so many obstructions and difficulties then lying across the path to their accomplishment, as might still prove strong enough, and obstinate enough, to defy removal. The heart of the Remonstrance lay here ; and its authors made no secret of their aim in so shaping and directing it. The malignant party, they frankly declared, representing still the authors and promoters of all the miseries and wrongs therein described, had taken heart again. Even during the present parliament, that party had been enabled again to prefer to degrees of honour, and to places of trust and employment, some of its own factors and agents; and had used this influence to work, in the King, ill impressions and opinions of the proceedings of the House of Commons: as if its members had altogether done their own work and not his, and had obtained from him many things very prejudicial to the Crown, both in respect of prerogative and profit. To wipe out which last-named slander, they thought it good to declare, that,—in voting 25,000*l.* a month for the relief of the Northern Counties, in voting 300,000*l.* by way of brotherly assistance to the Scots, and in voting above 50,000*l.* a month for the charge of the army, —all these sums, which, with the addition of monies yielded by assessments on merchandize, amounted to a million and a half sterling, had

Clauses 143-153.

Obstructions expected.

Preferment of evil counsellors.

Reproach against House :

of refusing to support the Crown.

been contributed to the greatnefs, the honour, and the fupport of the King. He was bound to protect his fubjects; and his fubjects might well have claimed exemption from contributing to the relief of burthens, created by the very wrongs inflicted on themfelves. Yet, out of their purfe fince the prefent parliament met, had this million and a half been voted to his Majefty, by thofe very members of the Houfe of Commons whom the ill-affected were now fo "impudent" as to reproach with having done nothing for the King! (143 to 153 inclufive.)

A million and a half voted for the King.

As to the other reproach put forth to juftify the flander, and touching mainly the queftion of prerogative, it was met with challenge as frank and refolute. While they acknowledged with thankfulnefs, and in the moft impreffive language, that the King had given his confent, during the preceding ten months, to more good bills for the advantage of the fubject than had been in many previous ages, they yet claimed to remember the venomous councils which had fince gone far to obftruct and hinder the benefits from thefe good acts. They proceeded to inftance, one by one, the four ftatutes,—the Triennial Bill, the Bill for Continuance of the Parliament, and the two Bills for Abolition of the Star Chamber and High Commiffion,—fingled out to eftablifh the charge of having prejudiced the Crown in prerogative as well as profit (in none other could be found fo much as the fhadow of pretence for fuch a charge); and they declared themfelves content to reft, upon no other than thefe four,

Claufes 154-161.

Popular bills paffed by King.

Four great acts recited.

the issue whether or not they had been careful, ever, to avoid desiring anything that should weaken the Crown in its just profit or its necessary power. The Star Chamber and High Commission had ceased, for some time before their abolition, to bring in any considerable fines; and, fruitful to the last in oppression, were so no longer in revenue. The Triennial Bill had fallen short of what the ancient law, existing still in two unrepealed statutes appointing parliaments each year, would have justified them in demanding. And though there might indeed seem to have been, in the Bill against putting an end without its own consent to the Parliament then sitting, some restraint of the royal power in dissolving parliaments, it was to be remembered that the design of that statute was by no means to take the authority out of the Crown, but simply to suspend its operation for the specific time and occasion. Without it, the great pecuniary charges heretofore described could never have been undertaken: the first consequence whereof must have been, the giving up of both armies to confusion and of the kingdom to plunder; and the first and greatest sacrifice, that of the public peace and of the King's own security. (154 to 161 inclusive.) *No intention to weaken Crown by them.*

Restraints necessary to safety.

Thus far the slander of the ill-affected had reached, in relation to the King. But it had taken also a wider range; and,—by such aspersions as that the House of Commons had spent much time and done little work, especially in the grievances concerning religion; and that it pressed itself upon the kingdom with peculiar *Clauses 162-168.*

Slanders against

burthens, not only by the voting of many fub-fidies heavier than any formerly endured, but by excefs in the protections againft fuits and debts granted to its members,—the attempt had been made to damage, with the people, the reputation of their reprefentatives, and to bring the Englifh nation out of love with Parliaments. Yet was there truly a ready anfwer, if they to whom fuch flander was addreffed would but look back and forward. Before they judged this Parliament, let them look back to the long growth and deep root of the Grievances it had removed, to the powerful fupports of the Delinquents it had ftruck down, to the great neceffities of the Commonwealth for which it had provided,—let them look forward to the many advantages which not the prefent only but future ages would reap, from the laws it had paffed and the work it had accomplifhed,—and where was the indifferent judgment, to which its burthen laid upon the fubject would not feem lighter than in any former example, and to which its time fpent in deliberation would not appear to have been better employed than a far greater proportion of time in many former parliaments put together? In the only direction where it was poffible that juft reafon for complaint might exift, already a bill was under difcuffion to provide a remedy; and any undue ftretching of thofe protections * from fuit and arreft which were neceffary to the difcharge of the

marginalia: the Parliament. Danger of hafty judgments. Comparifon with former parliaments. Alleged excefs of privilege.

---

* " By which the debts from parliament men, and their " followers, and dependants, were not recoverable." *Clarendon, Hift.* ii. 55.

functions of a legiflator, would now very speedily be removed. (162 to 168, inclusive.)

But what was the character of the men, and what their daily practices and efforts, by whom thefe flanders had been bufily difperfed? They were the fame men who moft bufily had fown divifion between the fifter kingdoms, and ftriven to incenfe againft each other the fubjects of one Crown: Who had been able fo to influence the bifhops, and a party of Popifh lords in the upper Houfe, as to create thofe very obftructions and delays for which the lower Houfe was affailed: Who had laboured, not unfuccefsfully, to feduce and corrupt fome even of the reprefentatives of the people, and to draw them into combinations againft the liberty of parliament: Who, by their inftruments and agents, had tampered with the King's army for the fame wicked and traitorous purpofe, and had twice engaged in plots to bring up a force to overawe the deliberations of the Houfe of Commons, and to feize the perfons of its leaders: Whofe defigns with this view, as well in Scotland as in England, had ftill been defeated, before ripe for execution, by the vigilance of the well-affected; but who had been fo far more fuccefsful in Ireland, that not till the very eve of the day when the main enterprife fhould have been executed at Dublin, was difcovery made, by God's wonderful providence, of their fcheme to poffefs themfelves of that whole country, to fubvert totally its government, to root out and deftroy the Proteftant religion, and to

Claufes 169-180.

The party hoftile to Parliaments.

Intriguers with Army.

Promoters of Rebellion.

maffacre all, without exception, of whatever fex or age, who were bred in it, or likely to be faithful to it. Which devilifh defign was fo far purfued notwithftanding, that open rebellion had broken out in other parts of the Irifh kingdom, many towns and caftles had been furprifed, many murders and villanies unutterable perpetrated,* all bonds of obedience to the King and the laws fhaken

The Irifh tragedy.

* It has been referved for our own time, after fuch a lapfe of years as might have feemed to render wholly incredible the poffibility of a recurrence of fuch horrors, to furnifh a parallel to the unfpeakable cruelties perpetrated in this Irifh Rebellion. "The innocent Proteftants" (I quote the hiftorian May, no vehement or exaggerated writer) "were upon a "fudden diffeifed of their eftates, and the perfons of above " two hundred thoufand men, women, and children murthered, " many of them with exquifite and unheard of tortures, with- " in the fpace of one month. . . Dublin was the fanctuary of " all the defpoiled Proteftants, . . and what mifchiefs foever " were acted in other parts, were there difcovered and lamented. " Their eyes were fad witneffes of the rebels' cruelty, in fuch " wretched fpectacles as daily from all parts prefented them- " felves : people of all conditions and qualities, of every age " and fex, fpoiled and ftripped . . . And befides the miferies " of their bodies, their minds tortured with the loffe of all " their fortunes, and fad remembrance of their hufbands, " wives, or children, moft barbaroufly murdered before their " faces . . . But that part of this woful tragedy prefented to " the eyes was the leaft, and but the fhadow of that other " which was related to their ears, of which the readers and all " pofterity may fhare the forrow. Many hundreds of thofe " which had efcaped,—under their oaths lawfully taken upon " examination, and recorded with all particulars,—delivered " to the Council what horrid maffacres the bloody villains " had made of men, women, and children ; and what cruel " inventions they had to torture thofe whom they murdered ; " fcarce to be equalled by any the moft black and baleful " ftory of any age. Many thoufands of them at feveral places " (too many to be here inferted), after all defpites exercifed " upon them living, were put to the worft of deaths : fome " burned on fet purpofe, others drowned for fport and paftime; " and if they fwam, kept from landing with poles, or fhot or " murdered in the water : many were buried quick, and fome " fet into the earth breaft high, and there left to famifh. But

Maffacres of Irifh Proteft-ants.

Narrative by May.

off, and such a fire in general kindled, as nothing but God's infinite blessing upon the measures and endeavours now at this time in progress would be able to quench. And to that so miserable tragedy in Ireland, but for the great mercy of Providence in confounding former plots, this country of England would have been made to furnish the lamentable prologue. (169 to 180 inclusive.) *Intended prologue to tragedy in England.*

7. Defence of the Popular Leaders.

"AND now," proceeded this memorable "most barbarous (as appears in very many examinations) was "that cruelty which was showed to pregnant women, whom "the villains were not content to murder, but——. But I "am loath to dwell upon so sad a narrative." Lib. 2, cap. i. 14. Let a brief passage from the authentic *Rushworth* (Part III. vol. i. p. 416-7) complete the horror, and with it the appalling parallel to incidents which have plunged this living generation into mourning. "For such of the English as "stood upon their guard, and had gathered together, though "but in small numbers, the Irish fairly offered unto them good "conditions of quarter, assured them their lives, their goods, "and free passage, and as soon as they had them in their "power, held themselves disobliged from their promises, and "left their soldiers at liberty to despoil, strip, and murder "them at pleasure . . . Their servants were killed as they "were ploughing in the fields, husbands were cut to pieces in "the presence of their wives, their children's brains were "dashed out before their faces . . their goods and cattle "seized and carried away, their houses burnt, their habita- "tions laid waste, and all as it were at an instant, before they "could suspect the Irish for their enemies, or any ways "imagine that they had it in their hearts, or in their power, "to offer so great violence, or do such mischief." Clarendon's own touching account (viii. 9, and elsewhere) of the barbarous circumstances of cruelty with which, in the space of less than ten days, an incredible number of protestants, "men, "women, and children promiscuously, and without distinction "of age and sex," were murdered, must be familiar to every reader of his History. *Clauses 181-191.* *Narrative by Rushworth.* *Clarendon's account.*

Declaration, in language which its authors might fairly have claimed to be appealed to on all occasions afterward when their deeds or their motives should be called in question—" And " now, what hope have we but in God? The " only means of our subsistence, and power of " Reformation, is, under Him, in the Parlia- " ment; but what can we, the Commons, with- " out the conjunction of the House of Lords? " and what conjunction can we expect there, " when the Bishops and recusant Lords are so " numerous and prevalent, that they are able " to cross and interrupt our best endeavours " for Reformation, and by that means give " advantage to this malignant party to traduce " our proceedings?

Hopes of leaders of Commons.

Reply to their affailants.

" They infuse into the people that we mean " to abolish all Church Government, and leave " every man to his own fancy for the service " and worship of God, absolving him of that " obedience which he owes under God to his " Majesty; whom we know indeed to be in- " trusted with the ecclesiastical law as well as " with the temporal, to regulate all the mem- " bers of the Church of England—though by " such rules of order and discipline only as are " established by Parliament; which is his great " council in all affairs, both in Church and " State.

Champions of Episcopacy:

" They have strained to blast our proceed- " ings in parliament by wresting the interpre- " tations of our Orders from their genuine " intentions. They tell the people that our " meddling with the power of Episcopacy hath " caused sectaries and conventicles, when it is

Abstract: Defence of the Popular Leaders.

" Idolatry,* and the Popish Ceremonies intro-
" duced into the Church by command of the
" Bishops, which have not only debarred the their
" people from them, but expelled them from flanders.
" the kingdom. And thus, with Eliab, we are
" called by this malignant party the troublers
" of the State; and still, while we endeavour
" to reform their abuses, they make us authors
" of those mischiefs we study to prevent.

" We confess our intention is, and our en- Design
" deavours have been, to reduce within bounds of the Bishops'
" that exorbitant power which the Prelates Bill.
" have assumed unto themselves, so contrary
" both to the word of God and to the laws of
" the land: to which end we passed the Bill
" for the removing them from their temporal
" power and employments, that so the better
" they might with meekness apply themselves
" to the discharge of their functions; which Bill
" they themselves opposed, and were the prin-
" cipal instruments of crossing.†

" And we do here declare that it is far from No inten-
" our purpose or desire to let loose the golden tion to
" reins of discipline and government in the relax just discipline.
" Church, leaving private persons or particular

---

* No expression was so hotly contested in the House as this Idolatry
of *Idolatry*. It was debated, as the reader has been already in the
told, with extraordinary vehemence; the clause containing it Church.
was recommitted twice; Falkland and Culpeper were added
to the Committee appointed " to prepare the clause in such a
" manner as may be agreeable to the sense of the House;"
and after a division taken on the question of whether it should
stand, which was carried by a majority of twenty-five, it was
again, on the final debate, vehemently discussed.

† This clause also was strenuously contested to the last, and
on the day when the final division on the Remonstrance was
taken, as will hereafter be seen, it was again put to the vote.

Conformity desired.

"congregations to take up what form of divine
"service they please: for we hold it requisite
"that there should be, throughout the whole
"realm, a conformity to that order which
"the Laws enjoin according to the word of
"God. But we desire to unburden the con-
"sciences of men of needless and superstitious
"ceremonies, to suppress innovations, and to
"take away the monuments of idolatry.*

Suggestion for a Synod:

"The better to effect which intended Re-
"formation, we desire there may be a General
"Synod of the most grave, pious, learned,

Authorship of Remonstrance.

* Clarendon more than once imputes the main authorship of the Remonstrance to Pym; but the share taken in it by that great statesman is yet more satisfactorily established by the extraordinary number of passages in it, identical in style, in manner, and often in the most precise expression, with his printed speeches. The passages on Church government quoted above are among the many such proofs from internal evidence. In themselves they are remarkable, and they agree exactly with the tone and terms of the brief but impressive "Declaration and Vindication" which the maligned leader of

Ascribed to Pym.

the popular party put forth, with his own name, against the calumnies of the royalists during the year preceding his death.
"That I am, ever was, and so will die, a faithful son of the
"Protestant Religion, without having the least relation, in
"my belief, to the gross errors of Anabaptism, Brownism, or
"any other revolt from the orthodox doctrine of the Church
"of England, every man that hath any acquaintance with
"my conversation can bear me righteous witness. These are
"but aspersions cast upon me by some of the discontented

Parallel passages from Pym's Vindication.

"clergy, and their factors and abettors; because they might
"perhaps conceive that I had been a main instrument in ex-
"tenuating the haughty power and ambitious pride of the
"bishops and prelates . . And was it not high time to seek
"to regulate their power, when, instead of looking to the
"cure of men's souls (which is their genuine office), they
"inflicted punishment on men's bodies, banishing them to
"remote and desolate places, bringing in papistical cere-
"monies by unheard of canons into the Church, imposing
"burdens upon men's consciences which they were not able
"to bear, and introducing the old abolished superstition of
"bowing to the altar?"

Abstract: Remedial Measures demanded. 269

"and judicious divines of this island, assisted
with some from foreign parts, professing the
same religion with us; who may consider of
all things necessary for the peace and good
government of the Church, and represent [to settle
the results of their consultations unto the Church
Parliament. There, to be allowed of, and Government.]
confirmed; and to receive the stamp of authority whereby to find passage and obedience
throughout the kingdom.

"We have been maliciously charged with [Desire to
the intention to destroy and discourage advance Learning:]
Learning, whereas it is our chiefest care and
desire to advance it, and to provide such
competent maintenance for conscientious and
preaching ministers throughout the realm as
will be a great encouragement to scholars,
and a certain means whereby the want, mean-
ness, and ignorance to which a great part of
the clergy is now subject, will be prevented.
And we have intended likewise to reform [by re-
and purge the Fountains of Learning, the forming
two Universities, that the streams flowing Universities.]
from thence may be clear and pure, and an
honour and comfort to the whole land."

So ran the clauses of the Great Remonstrance from the 181st to the 191st inclusive,
memorable always for their plain vindication of
the motives and meaning of its authors.

8. *Remedial Measures demanded.*

Fourteen clauses more, from the 192nd to [Clauses 192-206.]
the 206th, carried the Remonstrance to its close.
In these were frankly indicated the measures

Demands made. which the people were entitled to demand, as their only fafe or fufficient guarantee againſt the recurrence, at any moment, of the wrongs and ſufferings of the paſt ſixteen years. The groundwork of theſe meaſures, I may remark, was preciſely that which formed afterwards the *Settlement of Monarchy with limitations.* baſis of the ſettlement by which alone the Monarchy was again firmly eſtabliſhed in England. It compriſed ſafeguards againſt the Roman Catholic religion; ſecurity for the better adminiſtration of the laws; and conditions for the future ſelection of only ſuch counſellors and miniſters by the King, as the Parliament might have reaſon to confide in.

i. *Safeguards againſt Roman Catholic Religion.* For the firſt, it was laid down broadly that the principles of thoſe who profeſſed the Roman Catholic religion ſo certainly tended to the deſtruction and extirpation of all Proteſtants, whenever they ſhould have opportunity to effect it, that it was abſolutely neceſſary to keep them in ſuch condition, as that they might not be able to do any hurt;* and

Pym's view as to Popery: * The expreſſion is exactly that which Pym had employed in his ſpeech on grievances in the Short Parliament, in a paſſage which vindicates his memory from any imputation of intolerance. It is always with the prudent ſpirit of the ſtateſman, and never with the unreaſoning hatreds of the bigot, that this great ſpeaker adverts to the Roman Catholic religion. *diſlike of the ſtateſman, not the bigot.* "He did not deſire any new laws againſt Popery, or any "rigorous courſes in the execution of thoſe already in force. "He was far from ſeeking the ruin of their perſons or eſtates; "only he wiſht they might be kept in ſuch a condition as "ſhould reſtrain them from doing hurt ... The principles "of Popery are ſuch as are incompatible with any other "religion. Laws will not reſtrain them. Oaths will not. "The Pope can diſpenſe with both theſe; and where there is "occaſion, his command will move them to the diſturbance "of the realm, againſt their own private diſpoſition, yea againſt "their own reaſon and judgment, not only in ſpiritual matters

Abstract: Remedial Measures demanded.

that such connivance and favour, therefore, as had theretofore been shown to them, should thereafter be avoided.* With this view his Majesty was moved to grant a standing com-- mission to some choice men named in Parlia- ment, who might take watch of their increase, report upon their counsels and proceedings, and use all due means, by execution of the laws, to prevent mischievous designs, from that quarter, against the peace and safety of the

<small>Suggested Commission.</small>

" but in temporal. Henry III and Henry IV of France
" were no Protestants themselves, yet were murthered because
" they tolerated the Protestants. The King and the king-
" dom can have no security but in their weakness and dis-
" abilitie to do hurt."

* It is not necessary to multiply illustrations of the thorough understanding of the character of the King, which appears in, and justifies, the various urgent warnings of the Remonstrance against his dangerous tendency to intercourse with Rome. But let me refer the reader to one of the latest and most decisive evidences on this point, furnished in the very curious and interesting volume of Letters written by Charles to his Queen in 1646, published by the Camden Society in 1856, and most carefully edited by Mr. John Bruce. In these letters will be found the most satisfactory of all evidence, under his own hand, of the otherwise incredible and utterly insane scheme by which he proposed, to that congenial helpmate who did more than all the rest of his advisers to bring about the tragedy of his death, that she should "invite the Pope " and other Roman Catholics to help me for the restitution of " Episcopacy in England, upon condition of giving them free " liberty of conscience, and convenient places for their devo- " tions. . . I desire thee not," he adds, " to communicate " this motion to any of the French ministers of state, but I " would have thee to acquaint the Cardinal with it, requiring " his assistance, for certainly France is as much obliged to " assist me as honour can make it." p. 42. The intended mode of doing it was worthy of the thing to be done. The Queen was to get the French government to invade England with 6000 men, and with these, and double the number of Irish Roman Catholics, Charles proposed to provide for the safe re-establishment of the English Protestant Church and his own royal authority! *Letters in* 1646, p. 24 and 25. And see Clarendon's *State Papers*, ii. 262.

<small>The King's tendencies to Rome.

Compact for restoration of Episcopacy.

Proposed invitation to the French!</small>

realm. And it was further fuggefted, that fome fufficient tefts fhould be applied to that counterfeit and falfe conformity of Papifts to the Englifh Church, by colour of which perfons greatly difaffected to the true religion had been admitted into places of higheft authority and truft in the kingdom.

ii.
Securities for Adminiftration of Laws.

For the fecond, ftipulation was made, that, for the better prefervation of the liberties and laws, all illegal grievances and exactions fhould be prefented and punifhed at the feffions and affizes; that judges and juftices fhould be very careful to give this in charge to the grand juries; and that both the fheriff and the juftices fhould be fworn to the due execution of the Petition of Right and other laws.

iii.
Protection againft Evil Counfellors.

For the third, a feries of precautions were fuggefted to meet thofe cafes of not infrequent occurrence, when the Commons might have juft caufe to take exceptions at particular men for being felected to advife the King, and yet have no juft caufe to charge them with crimes. Seeing that there were grounds of diffidence which lay not in proof, and others which, though proveable, were yet not legally criminal (as, to be a known favourer of Papifts, or to have been very forward in countenancing

Parliament to be confulted in choice of Minifters.

and fupporting great offenders queftioned in Parliament, or to have become notorious for a ftudied contempt of Parliamentary proceedings), the moft cogent reafons might exift to be earneft with the King not to put his great affairs into fuch hands, though the Commons might be unwilling to proceed againft them in any legal way of impeachment. It was then plainly ſtated that ſupplies for ſupport of the King's own eſtate could not be given, nor ſuch aſſiſtance provided as the times required for the Proteſtant party beyond the ſea, unleſs ſuch Counſellors, Ambaſſadors, and other Miniſters only were in future employed as Parliament could give its confidence to; and unleſs all Counſellors of State were ſworn, as well to avoid receiving, in any form, reward or penſion from any foreign prince,* as to obſerve ſtrictly thoſe laws which concerned the ſubject at home in his liberty. *[margin: Miniſters to be made ſubject to laws.]*

And ſo this famous Declaration ended, with a prayer that his Majeſty might ever have cauſe to be in love with good counſel and good men; and, profiting by the humble and dutiful repreſentations therein made, might acknowledge how full of advantage it would be, to himſelf, to ſee his own eſtate ſettled in a condition ſufficing to ſupport his honour, to ſee his people united in ways of duty to him and in endeavours for the public good, and, by the influence of his own power and government, to ſee derived to his own kingdom, and procured to thoſe of his allies, Happineſs, Wealth, Peace, and Safety. *[margin: Cloſing prayer of Remonſtrance.]*

---

§ XIII. THE HOUSE AND ITS MEMBERS: 22ND NOV. 1641.

SUCH was the Declaration, the Great Remonſtrance, which lay engroſſed on the table *[margin: Monday, 22nd Nov. 1641.]*

* On Friday the 11th of December 1640, I find from a manuſcript report of the proceedings of that day, Pym handed in ſeveral petitions, and among them one from " Joſeph Engliſh ſtateſmen:

of the houfe on Monday the 22nd of November 1641, waiting the final vote. The King, eager at laft to reach London before that vote could be taken, was now haftening with all fpeed back from Edinburgh; and the fact that he was only diftant a two days' journey was doubtlefs known to Pym, Hampden, and Cromwell, when they paffed into the houfe that morning.

King approaching London.

The Speaker was late, probably in expectation that he fhould have to fit long; and prayers were not over until a little after ten. There is then fome bufinefs effential to be done, and honourable members eager for the great debate are fain to curb their impatience. Mr. Wheeler, the member for Weftbury, has to report concerning a delinquent involved in the recent confpiracies. Sir John Price, the member for Montgomeryfhire, has ill report to make of a Mr. Blany, a Welfh juftice of peace. Mr. Strode has to complain of an order of the Houfe as to a cafe in the Exchequer tending to throw difcredit on himfelf, and to obtain correction of the fame. Mr. Speaker has to prefer a petition from fome hundred or fo of the Moniers of the mint, claiming to be exempt, by the precedents of four centuries, from contributing to the payment of the laft fix fubfidies voted by the Commons; which petition, having been prefented to the King, his Majefty had commended

10 o'clock A.M. Speaker late.

Petition from moniers.

and foreign penfions.

" Hawes and other merchants touching the wrongs done them
" at fea by the Spaniards;" and moved that it fhould be referred " to the fame committee appointed to confider of the
" Turkifh pirates and Algiers, and to enquire what minifters
" of our State do receive penfions from foreign States."

§ XIII. *The House and its Members:* 1641.

to Mr. Speaker for presentation this day, and by the House was now ordered to be referred to the committee for poll-money, some not very courtly members remarking that " these " subsidies were given to the Commonwealth " and not to the King, and therefore they were " not freed by any charter of exemption." But, above all, Mr. Pym has to report the result of a conference with the Lords the preceding Saturday on Irish affairs, and sundry important matters relating thereto. He has evidence to offer that " this design of Ireland " was hatched in England." He has a petition bearing on these affairs to present from Sir Faithful Fortescue. He has to make an important suggestion for the transport, to Ireland, of the magazine at Hull; to get authority for the necessary estimates, from the officers of ordnance, as to the number of ships required for such transport; to take order for the immediate provision thereof; and to obtain means, by a vote of 4000*l*. to Mr. Crane, the victualler of the Navy, for the hastening away of other ships to guard the coast of Ireland.

Distinction between Commonwealth and King.

Pym on Ireland.

So the time passed until the clock had struck twelve, when, as the members began to hurry out for dinner, cries became loud for the debate on the Remonstrance. Thereupon, order having been made (so little in some quarters, even then, was any debate of unusual duration expected) that the Irish business should be resumed as soon as the debate on the Declaration was done, and the order of the day for resumption of the latter subject having been read, Mr. Hyde rose and desired that the

12 o'clock A.M. Dinner-hour.

Cries for order of day.

Serjeant might be sent with his mace to call up such members of the house as were then walking in Westminster Hall. It was a device to gain time, Mr. Hyde, we may presume, not liking to speak to thinly occupied benches; but, on the other hand, the liberal leaders were interested to have no time lost, and many resisted the proposal. After some debate, however, the objectors gave way, and the Serjeant with his mace departed accordingly.

Hyde's motion to gain time.

The old House of Commons, it may be well here to remind the reader, now that a generation has grown up who never saw the narrow, ill-lighted, dingy room, in which for three centuries some of the most important business of this world was transacted, ran exactly at right angles with Westminster Hall, having a passage into it at the south-east angle. The Hall itself, in those days, shared in all the excitements of the House; and nothing of interest went on in the one, of which visible and eager indications did not present themselves in the other.

The old House of Commons.

It was here, in the Hall, within an hour after the dissolving of the Short Parliament, that the cheerful and sanguine Mr. Hyde, with deeply despondent face, deplored gloomily that rash step to the dark and reserved Mr. St. John, who, with laughter lighting up features rarely known to smile, rejoined briskly that all was well, and it must be worse before it would be better. It was here, upon the assembling of the Long Parliament, that Mr. Hyde had walked up and down conferring on the state of affairs with Mr. Pym, when that worthy and

Westminster Hall.

Famous associations.

§ XIII. *The House and its Members: 1641.*

distinguished member told him they must now be of another temper than they had been heretofore, and must not only sweep the house clean below, but must pull down all the cobwebs which hung in the top and corners, that they might not breed dust, and so make a foul house hereafter. It was here the King himself was so soon to enter on his ill-fated errand against the Five Members, striking such a fear and terror, according to a manuscript report now before me, " into all those that kept shops " in the said Hall, or near the gate thereof, as " they instantly shut up their shops."* For here also such trades as those of booksellers, law-stationers, sempstresses, and the like, found customers among the variously idle, busy, or curious people, continually drawn together; and under the roof of the noble old Hall, whatever the business in progress might be within the Courts adjoining or in the Chapel beyond, might be heard the old city cry of *What d'ye lack?* addressed to lawyers walking up and down till their cases in the Bench or Exchequer come on, to clients in attendance to consult with their lawyers, to politicians anxious for news, and to members of either House escaping from committees or debates. —As those of the lower House, however, for whom Mr. Hyde sent the Serjeant and his mace, have doubtless by this time been col-

Side notes: Pym and Hyde. Shops in the Hall. Place of resort: for M.P.'s lawyers, and clients.

---

* Booksellers, law-stationers, sempstresses—these and other trades akin to these, now and for some time later, plied their callings in the place; and Laud notices in his Diary a narrow escape of the Hall from being burnt down, owing to a fire in one of the stalls. *Laud's Diary.*

lected, it is our bufinefs to enter St. Stephen's with them and obferve the afpect it prefents.

St. Stephen's Chapel. The entire length of the room in which the members fat was fomething lefs than the breadth of Weftminfter Hall; and, handfome as it originally had been, with its rich architecture and decorated paintings of the thirteenth century, it had loft all trace of thefe under boards and whitewafh immediately after *Its old interior.* the Reformation, when alfo a new floor above, and a new roof under, the old, ftill more abridged its proportions. At the weftern end, the entrance was between rows of benches, paffing the bar, and underneath a gallery into which members mounted by a ladder on the right-hand corner, near the fouthern window. At the eaftern end, a little in advance of a large window looking on the river, ftood the *Officers of Houfe.* Speaker's chair; and again, a little lefs in advance of that, towards the middle of the floor, ftood the Clerk's table, at which fat Henry Elfyng, and John Rufhworth his lately appointed affiftant, with their faces to the mace and their backs to the Speaker. Then, on right and left of the Speaker, in benches ftretching along and fpringing up as in an amphitheatre on either hand, were affembled *Honourable members.* the Honourable Members. There they fat, puritan and courtier, the pick and choice of the gentlemen of England; with bearded faces clofe-cut and ftern, or here and there more gaily trimmed with peak and ruff; faces for the moft part worn with anxious thoughts and fears, heavy with toil, weary with refponfibility and care, often with long imprifonment; there

§ XIII. *The House and its Members: 1641.*

they fat, in their fteeple hats and Spanifh cloaks, with fwords and bands, by birth, by wealth, by talents, the firft affembly of the world. And there, prefiding in his great chair furmounted by the arms of England, fat Mr. Speaker; alfo hatted, cloaked, and fworded like the reft; but not always treated by them, nor in footh always treating them, with the refpect which has gathered to his office in later time. *Position of Mr. Speaker.*

It was but a few weeks, for example, before the late recefs, that that honourable barrifter and member for Melcombe Regis, Mr. Richard King, took upon himfelf to declare, that, in a particular rebuke which Mr. Speaker had addreffed to another honourable member, he had "tranfgreffed his duty in ufing fo difgraceful "a fpeech to fo noble a gentleman;" and though the Houfe interfered to protect their Speaker, and Mr. King was commanded to withdraw into the Committee Chamber, the matter ended in but "a conditional apology "with which the Houfe was not fatiffied but "the Speaker was." The noble gentleman whom it vexed Mr. King to fee treated with difrefpect was the younger brother of Lord Digby, Mr. John Digby, member for Milborn Port; who, on the day when his brother would have been expelled the Houfe of Commons if the King's letters-patent had not iffued the night before calling him to the Houfe of Lords, "came into the houfe, and getting upon the "ladder that ftands at the door of the houfe "by which the members thereof ufually go up "to thofe feats which are over the fame door *Richard King's attack on Lenthal.* *Hon. Mr. John Digby:* *his difrefpect to Houfe:*

"under the gallery, he fat ftill upon the faid "ladder;"* whereupon the Speaker, doubt- lefs coupling the act, as a fign of difrefpect, with a difplay of infubordination by the fame young gentleman on difcuffion of his brother's cafe the previous day, "called out to him, and "defired him to take his place, and not to fit "upon the faid ladder as if he were going to "be hanged: at which many of the Houfe "laughed," and Mr. King, as aforefaid, was indignant. The incident leaves us at leaft no room for doubt, that, though the Speaker's powers were in their infancy as yet, and his claim to proper confideration only grudgingly admitted, he had neverthelefs as unruly an affemblage to deal with, as the powers and confideration conceded to him in modern par- liaments have found themfelves barely equal to govern.† Inceffant certainly were the rebukes

rebuked by Lenthal.

Mr. Speaker's powers.

Selden and the Digbys.

* Selden has a note in his *Table Talk* referring to this affair of the Digbys, and comparing the new-made lord, fafe from the wrath of the Commons, to an ape on the houfe-top grin- ning at the whip below, of which the farcaftic humour might probably enough have been fuggefted by the incident D'Ewes has preferved for us. If the learned member for Oxford Univerfity, as is moft likely, actually faw the younger Digby fneering at Mr. Speaker from the top of his ladder, the other image of the ape might naturally prefent itfelf. "My lord "Digby having fpoken fomething in the Houfe of Com- "mons, for which they would have queftioned him, was "prefently called to the Upper Houfe. He did by the Par- "liament, as an ape when he hath done fome waggery: his "mafter fpies him, and he looks for his whip, but before "he can come at him, 'whip,' fays he *to the top of the* "*houfe!*"—*Table Talk*, p. 175. (Ed. Irving, 1854.)

Digby on his ladder and the ape on houfe-top.

D'Ewes and Lenthal.

† Even Sir Simonds D'Ewes himfelf, one of the moft prim and precife of men, and a very Grandifon of propriety in regard to all cuftoms, orders, records, and authorities of the Houfe, in which he was a marvellous proficient, yet indulges himfelf without fcruple, when any occafion arifes, in a fneer-

§ XIII. *The Houſe and its Members:* 1641.

offered, and the rebuffs received, by Mr. Speaker Lenthal; who, ſetting aſide the one notable act of his career, had but commonplace qualities of his own to ſuſtain him; and who, in eſpecial, ſeems often to have found (herein perhaps not differing from later experiences in — *Lenthal's weakneſs.*

ing diſreſpect to Mr. Speaker. On the ſecond of December 1641, for example, there is quite a paſſage of arms between them. It begins with D'Ewes, "ſitting in my uſual place "near his chair," correcting Mr. Speaker on a point of order connected with a ſummons to conference with the Lords. Then, upon D'Ewes moving to have the Londoners' petition read over again, Mr. Speaker takes his turn by interpoſing that it is the worthy member's own fault to have been abſent at the reading on the previous day; but has to cry D'Ewes mercy, on the latter pleading his abſence that day at Hampton Court, by order of the Houſe itſelf, to aſſiſt in preſenting the Great Remonſtrance to the King. Then Mr. Waller gets up to ſpeak, and handles both the points ſtarted, as well the conference with the Lords as the Londoners' petition. To him ſucceeds D'Ewes, who alſo enlarges upon both ſubjects under various heads, until Mr. Speaker becomes manifeſtly uneaſy. "Having proceeded thus far or a little further, I "perceived the Speaker often offering to riſe out of his chair "as if he intended to interrupt me." An explanation follows. Mr. Speaker thinks D'Ewes out of order in not taking points ſeparately, firſt the matter of conference with the Lords, and then the Londoners' petition afterwards. "Whereupon "I ſtood up again and ſaid, 'Truly, ſir, I am much behold- "'ing to you for admoniſhing me, but if you had been but "'pleaſed to have informed the gentleman who ſpoke laſt "'before to both the particulars, you would have ſaved me "'my labour, for I did but follow his method;' at which "the Houſe laughed; and the Speaker being half aſhamed "of what he had done, ſtood up again and confeſſed that he "did permit Mr. Waller &c. and now he left it to the "Houſe, &c." Other ſimilar inſtances might be quoted. One had occurred in reference to a point on the paſſing of the Subſidy Bill, on the previous 13th of February, 1640-1, when the Speaker had predicted all ſorts of ill conſequences from a particular courſe of procedure, and D'Ewes is careful to inform him (and us) that "no inconvenience had fol-"lowed." Another involved a very ſharp encounter (26th Feb. 1641-2) with Sir Arthur Haſelrig. And any one who cares to purſue the ſubject will find additional illuſtrations in my *Arreſt of Five Members*, § xxiii. — *A quarrel on point of order. D'Ewes lectures Mr. Speaker. Lenthal's ſubmiſſion.*

Magister Venter. the fame feat) the dinner-hour an almoft infuperable difficulty. As it has been with many a modern Mr. Speaker between the hours of feven and eight in the evening, fo fared it with Mr. Lenthal between twelve and one mid-day.* Not a great many days before the prefent fitting, the rufh of members out of the Houfe at that hour, during a debate on fupply, had been fuch that he was fain flatly to tell them "they Houfe emptied by dinner bell. " were unworthy to fit in this great and wife " aſſembly in a parliament that would ſo run " forth for their dinners." † And now, though the Serjeant has returned with feveral members from the Hall, fo many more continue abfent from the Houfe at this clamorous hour, that Mr. Hyde ftill waits and defers to fpeak.

* There is a pleafant paffage in Clarendon's *Life* (i. 90), where he expreffly excepts certain leading members from this habit of ruſhing out at the time of dinner, and defcribes what plan they adopted. When their hours had become very diſorderly, he ſays, the Houfe feldom riſing till after four of the clock in the afternoon, he ufed to be frequently invited ("importuned" he calls it) to dine with the party of whom Pym was the leader, and often went with them accordingly to "Mr. Pym's lodging, which was at Sir Richard Manly's " houfe, in a little court behind Weſtminſter Hall, where he, " and Mr. Hampden, Sir Arthur Hafelrig, and two or three " more, upon a ſtock kept a table, where they tranfaƈted " much buſineſs, and invited thither thofe of whofe conver- " ſion they had any hope." It was after one of thefe dinners, the fummer evening being fine, that Nathaniel Fiennes having propofed to Mr. Hyde to ride into the fields and take a little air, they two fent for their horfes, and, while riding in the fields between Weſtminſter and Chelfea, Mr. Fiennes did his beſt to convert Mr. Hyde from his notions as to the government of the Church.

Pym's dinner parties.

An evening ride.

† This will explain a faying of Lord Falkland's reported in one of the fuppreffed paffages of Lord Clarendon's Hiftory, recently reftored (ii. 595, Appendix F), " that they who " hated biſhops, hated them worſe than the devil; and they " who loved them, loved them not fo well as they did their " dinners."

§ XIII. *The Houſe and its Members: 1641.*

While he does this yet a few minutes longer, let us ſeize the occaſion to obſerve where ſome of the prominent people ſit. The member whoſe manuſcript record chiefly has been quoted, Sir Simonds D'Ewes, will guide us to the knowledge here and there, in jotting down his own ſpeeches; for, as it was then the cuſtom to avoid mention as well of the place repreſented as of the member's name, the principal mode of indicating a previous ſpeaker was by ſome well known perſonal quality, or by his poſition in the houſe.* Sir Simonds himſelf ſat uſually by the Speaker's chair, on the lowermoſt form cloſe by the ſouth end of the clerk's table; and there, whatever the ſubject of debate might be, or the excitement going on around him, the preciſe ſelf-ſatiſfied puritan gentleman ſat, writing-apparatus forming part of his equipment, his eyes cloſe to the paper (for their ſight was defective), and ever buſily taking his Notes: but it was his cuſtom, when he ſpoke,

margin: Where leading members ſit.

margin: Sir Simonds D'Ewes:

margin: taking his notes.

---

* Thus old Sir Harry Vane, referring to D'Ewes himſelf (June 26, 1641) "is ſorry to miſs the gentleman out of his "place who is ſo well verſed in records;" and in like manner Sir Robert Pye characteriſes him (July 1, 1641) as "that learned "gentleman who was ſo well ſkilled in records—*and then he* "*looked at me.*" Sir John Evelyn is (4 March, 1641-2) "my very worthy friend on the other ſide." Sir Arthur Haſelrig is (26 February 1641-2) "that worthy gentleman in "the gallery." Sir Ralph Hopton is "that ancient parlia- "ment man." Mr. Cage, member for Ipſwich, is, "my old "neighbour behind me," or, "an old gentleman who uſed "to ſit here behind me." Sir Thomas Barrington, member for Colcheſter, is, "as ancient a parliament man as Mr. Cage, "though not of as many years." "No man did more honour "and love that worthy member that ſpake laſt than myſelf," are words in which an alluſion to Pym is conveyed. And Mr. Denzil Hollis is "the worthy gentleman whom I very "much reſpect."

margin: Places of members in Houſe.

284   *The Grand Remonſtrance.*

Marten and Pym. to go up two ſteps higher, that he might more eaſily be heard by the whole Houſe. In this poſition, Mr. Harry Marten, the member for Berkſhire, was "the gentleman below." Mr. Pym, the acknowledged chief of the majority of the Commons, is ever in his "uſual place "near the Bar," juſt beyond the gallery on the ſame right-hand ſide of the houſe at entering. Sir John Culpeper, member for Kent, and ſo ſoon to be Chancellor of the Exchequer, is "the Culpeper, "gentleman on the other ſide of the way."* Hyde, Falkland, He ſat upon the left-hand ſide; and near him, and moſt generally together, ſat Hyde and Falk-Palmer. land; Mr. Geoffrey Palmer, the member for Stamford, and Sir John Strangways, ſitting near. On the ſame ſide at the upper end, on the Speaker's right, ſat the elder Vane, member for Wilton, for a few days longer Secretary of State and Treaſurer of the Houſehold; near whom were other holders of office. Sir Vane and Thomas Jermyn, his Majeſty's Comptroller, King's who ſat for Bury St. Edmund's; Sir Edward miniſters. Herbert, the Attorney-General, who ſat for Old Sarum; Oliver St. John, the Solicitor-General, member for Totneſs, ſtill holding the office in the King's ſervice which had failed to draw him over to the King's ſide; Mr. Coventry, member for Eveſham and one of the King's houſehold;† and young Harry Vane, member for Hull, and as yet Joint-treaſurer of the Navy; all ſat in this quarter, on the Speaker's

---

* " I deſired that the gentleman on the other ſide of the " way—*and then I looked on Sir John Culpeper, &c.*"

† " For if the gentleman on the other ſide who laſt preſſed " it—*and then I looked towards Mr. Coventrie, &c.*"

§ XIII. *The House and its Members:* 1641.

right. Near them sat also Mr. Edward Nicholas, Clerk of the Council, soon to be *Sir Edward* and Secretary of State in place of Windebank, now an anxious auditor and spectator of this memorable debate, which he was there to report to the King. Between these members and Hyde, on the same side of the house, sat the member for Wilton, Sir Benjamin Rudyard; Sir Walter Earle; William Strode; and lawyer Glyn, the member for Westminster. Mr. Herbert Price, the member for Brecon, with Mr. Wilmot, member for Tamworth, and a knot of young courtiers, sat at the lower end of the house on the same side, immediately on the left at entering. John Hampden sat on the other side, behind Pym; and between him and Harry Marten, sat Edmund Waller; on one of the back benches, Cromwell; not far from him, Denzil Hollis; and under the gallery, the member for Oxford University, the learned Mr. Selden.* Near him sat lawyer Maynard, the other member for Totnes; and over them, in the gallery itself, that successful lawyer, Mr. Holborne; Sir Edward Dering; and the member for Leicestershire, Sir Arthur Haselrig. But our list must come to a close. The reader has been detained too long from the debate on the Great Remonstrance.

Independent members.

Hampden, Waller, Cromwell, Hollis, and Selden.

The lawyers.

---

* " I said that I did prize whatsoever should fall from the
" pen or tongue of that learned gentleman under the gallery
" —*and then I looked towards Mr. Selden, &c.*"

§ XIV. SPEECHES OF HYDE, FALKLAND, DERING, RUDYARD, AND BAGSHAW.

Eighth Debate: 22d Nov.

HYDE opened this remarkable debate in a speech of great warmth* and great length. The general ground of objection he took was that a Declaration so put forth was without precedent; and he questioned the power of the House, in so far as this was defined by the words used in the writs of election, to make, alone, a remonstrance to the people, without the concurrence of the Lords. Arguing from this, he asserted that the form of the Declaration touched the honour of the King, and that it ought not, for that reason, to be made public or be circulated among the people. Such a publication could only be justified by having peace for its end, and here every such object would be frustrated. In the Remonstrance itself, apart from these considerations, he did not deny that there might be a propriety. The members of the House were accused to have done nothing either for King or kingdom. It was right to repel that charge. But if a parliament must make an apology, let them show what they had done without looking too far back. They may desire themselves to see, but they should not divulge, their own infirmities, any more than a general the defects

Hyde speaks.

Doubts House's right to remonstrate.

Objections to form and language:

---

* Mr. Philip Warwick, young courtier as he was, and admirer of all things courtly, could yet detect the points in which the King's principal advocate in the House was weak, as well for himself as his cause. "Mr. Hyde's language *Hyde's* "and style," he remarks, "were very suitable to business, if *wordiness.* "not a little too redundant." *Memoires*, p. 196.

§ XIV. *Speeches of Hyde and Falkland.*

of his army to the enemy. All was true, if expreſſed modeſtly. But ſuch paſſages as Sir John Eliot's impriſonment under the King's own hand, and his wanting bread,* were ill-expreſſed. Let them be chary of Majeſty. They ſtood upon their liberties even, for the Sovereign's ſake: left he ſhould be King of mean ſubjects, or they ſubjects of a mean King.

<small>unjuſt to the King.</small>

Lord Falkland roſe immediately after Hyde, and, as his wont was, ſpoke with greater paſſion in his warmth and earneſtneſs; his thin high-pitched voice breaking into a ſcream, and his little, ſpare, ſlight frame trembling with eager-neſs. He ridiculed the pretenſion ſet up in the Declaration to claim any right of approval over the councillors whom the King ſhould name; as if prieſt and clerk ſhould divide nomination and approval between them. He

<small>Lord. Falkland ſpeaks.</small>

<small>King's right to name his own miniſters</small>

---

* In Sir Ralph Verney's Note of the debate (p. 121), this paſſage ſtands " Sir John Eliot's impriſonment, under the " King's own hand, and *the King's* wanting bread, ill ex-" preſſed." It is clear, however, that the words marked in italics are a repetition by miſtake from the previous line. Clarendon in his Hiſtory (ii. 51) affects to quote, in the exact words of the Remonſtrance as it paſſed ("after many unbe-" coming expreſſions were caſt out"), the paſſage reſpecting Eliot; and he quotes it in inverted commas, thus: " One of " which died in priſon, *for want of ordinary refreſhment,* " whoſe blood ſtill cried for vengeance." The "want of " ordinary refreſhment" in the hiſtory, is clearly the ſame as " wanting bread" in the ſpeech; yet certainly the Remon-ſtrance as printed ſays no ſuch thing, and the words, if ever there, muſt have been among the unbecoming expreſſions caſt out. The paſſage really runs thus: " Of whom one died by " the cruelty and harſhneſs of his impriſonment, which would " admit of no relaxation, notwithſtanding the imminent " danger of his life did ſufficiently appear by the declaration " of his phyſician. And his releaſe, *or at leaſt his refreſh-*" *ment,* was ſought by many humble petitions. And his " blood ſtill cries, &c."

<small>Allufion to Eliot in Remon-ſtrance: incor-rectly quoted by Hyde.</small>

denounced it as unjuſt that the concealing of delinquents ſhould be caſt upon the King. He ſaid (forgetting a former ſpeech of his own going directly to this point)* it was not true to allege that Laud's party in the Church were in league with Rome; for that Arminians agreed no more with Papiſts than with Proteſtants. And, with the power to make laws, why ſhould they reſort to declarations? Only where no law was available, were they called to ſubſtitute orders and ordinances to command or forbid. Reminding them of the exiſting ſtate of Ireland, and of the many diſturbances in England, he warned them that it was of a very dangerous conſequence at that time to ſet out any remonſtrance: at leaſt ſuch a remonſtrance as this, containing many harſh expreſſions. Above all, it was dangerous to declare what they intended to do hereafter, as that they would petition his Majeſty to take advice of his parliament in the choice of his privy council; and it was of the very worſt example to make ſuch alluſion as that wherein they declared that already they had committed a bill to take away biſhops' votes. He pointed out the injuſtice of imputing to the biſhops generally the deſcription of the Scotch war as *bellum epiſcopale*, which he aſſerted had been ſo uſed by only one of them. He very hotly condemned the expreſſion of "bringing in idolatry," which he characteriſed as a charge of a high crime againſt all the biſhops in the land. And he

Defends Laud.

Dangers of Remonſtrance.

Apology for biſhops:

---

* See *ante*, p. 217.

§ XIV. Speeches of Falkland and Dering.

denounced it as a manifest contradiction and absurdity, that after reciting, as they had indeed sufficient cause to do, the many good laws passed by a parliament of which bishops and Popish lords were component members, they should end by declaring that while bishops and Popish lords continued to sit in parliament no good laws could be made.

Falkland was followed by Sir Edward Dering, who was so well pleased himself with the speech he proceeded to deliver, that he afterwards committed it, with another spoken in the preliminary debates, to print, with a preface which cost him his seat in the House;* and

margin: and Popish Lords. Sir Edward Dering speaks: Dering's publication of his speeches. Ordered to be burnt. Origin of penny-a-lining.

* Under date the 2nd February, 1641-2, D'Ewes gives curious and amusing evidence in his Journal of the anger awakened in wise grave men by this very silly publication of Sir Edward Dering's. Oliver Cromwell takes the lead in vehemently denouncing the book. D'Ewes himself chimes in as violently, for that "in this scandalous, seditious, and "vain-glorious volume," he does " so overvalue himself as if "able of himself to weigh down the balance of this House "on either side, &c. &c." Then Sir Walter Earle moves to call in the book. But to this D'Ewes very sensibly objects, "for that by so doing the price of it would rise from fourteen "pence to fourteen shillings, and hasten a new impression." Finally, Cromwell moves and carries that the obnoxious volume shall be burnt "next Friday:" on which occasion doubtless Palace-yard was duly illuminated by the small bonfire. See this matter further treated in *Arrest of Five Members*, § xxiii. But perhaps there was really more reason than lies immediately on the surface for the resentment with which the House regarded the publication by its members of their speeches, unauthorised by itself. It gave some sort of sanction to another publication of a still more unauthorised description, which had lately become not uncommon, and by which many members suffered not a little. I quote one of the entries of D'Ewes in his Journal under date the 9th February, 1641-2. "After prayers I said that much wrong was "offered of late to several members by publishing speeches in "their names which they never spake. I had yesternight a "speech brought me by a stationer to whom one John Bennet, "a poet lodging in Shoe-lane, sold it for half-a-crown to be

until very recently, this publication by the member for Kent was fuppofed to be the only fragment which had furvived of the debates on the Grand Remonftrance.* Nor

<small>Reported fpeeches never fpoken:</small>

"printed. He gives it as my fpeech at a conference when "there was no conference." This is probably one of the firft glimpfes to be got in our hiftory of the now ancient and important penny-a-lining fraternity. The danger and the annoyance, however, were greater from the interpolated and falfified verfions, now alfo abundantly put forth, of fpeeches really fpoken in the houfe, than from the pure inventions of which D'Ewes complained. I may add that the inventions were not limited to fpeeches only. Petitions affecting to reprefent the feeling of large claffes of people were got up in the fame way! On the 25th of January, 1641-2, the matter of a Royalift petition from Hertfordfhire was before the

<small>Royalift petitions forged:</small>

houfe, and the fubjoined curious entry is made in D'Ewes's Notes. "Thomas Hulbert, one of the framers of the Hert- "fordfhire petition, fent for as a delinquent, alfo Martin "Eldred, one of the penners of the fame. The faid Martin "Eldred, being called into the houfe, did acknowledge that "Thomas Hulbert, a young fcholar of Cambridge, did draw "the faid falfe petition of Hertfordfhire in his prefence; and "that they fold it to the faid John Greenfmith, a ftationer, "for half-a-crown, which the faid Greenfmith, being called

<small>work of poor fcholars in ale- houfes.</small>

"in, did likewife confefs; and that he printed it. I faid "there were now abiding in, and about London, certain loofe "beggarly fcholars who did in ale-houfes invent fpeeches, "and make fpeeches of members in parliament, and of other "paffages fuppofed to be handled in, or prefented unto, this "houfe. That the licenfe of printing thefe fcandalous "pamphlets is grown to a very great heighth, &c." Where- fore the indignant Sir Simonds would have Mr. Thomas Hulbert, and Mr. Martin Eldred, and Mr. John Greenfmith forthwith conveyed to the Gate-houfe.

* The gloom was broken by fuch additional brief notices as were fupplied by the appearance, a few years ago, of Sir

<small>Verney's Notes.</small>

Ralph Verney's valuable *Notes of Proceedings in the Long Parliament*, moft intelligently edited by Mr. Bruce; but the exiftence of the manufcript materials which have fupplied me with the main portions of the account now laid before the reader in this Work, was not fufpected, even fo late as Mr. Bruce's publication. The report fupplied in my text of the particular debate now in progrefs, is the refult of a careful comparifon of the notes of Verney and D'Ewes, each having been ufed to correct and complete the other. Fragments of

§ XIV. *Speech of Sir Edward Dering.*

was it by any means a bad speech, though for the interests of his party it was hardly a discreet one. They would fain indeed have prevented his rising so early in the debate, but as yet Pym resolutely kept his place, and the field was open to all comers.

not discreetly.

Dering began by enlarging on the importance of the matter in discussion as far transcending any mere bill or act of parliament. Of what was so put forth, he warned them, the three kingdoms were but the immediate or first supervisors; for all Christendom would be attracted by the glass therein set up, and would borrow it to view their deformities. Then let them not dismiss in haste what others would scan at leisure. It was to be considered, first, whether their constituents were looking for such a Declaration. If not, to what end did the House so decline? Wherefore such descension from a parliament to a people? The people looked not up for any so extraordinary courtesy. The better sort thought best of that House; and why should its members be told that the people were expectant for a Declaration. "My constitu-
"ents," continued Sir Edward, "don't want
"it. They do humbly and heartily thank
"you for many good laws and statutes, and
"pray for more. That is the language best
"understood of them and most welcome to
"them. They do not expect to hear any
"other stories of what you have done, much

Urges importance of Remonstrance.

But why carry it to the people?

People want only good laws.

Verney's notes, I have already remarked, were known to Mr. Serjeant D'Oyley and Mr. Hallam some years before their publication by Mr. Bruce.

"less promises of what you will do. Mr.
"Speaker," he added, "when I first heard of
"a Remonstrance, I presently imagined that,
"like faithful counsellors, we should hold up
"a glass *unto his Majesty*. I thought to
"represent, unto the King, the wicked coun-
"sels of pernicious counsellors; the restless
"turbulency of practical papists; the treachery
"of false judges; the bold innovations, and
"some superstition, brought in by some prag-
"matical bishops and the rotten part of the
"clergy. I did not dream that we should
"remonstrate downward, tell stories to the
"people, and talk of the King as of a third
"person." The orator was here upon delicate
ground, and had perhaps some warning as he
spoke that his footing was unsafe. He did not
dispute, he already had remarked, the excellent
use and worth of many pieces of the Declaration; but what was that to him, if he might
not have them without other parts that were
both doubtful and dangerous? He felt
strongly, with the noble learned Lord who
spoke last (Falkland), that to attribute an
introduction of idolatry to the command of the
bishops was to charge those dignitaries with a
high crime. He did not deny that there had
been some superstition in doctrines and in practices by some bishops, but flat idolatry introduced by express command was quite another
thing. He objected that to refer to the decision
of Parliament the order and discipline that were
to regulate the Church, would be to encourage
sectarianism; and he further objected that these,
and other similar passages, appeared to have been

§ XIV. *Speech of Sir Edward Dering.*

introduced by the Committee without being first discussed and recommended to them from the House. Then, taking up the closing averments in the Declaration as to the desire of its promoters for the advancement of learning by a more general and equal distribution of its rewards, he avowed his opinion that this object would be defeated if the great prizes in the Church were abolished. "Great rewards," he said, "do beget great endeavours; and certainly, "Sir, when the great Basin and Ewer are taken "out of the lottery, you shall have few adventurers for small plate and spoons only.* If "any man could cut the moon out all into "little stars,—although we might still have "the same moon, or as much in small pieces, "yet we should want both light and influence."

[margin: Advocates prizes in church.]

[margin: Would not split moons into stars.]

Much beyond this flight even the member for Kent could not be expected to soar; and forcible and lively as many parts of his speech had been, its general tone and tendency had also been such, that the impatience and fears of party friends must greatly have been relieved by his preparation to resume his seat, after some further enlargements of his argument for the patronage and diffusion of learning. He ended by stating, that because he neither looked for cure of complaints from the common people, nor did desire to be

[margin: Final reasons for adverse vote.]

---

* There is no new thing under the sun; and it hardly needs to remind the reader that Sydney Smith's famous argument in defence of the "prizes in the Church," in those three letters to Archdeacon Singleton which rank among the wittiest prose compositions in the language, had been exactly and almost literally reproduced from this speech of Sir Edward Dering's.

[margin: Sydney Smith anticipated.]

cured by them; becaufe the Houfe had not recommended all the heads of the Remonftrance to the Committee which brought it in; and becaufe they paffed his Majefty, and remonftrated to the people; he fhould give his vote with Mr. Hyde.

Rudyard fpeaks.

When Dering refumed his feat, Sir Benjamin Rudyard rofe. It could hardly fail but that much intereft fhould be felt as to the part he would take on this occafion. He was not a leader in the Houfe; but his fpeeches had the influence derived from fingularly eloquent expreffion, from his age and character, from that long experience of parliaments in which he rivalled even Pym himfelf, and from his gravity, courtefy, and moderation of tone. In thefe qualities the Hiftorian of the parliament reports him as pre-eminent. "Cujus " erant mores," he fays, " qualis facundia;" inftancing his oration at the opening of the feffion as "a perfect exemplar" at once of the unfparing expofure of grievances, and of " the " way of fparing the King."* His known defire in this latter refpect gave peculiar fignificance to what fhould now fall from him.

His character by May.

Favourable to a Declaration.

He began by ftating that in his opinion it was abfolutely requifite that the Houfe fhould publifh a Declaration, becaufe this parliament had been flandered by fo many. Of the flanderers he then fpoke, as confifting of the papifts, to whom all parliaments were hateful, but this worft of all; of the delinquents, whom the parliament had punifhed; and of

* May's *Hiftory*: lib. i. chap. vii. Rudyard was now verging on his 70th year, having been born in 1572.

§ XIV. *Speech of Sir Benjamin Rudyard.*

the reckleſs claſs of libertines, who ſought ever to throw off the reſtraints of parliament and law. Next he commented on the malignancy of the libels they had propagated ſo buſily. Nevertheleſs, he continued, "whatſoever they "traduce, by God's aſſiſtance we have done "great things this parliament—things of the "firſt magnitude. We have vindicated the "liberty of our perſons, the freedom of our "eſtates. We have gotten, by the King's "grace and favour, a triennial, a perpetual "parliament, wherein all other remedies and "liberties are included. We have done ſome-"thing, too, for religion; though I reckon "that laſt, becauſe, I am ſorry to ſpeak it, "we have done leaſt in that." Then, as if to guard himſelf from a too deciſive tone againſt Hyde and his party, with whom he was never on unfriendly terms, he deſired Mr. Speaker not to imagine that he approved ordinarily of parliament putting forth what might be called an apology. Truly he thought it went hard with a parliament when it was put to make an apology for itſelf, becauſe apologies were commonly accounted ſuſpicious; but the malignity and machinations of the times had here enforced it, in this inſtance had made it neceſſary. To the particular Declaration before the Houſe, however, he had yet one objection to make. His vote went freely with the narrative part of it; but he muſt object to what he would call the prophetical part. He meant thoſe clauſes which ſet forth acts that were waiting to be paſſed, and meaſures intended hereafter. In that, it appeared to him, there was danger;

Great acts of the Parliament.

Neceſſity to defend it againſt libels.

States one objection to Remonſtrance.

and he doubted if there was precedent for it. It was to forefee the whole work of this parliament to come, and to bind it up by anticipation and engagement of votes beforehand. And he would humbly wifh the Houfe to confider, whether, if they failed in performing fome few of the things they fo promifed and the world would expect, they might not lofe more by non-performance of thofe few than they would be likely to get by all the reft of the Declaration. He refumed his feat with the remark that in any of thefe his doubts he fhould be glad to be refolved by better judgments.

<small>Would only mention Acts paffed: not Bills in progrefs or intended.</small>

This fpeech, moderate and temporifing as it was, was made matter of fuch grave reproach afterwards; and one of chronicler Heath's bafe inventions, which reprefented its fpeaker dying of remorfe as foon as the firft blood of the war was drawn, and complaining on his death-bed that Mr. Pym and Mr. Hampden always told him they thought the King fo ill-beloved by his fubjects that he would never be able to raife an army to oppofe them, has obtained fuch wide belief; that I paufe for a moment, before clofing the fection, to difpofe finally of that flander.

<small>Subfequent attacks on Rudyard.</small>

Rudyard had in his time played no undiftinguifhed part among the patriots, and he had talents and graces of mind, that, as they juftly entitled him to fuch praife at Jonfon's,*

<small>A poet and friend of poets.</small>

<small>Poem by Ben Jonfon.</small>

* " RUDYARD, as leffer dames to great ones ufe,
My lighter, comes to kifs thy learned, mufe;
Whofe better ftudies while fhe emulates,
She learns to know long difference of their ftates.
Yet is the office not to be defpis'd,
If only love fhould make the action prized;

§ XIV. *Speech of Sir Benjamin Rudyard.*

would have given any caufe new luftre. He was a mafterly orator, and no contemptible poet; and though, as I have faid, he was never a leader among thefe remarkable men, they might well boaft of the acceffion they received when fo courtly and accomplifhed a gentleman left his fafhionable haunts upon town and took his place among them. But his part was played out when the war of words became fo fharp as to forefhadow the fiercer conflict. He was in truth too good a fpeaker for the fervice which alone in other refpects he could render when the ftruggle took its graveft afpect. Shakefpeare knew a kind of men incapable even of their diftrefs, and Sir Benjamin was not altogether capable of his excellent oratory. His temperament was too delicate, anxious, and irrefolute, for all the tendencies and confequences of his own brave fpeech.

Joins the Parliament.

Unfit for all its duties.

> Nor he for friendfhip can be thought unfit,
> That ftrives his manners fhould precede his wit."

And again :

> " If I would wifh for truth, and not for fhow,
> The aged Saturn's age and rites to know ;
> If I would ftrive to bring back times and try
> The world's pure gold, and wife fimplicity ;
> If I would virtue fet as fhe was young,
> And hear her fpeak with one, and her firft tongue ;
> If holieft friendfhip, naked to the touch,
> I would reftore, and keep it ever fuch ;
> I need no other arts, but ftudy thee :
> Who prov'ft all thefe were, and again may be."

Epigrams addreffed to Rudyard.

And ftill again—this grand and brave old Jonfon could never fay too much for the men he loved and honoured :

> "Writing thyfelf, or judging others writ,
> I know not which thou'ft moft, candor, or wit ;
> But both thou haft fo, as who affects the ftate
> Of the beft writer and judge, fhould emulate."
>   Ben Jonfon's *Epigrams.*

Sayings and doings.

"He should be very glad," he said on one occasion, "to see that good old decrepit law " Magna Charta, which hath been kept so long " bedrid as it were, walk abroad again with " new vigour and lustre;" but nobody, not Charles himself, was so much alarmed as Sir Benjamin, when that good old law did in reality get upon its legs again. Yet in this he was no traitor; no renegade. It was the effect of timidity and of time. When these debates began, he had passed his seventieth year; and thus in all probability he found himself sinking bedwards, at the very time when the gigantic statute before named was rising out of its long sleep. Though he continued still to act with the parliament, therefore, it is no very grave reproach to him that during the progress of the war he should have cried out Conduct incessantly (as indeed it became old age when in old age. sensible of the grave's approach) for peace, for peace; and he is even supposed to have gone so far as to entitle himself to the (in that day) equivocal praise, recorded on the title-page of one of his published speeches, of having " nobly defended the Bishops." But, convert to the desire for compromise as he so became, he at least did not desert, or malign, the men with whom he had acted in riper years. The No apos- good old knight, to say nothing of his honesty, tate. was too much of a gentleman for that. Nor is there the remotest reason to infer, much as he disliked the conflict, that he was killed by it. He remained in his place in the House of Commons as long as he could; still, however feebly, acting with Pym and with his successors

§ XIV. *Speeches of Rudyard and Bagshaw.*

(as for example in his speech against the Court of Wards as late as '45); still inceffantly defiring a compromife; and, though he never regained any eminence in public affairs, not paffing from the fcene till he was eighty-feven. It feems quite clear, therefore, that the writers or politicians who want a precedent for the defertion and abufe of a great caufe, or a fet of great principles, muft not go to the life of the very eftimable Sir Benjamin Rudyard. They muft be fatisfied with the ftudy of the life of Hyde, which will fhow them, perhaps better than any other piece in hiftory, how it is poffible to act in intimate union with the principles and policy of a particular party at the commencement of a life, and to employ its clofe in fteadily blackening the characters and opinions of the men with whom one had fo acted cordially in earlier days. *Acting in Houfe till his death: æt. 87.*

When Rudyard refumed his feat, he was fucceeded by Mr. Bagfhaw, the member for Southwark, whofe effective fpeech on grievances at the opening of the feffion had for a time given him a place in the Houfe which he failed to make good. He had now joined Hyde's party, but did them fmall fervice in this difcuffion. All that has furvived of his fpeech are two objections to a paffage in the Declaration as to the abufes of the law courts; and againft the tendency of one expreffion, " the reft of the clergy," to comprehend and blame the whole of that profeffion. But he was followed by a more powerful fpeaker. *Mr. Bagfhaw fpeaks: againft the Remonftrance.*

§ XV. SPEECHES OF CULPEPER, PYM, BRIDG-
MAN, WALLER, AND HAMPDEN.

Sir John Culpeper speaks. SIR John Culpeper, Dering's colleague in the reprefentation of Kent, and, after Falkland, Hyde's ftrength and reliance in the debate, fpoke next after Bagfhaw; and we may well fuppofe the fpeech, from the fragment of it that remains, to have been highly charaƈteriftic of the man.* With a ready elocution, he had a rough and hafty temper; and though, when he pleafed, few were fo qualified by memory and quicknefs to feize *Manner of speaking.* and reproduce all the points in a difcuffion, he feldom faw, or cared to fee, more than that fingle point to which he chofe to addrefs himfelf. At all times in fpeaking, Hyde admits, he was warm and pofitive, uncourtly and ungraceful in his mien and motion, and fomewhat indifferent to religion. His firft objeƈtion now

Charaƈter of Culpeper. * "He feldom made an entire judgment of the matter in "queftion, for his apprehenfion was commonly better than "his refolution; and he had an eagernefs or ferocity that "made him lefs fociable than his other colleagues; (for his "education and converfe in the world had been in part "military) and his temper hafty."—Sir Philip Warwick's *Memoires*, p. 196. "He might very well be thought a man "of no very good breeding; having never facrificed to the "Mufes, or converfed in any polite company."—Clarendon's *Remark by Hyde:* *Life*, i. 106-8. In his *Hiftory* (ii. 94), he fays that he could upon occafion, when he fpoke at the end of a debate, as his cuftom often was, recolleƈt all that had been faid of weight on all fides with great exaƈtnefs, and exprefs his own fenfe with much clearnefs and fuch an application to the Houfe, that no man more gathered a general concurrence to his *more* opinion than he. This defcription, however, from other *applicable* accounts, would feem to be much more applicable to the *to Pym.* fpeaking of Pym.

§ xv. *Speeches of Culpeper and Pym.*

to the Remonftrance was that it fpoke of altering the government of the Church, and would therefore offend the people; an argument which certainly no other fpeaker would have had the boldnefs to put in that form. He then declared his oppofition to reft upon two grounds. The firft was, that the Declaration was unneceffary. The parliament had not been "fcandaled" by any public act, and therefore needed not to fend out any declaration to clear themfelves. The fecond was, that if this were not fo, it was yet both unconftitutional and dangerous in its prefent form. Going but from that Houfe, he faid, it went but on one leg. All remonftrances fhould be addreffed to the King, and not to the people, becaufe it belonged to the King only to redrefs grievances. Their writs of election did not warrant them to fend any declaration to the people, but only to treat with the King and the lords: nor had it ever been done by any parliament heretofore. It would be moft dangerous for the public peace.

Objects to Remonftrance:

not neceffary:

and dangerous in form.

People not to be addreffed alone.

The member for Taviftock rofe after him, and delivered a fpeech which in the manufcript record of the debate before me is characterifed as an anfwer to what had been faid by the various members who preceded him; and of which the fragment remaining, fcanty as it is, fhows that this was indeed its character. Even here its maffive and equal proportions are manifeft; and we may trace again the calm power and felf-poffeffion with which the veteran leader of the Parliament appears to have paffed in review the previous fpeakers, as his cuftom

Pym fpeaks.

Anfwers

preceding was in the great debates, and to have anfwered
fpeakers. each. The boldnefs and plain fpeaking of his
reference to the King was even for him remarkable.

To Hyde's appeal that the Houfe fhould be
chary above all things of the King's honour,
Replies Pym replied that the honour of the King lay
to Hyde: in the fafety of the people, and that the members of that Houfe had no choice now but to
tell the truth. They had narrowly efcaped
great dangers, and the time was paffed for concealment. The Plots had been very near the
King. All had been driven home to the Court
and the Popifh party. To what the noble
lord (Falkland) had objected againft the alleged
replies to neceffity of difallowing the votes of the Popifh
Falkland. lords and their abettors the bifhops, he anfwered
that good laws paffed in fpite of thofe votes
formed no anfwer to the affertion that the continued prefence of fuch voters would prevent
the future enactment of fimilar neceffary laws.
That debate itfelf might help to fhow how
their dangers were increafing upon them; and
" will any one deny," afked Pym, " that the
" Popifh lords and the bifhops *do* now obftruct
" us?" Nor could he fee any breach of
privilege in naming them; for had they not
heretofore often complained of particular lords
being away, and of mifcarriages that lords had
Claim of occafioned? Where alfo, he defired to know,
Parlia- fhould be the danger apprehended by " the
ment to " noble learned lord " in the recommendation
advife
King. to his Majefty not to choofe fuch counfellors
as that Houfe might be unable to approve?
" We have fuffered fo much by counfellors of

§ xv. *Speech of John Pym.*

" the King's choofing," faid Pym, " that we   *Right to*
" defire him to advife with us about us." He   *controul minifters.*
maintained that this courfe was conftitutional,
and where was the objection to it? Many of
the King's fervants were known to have moved
him about fuch counfellors, and why may not
the parliament? He enlarged upon this; and
illuftrated the mifchief of difregarding fuch
advice by that quarrel with the firft parliament
upon the unwife treaty of peace with Spain,
which had been fraught with fo many evils.
The fame worthy lord, and the knight who   *Replies to*
fpoke after him in the debate, had objected to   *Culpeper.*
the expreffion *idolatry*. But for himfelf, he
declared his opinion that altar-worfhip WAS
idolatry; and fuch worfhip had undoubtedly
been enjoined by the bifhops in all their ca-
thedrals. Coupling afterwards Sir John Cul-
peper's affertion as to the danger of difturbing   *Replies to*
the exifting Church government, with Sir   *Dering.*
Edward Dering's urgent appeal againft the
danger of permitting fectarianifm to intrude
into the liturgy or fervice, Pym avowed his
readinefs to join in a law againft fectaries, and
remarked that they would moft furely prevent
the evil by going to the root of what caufed
it. Let them take care, then, that no more of
fuch pious and godly minifters as were now
feparatifts beyond the fea, fhould be driven
out of England for not reading the Book of
Sports. Adverting next to what had fallen   *Slanders*
from opponents of the Declaration in admiffion   *againft Parlia-*
of the flanders thrown out againft parliament,   *ment.*
Pym challenged them to fhow that anything
but a Declaration could take away the accufa-

tions that had fo been laid upon the members of that Houfe. To Dering's remark againft the fuggeftion of a more equal provifion for minifters of the Church, that it would interfere with the great prizes, he replied that he held it beft that learning fhould be better provided for in the general than extravagantly rewarded in the particular. Another learned knight on the oppofite benches (Sir Benjamin Rudyard) had objected to what he termed the prophetical part of the Declaration; but he would remind the worthy member that the Declaration did not prophefy, but faid fimply that which it believed to be fit, and might eafily be done. The member who followed him (Mr. Bagfhaw) had queftioned the propriety of afferting that the Court of Chancery had grown arbitrary and unjuft in their jurifdiction, but to this he replied that not the Chancery alone but every Englifh court had of late years ufurped unjuft and arbitrary jurifdiction. To the worthy knight oppofite (Sir John Culpeper) who averred that a declaration going from this Houfe alone, without having defired the lords to join, went but upon one leg, he anfwered that the matter of this particular Declaration was in no refpect fit for the lords. Many of the lords were accufed in it. It alfo dealt throughout with fubjects which had been agitated only in that Houfe. The affertions made by the fame honourable perfon, that all remonftrances fhould be addreffed to the King, and that their writs of election did not warrant them to fend any declarations to the people, were not borne out by the practice. Remonftrances

§ xv. *Speeches of Pym and Bridgman.*

were not in truth directed either to the King or the people, but showed the acts of the House. If it were desired to present the Declaration now before them to the King, it must be done by Petition prefixed to it; and for his own part he inclined that such should be the course. Honourable speakers had complained of a direction to the people in this case, but where was it? Such had not been the purpose, nor was it necessary. It would suffice that its contents should reach the people, and be read by them. And when, by means of the Declaration, it became known throughout England how matters stood, and how the members of the House had been slandered, it would bind and secure to them the people's hearts. *An act of Commons, not of Lords or King.*

Appeal to people from representatives.

It was late in that November evening before Pym resumed his seat, but candles had been brought long ago, and the debate still went on. Orlando Bridgman, member for Wigan, so soon to be Sir Orlando and law dignitary to the King, rose next from among the group of lawyers seated near Hyde, and questioned Pym's view of the House's right to remonstrate or declare alone. They could only consent, counsel, and petition; and it was expressly said, in the indemnity of the Lords and Commons, that nothing should be reported out of either House, without consent of both Houses. As for what had been said of the separatists driven beyond sea, he thought them a condition of men to be taken away, being they were not at all moderate. To the right of approval sought by the House for ever over all counsellors selected by the King, he ob- *Orlando Bridgman speaks.*

Replies to Pym.

jected; and he thought the temporary ground alleged, of the neceffity fo to obtain fecurity for a proper ufe of the money to be voted for the affairs of Ireland, a reafon too particular to juftify fo general a demand.

Edmund Waller fpeaks. Edmund Waller ftarted up and fpoke after Bridgman, and with ingenious and lively turns of expreffion, as his cuftom was. He thought the Declaration ill-named, he faid. It was aimed more at the future than the paft, and expoftulated lefs with what had been done than with what was expected to be done. He thought it fhould be called, not a *Re*monftrance, but a *Pre*monftrance. And how unnatural were all fuch expedients for expreffing the will *Laws not to yield to Orders.* of that Houfe. Laws were the children of the parliament, and it did not become them to deftroy their offspring by means of orders and declarations. By what authority, too, did they claim the right to control the King in the choice of his counfellors? Freeholders had power to choofe freely the members of the *Why control the King?* Houfe of Commons to make laws, and yet the King muft not choofe counfellors to advife according to law without the approbation of the Houfe. In one fenfe it might indeed be a Remonftrance, but it was a Remonftrance againft the laws.

John Hampden fpeaks. John Hampden now rofe. Little remains of what he faid, but fufficient proof that he muft have fpoken, as he did ever, with calm decifion, yet with that rare temper univerfally attributed to him in debate, and which even to a difcuffion fo angry and paffionate as this, could bring its portion of affability and cour-

§ xv. *Speech of John Hampden.*

tefy. What were the objections, he afked, to this Declaration? When that Houfe difcovered ill counfels, might it not fay there were ill counfellors, and complain of them? When any man was accufed, might he not fay he had done his endeavour? "And," continued the member for Bucks, "we fay no more in this." The party oppofed to the members of the Houfe was prevalent, and it was therefore neceffary for them to fay openly that they had given their beft advice. That was declared in the Remonftrance, and no counter remonftrance could come againft them, being it was wholly true. Quiet and merely fuggeftive, however, as Hampden's general tone in this fpeech feems to have been, yet, once at leaft, in the courfe of it, he rofe to a higher ftrain. We have feen that Dering enforced his argument againft ufing the power and revenues of the bifhops in any attempt to ftrengthen the Church by fo giving influence and increafe to the general body of the clergy, by remarking that if any man could cut the moon out all into little ftars, although the fame amount of moon might ftill remain in fmall pieces, both light and influence would be gone. Taking up this extravagant illuftration, Hampden claimed to apply it differently. He afked the Houfe to remember what authority they had for believing that the ftars were more ufeful to the Church than the moon. And then he quoted from the Book of Revelations the paffage * under which the perfect Church, the

Why object to Declaration?

Replies to Dering.

Quotes and applies Revelations.

* "And there appeared a great wonder in Heaven: A
" Woman clothed with the fun, and the moon under her

spouse of Christ, is figured, and warned them that when the woman should be clothed with the sun, the moon would be under her feet, and her head would be circled with stars.

§ XVI. THE SPEECHES UP TO MIDNIGHT.

Hampden resumes seat: 9 o'clock, P.M.

THE House had now been sitting, without interval or rest, for a length of time unexampled in any one's experience. It was nearly nine o'clock before Hampden resumed his seat, yet still the cries for adjournment were resisted amid excitement and agitation visibly increasing. D'Ewes had himself left the House soon after four in the afternoon. He foresaw, as he tells us, that the debate in the issue would be long and vehement; and having been informed by Sir Christopher Yelverton, member for Bossiney, that those who wished well to the Declaration did intend to have it passed without the alteration of any one word, he did the rather absent himself ("being also somewhat ill of a cold taken yesterday") because there were some particulars therein which he had formerly spoken against, and could not in his conscience assent unto, although otherwise his heart and vote went with it in the main. His relation of what followed in his absence, therefore, was derived by him from other members of the House.

Why D'Ewes had left at 4 o'clock.

Attempts at compromise resisted.

The resolution of which Yelverton informed D'Ewes, though relaxed upon a few points, appears to have been in the main steadily

"feet, and upon her head a crown of twelve stars."—*Revelations*, xii. 1.

§ XVI. *The Speeches up to Midnight.*

adhered to; and it was this resolved determination to resist all attempts at any material compromise, which tended more than anything else to prolong and exasperate the opposition. Several such attempts were made, but without success. Though verbal changes were assented to,* and one clause was omitted, it may be inferred, from the two divisions which immediately preceded those taken upon the main question, that such few previous changes were not made under the pressure of any adverse vote. The first was upon a proposition by the promoters of the Declaration to remove a clause to which they had found reason to object, and this they carried, in a House of three hundred and ten members, by a majority of sixty-four.† The second division, which was taken on the clause avowing the necessity

Two divisions.

i. 187 to 123.

---

* I subjoin what appears as to this in the Journals of the House. " Resolved, That the Courts of Chancery, Exchequer " Chamber, &c. *are arbitrary and unjust in their proceedings,* " to be left out; and to be added instead thereof, *which* " *have been grievous in exceeding their jurisdiction.* ' *Loose* " ' *persons*' to be made ' *Libertines.*' Resolved upon the ques- " tion, that these words *which authority shall enjoin*, be made " *which the law enjoins.* Resolved, For to him they are best " *known*, that these words to be left out. Resolved, that the " word *First* be left out; and that the clause beginning with " the word *which*, and ending *kingdom*, be left out." This omitted clause, which had relation to the Court of Requests, was probably that to which D'Ewes referred when, after the remark quoted in the text, he added, " But those who desired " the declaration might pass, were compelled, contrary to " their resolution of which Sir Christopher Yelverton had in- " formed me, to suffer many particulars to be altered, and " amongst the rest that which I could not have assented " unto." See *Ante*, p. 257.

Subject of first division.

Remark by D'Ewes.

† Sir Thomas Barrington and Sir John Clotworthy were tellers for the ayes, Sir Frederick Cornwallis (member for Eye in Suffolk) and Mr. Stanhope (member for Tamworth, and fourth son of Lord Chesterfield) for the noes.

Tellers.

ii. and intention to reduce the exorbitant power of the bishops, ran closer, for, though in the interval, two members only had left the House, the liberal majority was only fourteen.*

161 to 147.

Still it sufficed; and no signs of receding were shown. More firmly than ever, therefore, as the night went on, the debate continued to rage; and what remains of the speech of Denzil Hollis gives proof of a less tolerant and more defiant temper than any previous speaker had exhibited. He plainly avowed with what belief and expectation he was there to support the Declaration. The kingdom, he said, consisted of three sorts of men, the bad, the good, and the indifferent. The indifferent could turn the scales, and that kind of men it was their hope to satisfy by publishing this Remonstrance. In denial of what had been averred by Culpeper, Bridgman, and other speakers, he declared the House to be expressly empowered, by their writs of election, to do this; and he quoted, in proof, the language of the writ by which they were called *ad tractandum de arduis negotiis, &c.* As to the ability residing in either branch of the legislature to make Declarations without the concurrence of the other, he said that it rested on grounds not to be assailed. The Lords had often made Declarations without the Commons, as about the Irish nobility; and the Commons without them, as about the

Denzil Hollis speaks.

People to be influenced.

Power of House to declare singly.

Second division.

* The numbers were 161 to 147, Sir Walter Earle and Mr. Arthur Goodwyn (Hampden's colleague in the representation of Bucks) telling for the majority, and Sir F. Cornwallis and Mr. Strangways for the minority.

§ XVI. *The Speeches up to Midnight.*

Duke of Buckingham. It had been objected that there were subjects on which they of that House were not entitled to advise his Majesty, but all necessary truths must be told. If kings were misled by their counsellors, the people's representatives may, nay they must, tell them of it. It was a duty which rested within safe limits. They only beseeched the King to choose good counsellors, for against such the House would never except. {Right to control King's advisers.}

Many members rose after Hollis, but Speaker Lenthal's eye (a rule of precedence only lately adjudged to be settled)* rested first on lawyer Glyn, the member for Westminster, soon to be recorder for London. There had been some doubt as to the line he would take, but he speedily removed it. It was against nature, he said, not to have liberty to answer a calumny, and there was no way but by Remonstrance to repel what had been laid upon them. They had made a Remonstrance in the first year of the reign, and that without the Lords; and in the third year, if the Speaker of the House had sat still in his chair, a Remonstrance would have been voted, and no fault found with it. The right was unquestionable. Both the Lords temporal and the Bishops had often severally protested without the Commons. He approved also of the matter of the Declaration. It was an honour {Glyn speaks. Precedents for remonstrance. Reasons in its favour.}

---

* " Then," says D'Ewes (in the course of his note describing the debate on the Canons, 26th November, 1640, after Glyn had done speaking), " long dispute ensued who should speak, divers stood up, and at last ruled for Mr. White, and the Speaker's eye adjudged to be the rule." {Speaker's eye rule of precedence.}

to let the world fee that in one twelvemonth they could reduce the diftempers of twelve years. The people trufted that Houfe, and it was therefore no difhonour to ftrive to fatisfy them.

From the anxious group of members who fat near Hyde, among whom were now gathered feveral fervants and officers of the King, Mr. Coventry, member for Evefham and fecond fon of the deceafed Lord Keeper, rofe after Glyn, and appealed to the Houfe at leaft to addrefs the Declaration to the King, if they fhould perfift in voting it. Though men build their monuments in their own time, he faid, yet a chronicle of any King's reign had never, until now, been written in his life-time, without his own confent. After him ftarted up Mr. Geoffrey Palmer, the well-known lawyer (he was Attorney-General at the Reftoration), member for Stamford, and Hyde's intimate friend and counfellor, who afferted with much vehemence that the Houfe could *not* declare without Lords and King, nor had ever done it, and that the beft way for the Commons to anfwer a fcandal was to negleƈt it. As to his friend's law, however, "honeft Jack Maynard" at once rofe and protefted, when Palmer refumed his feat. It was fully competent to the Houfe to declare to the people, for, he continued, if they fhould do nothing but what was ordained and fettled with the other branches of the State, they would affuredly fit ftill. They petitioned only for liberty to approve, they did not dictate the choice of, the counfellors of the King.

<small>Mr. Coventry fpeaks.</small>

<small>Geoffrey Palmer fpeaks.</small>

<small>Maynard fpeaks.</small>

§ XVI. *The Speeches up to Midnight.*

Meanwhile, as the debate thus continued to rage towards midnight, one counsellor of the King had silently and sadly withdrawn. His Majesty's correspondent Nicholas, under promise to inform him that night of the result of the discussion, had waited and watched until nearly worn out with fatigue, and had then of necessity repaired to Whitehall to close and forward his dispatch. He first added to it the subjoined words, little supposing that they would be rendered very memorable by what occurred in the House after his departure. " The Commons have been in debate about " their Declaration touching the ill effects of " bad councils ever since twelve at noon, and " are at it still, it being near twelve at mid- " night. I stayed this dispatch in hope to " have sent your Majesty the result of that " debate, but it is so late, as I dare not (after " my sickness) adventure to watch any longer " to see the issue of it: only I assure your " Majesty there are divers in the Commons' " House that are resolved to stand very stiff " for rejecting that Declaration, *and if they " prevail not then to protest against it.*" So thoroughly had Hyde's party previously resolved upon, and so unreservedly communicated to the ministers of the King, the step which they afterwards declared was quite unpremeditated, and indeed rendered suddenly necessary by the tactics of their opponents. But Nicholas would hardly have repeated it, even to his master, could he have seen the turn that affairs were to take.

Midnight approaching.

Secretary Nicholas retires.

Writes to the King.

Reveals Hyde's purpose.

§ XVII. QUESTION PUT, AND PALMER'S
PROTEST.

MR. Secretary Nicholas had not long left the Houſe when, a little after twelve o'clock, the main queſtion whether the Remonſtrance ſhould
Reſiſtance to putting queſtion. paſs was at laſt allowed to be put. In his Hiſtory, Clarendon admits that it was the party led by Mr. Hyde (himſelf) which ſo long had reſiſted the inceſſant calls for a diviſion ; and that they hoped to profit in numbers by ſo wearing out their opponents, is the plain and irreſiſtible inference. Neverthelefs, he proceeds to tell his readers that when midnight arrived, many were gone home to their lodgings out of pure indiſpoſition of health, having neither eat nor drank all the day ; and
Which ſide gained by delay. others had withdrawn themſelves, that they might neither conſent to it, as being againſt their reaſon and conſcience, nor diſoblige the other party by refuſing ;* leaving it to be inferred, that the gain from delay was entirely to the other party, not his own. In another paſſage † he conveys a ſimilar impreſſion, informing us that candles having been called for when it grew dark "(neither ſide being very
" deſirous to adjourn it till the next day,
" though it was evident very many withdrew
" themſelves out of pure faintneſs and diſ-
Hyde's ſtatement : " ability to attend the concluſion), the debate
" continued till it was after twelve of the
" clock, with much paſſion." And again he

* *Hiſt.* ii. 595. † *Ibid.* ii. 42.

§ XVII. *Question Put, and Palmer's Protest.*

says, in a third passage,* that the party led by Mr. Pym knew well enough that the House had not, at that time, half its members present, though they had provided that not a man of *their* party was absent; and that they had even then carried it by the hour of the night, which drove away a greater number of old and infirm opposers, than would have made those of the negative superior in number. Assuming for a moment that this was so; that the hour of the night did really carry it; and that it was, as Whitelocke affirms Sir Benjamin Rudyard compared it to, the verdict of a starved jury;† surely it is inexplicable that from Pym and his friends, who were to profit by the exactly opposite course, should have proceeded all the efforts that were made to force on the division at an earlier hour. But the first thing to settle, in disputes of this kind, is the authenticity of the point in dispute. We commonly are at "What's the reason "of it," as Selden says, before we are sure of the thing; and he interposes an excellent

Whitelocke's:

reasons to the contrary.

---

* *Hist.* ii. 44.
† "The sitting up all night caused many through weak-
"ness or weariness to leave the House, and Sir B. R. to com-
"pare it to the verdict of a starved jury" (*Memorials*, 51, ed. White-
1732). In reading the Memorials, however, valuable as locke's
they are, it is always necessary to keep in mind not only the *Memo-*
fact that they were compiled at a time not very favourable to *rials.*
the cause which the author had once strongly supported, and
that great portions of them consist of paragraphs taken not
very discriminatingly from Journals and Newspapers, but the
suspicion which there is good ground for entertaining that Not reli-
they were very greatly interpolated before publication. The able.
publication took place in Charles the Second's reign, twenty-
two years after the restoration, seven after Whitelocke's
death.

queftion of my Lady Cotton's, "when Sir
" Robert was magnifying of a fhoe, which
" was Mofes's or Noah's, and wondering at
" the ftrange fhape and fafhion of it, *but*, *Mr.*
" *Cotton*, fays fhe, *are you fure it is a fhoe ?*"
The real truth in this cafe appears to be, that
there is no fhoe. The evidence difproves the
affertion that a number of " old and infirm
" oppofers" had been driven away before the
vote by the latenefs of the hour. Very few
indeed, and thofe only occafional ftragglers,
had quitted the Houfe before the great divifion.
Two divifions on minor points preceded it,
as we have feen, with fome interval interpofed;
yet upon the firft, three hundred and ten
members divided, and upon the fecond, three
hundred and eight; and thefe, being more
than three fifths of the entire Houfe, were
certainly as large an affemblage as had been
muftered fince the Recefs within its walls.*

What, then, were the numbers on the third
and moft important divifion? They had been
reduced by fimply one vote, and this in all
probability the vote of Secretary Nicholas.
I quote the entry from the Journals.† " The

<small>Truth of the cafe.</small>

<small>Numbers on firft divifion: 310.</small>

<small>On fecond divifion: 308.</small>

---

* This point has already been adverted to *ante*, 163-4;
and I will only add that in a debate reported by D'Ewes on the
13th of the month following that in which the Remonftrance
was paffed, it appears that the exact number abfent on the latter
occafion were abfent ftill. The expreffion ufed is, " 200
" members ftill abfent after our recefs." And in this particular
debate, " Sir John Evelyn of Surrey" undertook to fhow that
that number " had not been here fince this fecond meeting."
On this fame occafion it was that Strode made the propofition,
already referred to, to fine a member 50*l*. or expel him, if he
quitted town without leave. " It was," fays D'Ewes, " much
" debated, but laid afide."

<small>Numbers commonly prefent.</small>

† *Commons' Journals*: ii. 322.

§ XVII. *Question Put, and Palmer's Protest.*

"question being proposed, whether this De-
"claration, thus amended, shall pass; the
"question was put, whether this question
"should be first put? and it went with the
"Yeas: And then the question was put, [On third
"whether this Declaration, thus amended, division:
"shall pass? The House was divided. Sir 307.]
"Frederick Cornwallis and Mr. Strangways,
"tellers for the Noe, 148; Sir John Clot-
"worthy and Mr. Arth. Goodwyn tellers for
"the Yea, 159. Resolved, upon the ques-
"tion, that this Declaration, thus amended,
"shall pass."

The question so long and desperately debated had hardly thus been settled, however,
when that new question arose which was to
create a new and worse agitation, and to carry [New ques-
almost to the pitch of frenzy the excited tion
passions of the House. As soon as the vote raised.]
was declared, Clarendon proceeds to say in his
History, "Mr. Hampden moved that there
"might be an order entered for the present
"printing it, which produced a sharper debate
"than the former. It appeared *then*" (as if
this had not been avowed all through the
debate), "that they did not intend to send it [Claren-
"up to the house of peers for their concur- don's Nar-
"rence; but that it was upon the matter an rative :
"appeal to the people, and to infuse jealousies 42.]
"into their minds. It had never* been the
"custom to publish any debates or deter-

---

* The first editors of Clarendon seem to have been so
startled by his use of this word, in direct contradiction of a
well-known fact, that they substituted "seldom" for it. The
genuine text was only restored in 1826-7.

"minations of the House, which were not regularly first transmitted to the house of peers; nor was it thought, in truth, that the House had authority to give warrant for the printing of anything; all which was offered by Mr. Hyde, with some warmth, as soon as the motion was made for the printing it: and he said, 'he did believe 'the printing it in that manner was not 'lawful; and he feared it would produce 'mischievous effects; and therefore desired 'the leave of the House, that if the question 'should be put, and carried in the affir-'mative, that he might have liberty to 'enter his protestation;' which he no sooner said than Geoffrey Palmer (a man of great reputation, and much esteemed in the House) stood up, and made the same motion for himself, 'that he might likewise protest.' When immediately together, many afterwards, without distinction, and in some disorder, cried out, 'They did protest:' so that there was after scarce any quiet and regular debate. But the House by degrees being quieted, they all consented, about two of the clock in the morning, to adjourn till two of the clock the next afternoon."

As to Hyde's protest:

as to Palmer's:

as to others:

as to close of debate:

So did the chief actor in a very memorable scene, writing deliberately in his exile a few years after the event, when nothing of the dignities, the responsibilities, or the trials incident to his later life, had occurred to impair or preoccupy his memory, describe the close of a stormy debate in which he had taken so

§ XVII. *Question Put, and Palmer's Protest.*

prominent a part. We shall shortly be able to test its accuracy. With how much accuracy the same writer had before described its commencement, has already been seen.* Of the similar spirit in which its progress had also been narrated, the reader who has here had all its details before him will be able to judge, as to when he is further informed, still on Lord Clarendon's authority,† that "the debate held "many hours, in which the framers and contrivers of the Declaration said very little, "nor answered any reasons that were alleged "to the contrary: the only end of passing it, "which was to incline the people to sedition, "being a reason not to be given: but still "called for the question, presuming their "number, if not their reason, would serve to "carry it; and after two of the clock in the "morning (for so long the debate continued, "if that can be called a debate where those "only of one opinion argued), when many had "gone home, &c. &c." It may be doubted if history contains such another instance of flagrant and deliberate falsification of the truth, committed by one to whom the truth was personally known. *[as to incidents in its progress.]* *[A tissue of misstatements.]*

Nor unworthy to rank beside it are the sentences first quoted, descriptive of what followed as to his own and Palmer's protestation when the Remonstrance had passed. It was not Hampden who moved the order for the printing,‡ but Mr. Peard, the member for *[Real mover of printing.]*

---

* See *ante*, p. 214.   † *Hist.* ii. 594-5.
‡ It is somewhat strange that this particular misstatement should have been made by Clarendon, whose habit it is to

320   *The Grand Remonſtrance.*

Mr. Peard. Barnſtaple, a lawyer of the Middle Temple in good repute in his profeſſion, and who had ſat in the laſt as well as the preſent parliament. It was not then announced for the

repreſent Hampden as invariably, on ſuch occaſions, reſerving himſelf in the background and putting others in the front. I am bound to add that Clarendon ſeems to have ſhared with others this habit, which I once thought peculiar to himſelf. For, as it is one of the objects of this Work to ſhow how entirely untruſtworthy is his authority for any ſtatement adverſe to the leaders againſt Charles I, it is the more neceſſary not to omit any inſtance in which ſuch ſtatements made by him find unexpected ſupport. Thus, in an entry of D'Ewes's Journal relating to the debate of "the Bill of Epiſcopacy," on the 10th June, 1641, after mentioning that the bill was moved by Sir Robert Harley, the member for Herefordſhire, Sir Simonds adds: " Mr. Pym, Mr. Hampden, and others, with " Mr. Stephen Marſhall, parſon of Finchingfield in the county " of Eſſex, and ſome others, had met yeſternight and appointed " that this bill ſhould be proceeded withal this morning, and " the ſaid Sir Robert Harley moved it firſt in the Houſe : for " Mr. Hampden, out of his ſerpentine ſubtlety, did ſtill put " others to move thoſe buſineſſes that he contrived." It is impoſſible not to compare this with what Clarendon ſays (*Hiſt.* iv. 93) of Hampden's moderation during the firſt year of the Long Parliament, "that wiſe and diſpaſſioned men " plainly diſcerned that that moderation proceeded from pru- " dence, and obſervation that the ſeaſon was not ripe, rather " than that he approved of the moderation ; and that he be- " gat many opinions and notions, the education whereof he " committed to other men, ſo far diſguiſing his own deſigns, " that he ſeemed ſeldom to wiſh more than was concluded." The reader will at the ſame time not too haſtily conclude, that, even aſſuming the feeling reflected in theſe paſſages to have been entertained by members on both ſides of the Houſe, it is neceſſarily the true one. Hampden's was a character, more than moſt men's, open to miſconception. He was peculiarly ſelf-reliant and ſelf-contained, and in a remarkable degree he had the faculty of ſilence. Until the time arrived for ſpeaking, he had never the leaſt diſpoſition to utter what lay within the depths of his breaſt—*altâ* mente repôſtum. On no man of this great period is ſo unmiſtakeably impreſſed the qualities which ſet apart the high-bred Engliſh gentleman, calm, courteous, reticent, ſelf-poſſeſſed ; yet with a perſuaſive force ſo irreſiſtible, and a will and energy ſo indomitable, lying in thoſe ſilent depths, that all who came within their reach came alſo under their control. Clarendon, though he ſtill

Hyde and Hampden.

D'Ewes on Hampden.

Art of making uſe of others :

open to miſjudgment.

§ XVII. *Question Put, and Palmer's Protest.*

first time, but had substantially been confessed all through the debate, that the Declaration was meant as an appeal to the people. And so far from the desire to "protest" having arisen naturally and suddenly out of that announcement, we have seen, by the irrefragable evidence unconsciously afforded in Secretary Nicholas's letter to the King, that the protest had been concerted as a party move, and made known to the King's servants before the Declaration was voted. The intention was obvious. It was meant to divide, and by that means destroy, the authority of the House of Commons. It was a plan deliberately devised to exhibit, before the face of the country, the Minority as in open conflict against the Majority, and as possessed of rights to be exercised independently. The

True object of "protesters."

To divide and destroy authority of House.

imparts his own colour to the feeling, gives it fairer expression in the passages where he speaks of his possessing "that seeming "humility and submission of judgment as if he brought no "opinion of his own with him, but a desire of information and "instruction; yet had so subtle a way of interrogating, and, "under the notion of doubts, insinuating his objections, that "he left his opinions with those from whom he pretended to "learn and receive them." And again he says: "He was "not a man of many words, and rarely begun the discourse, "or made the first entrance upon any business that was "assumed; but a very weighty speaker, and after he had "heard a full debate, and observed how the House was like "to be inclined, took up the argument, and shortly, and "clearly, and craftily, so stated it, that he commonly con- "ducted it to the conclusion he desired; and if he found he "could not do that, he was never without the dexterity to "divert the debate to another time, and to prevent the deter- "mining anything in the negative which might prove incon- "venient in the future." *Hist.* i. 323-4. Here we have again the craft and the subtlety, but it is less "serpentine." I have enlarged upon this theme in my *Arrest of the Five Members*, § xvii.

Claren- don : Hist. iv. 92.

A go- vernor of men.

Y

322   *The Grand Remonſtrance.*

Why ſo reſolutely reſiſted.
balance would be thus redreſſed; and the King's party, outvoted in the Houſe, would yet be a recogniſed power without its walls, and would carry thenceforward a ſhare of its authority. Happily, the leaders ſaw the intention, and on the inſtant met and defeated it. The right to proteſt, they ſaid, never had been, and never could be, admitted there. The Houſe of Commons was indiviſible. It acted with one will, and one power; and it exerciſed rights with which individual claims were incompatible. Its authority derived from the people, its privilege to addreſs them, its power to tax them, reſted upon a foundation that would at once be undermined and overthrown by what Hyde and his friends had aſked for.

Exiſtence of Houſe involved.

To uſe merely the language of Clarendon in giving account of what followed thereupon, and ſimply to ſay that many members roſe to ſpeak without diſtinction and in ſome diſorder, ſo that there was after ſcarce any quiet and regular debate, were to offer a faint verſion indeed of the truth. Never had thoſe walls witneſſed ſuch a ſcene as now, from the report of eye-witneſſes leſs prejudiced and partial, waits to be deſcribed.

Unexampled ſcene.

§ XVIII. VALLEY OF THE SHADOW OF
DEATH.

Remonſtrance carried by 159 to 148.
HARDLY had announcement been made of the diviſion which carried the Remonſtrance by a majority of eleven votes, when one more ſtrenuous effort was made to have it addreſſed

§ XVIII. *Valley of the Shadow of Death.*

to the King. This was fuccefsfully refifted;
Denzil Hollis expreffing his intention to move, *Poſt,* 343.
on another occafion, that it fhould be referred
to a committee to give effect to the modified
fuggeftion already thrown out by Pym. Mr.
Peard then moved that the Declaration might Peard
be printed, which was oppofed with the greateft moves
warmth and vehemence by Hyde and Culpeper; printing.
Hyde again giving utterance to the extraordinary opinion he had ventured to exprefs in the
debate, that the Houfe of Commons had no Hyde.
right to print without the Lords' concurrence. oppofes.
Wherefore, he added, if the motion were perfifted in, he fhould afk the leave of the Houfe
to have liberty to enter his proteft. Culpeper's fpeech in the fame ftrain, replying to
the determined objection made upon this, firft Confufed
very calmly by Pym, and then more excitedly debate.
by Denzil Hollis, carried the excitement ftill
higher; and in the midft of it were now heard
feveral voices, and among them very con-
fpicuoufly that of Palmer, crying out that they
alfo protefted. Some one then rofe, and
moved that the names of the protefters might Members
be taken; but this, being declared againft the protefting.
forms and orders, was not at the moment
preffed. "So," according to D'Ewes's account,
derived from Sir Chriftopher Yelverton, " this
" matter was underftood to be laid afide until
" a further time of debate, when everybody
" thought the bufinefs had been agreed upon,
" and that the Houfe fhould have rifen, it
" being about one of the clock of the morning Palmer
" enfuing, when Mr. Geoffrey Palmer, a moves to
" lawyer of the Middle Temple, ftood up." take down
names

He should not be satisfied, he said, for himself or those around him, unless a day were at once appointed for discussion of whether the right to protest did not exist in that House; and meanwhile he would move, with reference to such future discussion, that the Clerk should now enter the names of all those whose claim to protest would then have to be determined. At these words the excitement broke out afresh; loud cries of "All! All!" burst from every side where any of Hyde's party sat; and Palmer, carried beyond his first intention by the passion of the moment, cried out unexpectedly that he *did* for himself then and there protest, for himself and all the rest—"of his "mind," he afterwards declared that he meant to have added, but for the storm which suddenly arose.

The word *All* had fallen like a lighted match upon gunpowder. It was taken up, and passed from mouth to mouth, with an exasperation bordering on frenzy; and to those who in after years recalled the scene, under that sudden glare of excitement after a sitting of fifteen hours,—the worn-out weary assemblage, the ill-lighted dreary chamber, the hour sounding One after midnight, confused loud cries on every side breaking forth unexpectedly, and startling gestures of violence accompanying them,—it presented itself to the memory as a very Valley of the Shadow of Death. "All! "all!" says D'Ewes, was cried from side to side; "and some waved their hats over their "heads, and others took their swords in their "scabbards out of their belts, and held them by

[margin notes: of all claiming to protest. Cries of "All! All!" Palmer protests for "all." Sudden fury of excitement. "I thought we had all sat in the Valley of the Shadow of Death."]

§ XVIII. *Valley of the Shadow of Death.* 325

"the pummels in their hands, setting the lower Swords
"part on the ground; so, as if God had not ready for mischief.
"prevented it, there was very great danger
"that mischief might have been done. All
"those who cried *All, all,* and did the other
"particulars, were of the number of those
"that were against the Remonstrance." And
among them was the promising young gentleman of the King's house, Mr. Philip Warwick,
the member for Radnor, who bethought him,
as we have seen, of that brief scriptural comparison from the wars of Saul and David,* Parallel from Saul's wars.
his application of which comprised all that,
until now, was known to us of this extraordinary scene. He thought of what Abner said
to Joab, and Joab to Abner, when they met
on either side of the pool of Gibeon; and how,
having arisen at the bidding of their leaders to
make trial of prowess, their young men caught
every one his fellow by the head, and thrust
his sword in his fellow's side, and so fell down
together; a result which might have followed Calmness of Hampden.
here, had not the sagacity and great calmness of
Mr. Hampden, by a short speech, prevented it.

It is not perhaps difficult to imagine, from
what D'Ewes goes on to say of the short but
memorable speech, with what exquisite tact
and self-control this profound master of debate
calmed down the passions of that dangerous
hour. He saw at once that the motion for Shows Palmer's presumption.
printing could not then with safety be persisted
in; and, reminding the House that there might
be many who, having supported the Remon-

---

* Samuel II. Chap. ii. v. 12-16. And see *ante*, p. 112.

ſtrance, might yet be oppoſed to the printing of it, he aſked how any one could ſo far know the minds of ſuch as to preſume to enter a proteſt for *them* ? " Some who were againſt " the printing of the Remonſtrance," ſays D'Ewes, " yet diſavowed Mr. Palmer's deſiring " to have a proteſtation entered in their names; " *and Mr. Hampden demanded of him how he* " *could know other men's minds?* To whom " Mr. Palmer anſwered, having leave of the " Houſe to ſpeak, that he having once before " heard the cry ' All, All,' he had thereupon " deſired to have the ſaid proteſtation entered " in all their names."

How ſhould he anſwer for "all."

The Houſe calmed.

The mere queſtion and anſwer had quelled the unnatural excitement, and brought the Houſe again, as Hampden anticipated, within government and rule. Agreement was then come to, that the queſtion as to the printing of the Declaration ſhould for the preſent be left undetermined, with the underſtanding that it was not to be printed without ſpecial leave. Hyde's party would further have reſtricted this order, by introducing the word "publiſhed" into it; but Pym, refuſing to conſent to that addition, divided the Houſe once more, and carried the original propoſal, " that this Decla- " ration ſhall not be printed without the par- " ticular order of the Houſe," by a majority of twenty-three : thus leaving the publication free, and reſtraining the printing only until further order. The numbers were 124 to 101 ; Sir Edward Dering and Sir Robert Crane, D'Ewes's colleague in the repreſentation of Sudbury, being tellers for the minority;

Printing to be left unſettled.

Fourth Diviſion: 124 to 101.

§ XIX. *Sitting of Tuesday, the 23rd Nov.* 327

and for the majority, Sir Walter Earle and Mr. Richard Knightly, the member for Northampton. Between the laſt diviſion and the preſent, thirty-five of Pym's party and forty-ſeven of Hyde's had quitted the Houſe. And ſo, ſays D'Ewes, "the Houſe aroſe juſt "when the clock ſtruck two the enſuing "morning." Houſe riſes 2 A.M.

In the ruſh to the door after their weary ſitting of eighteen hours, Falkland and Cromwell paſſed out together; and Hyde afterwards reported, on the relation of his friend, that even the member for Cambridge, uſually ſo "tempeſtuous" in behaviour, ſhowed no exultation at the victory his party had gained. Not as of a triumph won, but as of a danger narrowly eſcaped, was Cromwell's reference to the vote which had cloſed this momentous debate. If it had gone againſt them in that vote, he ſaid, he and many other honeſt men he knew would have ſold all they had this very morning, and never have ſeen England more. And though the ſpeaker is not, perhaps, likely in expreſs terms to have ſaid this, any more than to have acted in any ſuch faſhion, the anecdote doubtleſs repreſents what ſubſtantially was not untrue. The turning point of freedom or deſpotiſm for two more centuries in England was probably paſſed that night. What Cromwell ſaid of the vote.

Turning point of freedom or deſpotiſm.

§ XIX. SITTING OF TUESDAY, THE 23RD NOVEMBER.

CLARENDON fixes as late as three o'clock the hour of meeting on the day following the Tueſday, 23rd Nov.

famous fitting of which I have thus, for the first time, given all the impreffive details. But in reality the Houfe affembled only a little later than the ufual hour. Much important bufinefs, not admitting of delay, was in hand; and the further loan of fifty thoufand pounds from the City for the Irifh affairs, to bear intereft at eight per cent., had this day to be completed. A little incident marked the temper of the Houfe. Early in the month the Queen's confeffor, Father Philips, had for contumacious conduct been committed by the Lords to the Tower, and no order was to be given for his releafe without the knowledge of the Commons. He had now made fubmiffion, and in deference to an urgent meffage from the Queen, the Lords had ordered his releafe; but on their meffenger bringing this intimation to the Commons, a peremptory refufal was fent back, and Father Philips had to return to the Tower. This incident had paffed, and it was nearly four o'clock in the afternoon, when Pym arofe, and made allufion to the fcene of the night before. He lamented the diforder on that occafion, which, he faid, might probably have engaged the Houfe in blood. It proceeded principally, he continued, by the offering a proteftation, which had never before been offered in that affembly; and was a tranfgreffion that ought to be feverely examined, that mifchief hereafter might not refult from the precedent. He therefore propofed that the Houfe fhould the next morning enter upon that examination: and in the meantime he advifed that men might recollect themfelves,

§ XIX. *Sitting of Tuesday, the 23rd Nov.* 329

and they who used to take notes might peruse their memorials; to the end that the persons who were the chief causers of the disorder might be named, and defend themselves the best they could. "And with this resolution," adds Clarendon, "the House rose; the vex-
" ation of the night before being very visible
" in the looks and countenances of many."* {to be discussed next day.}

How far the further statement made herein by Clarendon is to be believed, must be judged upon the facts. He says, as we have seen, that the House did not meet till three in the afternoon: But the statement in D'Ewes's Notes (and this is borne out by the Journals) leaves no doubt that the House was in debate soon after ten o'clock. He asserts that the most part of the day had been passed by the leading men in private consultations, having for their object how to chastise some of those who most offended them the night before, and how to punish the attempt to introduce the dangerous and unheard-of precedent of pro- testing against the sense of the House: But the private consultations must in that case have been held during the open sitting, for the leading men on Pym's side were unquestionably engaged, in public, upon the bill for deter- mining parliamentary privilege, upon the Committee of Irish affairs, upon the bill of tonnage and poundage, upon the City loan, and upon the case of the Queen's confessor. He explains that the subject of private consul- {The truth, and Clarendon's version of it. As to party counsels. Impossible as stated.}

---

* *Hist.* ii. 46. D'Ewes simply says of the rising of the House, that " they appointed to meet to-morrow at ten, and
" rose between four and five of the clock."

tation was all the more grateful to the "leading "violent men who bore the greateſt ſway," becauſe they ſhould thereby take revenge upon Mr. Hyde (himſelf), whom they perfectly hated above any man, and to whoſe activity they imputed the trouble they had ſuſtained the day before; only they encountered an unexpected difficulty from an important ſection of their ſupporters, the Northern men as they were called, led by Sir John Hotham, Sir Hugh Cholmondeley, and Sir Philip Stapleton, members for Beverley, Scarborough, and Boroughbridge, who were ſo grateful to Mr. Hyde for his ſervices in overthrowing the monſtrous oppreſſion of the Court of York, that they refuſed to join againſt him, though very eager to make others reſponſible; and he adds that this diſpute, which broke out in the private council in the morning, occupied all that day and night, and was only terminated by the compromiſe of ſelecting another perſon, Palmer, to bear the brunt of puniſhment: But if all this were ſo, it is ſtrange that neither Sir Simonds D'Ewes nor Sir Ralph Verney, in Notes ſtill preſerved exactly as they were taken at the moment, ſhould in any form confirm or make alluſion to it; and ſtill more ſtrange that the leaders ſhould have propoſed to make Hyde reſponſible for the minor offence of aſking leave to proteſt, which had led to no diſturbance, and to paſs by the real offence of Palmer, who reopened the queſtion that had been laid aſide, did actually proteſt without aſking leave,* and brought on the ſcene that

As to a purpoſe againſt himſelf:

rejected by Northern men.

As to diſputes among the leaders.

Not confirmed by D'Ewes or Verney.

* Clarendon is obliged to admit this diſtinction, even where

followed. It will be perhaps the more natural, and certainly no unfair, conclufion to form, that the writer who deliberately had mifreprefented and mifftated every fingle fucceffive incident in thefe memorable debates, has mifreprefented this alfo. Happily the means of refutation are at hand; and from records taken at the moment, and quite above fufpicion, the account given by Clarendon can be corrected, and the ftory of the Grand Remonftrance be faithfully carried to its clofe. It is but another chapter of the fame great theme that prefents itfelf in the Debate on Palmer's Proteft.

Why not credible.

Refuted by MS. of D'Ewes.

§. XX. DEBATE ON PALMER'S PROTEST.

ON Wednefday, the 24th of November, the Speaker arrived at the Houfe at about ten o'clock, when, after prayers were read, certain neceffary bufinefs of no great intereft was done, and Pym moved the appointment of fome committees. He then, producing a printed pamphlet, purporting to be Articles of Accufation preferred againft Father Philips, and containing matters of fcandal againft the French Ambaffador, pointed out the grave offence of difseminating fuch falfehoods, and called the printer to the bar. Hereupon Mr. Ralph Goodwin, the member for Ludlow (he who

Ninth Debate: Wednefday, 24th Nov.

Pym denounces fcandalous prints.

he is doing his beft to exaggerate the caufe of offence he had himfelf given. "He was the firft" (he is fpeaking of himfelf) "who made the proteftation, that is, *afked leave to do it*; "which produced the other *fubfequent clamour*, that was ' indeed in fome diforder."

Clarendon: Hift. ii. 45.

was afterwards fecretary to Prince Rupert), took the fame opportunity of complaining, that a pamphlet fcandalous to the King himfelf had alfo juft been printed, purporting to be the account of a duel between Sir Kenelm Digby and a French Lord, as to which he moved that the printer thereof might alfo be queftioned. To whom, with a fimilar complaint of unauthorifed printing, fucceeded Mr. Robert Reynolds, who fat for Hindon in Wiltfhire, and was afterwards one of the King's judges, and who brought before the Houfe the fact, that the examination of a delinquent prieft, taken by one of their committees, ftill remaining in his own poffeffion, and not yet reported to the Houfe, had been fuddenly iffued in print; an offence which alfo called for punifhment. "Upon all which motions," D'Ewes adds, "it was ordered that the former com-
" mittee for printing (of which I was one)
" fhould meet to-morrow morning at feven
" of the clock, in the Inner Court of Wards,
" and fhould examine thefe abufes now
" complained of, and all other abufes of the
" kind, and to confider of fome way for the
" preventing thereof."

Complaints of Pamphleteers.

Referred to Committee for abufes of printing.

Pym fpeaks againft "proteft."

Then fucceeded the more interefting bufinefs of the day, introduced as ufual by the member for Taviftock. He called the attention * of

Hift. ii. 46-7.

* This opening of the proceedings, down to the appearance of Hotham in the debate, is taken from Clarendon. It is here given becaufe, although neither in the notes of D'Ewes, nor thofe of Verney, is there any mention of it,—both beginning their account with Hotham's fpeech,—it is not only quite poffible that Hyde may have fpoken what he here attributes to himfelf, but it is even likely that he fo endeavoured

§ xx. *Debate on Palmer's Protest.* 333

the House to the offence which had been com- *Shows its*
mitted on Monday night. He enlarged upon *danger.*
the mischief it was then like to have produced,
and which would unavoidably be produced, if
the custom or liberty of individuals protesting
against the sense of the House should ever be admitted. That was the first time it had ever been
offered there, and care ought to be taken that it
should be the last, by severe judgment upon
those who had begun the presumption. Where- *Hyde*
upon Hyde rose and said, that it concerned *defends it:*
him to justify what he had done, being the
first man who mentioned the protestation.
But he was interrupted by a general noise and
clamour, one half the House crying to him *amid cla-*
to "withdraw," and the other half to "speak." *mour.*
He waited awhile, and then resumed. He
was not old enough, he said, to know the
ancient customs of that House; but he well
knew it was a very ancient custom in the
House of Peers. Leave was never denied *Why not*
there to any man who asked that he might pro- *Commons as well as*
test, and enter his dissent, against any judgment *Lords?*
of the House to which he would not be understood to have given his consent; and he did
not understand any reason why a commoner
should not have the same liberty, if he desired
not to be involved in any vote which he
thought might possibly be inconvenient to him.
He had not offered his protestation against the
Remonstrance, though he had opposed it all he

to put himself forward, when he found that his friend Palmer *Hyde and*
was to be called to account. The matter of the so-called *Palmer.*
private dispute raised as between Hyde and Palmer, which I
altogether disbelieve in, is not affected by it either way.

could, becaufe it remained ftill within thofe walls. He had only defired leave to proteft againft the printing it; which, he thought, was in many refpects not lawful for them to do, and might prove very pernicious to the public peace.

This was liftened to with fome impatience; and at its clofe the member for Beeralfton, always impetuous and forward on fuch occafions, was for having the Houfe to call upon Mr. Hyde to withdraw, fince he confeffed that he firft propofed the proteftation; but Mr. Strode's fuggeftion was difregarded, and not the leaft notice appears to have been taken of Mr. Hyde's own propofal to make a martyr of himfelf.

Mr. Hotham, the member for Scarborough, familiarly called Jack Hotham, the fon of Sir John, and fo foon to perifh with him on a public fcaffold for treafon to the Parliament, rofe now and faid that the offence committed on Monday night which the Houfe was called to vifit with its fevereft cenfure, was committed by Mr. Geoffrey Palmer, the member for Stamford. A gentleman on that occafion had offered, with the leave of the Houfe, to make a proteftation, and another had feconded him; upon which the faid Mr. Palmer had without leave cried out, *I do proteft*, and, further encouraging men to cry out every man the fame, had faid that he protefted "for himfelf and "the reft." Many voices here interrupted Hotham, fhouting out that Palmer's words were "*all* the reft." The fpeaker proceeded, and fhowed that fuch words in the mouth of

§ xx. *Debate on Palmer's Protest.*

any member, tended to draw on a mutiny; *of a mutiny.* and that if this were permitted in the Houſe, any one might make himſelf the head of a faction therein, and there would ſoon then be an end of the liberty and privileges of Parliament, and they might ſhut up their doors. *Moves to have him ſent for.* He therefore deſired that Mr. Palmer, not being in the Houſe, might be ſent for.

Several members of Hyde's party next roſe, and objected to Palmer's being ſent for; and ſome wiſhed to know by what right Mr. Hotham had applied the word "faction" to any ſection of members in that Houſe. But, adds D'Ewes, "whilſt we were in debate about *Palmer enters.* "ſending for him, Mr. Palmer came in; " and then Mr. Hotham laid the ſame charge " againſt him which he had done before, for " the ſubſtance thereof." Hereon, he continues, ſome would have had Mr. Palmer to make his anſwer, and then to withdraw into the Committee Chamber, that ſo they might proceed to cenſure; but others ſaid, that either he had committed no fault to which he was to anſwer, or, if he *had* ſpoken anything amiſs, he was to have been queſtioned for it at the time when he ſpake it, and not at this time, *Conflict of friends and foes.* which was two days ſince the pretended words were uttered. "And this was maintained," ſays D'Ewes, "with great vehemence by thoſe " who ſpake for Mr. Palmer."

Hyde and Culpeper were as uſual the moſt vehement. Speaking to the orders of the Houſe, Hyde ſaid * the charge againſt Palmer

---

* Clarendon's own account of his ſpeech is, that, upon Mr. Palmer being called upon to explain, " Mr. Hyde (who

Hyde supports Palmer.

was againſt the orders, being he was only charged with words, not with any ill carriage. This being ſo, and the words not having been excepted againſt at the time they were ſpoken, it was now no orderly charge. For, in that caſe,

Too late to require him to anſwer.

a man might be queſtioned for words ſpoken a month or a year ago, as well as for thoſe ſpoken on Monday laſt. Words might be forged, too, and then how could a man anſwer for himſelf? It would take away the great privilege of freedom of ſpeech. Culpeper went ſtill further. Alſo ſpeaking to the orders of the Houſe, he took the objection, that the members aſſembled

Culpeper on ſame ſide.

on that day, Wedneſday the 24th, could not be competent judges of words ſpoken on Monday the 22nd, becauſe divers were on this occaſion preſent who on the former were abſent; although he did not deny that the Houſe was the ſame in reſpect of the power of it. And what could be more dangerous than for a man to be queſtioned for words ſpoken in the

Members to be queſtioned only at ſpeaking.

Houſe after the time he ſhould ſpeak them; for might he not in ſuch caſe be alſo queſtioned in another parliament after? Theſe confident opinions appear to have ſhaken ſome of the members preſent; the

Hyde reported by himſelf: Hiſt. ii. 48.

" loved him much, and had rather have ſuffered himſelf,
" than that he ſhould) ſpoke to the order of the Houſe, and
" ſaid that it was againſt the orders and practice of the Houſe
" that any man ſhould be called upon to explain, for anything
" he ſaid in the Houſe two days before ; when it could not be
" preſumed that his own memory could recollect all the words
" he had uſed ; or, that anybody elſe could charge him with
" them ; and appealed to the Houſe whether there was any
" precedent of the like—and there is no doubt there never had
" been ; and it was very irregular." The account of the ſpeech in the text, however, is manifeſtly more correct than this notice of it preſerved by its author.

§ xx. *Debate on Palmer's Protest.* 337

debate went on with increasing heat; and three hours had been so passed, when Denzil Hollis got up, and declared that he would charge Mr. Palmer with a new charge, in making a pernicious motion. But now, Sir Simonds D'Ewes, fortified with precedents, advanced to the rescue; undertaking to prove that the original proposition to make Palmer responsible for the words he had uttered, was strictly in accordance with the usage, and no violation of the orders, of the Commons.

Denzil Hollis makes new charge.

He began by saying he was sorry, with all his heart, that the House should already have lost so much time about this business, and the more because it concerned a gentleman whom he had long known, and knew to be learned in his profession. But he wondered to see any member of that House, and much more (alluding to Hyde) any of the long robe, affirm that they could not question words spoken therein any day after they were spoken, unless exception to the words were taken at the time of speaking. "I dare be bold to say," continued Sir Simonds, warming into confidence, as his well-beloved records and precedents came to him at need, " there " are almost precedents in every Journal we " have of the House of Commons. Some " I can remember upon the sudden, as Mr. " Copley, in the time of Queen Mary; Mr. " Peter Wentworth, in 35th Elizabeth;* and, " in 43d and 44th of the same Queen, either

D'Ewes speaks.

Replies to Hyde.

Exhibits precedents.

* " I was mistaken in the year," notes the particular D'Ewes in the margin of his Journal, " for it was in—" but alas! the correction is not legible to me.

z

"one Haſtings took exception at Mr. Francis
"Bacon, or he to Haſtings, for I dare not
"truſt an ill memory with the exact relation
Members "of it upon the ſudden. And all theſe were
not quef- "queſtioned in this House after the day was
tionable
elſewhere: "paſſed in which the words were ſpoken.
"This, indeed, is the true, ancient, funda-
"mental right of parliament, that we ſhould
"not be queſtioned anywhere elſe for things
"ſpoken within theſe walls. But that we
"ſhould not have power here to queſtion our
"own members for words ſpoken within theſe
"walls, either at the time when the ſaid words
"were ſpoken, or at any time after alſo, were
but by the "to deſtroy thoſe very liberties and rights of
Houſe at
any time. "parliament."

Having laid down thus clearly and boldly the undoubted parliamentary rule, D'Ewes went on to apply it to Palmer's caſe. Pre-miſing that the words ſpoken, and matter of fact in iſſue, muſt be ſtated exactly, he ſhewed that to refiſt any propoſal to queſtion the ſame,
Judgment whether at the moment of delivery, or at any
of Houſe time after, would be to decline the juſtice of
never
avoidable. the Houſe; which for his part he ſhould never do, but ſhould always be ready to anſwer, at any preſent or future time, to anything he ſhould there ſay. As for that which was ob-jected, he continued, by the gentleman on the other ſide (and he pointed to Sir John Cul-peper), that it were a dangerous thing for them to admit that a ſucceeding parliament might
Error in queſtion what was done in a former, there was
Culpe-
per's nothing more ordinary or more uſual. There
argument. was no doubt whatever but that a ſucceeding

§ xx. *Debate on Palmer's Protest.*

parliament might not only queftion any par- Future
ticular thing done by them, as, for example, parlia-
what was in progrefs at that moment, but queftion
might alfo revoke and repeal all the acts and paft.
ftatutes which they had paffed. And the reafon thereof was evident and plain. For they
fat not there in their own right, but were fent
thither, and entrufted by the whole kingdom;
the knights being chofen by the feveral counties, and the reft by the feveral cities and towns.
And, for that which was objected by the fame
worthy gentleman oppofite, that, there being
divers others in the Houfe who were not there
when the words were fpoken, therefore the Houfe un-
Houfe was not the fame, he (Sir Simonds changed
D'Ewes) faid confidently that the Houfe was of mem-
the fame to all intents and purpofes, not only bers.
quoad poteftatem, but *quoad notionem* alfo; for
of courfe he affumed there muft be a perfect
agreement as to what the words were that were
fpoken, before they could proceed to a cenfure
of them. Whereupon, as though remember-
ing his own abfence at the extraordinary fcene,
he thus proceeded:

" And truly they may well be excufed that D'Ewes's
" were abfent out of this Houfe at midnight, own
" for it was about that time on Monday night midnight
" laft when thefe words were fpoken; and I of Mon-
" do as much wonder that fo many in this day.
" Houfe fhould object that the fpeaking of
" words is not an action, when that old verfe
" affures us of the contrary—' Quatuor et
" ' dentes et duo labra fimul, &c.' And more
" ftrange it feems to me alfo, that when this
" worthy gentleman himfelf (and I pointed to

z 2

"Mr. Palmer) hath so often stood up, himself, to speak, so many should hinder him;
for if they will not let him speak by way of
answering, yet let him speak by way of
speaking.—Some laughed at this, thinking I
had been mistaken; but I proceeded and
told them, that I should be sorry to speak
anything in that House which I could not
make good logic of; and therefore I still
pressed, that if we would not let him speak
by way of answering, that is by coaction
and as a delinquent, then let him speak by
way of speaking, that is *sermoni libero et spon-
taneo*. And who knows," concluded the
precise and learned orator, " but that he may
give much satisfaction to this House by his
speaking? And therefore, Sir, I desire that
he may be heard."

Would have Palmer speak.

D'Ewes proud of his logic.

Palmer's friends prevent his rising.

The desire of the worthy Sir Simonds, however, failed to convince Mr. Palmer's friends
of the expediency of yielding thereto. In vain
the Speaker renewed the proposition that the
member for Stamford should be heard. In
vain was it urged that no man was entitled to
object because none knew what he would say.
The objectors stood so firm, that it became
clear it would have to come to a division, and
Hyde and Culpeper violently called out to
divide. Palmer withdrew into the Committee
Chamber, and the Speaker put the question—
As many as are of opinion that Mr. Palmer
shall be required to answer to the charge laid
against him, let them say Aye. "But then,"
interposes D'Ewes, " Mr. Palmer's friends
would have had these words to have been

A division called for.

Hyde moves addition

§ xx. *Debate on Palmer's Protest.* 341

" added to the queftion, namely, 'for words to quef-
" 'by him fpoken on Monday night laft;' tion.
" but we that thought Mr. Palmer deferved
" to be queftioned, would not agree to that
" addition. Whereupon it came to a divifion
" upon the queftion."

The tellers appointed on the one fide were Hyde and Sir Frederick Cornwallis, and on the other Sir Thomas Barrington and Sir Martin Lumley, the member for Effex. The Ayes went out, and proved to be but 146; the Defeated Noes (of whom D'Ewes was one) fat ftill, and by 192 to 146. were 192. It being directed, upon this, that Hyde's addition fhould not be made, Sir Robert Hatton, the member for Caftle Rifing, and a determined royalift, jumped up to fpeak againft the other queftion; but Mr. Speaker interrupted and told him he was out of order, for he could not now fpeak until the queftion had been put. It was put accordingly, the fame tellers being Original appointed on both fides; and the Ayes (of queftion carried by whom D'Ewes was one) going out, were 190, 190 to whereas the Noes, fitting ftill, were but 142. 142. It was thereupon immediately ordered, that Mr. Palmer fhould be required to fpeak; and being called down from the Committee Chamber, in which he had remained fince before the firft divifion, he was informed by the Speaker Palmer that the Houfe required him to make anfwer required to fpeak. to the charge laid againft him.

He prefently arofe, and, profeffing his innocency as to the particular matter alleged, made relation of fome foregoing paffages. That when, upon the vote being determined that the Declaration fhould pafs, a motion was

His defence.

Hampden's question.

Apology.

Whitelocke supports Palmer.

Mr. Speaker cannot see hon. members.

made by Mr. Peard that it should be printed, divers protested against it; and that himself desired also to have his protestation entered, against the printing but not the passing; and that when, afterwards, it was moved that the names of such as had protested might be entered, he being unsatisfied, and desiring it might be debated first whether such a protestation might be made or not, wished a day to be appointed for that end, and thereupon desired that his own name, and the names of the rest who had protested, might be entered by the Clerk. And that, Mr. Hampden thereupon asking him, how he knew other men's minds, he answered, because he had heard others desire their names to be entered, and heard them cry "All, all." But for the other words charged upon him, that he had protested "in the name of himself and "the rest," he declared he did not remember that he had spoken them. But he was very sensible of his own misfortune, and sorry for having given that occasion to the House to question him. And so, having ended, he withdrew again into the Committee Chamber.

Bulstrode Whitelocke, member for Marlow, and a personal friend of Palmer's, though himself a supporter of the Remonstrance, rose immediately after to confirm generally, by his own recollection, the substance of the statement just made: but the hour was now late, it having long struck four, and it had grown so dark that the Speaker was no longer able to discern who stood up. Cries from both sides became loud for an adjournment, and order was accordingly made that the further consideration of

Mr. Palmer's offence should be resumed at ten o'clock the next morning. Dark as it was, however, the House was not allowed to rise until the indefatigable Mr. Pym had obtained direction for a committee, consisting of himself, Mr. Denzil Hollis, and others, to take examinations of divers Irishmen* then in the serjeant's custody, suspected of privity in the late horrible design; and his purpose in so demanding this immediate committee was, that those who on examination might be found not fairly obnoxious to suspicion might at once be dismissed. Through all the frequent conspiracies and dangers of this troubled time, the reins of authority seized by the House were held with a firm, yet wise and temperate, hand; and no strain upon the liberty of the subject that could be safely spared, was countenanced or permitted by its great leader.

Subject to be resumed tomorrow.

Adjournment at dark, 4·30.

§ XXI. PALMER'S PUNISHMENT AND SUBMISSION.

ON Thursday, the 25th of November, the Speaker took the chair at ten o'clock; but Mr. Solicitor St. John interposed before the resumption of Palmer's business, to obtain leave to bring in a short bill for the levy of tonnage and poundage, and after him Denzil Hollis rose to remind the House of that suggestion of the worthy member sitting below him by the

Tenth debate: Thursday, 25th Nov.

Petition to accompany

---

* " He hoped also," the liberal leader told the House on this occasion, " that they had the woman in hold who had " conveyed letters into Ireland."

bar (defignating Pym) which had found favour on Monday night, to accompany the Remonftrance by a Petition to his Majefty; as to which he moved accordingly that fome might be appointed to draw this Petition, in fuch manner as to fhow what had neceffitated them to make their Declaration. Some little debate enfued hereon, and ended in the adoption of Hollis's motion that the Petition fhould be prepared and prefented by the fame committee that had drawn the Declaration; to which was added an order, on the motion of Sir Gilbert Gerrard, member for Middlefex, that they fhould include in the faid Petition a form of congratulation for his Majefty's fafe return from Scotland, which fhould alfo be prefented to him in the name of the Houfe.

D'Ewes had left his place while Hollis was fpeaking, and when he returned to it, between eleven and twelve o'clock, he found the Solicitor-General preffing his bill of tonnage through the neceffary ftages to obtain its enactment before the exifting bill fhould expire. After this, fome other bufinefs of moment prefented itfelf, but members grew impatient for the conclufion of the debate refpecting Palmer; and on the motion of Sir Robert Cook, who fat for Tewkefbury, and who urged with fome vehemence the propriety of not delaying cenfure in a matter affecting the high privileges of the Houfe, that fubject was refumed. "We "then," fays D'Ewes, "proceeded before "twelve of the clock with the debate and "confideration touching Mr. Palmer's offence. "That held till about three of the clock in

§ XXI. *Palmer's Punishment and Submission.* 345

"the afternoon, before we proceeded to debate
"of his punishment."

. The substance of the speeches on either side
will sufficiently indicate the character of the
early part of the debate. In aggravation it
was insisted on, that as to the particular
matter, Palmer's great ability in his profession,
his very temperateness of nature in the general,
and the fact of his being a gownsman, much
increased his offence. "That after the first
"distemper of the House was well pacified
"which arose about the protestation-making,
"he, by his new motion to have a protesta-
"tion entered in his own name and the name
"of all the rest, did again raise the flame to
"such an heighth, as, if God had not pre-
"vented it, murder and calamity might have
"followed thereupon, and this parliament
"with our posterity and the kingdom itself
"might have been destroyed. For, upon
"Mr. Palmer's said motion, some waved their
"hats, and others took their swords with the
"scabbards out of their belts and held them
"in their hands." On the other side, in
extenuation, it was urged, that Palmer had in
no respect forfeited his reputation as a sober,
learned, and moderate man. That his only
intent in the motion he made was to put an
end to the particular night's debate, it being
so far spent; and to put off to a further day
the dispute of the question whether the members of that House might protest or not.
There had been an earnest offer to protest on
the part of Mr. Hyde, then a motion to take
names by others, and then Palmer moved in

Speeches on either side.

In aggravation of offence.

Scene it had occasioned.

In extenuation of offence.

the name of himfelf and all others of his mind; but whether this was to proteft, or to take names, was yet a queftion. Afterwards, indeed, Palmer was queftioned by Mr. Hampden, and he ftood up, and the Houfe cried, "All, "all." But there was no proof that he had an intention to raife any heat or combuftion. He had done very good fervice in the Houfe, and particularly in the enquiries into foreft abufes, where he occupied the chair; and he was entitled to have that remembered now. Some, however, went ftill further in extenuation, and others even juftified what he had done to be no offence at all.

Interference of Hampden.

Palmer's previous fervice.

The afternoon wore away in fuch debate, but it was in vain that Palmer's friends exhaufted every refource to avert what they too plainly felt muft inevitably come. The popular leaders were not to be turned from their purpofe. The offence committed, and the perfon committing it, were of no ordinary kind. The offence ftruck at the very fource and foundation of the power of the Houfe, breaking down all the barriers which old ufage and cuftom had thrown up, to keep before the people fole and intact, no matter what their internal divifions might be, the authority and influence of the Commons. The offender in himfelf reprefented a new and powerful party, bred within the Houfe itfelf, who would have entered through the breach fo made, and turned that very influence and authority to the fecret fervice of the King. Palmer's fuccefs would have divided the Houfe againft itfelf; into a Minority claiming to be free from undue ftrain

Delays reforted to.

Refolution of majority to punifh.

Gravity of the act attempted:

§ XXI. *Palmer's Punishment and Submission.*

and preſſure upon their conſciences, oppoſed to a Majority claiming predominance incompatible with the exerciſe of individual rights, and coercing free deliberation. Once admit ſuch diviſion, all the votes of the paſt year would loſe their claim to continued reſpect,* and the Sovereign would again be uncontrolled. No jot would Pym and Hampden conſent to abate, therefore, from what was ſtrictly neceſſary to ſingle out and ſet aſide what Palmer had done, as matter of high and weighty cenſure. But they did not go beyond it. They demanded his committal to the Tower until due ſubmiſſion and retractation were made.

[Sidenotes: to place minority above majority. Puniſhment demanded.]

Some indeed were eager to have gone farther, demanding his expulſion; but none of the great names on the liberal ſide appear among theſe, who were in truth led by the very man, Sir John Hotham, whom Clarendon repreſents as moſt oppoſed to what the leading men deſired as to himſelf. Sir Robert Cook, the member for Tewkeſbury, would

[Sidenote: Hotham and others for expulſion.]

* Clarendon occaſionally, to uſe an expreſſion of his own, " lets himſelf looſe " (*Hiſt.* i. 7: as if, to quote Warburton's ſhrewd comment on the phraſe, he were ſpeaking againſt his duty when he cenſures the Crown); and there is a remarkable and moſt weighty paſſage in his *Hiſtory* (ii. 252), in which he diſtinctly admits that it was the King's habit to conſent to particular meaſures (in this caſe he is ſpeaking of the bill for taking away the legiſlative power of the biſhops) from an opinion that what he held to be the violence and force uſed in procuring them, rendered them abſolutely invalid and void, and " made the confirmation of them leſs conſidered, as not " being of ſtrength to make that act good, which was in " itſelf null. And I doubt," he adds, " this logic had an " influence upon other acts of no leſs moment than theſe." Thoſe are ſurely very ſignificant and pregnant words. See *ante*, p. 155.

[Sidenotes: Clarendon " letting himſelf looſe." *Hiſt.* ii. 252.]

have had the offender not only sentenced to the Tower, but turned out of the House as well: whereupon Sir John Strangways got up and reminded that worthy member, that as he had been sworn since the last Lord Steward surrendered his staff, some doubts existed how far there was any legal commission to swear him,* and perhaps he might himself, by the statute 21st of James, be turned out of the House before Mr. Palmer. The member for Southwark, Mr. Bagshaw, rose next, and, as a brother barrister of Palmer's, took the liberty to doubt whether, having denied the fact charged, he was fit to be sentenced; seeing that the charge had really not yet been proved by any one man, and all judges should go *secundum allegata et probata.* But Palmer found a more effective advocate in Mr. John Crew, the member for Brackley.

Crew, a man of great fortune, and of principle as firm and unassailable as he was generally moderate in speech (it was by his help chiefly that Vane and Cromwell were able subsequently to pass the Self-Denying Ordinance), had voted uniformly with Pym and Hampden throughout the debates on the Remonstrance,† and he now thought that the

Speeches by friends of Palmer.

Strangways and Bagshaw.

Crew comes to rescue.

Pembroke Lord Steward. * Three days subsequent to this, an order was made to move the Lords to join with the Commons in moving his Majesty " to appoint the Earl of Pembroke Lord Steward of " his Majesty's household: for that this House is deprived of " certain members, by reason there is no Lord Steward, to " give or authorise the giving of the oaths of allegiance and " supremacy."

Crew at Uxbridge. † It is worth mention, perhaps, that in the famous treaty of Uxbridge, nearly four years after this date, Crew was one of the commissioners on the side of the Parliament, with

§ XXI. *Palmer's Punishment and Submission.*

justice of the case, which he considered to have been fully admitted, would be satisfied sufficiently by such admonishment as the Speaker standing in his place might then and there administer. For himself, he would interpret things doubtful ever in the best sense; and he could not forget such service as Mr. Palmer had heretofore rendered to the cause which in this late matter had received some offence from him. "Sir," continued this discreet and temperate advocate, "though none can plead "his merits to excuse a fault, yet if I have "received many favours from a man that "now doth me injury, I shall not forget "those benefits, but be the willinger to for- "get the injury, and the rather in this place, "because we have power to punish our own "members when they offend, but not to "reward them when they do well." It was impossible that such an appeal as this should fail of effect; but the effect was in a great degree removed by a speech in which Waller meant to have followed up the advantage, but, in his lively audacious way, seeking to please both sides, satisfied neither, and almost wholly lost what Crew had gained. He desired the House not to permit a man's success to be the proof of his delinquency. All their punishments were but the Tower and the Bar, and those were great punishments, when they were inflicted for great offences. But the custom had arisen, both within and without those

Suggests reprimand by Mr. Speaker.

Reminds House of Palmer's services.

Waller on same side;

less discreet.

Geoffrey Palmer opposed to him on the King's side. See Clarendon, *Hist.* iii. 37, 76, and 90.

walls, of punifhments difproportioned to the offence. In former days, while Queen Elizabeth reigned, a check from the Council Table, or a fentence in the Star Chamber, was of fuch repute that none efteemed men who were fo checked or fentenced: but what was it their Remonftrance had juftly taken exception to? Of late thefe punifhments had been inflicted for fuch fmall offences, that all men did rather value and efteem thofe as martyrs who fuffered in that way, than difefteem them for it. He adjured them, therefore, to let no man be punifhed for temperance, left they fhould feem to punifh virtue.—The refult of which homily, by one whofe great wit and parts had brought himfelf fuch fmall efteem, may perhaps be meafured by what followed immediately after. Sir John Hotham declared that if by the rules of the Houfe any greater cenfure than expulfion and the Tower could be laid upon the offender, he would gladly go higher than even thofe. Happily the majority were not of that opinion.

"This laft debate," fays D'Ewes, "held
" till paft four, at which time I withdrew out
" of the Houfe. When I returned again, the
" debate was, which of the two queftions
" fhould be put firft: whether for his fending
" to the Tower, or for his being expelled
" out of the Houfe." Upon this, Sir Ralph Hopton, member for Wells, afterwards fo confpicuous on the King's fide in the war as "Hopton of the Weft," appears to have taken the lead. He moved that the queftion of fending to the Tower fhould be firft put;

§ XXI. Palmer's Punishment and Submission.

because, he argued, if that for expulsion were put first, being the greater, the judgment of the House would be passed by it, and then the lesser question could not be put. Such a point mooted as this rarely failed to call up D'Ewes. *Replied to by D'Ewes.* He rose accordingly, and craved leave rather to speak to the orders of the House than to the order of putting the questions. In respect of the remarks which had been last made, he wondered to hear such from an ancient parliament man; for it was not the putting and voting of one, two, three, or four questions there, that made the judgment of the House. "That, Sir," continued the precise Sir Simonds, "is to be pronounced by yourself, our Speaker, to whom we direct our speeches; and then, and not till then, is the judgment of this House past." *Usages of the House.* He added that, if they could not agree which of the two questions should be passed first, for his part he should be content to have them passed together.

The result is thus succinctly recorded by the same veracious and conscientious witness. "Others spake after me, and the contention "which question should be first put was again "set on foot: till at last it was resolved, by "question, that the matter touching Mr. "Palmer's going to the Tower should be first "determined; and thereupon the Speaker did "first put this question—As many as are of "opinion that Mr. Palmer should be sent to "the Tower, there to remain during the "pleasure of the House, let them say Aye. "Upon which followed a great affirmative; "and the question being put negatively, there *Questions put: Shall Palmer be sent to Tower?*

352   *The Grand Remonstrance.*

<small>Yes: by 169 to 128.</small>

<small>Shall he be expelled?</small>

<small>No: by 163 to 131.</small>

<small>House adjourns.</small>

<small>Friday, 26th Nov. Palmer appears at Bar.</small>

"were many Noes: whereupon there followed
"a division of the House, and the Speaker
"appointed Sir Thomas Barrington and Sir
"John Clotworthy tellers for the Ayes, of
"which I was one, and we went out and were
"in number 169; the tellers appointed for
"the Noes, who stayed in the House, being
"the Lord Falkland and Mr. Strangways"
(the member for Bridport), "and the number
"of them was 128. Then the Speaker put
"the second question, namely—As many as
"are of opinion that Mr. Palmer shall be
"expelled from being a member of this House
"during this parliament, let them say Aye.
"Upon which followed a lesser affirmative
"than formerly; and upon the negative, a
"greater number of Noes. The House was
"again divided, and the same tellers appointed
"both for the Ayes and Noes as before. I
"was an Aye, and the Ayes went out again,
"and were in number 131. The Noes that
"continued in the House were 163. And so
"Mr. Palmer escaped expulsion out of the
"House, which his offence had deserved in a
"high measure. We appointed to meet to-
"morrow morning by ten of the clock, and
"so the House rose between six and seven of
"the clock at night."

On the next day, Friday the 26th of November, Palmer, "in his barrister's gown,"
appeared at the Bar to receive sentence; and,
kneeling there, was informed by Mr. Speaker
that the judgment awarded to his offence was
committal to the Tower during the pleasure
of the House. To the Tower he was com-

§ XXI. *Palmer's Punishment and Submission.* 353

mitted accordingly, and there remained until Wednesday the 8th of December; on the morning of which day "the humble petition "of Geoffrey Palmer was read, wherein he "did acknowledge his offence and the justice "of the House, and his sorrow that he had "fallen into its displeasure;" upon which an order passed for the discharge of Mr. Palmer from his imprisonment in the Tower.

As to this submission of his friend, Clarendon is wholly silent; and, in so far as the sin of suppression may be less than that of deliberate falsification, the circumstance should perhaps be mentioned to his praise. He also unconsciously renders tribute to the sagacity and steadiness of purpose with which the leaders had pursued and obtained their object in these long and passionate debates, when he says, that, having compassed their main end, they found the sense of the House more at their devotion from that time, and admits that the minority grew so cast down and dejected, that the leading men ever after met no equal opposition within its walls. But in every other point of these later, as of the earlier proceedings, every single sentence he utters is a misstatement. He says there was not the least doubt that there never had been any precedent for calling a member to account for words spoken except at the moment of their utterance: Whereas D'Ewes's precedents have been seen. He says that, after two hours' debate, additional delays and bitterness were only spared by Palmer's own voluntary offer that to save the House farther trouble he might answer and withdraw:

Is committed.

8th Dec. Sends in petition and is released.

Results of Palmer's punishment.

Clarendon's *Hist.* ii. 61-62.

Series of misstatements.

A A

Whereas the anfwer was only given upon compulfion, after a formal divifion had left no alternative. He fays that the real fecret of the hoftility difplayed to Palmer, and the reafon why the angry men preffed with all their power that he might be expelled the Houfe, was that they had borne him a long grudge for the civility he fhowed as one of the managers in the profecution of the Earl of Strafford, in that he had not ufed the fame reproachful language which the others had done: Whereas the men moft eager to protect Palmer were notorioufly thofe who, like Culpeper, Falkland, and even Hyde himfelf, had fhown leaft mercy or forbearance to Strafford. Finally he fays,[*] that in the clofe of the day, when the divifion was taken againft Palmer, and on the rifing of the Houfe, an order was obtained, without much oppofition, for the printing of the Remonftrance: Whereas two days were occupied by the Palmer debate, and not even an attempt was

Marginal notes: Alleged ground of hoftility to Palmer. No truth therein. Falfe averment

---

[*] I give the entire paffage, taking it up from where the paffage previoufly quoted (*ante*, p. 336) ends. As he there mentions, he had appealed to the Houfe whether there was any precedent of the like: "and there is no doubt," he continues, "there never had been; and it was very irregular. But they were too pofitively refolved to be diverted; and, after two hours debate, he himfelf defired, 'that to fave the 'Houfe farther trouble, he might anfwer and withdraw'— which he did. When it drew towards night, after many hours debate, it was ordered that he fhould be committed to the Tower; the angry men prelfing with all their power, that he might be expelled the Houfe: having borne him a long grudge, for the civility he fhowed in the profecution of the Earl of Strafford; that is, that he had not ufed the fame reproachful language which the others had done ... And in the clofe of that day, and the rifing of the Houfe, without much oppofition, they obtained an order for the printing their Remonftrance."

Marginal note: Clarendon *Hift.* ii. 48-9.

§ XXII. *Debate on Petition.* 355

made during either to fmuggle in any order for the printing. When it was done, it was done openly, but the time for it was even yet not come.

Such are the deliberate averments of Clarendon; and fuch in each cafe the complete difproof which a fimple ftatement of the fact enables me to give.

§ XXII. PETITION TO ACCOMPANY REMONSTRANCE.

SATURDAY, the 27th of November, was the day named for reception of the report of the Committee appointed to draw the Petition to the King; defigned, in accordance with Pym's fuggeftion, to accompany the Remonftrance. It was ufhered in by threatening omens. Charles was now arrived from Scotland, and had been received with magnificent entertainment in the City, on the previous Thurfday. He had returned afterwards to Whitehall in fuch elation and excitement as rarely was witneffed in him; between that evening and the following day, when he proceeded to Hampton Court, had given Nicholas the feals which were held by Windebank; had deprived old Vane (whofe Treafurer's ftaff had been taken from him at York) of his Secretaryfhip; had feen privately Culpeper, Falkland, and "Ned Hyde;" had directed a proclamation to be iffued for more implicit obedience to the laws eftablifhed for the exercife of religion; and had given order for the immediate difmiffal of thofe Trained Bands employed upon guard at the two Houfes, which, as we have feen, upon the receipt of

as to printing.

Eleventh Debate: 27th Nov.

King's arrival.

Impolitic acts.

Order as to Religion.

A A 2

Hampden's difpatch out of Scotland announcing the plots againſt the leaders of the Covenant, had been ordered up for their protection, and fince had guarded them by night and day.* He had alſo taken the refolution, though the act was deferred for yet a few days, to remove Col. Balfour from the command of the Tower, and to appoint Col. Lunsford in his place. The temper of the Houſe at ſuch report as had reached them of theſe incidents was not flow in revealing itſelf.

Prayers had juſt been ſaid when Hampden roſe in his place; made a ſtatement as to a Buckinghamſhire papiſt, one Adam Courtney, ſuſpected of connivance in the plot now proved againſt the King's officers to bring up the Army to overawe the Parliament; and, producing the minute pieces and fragments of certain letters which Courtney had torn up on his arreſt, defired that they ſhould be deciphered by the army committee then fitting, by whom alſo the delinquent could be

Marginalia: Guard to parliament difmiſſed. Excitement in Houſe. Hampden ſpeaking.

* The order had been given by the King on the evening of his arrival, Thurſday, the 25th. Early on Friday morning Pym reported to the Houſe that, whereas, heretofore, a Guard had been ſet, at the defire of the Commons, in reſpect of the multitude of ſoldiers, and other looſe perſons, infeſting the precincts of Weſtminſter, and was afterwards continued by both Houſes, and the Lord Chamberlain [Eſſex], who had a commiſſion to be Lord General on this ſide Trent, took a care concerning the fame; but now, upon His Majeſty's return, he hath ſurrendered his commiſſion, and the Lords have received a meſſage from his Majeſty, to be communicated to both Houſes, "that the Guard, that had been ſet in his ab-
" ſence, perhaps was done upon good grounds, but now his
" preſence is a ſufficient guard to his people; and therefore
" it is his pleaſure they ſhould be difcharged; and, if need be
" to have a Guard hereafter, his Majeſty will be as glad to
" have a Guard as any other."

Marginalia: Queſtion as to Guard. King's meſſage.

§ XXII. *Petition to accompany Remonstrance.* 357

brought up from Aylesbury gaol and examined. After him rose Mr. Oliver Cromwell, to call attention to a gross slander against the House of which he held the proofs in his hand, and by which it seemed that "one "whom he named not left he should withdraw himself" had given out that the principal members had been alarmed on seeing the intended City entertainment to his Majesty announced, and had sent privately to the said City to induce them not to entertain him. After Cromwell, Mr. Strode presented himself, to move that some course might be taken for putting the kingdom in a posture of defence, in which he was seconded by Sir Thomas Barrington and Sir Walter Earle; and, upon the suggestion of the same active member, a committee of seven was named to draw up the whole proof of the first design to bring up the Army to overawe the House, and to prepare for introduction at the next sitting a bill for the "future commanding of "the Arms and the Trained Bands of the "kingdom." The member for Beeralston also moved that reasons should at once be presented to his Majesty for the continuance of the Guard over both Houses,* and that these

Oliver Cromwell.

Suggestion for defence of kingdom.

Referred to Committee.

---

* This was on Saturday; and on the morning of the following Tuesday, the 30th of November, Pym presented those reasons in a remarkable report which shows how thoroughly existing dangers were appreciated, and how much was thus early suspected of the King's most cherished design. Already, in a second reply to a further petition on the subject of the continuance of the Guard, his Majesty had all but confessed his purpose of gathering an armed force around his person. So tender was he of the Parliament's safety, he protested, "that to "secure them, not only from real, but even imaginary dangers,

Tuesday, 30th Nov.

King's design as to Guard.

The Grand Remonstrance.

should be drawn by the same committee to whom it had been referred to prepare the Petition to accompany the Remonstrance.

Personal reasons.

"he had commanded the Earl of Dorset to appoint some of "the Trained Bands to wait upon the Parliament for a few "days; in which time, if he should be satisfied that there is "just reason, he would continue them, and likewise take such "a course *for the safety of his own person* as should be fit." Quietly disregarding this intimation, Pym's report was an elaborate exposition of reasons for continuing the existing Guard, under their own officers. It adverted to the great number of disorderly, suspicious, and desperate persons, especially of the Irish nation, lurking in obscure alleys and victualling houses in the suburbs and other places near London and Westminster. It described the jealousy conceived upon discovery of the design in Scotland, for the surprising of the persons of divers of the nobility, members of the parliament there, which had been spoken of here, some few days before it broke out, not without some whispering intimation *that the like was intended against divers persons of both Houses:* which had found the more credit, by reason of the former attempt of bringing up the army, to disturb and enforce this parliament. It enlarged upon the conspiracy in Ireland, and indicated the alarming evidence existing that *something of the like was designed in England and Scotland.* It hinted at divers advertisements coming at the same time from beyond sea, " that there should be a great alteration of religion in England " in a few days, and that the necks of both the parliaments " should be broken." It instanced the recent divers examinations and dangerous speeches of the popish and discontented party; and the secret meetings and consultations of the papists in several shires and districts. And its authors concluded that for these considerations a Guard was necessary; for they did conceive there was just cause to apprehend that *there was some wicked and mischievous practice still in hand to interrupt the peaceable proceedings of the parliament.* Nor less necessary did they consider it that the Earl of Essex should be continued in the command. " For preventing whereof it " is fit the Guard should be continued under the same com- " mand, or such other as they should choose; but to have it " under the command of any other, not chosen by themselves, " they can by no means consent to; and would rather run any " hazard, than admit a precedent so dangerous both to this " and future parliaments. And they humbly leave it to his " Majesty to consider whether it will not be fit to suffer his " High Court of parliament to enjoy that privilege of providing " for their own safety, which was never denied other inferior

Pym's counter reasons.

Plots in progress.

Attack on Parliament expected.

Unsafe without

§ XXII. Petition to accompany Remonstrance.

After this the House went into committee on the Tonnage and Poundage bill, with Mr. Lisle, the member for Winchester (he who afterwards sat on the King's trial), in the Clerk's chair; and on the Speaker's resumption of his seat, between one and two o'clock mid-day, Pym entered with the Petition just named in his hand. He craved permission at once to be permitted to read it; and having done this, it was handed over to the Clerk, who "loudly and deliberately" read it over again. *Remonstrance petition brought in.*

It was to the effect that his Majesty's faithful Commons did with much thankfulness and joy acknowledge the great mercy and favour of God, in giving his Majesty a safe and peaceable return out of Scotland into his kingdom of England, where the pressing dangers and distempers of the State had caused them, with much earnestness, to desire the comfort of his gracious presence, to help the endeavours of his Parliament for the averting of that ruin and disaster with which his kingdoms at this time were threatened. For having convinced themselves of the existence of a malignant party who had access to his person and councils, and whose unceasing endeavours were to discredit his Parliament and to create a faction among his people, they had, for the prevention thereof, and the better *Abstract of its contents.* *Why King's presence desired.* *Zeal of evil councellors.*

"Courts: and that he will be pleased graciously to believe,
"that they cannot think themselves safe under any Guard,
"which they shall not be assured that it will be as faithful in
"defending his Majesty's safety as their own; whereof they
"shall always be more careful than of their own." *their own Guard.*

information in fundry important particulars of his Majefty, the Peers, and all other his fubjects, been neceffitated to make a Declaration of the ftate of the kingdom as well before as after the meeting of the parliament now affembled. Before fubmitting which, they defired frankly to point out with what danger to the country, and grievous affliction to all loyal dwellers therein, the practice was attended of placing in employments of truft and nearnefs about his Majefty, the Prince, and the reft of his Royal children, active members of the malignant party before mentioned, favourers in all refpects of popery, and mere engineers or factors for Rome; fince it was by fuch, to the fore difcontent of his loyal fubjects, that divers of his bifhops, and others in prime places of the Church, had been corrupted. They juftified their right to give this warning, by the diftractions and fufferings fo caufed; by the continual tamperings with the army in England; by the miferable incidents and jealoufies in Scotland; by the papift infurrection, and moft bloody maffacre, in Ireland; and by the great neceffities which had in confequence arifen for the King's fervice, impofing upon themfelves the tafk of burdening the fubject for contributions to the extent of a million and a half fterling. Not diftantly pointing at the Queen, they then urgently entreat his Majefty not to fuffer any folicitation to the contrary " how power- " ful and near foever," to turn afide the three requefts with which they concluded.—(1.) That for the preferving the kingdom's peace

§ XXII. *Petition to accompany Remonſtrance.*

and ſafety from the deſigns of the popiſh party, his Majeſty will, in regard to the biſhops,* concur with and ſecond his people's humble deſires in a parliamentary way † to abridge their immoderate power uſurped over the clergy; to deprive them of their temporal juriſdiction in parliament; to take away ſuch oppreſſions ‡ in religion, church government, and diſcipline, as had been brought in and fomented by them; and to abate their preſſure upon weak conſciences by removing thoſe oppreſſions and unneceſſary ceremonies. (2). That the malignant and ill-affected be removed from their places of influence, and that in future his Majeſty vouchſafe to employ near him, and in great public offices, only ſuch perſons as his parliament had cauſe to confide in. (3). That ſuch lands in Ireland as may be forfeit to the Crown in conſequence of the Rebellion, be not alienated from it, but applied to the public neceſſities. —Which humble deſires being fulfilled, the authors of the Remonſtrance undertook, by the bleſſing and favour of God,§ moſt cheerfully to undergo the hazard and expenſes of the war againſt the Iriſh rebels, and to apply themſelves to ſuch other courſes and counſels

i. To abridge biſhops' power.

ii. To remove ill counſellors.

iii. To apply Iriſh forfeitures to public needs.

Changes propoſed in Petition.

---

* A great attempt was made, as ſtated in the text, but unſucceſsfully, to limit the expreſſion here to "divers of the "biſhops," as in a previous paſſage.

† Theſe words, "in a parliamentary way," were moved to be added after the Petition was brought in.

‡ The word "oppreſſions" had originally ſtood "corruptions," and ſeems to have been changed on Mr. Coventry's ſuggeſtion.

§ "By the bleſſing and favour of God" were words added, upon ſpecial motion, during the debate.

as might, with honour and plenty at home, with power and reputation abroad, support the Royal eftate, and, by their loyal affections, obedience, and fervice, lay a fure and lafting foundation for the greatnefs of the King, and the happinefs of his pofterity in future times.

Pym anfwers objections. After the Clerk had finifhed his reading, feveral members of Hyde's party ftated objections; "to whom," fays D'Ewes, "Mr. "Pym anfwered. Then Sir John Culpeper "anfwered much of that Mr. Pym had faid, "and made fome new objections. Mr. *A point of order.* "Pym ftood up again." But he was not permitted to fpeak. Mr. Strangways rofe to order, many others rofe to order, and the interruption was long and vehement. Hampden's *Hampden reftores quiet.* authority at length again reftored fome quiet, upon his fuggefting that it would probably be found within the rules of the Houfe that Mr. Pym, being the reporter from the committee which prepared the Petition, might fpeak more than once, and might anfwer all objections. Here was opportunity made for D'Ewes; and that great mafter of precedents, and voucher of records, was not flow to take *D'Ewes explains ufage of Houfe.* advantage of it. He got up and faid that it was very true that the worthy gentleman at the Bar (indicating Mr. Pym), being the reporter, might fpeak as often as occafion fhould ferve; and yet it was as true, alfo, that he might fpeak out of order. For, though he was at liberty to anfwer new objections that were made, yet, if thofe anfwers of his were replied upon, he was not at liberty to fpeak

§ XXII. *Petition to accompany Remonstrance.* 363

again to those particular points to which he had spoken before, by way of mere answer to him that did reply upon him. There was, however, no question but that the gentleman on the other side who first interrupted him, did himself break the orders of the House in doing so; because it did not then appear whether the gentleman at the Bar would have answered any new objection, or would simply have spoken again to any of those particulars whereto he had formerly spoken.

<small>Culpeper in fault, not Pym.</small>

" The distinction I gave," continues D'Ewes,
" being well approved by the House, and some
" few having spoken after me, the Speaker
" directed Mr. Pym to speak again to any
" new objection, but not to touch upon any
" thing to which he had formerly spoken.
" And so he spake again, and answered those
" new objections Sir John Culpeper had made.
" Others spake also, after him, to the said
" Petition in general. Then others moved
" that it might be read over again, that so
" every particular might be debated; which
" was at length agreed unto. So the Clerk
" read it again, and staid at every clause
" awhile; and so some clauses were spoken
" against, and others were agreed unto without
" any opposition. In one part of it, we
" alleged that the popish and malignant party
" had corrupted divers of the bishops with
" popery. In another part, that all the bishops
" had exercised usurped authority. Where-
" upon it was moved, by one or two, that we
" would not make the crimination general
" here, but that we would put in the word

<small>"Well moved."</small>

<small>Pym answers Culpeper.</small>

<small>Petition read again:</small>

<small>and debated in detail.</small>

"'divers' as we had done in the former place.
"To which I stood up and answered, that
"though some of the bishops were of them-
"selves so corrupt and bad as they could not
"well be made worse, yet the word 'divers'
"was necessarily added in that clause, because
"they were not all so: this being but a per-
"sonal crimination. But in the other clause,
"the complaint having reference to their pre-
"latical jurisdiction, which was equally exer-
"cised by them all and defended and main-
"tained by them all, we should as much err
"on the other hand to add the word 'divers'
"in this place, as we should have done to
"omit it in the former place."

D'Ewes attacks bishops.

House adopt his views.

This lucid argument of the correct and learned baronet was doubtless very favourably received, for the word so much desired by Hyde and his friends was not allowed to limit the force of the sentence. But a further stand was attempted to be made against the use of the words "corruptions" and "unnecessary ceremonies," in speaking of the necessity of abating the immoderate power of the bishops;

Further objections by Hyde:

Hyde urging strongly that such words laid a scandal upon the law itself, in so characterizing a church discipline it had established. His friend Mr. Coventry also put another objec- tion, whether, seeing the intention was to have

and Mr. Coventry.

those particulars in the discipline of the church altered by law, it was not quite out of rule to "preoccupate" his Majesty with it beforehand. Surely, when the new church-regulation acts should have once passed both Houses, then it would be seasonable, and not before, to move

§ XXII. *Petition to accompany Remonstrance.*

his Majesty about it. This, however, again called up D'Ewes. He could not admit the force of the objection taken. It was an old, and he thought a wife usage, when the means offered, to move the sovereign beforehand as to particulars proposed to be passed by act of parliament. For, if the gentleman on the other side who last pressed it ("and then I looked "towards Mr. Coventry"), had but had time to peruse the Parliament Roll de an°. 2do. H. IV. no. 23, he would have found that the same course was then advised upon: to the end that so, by knowing the King's inclination beforehand, they might save much time in avoiding to treat of particulars which there was no hope of obtaining his assent unto. And, holding that if it were ever needful to take that course to gain time, it was so at this moment, he thought the word "corruption" might very well stand. On the whole, however, Pym seems to have thought differently; whether or not from some feeling of distaste to the logic employed, or to the sentiments expressed, by Sir Simonds: and "corruption"*

Replied to by D'Ewes.

Urges study of Rolls.

Pym's moderation.

---

* Nevertheless, and notwithstanding the change of this word, it is remarkable that in the answer which the King sent to the Petition (in which he stigmatises the Remonstrance as "unparliamentary," and intimates his surprise that "our "express intimation by our Comptroller to that purpose," should not have restrained them from the publishing of it till such time as they should have received his answer), he quotes, not from the Petition as amended, but from some copy of it which he had received in its original form. "Unto that "clause," he says, "which concerneth Corruptions (as you "style them), in Religion, in Church Government, and in "Discipline, and the removing of such unnecessary cere- "monies, &c." Again he says, "We are very sorry to hear "in such general terms, Corruption in religion objected, &c."

Unaltered Petition sent to Court.

having been withdrawn, and "oppreſſion" ſubſtituted, the Petition paſſed.

§ XXIII. THE KING RECEIVES REMONSTRANCE AND PETITION.

Tueſday, 30th Nov. Petition engroſſed.

IT now remained to preſent the Petition, and with it the Remonſtrance it was deſigned to accompany, to the King; and with this view it was ordered to be engroſſed: direction being given that the Clerk ſhould alſo cauſe two copies of the Remonſtrance itſelf to be fair written, one for his Majeſty to be preſented with the Petition, the other for the Lords; and that the Committee for preſenting it ſhould be named at the next ſitting but one. On Tueſday, the 30th, it was accordingly moved that this committee ſhould conſiſt of twelve members; and the twelve ſelected were, Sir Simonds D'Ewes; Sir Arthur Ingram, member for Kellington; Sir James Thinne, who

Committee named to wait on King.

Secret communication with the King.

Now, in the Petition as publiſhed by the Houſe, it will be found that the clauſe ſtands expreſſly as concerning "Oppreſſions in " Religion, Church Government and Diſcipline," and again as referring to "ſome Oppreſſions and unneceſſary cere-" monies;" bearing out and confirming exactly the narrative given in my text. This clearly exhibits that ſecret communication between the King and his friends in the Houſe which is the ſubject of frequent alluſion by D'Ewes. So, in a ſubſequent debate in reference to the King's complaint of certain expreſſions in one of Pym's publiſhed ſpeeches (on Thurſday 24th March, 1641-2), Sir Edward Bainton, member for Chippenham, who had been one of a deputation to the ſovereign to preſent a meſſage from the Houſe, "ſtated that he had gathered " from ſome expreſſions of his Majeſty that he had ſeen the " ſaid meſſage before they gave it him." For further proofs on this point ſee *Arreſt of the Five Members*, § xxii. The member of the Houſe to whom ſuch unauthoriſed communications with the Court were brought moſt directly home, was undoubtedly Mr. Edward Hyde.

§ XXIII. *King Receives Remonstrance & Petition.* 367

sat for Wiltshire; Mr. Henry Bellasis, and Lord Fairfax (Ferdinando), who both sat for Yorkshire; Lord Grey of Groby, member for Leicester, Earl Stamford's second son, and hereafter to sit among the regicides; Sir Christopher Wray, who represented Great Grimsby, father-in-law of the younger Vane; Sir John Corbet, member for Shropshire; Sir Richard Wynne, member for Liverpool, who held an office in the King's house; and Sir Ralph Hopton, Sir Edward Dering, and Sir Arthur Haselrig. There was here a liberal apportionment of those who, being known to have opposed the Declaration, were less likely to be unwelcome to the King; and that the same tenderness on this point determined Pym to withdraw his own name, which appeared among those first selected,* hardly admits of a doubt. The same deference to the feelings of the Sovereign seems also to have suggested a resolution moved the next morning (when the Committee were in waiting in the House to receive the Petition and Remonstrance, and repair therewith to Hampton Court) to the effect " that Sir Edward Dering should present " and read the Petition unto his Majesty." The Petition only was to be read, after which the Remonstrance was to be placed in his hands. Sir Edward Dering, however, probably suspecting that into much consideration for the King in this matter had entered not a little want of consideration for himself, quietly withdrew from the House while the resolution

Its members.

Several King's friends.

Pym withdraws his name.

Dering to read petition to King.

* See *Rushworth*, vol. i. part iii. 486.

was in hand ; and upon difcovery of his abfence another order had to be fubftituted, "that
"Sir Ralph Hopton, in the abfence of Sir
"Edward Dering, fhall read the Petition and
"prefent that and the Declaration unto his
"Majefty."

Declines, and Hopton chofen.

And fo, the Speaker calling to Sir Simonds D'Ewes to receive Petition and Remonftrance, to which Sir Simonds refponds by advancing from the lower end to the table, making three congees as he moves along, the Committee get poffeffion of their important charge, and betake themfelves to Hampton Court.

Thurfday, 2nd Dec. Hopton's report.

The next day, Thurfday the 2nd, Sir Ralph Hopton reported to the Houfe what had paffed at the interview. With the exception of Sir Edward Dering, all the deputation affembled ;* and on arrival at the palace, the member for Liverpool, who had familiar entrance therein, having announced them, they had to wait but a quarter of an hour before the King invited them to his chamber. Here they fank upon the knee, and in this pofture Sir Ralph began to read the Petition. But Charles would not have it fo; and, making them all rife, liftened attentively as Sir Ralph proceeded; until he came to the paffage charging the malignant party with a defign to change the eftablifhed religion, when his Majefty fuddenly interrupted him, exclaiming with a great deal of fervency, "The Devil take him, whom-

Reception by Charles.

Hopton reading Petition.

---

* D'Ewes has fubfequent occafion to refer in his Journal to the Remonftrance " prefented at Hampton Court by my- " felf and ten other members of the Houfe," which fhows that the only defaulter in attendance, out of the twelve named, was Sir Edward Dering.

§ XXIII. *King Receives Remonstrance & Petition.*

"soever he be, that hath a design to change "our religion!" Then Sir Ralph resumed; but, just after reading the sentence towards the close about reserving the disposal of the rebels' lands in Ireland, his Majesty again broke in and was pleased to say, "We must not dispose "of the Bear's skin till the Bear be dead." His Majesty, in short, was in excellent spirits; showed none of his usual short sharp ways; and, after they had finished reading the Petition and had placed the Remonstrance before him, seemed entirely disposed to have some familiar talk with the Committee. Its object, however, speedily revealed itself on his desiring merely to ask the worthy members a few questions touching this Remonstrance and the Petition they had read. Royalist as he was, Sir Ralph Hopton saw the danger, and made reply respectfully that they had no commission to speak anything concerning the business. "Then," the King quickly rejoined, "you "may speak as particular men. Doth the "House intend to *publish* this Declaration?" But not so were those ancient parliament men to be thrown off their guard; and they answered simply that they could give no answer to it. "Well then," said the King, "I suppose "you do not expect *me* to answer now to so "long a Petition. But this let me tell you, I "have left Scotland well, and in peace; they are "all satisfied with me, and I with them; and "though I stayed longer there than I expected, "yet I think, if I had not gone, you had not "been rid so soon of the army. And as to "this business of yours, I shall give you an

Interruptions by King.

The Bear and the Bear's skin.

Committee questioned:

"Do you mean to *publish*?"

King's answer to Petition.

Close of interview.
"answer with as much speed as the weightiness of the business will permit." With which he gave them his hand to kiss; committing them to the entertainment of his comptroller, and the lodgment of his harbinger; both being of the worthiest. And Sir Ralph craved to conclude his report with faithful repetition of the royal message which, just as they were on the point of leaving the palace,
Message before departure.
was brought to them with request for its immediate delivery to the House of Commons: "*That there might be no publishing of the De-*" "*claration till the House had received his Ma-*" "*jesty's Answer.*"

The reader will now judge to what extent the facts justify Clarendon in stating, that, when it was finally resolved to publish the Remonstrance, this was done in violation of a compact or understanding against any such step until the King's answer was received. On the
No pledge not to publish.
one side there was a strong wish expressed undoubtedly, but on the other this wish was met by neither compact nor understanding. If indeed there were any violation in the case, it might more fairly be charged upon the King. He told the Committee that he did not at that time design to answer their Remonstrance, yet there was hardly an act at this moment contemplated by him, or to which he had set his
Incitements to publication.
hand since his arrival in London, which did not practically express his answer. It was in his proclamation for obedience to the laws regulating worship; in his order for the dismissal of the City Guard over the Houses; in his direction that they should in future be

§ XXIII. *King Receives Remonstrance & Petition.*

guarded by the bands of Westminster and Middlesex, officered by his own servants; and in his proposed removal of Balfour from the command of the Tower. Already he had ended all doubt as to the temper in which he had returned; and many to whom even the voting of the Remonstrance had appeared of doubtful expediency, now saw and admitted the necessity of publishing it to the people. Manifestly had its promoters succeeded in its first design at least; for the challenge it threw down had been promptly taken up. If the King had been sincere in his former professions of an intention to govern for the future within the limits of the laws he had himself assented to, there was nothing in the Remonstrance to defeat that intention; but if he had any other desire or purpose as yet masked, such was no longer maintainable. He never had a better opportunity than the present for betaking himself to parliamentary ways of asserting his power and prerogatives, but events were speedily to show with what far other views he was now inviting into office two out of those three of the House of Commons (calling also into secret council the third) who had organised and led the new party of his friends within its walls. Something less than twelve days are to pass before the debate which is to put finally before the people the Grand Remonstrance, and if the wish still lingered with Hampden or with Pym to have been saved, if possible, the necessity of that appeal, each day supplied its argument against such a possibility. I will select but a few, from the manuscript records before

Hostile acts against House.

King's purpose unmasked.

Hyde and friends invited to office.

me, to fhow with what refiftlefs march, as day followed day, the crifis came on.

§ XXIV. RETALIATION AND REVENGE.

Tamperings with command of Tower. The rumoured removal of Balfour from the command of the Tower was the firft direct challenge to the Houfe. Balfour ftood high in their confidence for his unfhaken fidelity in preventing the efcape of Strafford, whereas Clarendon himfelf admits * that Lunsford, felected to replace him, was a man of no education, of ill character, and of decayed and defperate fortune, who had been obliged, but a few years before, to avoid by flight into France the penalty of punifhment for a grave mifdemeanour. Such indeed was the feeling in the City aroufed by his appointment when, in lefs than three weeks from this time, it actually *Popular commotion.* took place, that under the preffure of very alarming indications of riot, the King had to withdraw it. Even already, a certain uneafy feeling in the City connected itfelf with a fenfe of the infecurity of the Tower; and the report of Balfour's removal led to fome tumultuous

Preparing for act of violence. * Though of courfe, as with all the acts of the King which had immediately difaftrous iffue, he makes Lord Digby the fcapegoat, and charges the ill counfel upon him. *Hift.* ii. 123. The King's object, as Clarendon frankly admits, was, that having now fome fecret reafon to fill the place with a man who might be trufted, he felected Lunsford as one who would be faithful to him for this obligation, and execute anything he fhould defire or direct. In other words, as is remarked by Warburton (vii. 547), who puts in plain fpeech Clarendon's laboured periphrafis, "*to keep the Five Members " fafe whom it was determined to arreft.*" This fubject is treated in detail in my *Arreft of the Five Members.*

§ XXIV. *Retaliation and Revenge.* 373

gatherings on the Monday after the King's return, and spread great alarm among the well-affected.

That was on the 29th of November. On the morning of that same day, the new Guard to the Houses was sent under the command of Lord Dorset by the King, by way of reply to the reasons drawn up by Pym* and presented in the name of both Houses; and before the day had closed, swords were drawn and muskets fired upon the people.† It was thus fast coming to an issue outside the walls of parliament, upon the suggestion or incitement of the sovereign; invitations were going out to the people, to throw on either side their weight into the scale; and soon perforce the question must arise, to which of the contending parties that power would most freely lend itself, to uphold monarchical pretension, or to strengthen and establish parliamentary privilege.

<small>New King's Guard.</small>

<small>People fired upon.</small>

On the morning of the 30th of November, Pym, Hampden, and Hollis went up to the Lords with a message for the discharge of the trained-bands which the King had so substituted for their own. As Clarendon puts it, "since they could not have such a guard as "pleased them, they would have none at all."‡ And so, the Peers consenting, Lord Dorset and his followers were dismissed; the Commons

<small>30th Nov. A.M. Houses dismiss King's Guard.</small>

<small>Lord Dorset.</small>

---

* See *ante*, p. 357-8.

† "The Earl of Dorset's indiscreet rashness this day," writes D'Ewes, on the 29th, "might have occasioned the "shedding of much blood—he commanded some of the "guard to give fire upon some of the citizens of London in "the Court of Requests or near it."

‡ *Hist.* ii. 86.

at the fame time declaring that it fhould be lawful, in the abfence of a Guard duly appointed, for every member to bring his own fervants to attend at the door, armed with fuch weapons as they thought fit.* No needlefs or unprovoked precaution; for the danger, and the direction it would take, were now not diftantly revealing themfelves. What fecretly was already refolved upon could not much longer be concealed. As Selden wittily puts it in his Table Talk (and a calmer or lefs partial witnefs of the events now rapidly moving to their iffue could not be named), "the King was "ufing the Houfe of Commons in Mr. Pym "and his company, that is, charging *them* with "treafon becaufe they charged my lord of "Canterbury and Sir George Ratcliffe, with "juft as much logic as the boy that would have "lain with his grandmother ufed to his father: "You lay with my mother, why fhould not I "lie with yours?" † Thus early were people talking of his purpofe, almoft openly. On this very day (the 30th), when the Commons difmiffed Lord Dorfet and his band, D'Ewes tells us "upon Mr. Pury's motion, that "one William Chillingworth, doctor of divi- "nity, had faid that fome members of this

Marginalia: Ominous precaution. The end approaching. Witty remark by Selden. Commons' Journals: 30th Nov.

---

* Such is Clarendon's account (*Hift.* ii. 86), but the notice in the journals fimply fays: "Ordered that the Guard fhall "be difmiffed; and that Mr. Glyn and Mr. Wheeler do "require the High Conftable of Weftminfter to provide a "ftrong and fufficient watch in their fteads."

† *Table Talk*, p. 96. The fubftitution of Ratcliffe for Strafford, in this report by Selden of the plea or pretence of the Court party, is highly characteriftic. Strafford could not in decency be put forward, with fo many who had perfecuted him to the death now ranged on the fide of the King.

§ xxv. *Alleged Intimidation of Parliament.* 375

"Houfe were guilty of treafon, and that they *Doctor*
"fhould be accufed within a day or two, it was *Chilling-*
"ordered that the ferjeant's deputy fhould *difclofure.*
"bring him forthwith to the Houfe, and if he
"fhould refufe to come, then to apprehend
"him as a delinquent, and bring him." So
rapidly were the lifts clofing up on both fides,
and fo narrowed the opportunities on either for
efcaping a fatal iffue.

§ xxv. ALLEGED INTIMIDATION OF
PARLIAMENT.

The next move in the perilous game was *Hyde's*
made by Hyde and his party, bent upon effect- *plot.*
ing fome diverfion from the fufpicions and
agitations let loofe by Doctor Chillingworth's
difclofure, and to whom the popular riot of
Monday offered good pretence for complaint
of fuch preffure and coercion as " confifted
" not with the freedom of parliament." In *Parlia-*
that expreffion their whole policy revealed it- *ment' "not*
felf; its entire aim and end lay there ; and, in *free.'*
the fame temper which had now fupplied the
occafion, it was eagerly followed up. It is not,
I think, poffible to doubt, that, from the day
when Charles had left for Scotland in the
autumn, his cherifhed and fteadily purfued
purpofe was to find ground for revoking whatever had been done that was unpalatable to *King's*
him during the paft year ; and fuch ground *plea of*
would be furnifhed by the pretence that parlia- *coercion.*
ment had not been free, but that coercion had
been put upon it by certain leading members,
by whom penalties of treafon to the State had

otherwife alfo been incurred. Every act of himfelf or his partizans, therefore, affumed now that fpecific form and direction. The cafe of the protefters againft the Grand Remonftrance he took where they left it, and made his own. Not they who paffed it, but they who protefted againft it, were his faithful Commons. But they were under a tyranny both within and without the Houfe which prevented fair expreffion of opinion.

On the return of the leaders to their feats after removal of Lord Dorfet's men, in the afternoon of the 30th of November, Hyde rofe, and craving leave to advert again to the incident of the Guard, taxed the London citizens and apprentices with having come on the previous day armed with fwords and ftaves to Weftminfter, fpecially to overawe particular members from voting as they wifhed. He was interrupted by the demand for inftances; upon which Sir John Strangways faid afide to thofe who fat near him, that he could extinguifh fome loud talkers and interrupters in that Houfe perhaps, were he to tell what he knew. "Tell "it, then," was the cry of one who overheard him; and the member for Weymouth rofe, nothing loath. He wifhed Mr. Speaker to inform him whether the privilege of parliament was not utterly broken if men might not come in fafely to give their votes freely? Well, then, he muft tell them that he had received information of a plot or confpiracy for the deftruction of fome of the members of that Houfe, which he conceived to be little lefs than treafon; and he had moreover grounds

§ XXV. *Alleged Intimidation of Parliament.* 377

to believe that some other of the members of
that House were either contrivers of it, or had
consented to it; and he therefore desired that
the Lord Falkland, Sir John Culpeper, and
some three others, might be appointed a select
committee to examine the matter. Upon
which not very impartial proposal arose, not
unnaturally, great murmurs; ending in a peremptory order that Sir John should presently
declare the whole matter in particulars, and not
lay suspicion and charge indiscriminately upon
members of the House. Authority for the
statement was handed in accordingly; and
proved to be to the effect* that a certain
" lusty young man," a haberdasher's apprentice
in Distaff Lane, had boasted to certain parties
of having been one among a thousand or so,
who with swords and staves had betaken themselves to Westminster Palace Yard; his master,
who was a constable, having given him a sword
and ordered him to go; in fact, that some parlia-

Strang-
ways asks
for com-
mittee.

Is required
to state
complaint.

Story
of an ap-
prentice.

* I furnish these curious details from the Journal so often
referred to; the paper produced by Strangways being entitled
" A brief of the Discourse had between one Cole, an appren-
" tice to Mr. Mansfield, an haberdasher in Distaff Lane, and
" one John Nicholson, DD, in the presence of Stephen
" Tirrett, uncle to the said Cole, and John Derivale, both
" Chelmsford men." The Rev. Doctor is the informant,
and appears to have been fitting conversing with the said
Tirrett and Derivale, probably on theological subjects, " in
" his lodgings in Gracious [Gracechurch] Street, between
" nine and ten of the clock," when that very respectable lad,
Stephen, came in somewhat elatedly to tell his uncle the news
above mentioned. Mr. Kirton's respectable citizen, on the
other hand, whose man came to him when he was smoking
with his friend Mr. Farlow of Wood Street, was one Mr.
Lavender; and the witnesses who signed the relation averred
that when Mr. Lavender heard what his man told him, he
instantly departed, " and the rest of the company were much
" troubled."

D'Ewes's
MS.

A scene
in "Gra-
cious"
Street.

ment men had fent for them; and that the intent of their going was becaufe of news of fome certain divifion among the members of the lower Houfe, in which the beft-affected party, whom they were to affift, were likely to be overborne by the others; but that finding all quiet, and both fides agreeing well together, they had come home again.

Some members to be over-awed by others.

Yes, well, and is this all? became the cry when Sir John Strangways' relation was ended. Where, then, is the evidence againft members of this Houfe, and *who are* the members impugned? "That *I* can anfwer," cried an active partizan of Hyde's, Mr. Kirton, the member for Milborn Port; who thereupon handed in a further piece of evidence, to the effect that a worthy London citizen, being in Wood Street taking tobacco with fome friends on the day in queftion, there came his man to him and brought him word that a meffage was arrived from Captain Ven (member for London, he who afterwards fat on the trial of the King) to defire him to come away fpeedily armed to the Houfe of Commons, for fwords were there drawn, and the well-affected party was like to be overborne by the others. During the reading of this paper, Captain Ven came into his place, and would at the moment have anfwered to it; but the Houfe thought it not fit till fomewhat were proved, and, as to the preceding relation, conceived that Sir John Strangways had confiderably overftated himfelf, and had ventured upon an accufation which his information in no refpect warranted. On which Pym, rifing with unufual gravity of

"Name! Name!"

Kirton names Ven.

Houfe prevents Ven's anfwer.

§ xxv. *Alleged Intimidation of Parliament.* 379

manner, put this very significant question to Mr. Speaker: "Whether, though the worthy "member had failed to prove his charge of "a conspiracy, either contrived or consented "to by members unnamed, for the destruc- "tion of other members more plainly referred "to, he had yet not succeeded in proving very "fully, that there WAS *a conspiracy by some* "*members of this House to accuse other members* "*of the same of Treason?*" [Pym's question to Mr. Speaker.]

On the second of December, and on the third, the subject of these out-of-door demonstrations continued still under debate. Edmund Waller inveighed much against the Londoners for coming to Westminster in so tumultuous a manner and crying openly, No Bishops! No Bishops! and boldly justified the Earl of Dorset in the course he had taken, saying he had done nothing but what he was necessitated unto. Strode took the other side as warmly, declaring that the citizens had *not* come in any tumultuous or unlawful manner. Culpeper answered him, and in rough overbearing speech reiterated the charge that there had been a very unjustifiable tumult. To him succeeded D'Ewes, who declared himself of Mr. Strode's opinion, and that it was matter for grave inquiry that the Lord Dorset should have advised his musqueteers to shoot the citizens, and his pikemen to run them through, when they came simply, with all affection and faithfulness to the House, to attend the issue of their petitions to the high court of Parliament. Whereupon again started up Sir John Culpeper, speaking to order, and calling upon Sir Simonds [2nd & 3d Dec. Debates on popular gatherings.] [Waller, Strode, and Culpeper.] [D'Ewes defends the citizens.] [Culpeper interrupts.]

D'Ewes to explain what he meant by talking of—— But then Sir Walter Earle rofe to order from the other fide, and faid that no individual had the right, except with authority of the whole Houfe, to take exceptions to what had fallen from any member. Culpeper hereon refumed his feat, and D'Ewes himfelf was heard to the point of order. He fimply defired the gentleman on the other fide of the way might be allowed to fpeak, and to name the words he would except againft. On which Culpeper ftood up again and faid, more mildly, that what he intended to have remarked was out of a great deal of refpect to the worthy member who had juft fpoken, well knowing he had no ill intention, whatever words might flip from him. But, what did he mean by mentioning the citizens' "loyalty" to that Houfe? Was loyalty due, and to be paid, there or elfewhere? "Which very words," interpofes D'Ewes in his Journal, "I either certainly fpake not at "all, or not in one common claufe together." (In his own report, in the fame manufcript record, the words are "affection and faithful-"nefs," not loyalty.) "Wherefore I ftood up "myfelf, not one man calling on me, to ex-"plain; and I faid 'For the words themfelves, "'I do not remember that I fpake them, "'and for that I appeal to the whole Houfe' "(upon which there followed a great filence, "and I did not hear one man fecond Sir John "Culpeper's charge). 'But if I had fpoken "'the words, I conceive that gentleman would "'take no exception to them if he will but "'perufe Littleton in his chapter of Homage,

Earle and D'Ewes to order.

Culpeper explains.

D'Ewes replies.

Houfe fupports D'Ewes.

§ xxv. *Alleged Intimidation of Parliament.*

"'where he will find that one subject may owe
'loyalty to another without breach of his
'loyalty to the King.' Whereupon the
House rested satisfied. Sir John Culpeper
sat silent; and many laughed at the imperti-
nence of his exception, hearing how fully I
had answered him upon the sudden. In
which," adds the good Sir Simonds in
parenthesis, "I did very much acknowledge
God's assistance in furnishing me with so apt
and present a reply." {Culpeper silenced.}

The temper of the Majority of the House, {Pym's motion against upper House.} in close juxtaposition and contrast with that of its Minority of royalist opposition, appears in these curious and valuable records; and still more unmistakeably was it shown in the afternoon of that same 3d of December, when Pym rose and called attention to the stoppage of all legislative business by the rejection of, or refusal of the Lords to proceed with, various bills that had been sent to the upper House. He moved for a committee to review what bills the Commons had passed and the Lords had rejected, and the reasons why; and, if the Lords would not join with them,* then let them go to the {Stoppage of useful Bills.}

---

* It was but a few weeks after this that Pym summed up these and similar obstructions made by the Lords, at a conference with that House, and closed his speech in these very memorable words: {Obstructions in upper House.}

"We have often suffered under the misinterpretation of
"good actions, and false imputation of evil ones which we
"never intended; so that we may justly purge ourselves from
"all guilt of being authors of this jealousy and misunder-
"standing. We have been, and are still, ready to serve his
"Majesty with our lives and fortunes, with as much cheer-
"fulness and earnestness of affection as ever any subjects
"were; and we doubt not but our proceedings will so mani-

King; having firſt put their Declaration before the people, which would enable *them* to ſee where the obſtructions lay. "We may have our part in the miſery occaſioned," he ſaid, "let us be careful that we have no part in the "guilt or the diſhonour." He further threw out the ſuggeſtion, that, ſince the Lords poſſeſſed the undoubted right to proteſt in their individual capacity, and were not conſtitutionally involved by the major part, it would be well that they ſhould take thoſe proteſting Lords with them, and repreſent jointly to the King the cauſes of obſtruction. A propoſal which called forth inſtantly a retort from the quarter where Hyde's party ſat; for, up ſprang Mr. Francis Godolphin, Edmund Waller's colleague in the repreſentation of St. Ives, and aſked Mr. Speaker to inform him, whether, if the majority of that Houſe went to the King with the leſſer part of the Lords, "*the greater* "*part of the Lords might not go to the King*

Will minority of Lords join majority of Commons in a proteſt.

Counter propoſition by Godolphin.

Pym's appeal to Lords:

"feſt this, that we ſhall be as clear in the apprehenſion of the
" world, as we are in the teſtimony of our own conſciences.
" I am now come to a concluſion. I have nothing to pro-
" pound to your Lordſhips by way of requeſt or deſire from
" the Houſe of Commons. I doubt not but your judgments
" will tell you what is to be done: your conſciences, your
" honours, your intereſts, will call upon you for the doing of
" it. The Commons will be glad to have your concurrence
" and help in ſaving of the kingdom; but if they fail in it,
" it ſhall not diſcourage them in doing their duty. And
" whether the kingdom be loſt or ſaved, (but I hope, through
" God's bleſſing, it will be ſaved!) they ſhall be ſorry that
" the ſtory of this preſent parliament ſhould tell poſterity,
" that in ſo great a danger and extremity the Houſe of Com-
" mons ſhould be enforced to ſave the kingdom alone, and
" that the Peers ſhould have no part in the honour of the
" preſervation of it; having ſo great an intereſt in the good
" ſucceſs of thoſe endeavours, in reſpect of their great eſtates
" and high degrees of nobility."

Do not leave us to ſave the country alone.

§ xxv. *Alleged Intimidation of Parliament.* 383

"*with the leſſer part of us.*" Mr. Godolphin's ſuggeſtion was ſtartling, and he was reprimanded and had to make due ſubmiſſion for it;* but nothing could more perfectly have revealed all that at this time filled the minds and hopes of the King and his friends. If the right blow could only be aimed, at the right time, againſt the leaders of the Commons, the way to its accompliſhment ſeemed not remote. And what view Lenthal himſelf, the Speaker of the Commons, ſeems now to have been diſpoſed to take, as between King and Parliament, of the ſide to which victory was likely to incline, is expreſſed by a ſervile letter he wrote privately on this very third of December to the King's new Secretary of State, Sir Edward Nicholas, praying to be relieved of the too onerous dignity of the Chair, and to be ſuffered to become, once more, the meaneſt ſubject of the beſt of ſovereigns.†

That was on Friday, the day of Godolphin's ſtartling propoſal to piece out the minority of the Commons by a majority in the Lords. On Monday the 6th, Cromwell brought forward a

Side notes: Hopes of Court party. Views of Mr. Speaker. Monday, 6th Dec. Cromwell

---

* "Ordered that on Tueſday next the Houſe ſhall take into "conſideration the offence now given by words ſpoken by "Mr. Godolphin." The offence is not further ſpecified. On the Tueſday named, an order appears "that the Houſe "do take into conſideration, on Thurſday next, ſuch words "ſpoken by members of this Houſe, to which formerly ex-"ception hath been taken." Alas! however, on the Thurſday named (the 16th), occurred the King's great breach of privilege in taking notice of a Bill while in progreſs; and the matter was again deferred. I have not cared to purſue it further.

Side notes: Commons' Journals: 3rd Dec. and 7th Dec.

† See *Arreſt of the Five Members*, § iii. I have ſince found, however, that Nalſon had anticipated me in printing (*Collections,* ii. 713), alſo from the State Paper Office, this letter of Lenthal.

case of interference by a peer with Houfe of Commons privileges, which had no tendency to abate the prevailing excitement. He charged Lord Arundel with having fought unduly to influence and intimidate burgeffes of the borough of Arundel in regard to new elections. This appears to have raifed an animated debate, in the courfe of which a doctrine laid down by Hyde and Culpeper, to the effect that Lords *might* " write commendatory letters " during the progress of an election, was fomewhat roughly handled. But Tuefday the 7th faw a ftill more ftartling propofition launched from the other fide ; a propofition fo notable indeed, that Clarendon in his Hiftory is difpofed to fingle it out, and fet it apart, as the fole caufe and ground of all the mifchiefs which enfued. Neverthelefs it will probably feem to us, after watching the courfe of events immediately before and fince the return of the King, but as an advance or ftep onward, hardly avoidable, in the hazardous path which had been entered. The neceffity of greatly increafing the forces of the realm was not more obvious, than the danger of entrufting to an executive in whom no confidence was placed, the uncontrolled power of difpofing thofe forces. The difaffected fpirit of the army, as now officered, and in the midft of a frightful rebellion raging in one of the three kingdoms, was no longer matter of doubt. Irrefragable proofs of the fecond army plot had been completed ; and refolutions were at this time prepared, to take effect on the day after that to which my narrative has arrived, difabling four of thofe officers (men high in the

§ XXVI. *An Ominous Proposal.*

King's confidence and to whom he afterwards gave peerages) from their feats in the lower Houfe, as guilty of mifprifion of treafon, by name Wilmot, Pollard, Afhburnham, and Percy, members for Tamworth, Beeralfton, Ludgerfhall (Wilts), and Northumberland. The diftruft felt by the Commons on the King's removal of their Guard, and the refolutions as to the defence of the kingdom which they paffed on that troubled Saturday after his return, receive only their full explanation from keeping fuch facts in view; and they led, almoft unavoidably, to the more momentous ftep now waiting to be detailed.

Dangers from army intrigues.

Diftruft of the King.

§ XXVI. AN OMINOUS PROPOSAL.

ON Tuefday, the 7th of December, Sir Arthur Hafelrig rofe in his ufual place in the gallery of the Houfe, and prefented a Bill for fettling the Militia of the kingdom by fea and land, under a Lord General and a High Admiral, to whom it gave great powers to raife and levy forces. It was ftyled An Act for the making of (Blank) Lord General of all the forces within the kingdom of England and dominion of Wales, and (Blank) Lord High Admiral of England. Clarendon fays that this bill had been privately prepared by the King's folicitor, St. John; and that his influence as a lawyer, on his declaring the exifting law to have been fo unfettled by difabling votes of the two Houfes that a fpecial enactment was become abfolutely neceffary, mainly led to the bill being permitted to be read. But, while his ftatements here are to be taken with even more

Tuefday, 7th Dec. Bill prefented by Hafelrig:

for fettling the Militia.

than the usual caution, it is to be remarked that D'Ewes, though he says nothing absolutely inconsistent therewith, does not expressly confirm them; and D'Ewes's account, of which I proceed to give an abstract from his manuscript, is the only other on record, so far as I am aware, of this memorable debate.

Haselrig had scarcely named the provisions of the bill, when a great many members cried, " Away with it ! " and others, that they should " Cast it out ! " Sir John Culpeper started up on the instant of Haselrig's resuming his seat; and, after wondering that the gentleman in the gallery should bring in such a bill, moved that it be at once rejected. Sir Thomas Barrington, though he had voted with the majority in all the Remonstrance debates, regretted that he could not support the particular measure, and wished it might be thrown out; but he thought another less objectionable should be brought in with similar design. Strode "and others" spoke for it strongly; and then D'Ewes himself rose and made a lengthy speech in its favour, duly self-reported, but with which the reader need not be troubled. Divers followed him, speaking on either side, some for, and others against the bill, and many using violent expressions against it. Mr. Thomas Cook, for example, the member for Leicester, declared that one Hexey in Richard the Second's time, for introducing, in the twentieth year of that reign, a bill against the King's prerogative of far less consequence than this, had been condemned as a traitor. Nor did Mr. Mallory, the member for Ripon,

§ XXVI. *An Ominous Proposal.*

speak less violently on the same side. He denounced the bill as fit to be burned in West- minster Palace Yard, and the gentleman who brought it in as deserving to be questioned. On the other hand, several rose and excepted against Mr. Mallory's speech, as rather thinking *it* more worthy to be questioned; but thereupon Strode got up and remarked that he thought Mr. Mallory's speech in some sort excusable, as having been occasioned by the speech of a gentleman that sat near him (alluding to Mr. Cook), who had once before cited in that House a highly dangerous precedent. Great cries of assent followed this remark, and many rose in succession to enforce it, until, in spite of dissentients, Mr. Cook was called up to explain. But, what he said not satisfying the House, he was ordered to withdraw, while some would have had his further attendance suspended. Meanwhile a sudden thought had occurred to D'Ewes, which he had immediately proceeded to execute. " During this debate," he says, " I retired " out of the House to my lodging in Goats- " alley, near the Palace, and there searched " out the precedent. On my return, I said " that the gentleman now withdrawn was a " young man, and a man of hope, and there- " fore I desired that he be not too much dis- " heartened. I thought him more punishable " for mis-reciting than for citing precedents. " The precedent in question was not against " the King's prerogative, but against the " excessive expenses of the King's household; " and though Hexey was sentenced, he was

Mallory would have bill burnt.

Cook called up :

ordered to withdraw.

Had mis-quoted precedent.

D'Ewes exposes

afterwards cleared by Parliament. Therefore the greateſt cenſure I would have laid upon this gentleman is, that he would cite no more records till he ſhall have ſtudied them better. At which divers of the Houſe laughed;" and Cook having been called in, and admoniſhed by Mr. Speaker,* Haſelrig's bill paſſed to a diviſion. Sir John Culpeper and Sir Frederick Cornwallis were tellers for the Yeas, which were 125, to reject it; and Denzil Hollis and Sir William Armyn, member for Grantham, for the majority of 158 in its favour: and the bill was read a firſt time.

And now let me append to this truſtworthy account, taken from the notes of a member preſent while the debate was in progreſs, the narrative of the ſame incident as related by Clarendon. Perhaps no more remarkable warning could be given of the ſcrupulous care with which his *Hiſtory* ſhould be read, and of

and laughs at him.

Cook admoniſhed.

Bill read a firſt time: 158 to 125.

Same incident:

Commons' Journals. ii. 334.

Verney's Notes, p. 132.

* The only notices hitherto given of this incident appear in the *Journals* and in Verney's *Notes*. " Some exceptions were taken to Mr. Coke for the miſalleging of precedents; and after he had explained himſelf, he was, according to the order of the Houſe, commanded to withdraw. Reſolved upon the queſtion, That Mr. Coke ſhall be called down, and in his place, have an admonition for the words that fell from him. The Speaker told him in his place that he was commanded to admoniſh him, that he ſhould take a care hereafter, how he did allege or apply precedents in this Houſe." Verney ſays in his *Notes*: "Sir Arthur Haſelrig did bring in a bill to diſpoſe all the Militia of England into two generals for life. This bill was thought fit by ſome to be rejected, and Mr. Thomas Cook ſaid, it was in his judgment worſe than the bill brought in by Hexam in Richard the Second's time, by which he was accuſed of high treaſon. For this ſpeech he was queſtioned and taxed, for citing but half the precedent, for Hexam was afterwards cleared by parliament. For this offence he received an admonition in his place, by the Speaker."

§ XXVI. *An Ominous Proposal.*

the danger of trusting to its statements even where there is no suspicion of bad faith, than is afforded by the manner in which he recounts the first introduction of this Bill for putting the power of the Militia substantially into the hands of the House of Commons.

told with strange variations.

In his Fourth Book, speaking of the exact period to which reference already has been made, he says that there was "at this time, or thereabout," a debate started in the House, as if by mere chance, which produced many inconveniences thereafter, and indeed, if there had not been too many concurrent causes, might be thought the sole cause and ground of all the mischiefs which ensued. And then he describes " an obscure " member" moving unexpectedly " that the " House would enter upon the consideration " whether the Militia of the kingdom was so " settled by law that a sudden force, or army, " could be drawn together for the defence of " the kingdom, if it should be invaded, or to " suppress an insurrection or rebellion, if it " should be attempted." He goes on to say that the House kept a long silence after the motion, the newness of it amazing (until the edition of 1826, this word had been printed " amusing ") most men, and few in truth understanding the meaning of it; until sundry other members, not among the leading men, appeared to be so moved by the weight of what had been said, that it grew to the proposition of a committee for preparing such a bill, whereupon Mr. Hyde so strongly opposed it as encroaching on the royal prerogative, that the

Clarendon's Hist. ii. 76-80.

Motion made as to militia:

how treated.

Houſe appeared ſatisfied to take up another ſubject: when the King's Solicitor, St. John, "and the only man in the Houſe of his "learned council," got up and diſputed Mr. Hyde's law, obſerving that the queſtion was not about taking away power from the King (which it was his duty always to oppoſe), but to inquire if the ſufficient and neceſſary power exiſted at all. This he regretted to ſay he did not believe, ſupporting his opinion by the many adverſe votes which that Houſe had paſſed againſt the ordinary modes of levy in the King's name, by means of commiſſions to Lord Lieutenants and their ſubordinates; and the reſult of his diſplay of learning was, that in the end he was himſelf requeſted to introduce ſuch a bill, which, within a few days after, was actually brought in, enacting "that hencefor- "ward the Militia, and all the powers thereof, "ſhould be veſted in ——;" and then a large blank was left for inſerting names, in which blank, the Solicitor urged, they might for aught he knew inſert the King's, and he hoped it would be ſo. This bill, Clarendon con- cludes, not withſtanding all oppoſition, was read, "they who had contrived it being well "enough contented that it was once read; "not deſiring to proſecute it, till ſome more "favourable conjuncture ſhould be offered; "and ſo it reſted."

Now, having proceeded ſo far, let the reader turn back to the Third Book of the ſame Hiſtory, and he will there find that the ſame hiſtorian, profeſſing to ſpeak of the period im- mediately before the King's departure for Scot-

§ XXVI. *An Ominous Proposal.*

land, antedates the whole of the tranfaction juſt defcribed; and narrates quite differently, and as though impelled by motives and inducements altogether different, events precifely the fame. His object now is to ſhow that the leaders of the Houſe were anxious to prevent the King's departure by warning him that he was leaving affairs in a dangerouſly unfettled ſtate, and without fufficient powers inherent in the laws and conſtitution to meet the danger. "And "therefore," he continues, "one day Sir Ar- "thur Hafelrig (who, as was faid before, was "ufed by the leading men, like the dove out "of the ark, to try what footing there was) "preferred a bill for the fettling the Militia of "the kingdom both by fea and land in fuch "perfons as they ſhould nominate." He adds that there were in the bill no names, but blanks to receive them, when the matter ſhould be paffed; and that when the mere title of the bill was read, it gave fo general an offence to the Houſe that they feemed inclined to throw it out, without fuffering it to be read: not without fome reproach, to the perfon that brought it in, "as a matter of fedition:" till Mr. St. John, the King's Solicitor, rofe up and fpake to it, and ("having in truth himfelf "drawn the bill") defended its provifions, declaring his belief as a lawyer, that the power it propofed to fettle was not yet by law veſted in any perfon or in the Crown itſelf, the Houſe by their votes having blaſted the former modes of proceeding by the ordinary royal commiſ- fions to Lord Lieutenants and their deputies; that fuch a bill therefore was neceffary; and

Same incident again told.

Quite different account of fame facts.

Bill brought in by Hafelrig:

drawn by St. John:

who defends

The Grand Remonstrance.

and explains it. that for the nomination of perfons under it, this was a matter not requiring to be fettled on the reading of the bill, for if it feemed too great for any fubject it might be devolved upon the Crown. " Upon which difcourfe," *Never read fecond time.* Clarendon concludes, " by a perfon of the King's fworn council, the bill was read; " but with fo univerfal a diflike, that it was " never called upon the fecond time, but flept, " till, long after, the matter of it was digefted " in ordinances."*

Great of courfe has been the confufion, to readers, confequent on thefe two verfions of the fame incident, dated at different times, and *Alleged rejection.* having objects quite diffimilar; and it has been further increafed by a ftatement of Nalfon's,† that Hafelrig's bill was rejected indignantly on its introduction, by a majority of 158 to 105. But the one point on which Clarendon is not inaccurate is, in affirming, in both *Error as to firft reading.* narratives, that the bill *was* read. The error in this refpect has arifen from a too hafty reading of the Journals,‡ where the Yeas at the divifion appear undoubtedly as 125 (not 105), and the Noes as 158; but it has been overlooked that the divifion was taken not on the queftion whether the bill fhould be read, but whether it fhould be rejected. The names of *Carried by 158 to 125.* the tellers are quite decifive, Culpeper and Cornwallis being for the Yeas, and Denzil Hollis and Sir W^m. Armyn (member for Grantham, and afterwards a king's judge) for the Noes. Even that generally accurate and

---

* *Hift.* i. 486-8.   † Nalfon's *Collections*, ii. 719.
‡ *Commons' Journals*, ii. 334.

reliable writer, Mr. Bruce, has fallen into error on this point,* and suppoſes the bill to have been rejected. Mr. Hallam alſo has been led into ſome confuſion † from not examining Clarendon's text with ſufficient minuteneſs. I take the opportunity of adding that Nalſon's *Collections*, which, by ſome extraordinary chance in the fortunes of books, has been too commonly accepted as an authority on theſe times, is an utterly untruſtworthy gathering of the moſt violent party pamphlets and libels, got together towards the cloſe of Charles the Second's reign for the ſpecial delectation of his Majeſty and as an antidote to Ruſhworth, by a compiler who had himſelf no perſonal knowledge of the men or the events, over which he exerciſed an unlimited right of the groſſeſt abuſe and moſt unwearied miſrepreſentation.

<small>Miſtakes and confuſion.</small>

<small>Hiſtorians miſled.</small>

<small>Nalſon no authority.</small>

§ XXVII. THE CITY PETITION.

ON the day following Haſelrig's introduction of the Militia Bill, Wedneſday the 8th, Geoffrey Palmer made his ſubmiſſion and was releaſed from the Tower. The day following, the expulſion of the officers convicted of complicity in the ſecond army-plot took place; and on the morning after, Friday the 10th of December,‡ the members were ſtartled, on

<small>Wedneſday, 8th Dec.</small>

<small>Friday, 10th:</small>

---

* See Verney's *Notes*, p. 132.   † *Conſt. Hiſt.* ii. 128, 9.

‡ On the ſame morning I find a point of order and reverence ſettled by Mr. Denzil Hollis. "On Mr. Hollis' motion," ſays D'Ewes's Manuſcript, "it was declared the ancient order <small>Points of</small>

coming to take their feats, to find a new Guard of Halberdiers fet upon the doors. A debate upon the report as to the Public Debt handed in by Sir John Hotham the previous day, and upon the immediate neceffity of raifing men and money for the requirements of the Irifh Rebellion, was in progrefs, when Sir Philip Stapleton ftood up and called attention to the fact that there was a new Guard fet upon the Houfe of two hundred men with halberts. Much agitation enfued upon this, the bufinefs immediately in hand was dropped, and fome fear and trouble found expreffion. Upon particular inquiry it was difcovered, that the plea for fuch new fhow or threatening of force was a report which had gone abroad of a great Petition coming from the City againft the Bifhops' votes, and againft the obftruction by the Lords of other matters whereof the fettlement was much to be defired, which Petition, accompanied by large numbers of citizens, was to be prefented the following day. " Then we were " informed," fays D'Ewes, " from feveral " hands, that the original ground of thofe men " affembling was upon a writ from the Lord " Keeper pretended to be warranted by the " ftatute of Northampton (13 Henry IV.) for " the better fuppreffing of Routs and Riots :" in obedience to which writ the under-fheriff and magiftrates of Middlefex had iffued order

New Guard on Houfes.

Agitation thereat.

By whom placed.

Writ from Lord Keeper.

form and order. " of the Houfe that when men came in and went out of the
" Houfe, they ought to make three reverences; and that if
" any were fpeaking on the lower form, they ought to go
" about, and not to come up towards the table"—interrupting
honorable fpeakers!

§ XXVII.   *The City Petition.*   395

for the placing of the Halberdiers. The matter was debated with unusual gravity and earnest- ness; and, upon the motion of Pym, not only was a resolution passed that the placing of such a Guard without consent of the House was a breach of privilege, but orders were issued for bringing before them at nine o'clock on the following morning the various magistrates by whom the warrants had been signed. Instant steps were at the same time taken for removal of the Halberdiers ;* and while these were in progress, at about two o'clock in the afternoon, Sir Christopher Yelverton entered, and said that divers of the Lords were now come, knowing nothing at all of the setting of this new Guard, and were startled at it " as much as " ourselves." A characteristic incident of the debate, as related in D'Ewes's manuscript, should not be omitted. One of Hyde's party, Mr. Francis Newport, the member for Shrewsbury, " during our debate offered to go out " of the House, and there was great cry, " ' Shut the door ! Shut the door !' and yet " he would go away. The Serjeant not being

<small>Voted breach of privilege.

Halberdiers removed.

Lords startled as well as Commons

"Shut the door!"</small>

<small>* The subjoined order and resolutions appear upon the *Journals*, " Ordered that the serjeant shall require some of the " Halberdiers, or some of those that have the command of " them, to come hither to the bar. The bailiff of the Duchy " of Lancaster being called in, was demanded by what au- " thority he brought down men armed : He said the Sheriff " received a writ from the Lord Keeper, and that the Under- " sheriff gave him warrant to do it. . . . Resolved upon the " question, That the setting of any guards about this House, " without the consent of this House is a breach of the privi- " lege of the House : And that therefore such guards ought " to be discharged. Resolved upon the question, That this " Guard shall be immediately discharged by the command of " this House."

Commons Journals: ii. 338.</small>

"in the House, Mr. Rushworth, the clerk's
"assistant, was sent after him; who called him
"back. He being come into the House, the
"Speaker declared to him that when the sense
"of the House was that the door should be shut,
"no member ought to go out. Mr. New-
"port said he knew of no order that had been
"made to that end: but Mr. Pym showed,
"that, besides the general sense of the House,
"expressed by so many calling out to have the
"door shut, the greatness and weight of the
"agitation might persuade any man to forbear
"going out."

Member quits House without leave.

Rebuked by Pym.

11th Dec. Sheriff and Magistrates reprimanded.

The next morning, Saturday the 11th of December, the under-sheriff and Westminster justices appeared, and, having been duly examined and reprimanded, and the under-sheriff having been committed to the Tower, there shortly afterwards arrived, at the House, the Petition upon whose presentation the King had been so eager to impose that check of armed men. The intention of its originators had been to disabuse his Majesty of the fatal notion which seems to have been suddenly engendered in him by his recent grand entertainment in the City, and by the eager royalist tendencies of the Lord Mayor, that there was any real defection from the popular cause in that its most powerful stronghold;* and so eagerly had it been signed

The City petition.

---

* I venture here to subjoin a passage from my *Arrest of the Five Members* (§ xxiv.), in explanation of what the City at this time represented and was. "Of the power and the im-
"portance of the City of London at this time, it is needless
"to speak. It represented in itself the wealth, the strength,
"and the independence which had made England feared and
"honoured throughout the world. Within its walls, and

The City 220 years ago.

§ XXVII. *The City Petition.* 397

by all claſſes with this view, that, up to that date in the world's hiſtory, no petition of equal ſize and dimenſions had yet been ſeen. One of the members for London, Alderman Pennington, who afterwards ſat as one of the King's judges, announced its arrival. He ſaid that divers able and grave citizens were waiting without, to preſent the Houſe with that formidable Petition of which they had been told that ten thouſand perſons were coming to preſent it; but a ſmall number only had come with it, and in a humble and peaceable manner. To avoid all poſſibility of commotion or undue excitement in connection with it, it had been brought by twelve leading citizens. Upon this the Houſe laid aſide all other buſineſs; the Speaker called in the deputation; and Mr.

Its arrival announced.

Brought by twelve citizens.

" under the ſhadow and protection of its franchiſes, ſlept
" nightly between three and four hundred thouſand citizens.
" The place of buſineſs of the merchant in thoſe days, was
" alſo his reſidence and home. The houſes then recently
" built by nobles beyond its precincts, along the Strand of the
" magnificent river, ſcarcely tranſcended in extent or ſplen-
" dour thoſe palaces of its merchant princes, which lurked
" everywhere behind its buſy wharves and crowded counting-
" houſes. But, beyond every ſuch ſource of aggrandiſement,
" its privileges were its power. From its guilds, charters,
" and immunities, wreſted from the needs, or beſtowed by the
" favour, of ſucceſſive princes; from its own regulation of its
" military as well as civil affairs; from its complete and
" thoroughly organiſed democracy, governed and governing
" by and within itſelf; it derived an influence which made it
" formidable far beyond its wealth and numbers. . . . . To
" its honour, be it ſaid, that from the hour when the cauſe of
" public freedom was in peril, the City of London caſt in its
" fortunes unreſervedly with the oppoſition to the Court. Its
" reſolute refuſal to join the league againſt the Scottiſh Cove-
" nant, had baffled the counſels and waſted the energies of
" Strafford; and its Trained Bands, under Skippon, were
" deſtined largely to contribute to the final defeat of the
" King."

Source of its power.

Its ſupport of popular cauſe.

Fouke, a merchant dwelling in Mark-lane, appeared at their head, and prefented it as the humble Petition of Aldermen, Common Councilmen, Subfidymen, and other inhabitants of the City of London and fuburbs thereof. Then, fays the precife Sir Simonds D'Ewes, " the Clerk of the Houfe did thereupon go down to the bar, and received it of him, and brought it up, and laid it on the table. The faid Petition was not very long, but there were fome fifteen thoufand names fet to it. It was about three-quarters of a yard in breadth, and twenty-four yards in length." Nor did it feem that even thefe unufual proportions had quite fatisfied its promoters; for the worthy citizen at the head of the Deputation, having liberty to addrefs the Houfe, informed them that they fhould have got before that day many thoufand hands more to it, but that they found many obftructions and much oppofition from the Lord Mayor, *and others*. And fuch, faid Mr. Fouke in conclufion, was the feeling excited by thefe difficulties interpofed, that it was God's mercy the petitioners had not come in numbers yefterday, when the Halberdiers were affembled, and when there muft have been bloodfhed. To which Mr. Speaker replied with gracious words, telling the citizens of London, through the worthy gentlemen then ftanding at their bar, that the Houfe gave them thanks for their readinefs on all occafions to comply with fupplies for the public; that they would take into confideration, in due time, the particulars defired in the Petition; and that they hoped to

§ XXVII. *The City Petition.*

bring things to such result as would give them satisfaction.

When the Deputation left, a debate arose as to the necessity for immediate provision of the supplies which had been voted for Ireland, and as to the best mode of providing such satisfaction for the people as had just been promised to the London petitioners: and again the debate pointed in the old direction, which was that of printing, and circulating through the country, their Grand Remonstrance. The course taken by the King's advisers, indeed, had so far gone in the same direction, that even some royal partizans among the members had been constrained to admit the unlawfulness of the recent attempt to put external pressure on the Houses by means of armed watches and guards. The result of the present deliberation, therefore, appears to have been a kind of silent or unopposed understanding, that the printing of the Remonstrance should be considered as soon as the bill then depending for the pressing of soldiers to serve against the Irish Rebellion should have been disposed of.

But again the ill-advised monarch precipitated this determination. The bill for raising such soldiers by Impressment was under debate on the morning of Tuesday the 14th of December, when a message was unexpectedly brought in, to the effect that his Majesty desired the Commons to attend him in the Lords' House. There, in brief intemperate phrase, he adverted to the Impressment bill which they were then discussing; warned them that, in the event of its passing, he should give his consent

Debate as to Ireland.

Question of printing Remonstrance revived.

Resolve thereon.

Tuesday, 14th Dec. Message from King:

The Grand Remonstrance.

<small>respecting bill under discussion.</small> to it only with an exprefs faving of his prerogative; and fignificantly added, that he was little beholding to " him whoever at this time " began this difpute." The Commons immediately returned to their Houfe; voted it, upon the motion of Pym, a breach of all the ancient privileges both of Lords and Commons that his Majefty fhould fo have taken notice of a <small>Voted breach of privilege.</small> bill whilft in progrefs; demanded a conference with the Lords; and, before the day clofed, had obtained their full co-operation in drawing up "a declaratory Proteftation" of their privileges and liberties, and " a petitionary Remon- " ftrance "* againft his Majefty's violation of <small>Proteft carried to King.</small> them. Eighteen of the Lords, and double the number of the Commons, went at once with this Proteftation to Whitehall;† and on the

---

<small>Charge againft St. John.</small> * The petitionary Remonftrance further requires that " his " Majefty will be pleafed to difcover the parties by whofe " information and evil counfel his Majefty was induced to " this breach of privilege, that fo they may receive condign " punifhment for the fame." In the face of which, Clarendon neverthelefs hazards the ftatement in his *Hiftory* (ii. 70-1) that the man who had advifed this breach of privilege, was, of all men in the world, Mr. Solicitor St. John! As if, fuppofing this were fo, the King, who hated no one fo much, would not thereon have been eager to give him up as his advifer in fo direct an attack upon his own party! From the account of <small>Not credible.</small> the matter I find in D'Ewes's Journal, I am convinced, on the other hand, that the perfons fufpected were Culpeper and Hyde, and that the claufe requiring the King to furrender the names of his ill advifers was directed fpecially at them. D'Ewes would have had the claufe rejected, on the ground that it was " very poffible that his Majefty received his in- " formation and ill counfel from fome third perfon and from " no member of either Houfe ;" but Pym ftrongly oppofed this, and the claufe was retained.

† D'Ewes attended, as one of the Deputation of the Commons, both on the occafion of the prefenting of the Protefta- <small>Curious notices</small> tion, and on that of receiving the King's Anfwer, and his notices of both are highly curious and interefting. I quote

§ XXVII. *The City Petition.* 401

day following the King's churlish reception of them, the step was taken from which no further retreating was possible, and the Remonstrance was committed to the people.

Resolve taken.

from his manuscript Journal. "I departed with divers others from the
" to the Court at Whitehall, being one of the select commit-
" tee of thirty-six appointed by the House of Commons to
" attend his Majesty there this afternoon at two o'clock, with
" a select committee of eighteen of the Lords' House, with
" that petitionary Remonstrance. The eighteen Lords were
" at Whitehall before us; and having staid awhile in the
" Privy Chamber, the Earl of Essex, Lord Chamberlain of
" his Majesty's household, came out to us, and told us that
" the King expected our coming to him. Whereupon divers of
" the Lords, and we of the House of Commons, followed him
" in through two or three rooms, into a fair inward chamber
" where the King was. Dr. Williams, Archbishop of York,
" was appointed to read the said Petition or Remonstrance.
" He, passing from the lower end of the room towards the
" King, made three reverences, as most of us also did with
" him; and then he, coming near the King, kneeled down,
" and showed his Majesty that he had a Petition or Remon-
" strance from both Houses to be presented to him. The
" King then caused him to stand up, and so he read the said
" Petition. I stood all the while close to him on his left
" hand. After he had read it, he kneeled again, and pre-
" sented it to his Majesty, being fairly engrossed in parchment.
" The King spake so low as I could not hear him; but the
" Archbishop of York told me after we were come out 'that
" 'he would take some time to advise,' &c. And so, making
" like reverence at our going out as we did at our coming in,
" we departed." In like manner he describes the more striking
scene of receiving the King's Answer. Between the two
occasions the reader will remember, the Commons had not
only voted the printing of their Grand Remonstrance, but
had issued it in print; a circumstance which may account for
the increased sharpness of the King's manner. "Went to
" Whitehall," says D'Ewes, "to receive the King's Answer.
" We were admitted into the same room again (being a fair
" chamber within the privy gallery) where we had delivered
" the said Petition. The King, looking about, asked to
" whom he should deliver his Answer; because he saw not
" the Lord there from whom he received our Petition. But it
" was answered his Majesty, that he, being to preach before the
" Lords at the Fast on Wednesday next, was now absent on
" that occasion. His Majesty demanded further to what other
" Lord in his absence it was to be delivered? It was an-

D'Ewes MS.

Deputation presented.

Arbp. Williams reads it.

King's answer:

§ XXVIII. THE LAST DEBATE.

Twelfth and laſt Debate: 15th Dec.

Purefoy moves printing.

ON Wedneſday morning, the 15th of December, an unuſual number of members were in attendance at an early hour in the Houſe of Commons, and a ſuppreſſed excitement ſhowed itſelf, as of ſome undertaking of weight in hand as yet not generally known. Then Mr. Purefoy, the member for Warwick, who afterwards ſat upon the trial of the King, ſtood up and ſaid, that they did now ſtand ſorely in need of money, and he conceived that any propoſition for the bringing in of money would be very ſeaſonable and acceptable. "Whereupon,"

A great ſilence.

ſays D'Ewes, "there enſued a great ſilence." Mr. Purefoy then proceeded, and ſaid he conceived that there was but one mode of obtaining what they deſired in this reſpect, and that was by imparting to their conſtituents, and the people generally, ſome ground for greater confidence than they could derive from recent and exiſting events. He pointed out

Argument for printing:

that all men's minds were unſettled by the many ſlanders which had freely gone abroad,

read by Nicholas.

Anger of the King

" ſwered, to the chief of the Lords who were preſent. His
" Majeſty then calling to Sir Edward Nicholas, lately made
" Secretary of State, delivered to him his Anſwer written on
" a ſheet of paper, which the ſaid Sir Edward received kneel-
" ing, and then, ſtanding up again, read it ; and his Majeſty,
" after the delivery of it to the ſaid Earl (Briſtol), juſt as we
" were all making reverences and departing forth, paſſed
" through the midſt of us with a confident and ſevere look,
" and ſo went into the privy gallery, where he ſtood looking
" towards us, as we came forth and made our obeiſances to
" him."

§ XXVIII. *The Laſt Debate.* 403

and that if, as a worthy member had ſaid on a former occaſion, it was deſirable to recover and bind to that Houſe the hearts of the people, now was the time and the opportunity. In a word, he conceived there were no readier means to bring in money than to cauſe their Declaration to be printed; that ſo they might ſatisfy the whole kingdom. At this there were loud cries of agreement; but upon ſeveral even of the majority the propoſal fell with a ſurpriſe, and D'Ewes was one of them. "It "ſeems," he ſays, "that many members were "privy to this intended motion, which I con-"feſs ſeemed very ſtrange to me; for they "cried *Order it! Order it!*" Then the Speaker roſe, and, as if to ſhow that he at any rate had been no party to the preparing of the motion, aſked the member who had ſpoken, what Declaration he meant, for (alluding to the declaration as to breach of privilege voted the preceding day) there were two. This called up Mr. Purefoy again, who ſaid he meant the Declaration that had been preſented to the King, the great Remonſtrance; and he was ſeconded by Mr. Peard, who had firſt moved the printing on the memorable night of the 22d November, and who now moved that the Petition accompanying it might alſo be printed: to which again reſponded loud cries of *Order it! Order it!* Edmund Waller next took the lead in a deſperate attempt to pro-,tract and delay the vote, which in ſo much was ſuccefsful that it laſted far into the afternoon; but of which, unfortunately, ſmall record remains, for in the midſt of it D'Ewes,

will re- cover Peo- ple to Houſe.

Surpriſe of D'Ewes and others.

Peard ſeconds Purefoy.

Waller oppoſes.

D D 2

apparently in some dudgeon at the want of confidence in him displayed by the leaders, left the House for some time. Then the putting of the Resolution having been fought off until daylight began to decline, the coming on of dark was made the excuse for a further attempt to prevent its being put at all. So dark it became, that the Clerk could no longer see to read; but, on a proposal for bringing in candles, Sir Nicholas Slanning, the member for Penryn, made urgent representation of the propriety of adjourning the debate, reminded the House of the scene which had been witnessed when this question was before discussed in the night, and threw out warnings of some similar danger now. Against any possible recurrence of that danger, the majority was on this occasion thoroughly guarded; but, if it had not been so, few were better entitled than Slanning to give the warning. Himself one of those who early and eagerly exposed and lost their lives in the war, he was also ever at the head of the young and ardent spirits of the House of Commons, with whom it was matter of chivalry to resent every encroachment on the power and pretensions of the sovereign; and Clarendon (in one of those charming character pieces of his History which will survive to keep it still the most delightful reading in the world, long after the conviction of its untrustworthiness and bad faith shall have entered into every mind) has celebrated his youth, his small but handsome person, his lovely countenance, his admirable parts, and his courage

Debate prolonged to evening.

Candles called for.

Sir Nicholas Slanning opposes.

An eager Royalist.

"so clear and keen."* He failed for the Forces present, however, to turn the House from their purpose, though not till he had forced on a division.

Division:

* See *History*, iv. 150, and 612-13. Slanning was one of Great men the little men; "and it was an age," says Clarendon, "in of little "which there were many great and wonderful men of that size. "size" (*Life*, i. 62), among the men of learning as well as of action. One of the least men in the kingdom he celebrates as one of the greatest scholars of Europe, in the person of the ever to be remembered Mr. Hales of Eton—"who "would often say that he would renounce the religion of the Hales of "Church of England to-morrow, if it obliged him to believe Eton. "that any other Christians should be damned; and that "nobody would conclude another man to be damned, who "did not wish him so;—than whom no man was more "strict and severe to himself, yet to other men so charitable "as to their opinions, that he thought that men not erring "were more in fault for their carriage towards men who "erred, than the men themselves were;—and who thought "that pride and passion, more than conscience, were the "cause of all separation from each other's communion; and "frequently said, that that only kept the world from agreeing "upon such a liturgy as might then bring them into One "communion" (*Life*, i. 60-1). Chillingworth was another Chillingof the very little men. Sidney Godolphin, also belonging to worth. the same diminutive class, amazed the tall and well-formed Mr. Hyde by presenting so large an understanding and so unrestrained a fancy in so extremely small a body as he possessed: Sidney the smallest indeed of all, as it would seem, for Falkland Godolused merrily to say that he thought what charmed him most phin. to be so much in Godolphin's company was the sense of finding himself there "the properer man." But the prince of the little men was Falkland himself. Observe with what exquisite art Clarendon puts forward his disadvantages of person simply to make more lovable the attractions of his mind. "His stature was low, and smaller than most men; Falkland. "his motion not graceful; and his aspect so far from inviting, "that it had somewhat in it of simplicity; and his voice the "worst of the three, and so untuned, that instead of recon"ciling, it offended the ear, so that nobody would have "expected music from that tongue: and sure no man was "less beholden to nature for its recommendation into the "world. But then no man sooner or more disappointed this "general and customary prejudice. That little person and Picture by "small stature was quickly found to contain a great heart, a Claren"courage so keen, and a nature so fearless, that no composi- don:

on ques-
tion for
candles.

D'Ewes returned to his feat juft as they were about to divide on the queftion for candles, and by the very found, he fays, the Ayes declared themfelves to be far more than the Noes; but the Noes perfifted in dividing, and "fitting ftill" in the Houfe with Sir Robert Hatton and Mr. John Ruffell (who had fucceeded Lord William on the old Earl's death,

152 to 53.
Candles
brought.

as Pym's colleague in the reprefentation of Taviftock) for tellers, proved to be only 53 in number, whereas the Ayes who went out, with Denzil Hollis and Sir John Clotworthy as tellers, were 152. Upon this, candles were brought; and again the debate went on, not lefs warmly than before. For more than two hours longer, fays D'Ewes, it was argued with

Divifion
for print-
ing.

great vehemence pro and con; until at laft the queftion was put for the printing. Then went forth the Yeas, in number 135, with Denzil Hollis and Sir Walter Earle for tellers; the tellers for the Noes, who ftayed in the Houfe, being Sir John Culpeper and Mr. John Afhburnham, the member for Haftings, and

Carried:
135 to 83.

their numbers 83. Amid confiderable excite-

" tion of the ftrongeft limbs, and moft harmonious and pro-
" portioned prefence and ftrength, ever more difpofed any
" man to the greateft enterprife, it being his greateft weaknefs
" to be too folicitous for fuch adventures; and that untuned
" tongue and voice eafily difcovered itfelf to be fupplied and

Life i.
43-4.

" governed by a mind and underftanding fo excellent, that
" the wit and weight of all he faid carried another kind of
" luftre and admiration in it, and even another kind of ac-
" ceptation from the perfons prefent, than any ornament of
" delivery could reafonably promife itfelf, or is ufually
" attended with; and his difpofition and nature was fo gentle
" and obliging, fo much delighted in courtefy, kindnefs, and
" generofity, that all mankind could not but admire and love
" him."

§ XXVIII. *The Laſt Debate.*

ment, the order was then given for immediate printing of the Remonſtrance concerning the ſtate of the kingdom; the Grand Remonſtrance, as thereafter it came to be called, to diſtinguiſh it from the many other ſimilar State Papers of leſs importance, and leſs intereſt for the people, which were iſſued during the war. Even now, however, it required all the temper and control of the leaders to avoid a mutiny. The claim to proteſt was, at this point, once more revived; and Sir Nicholas Slanning, heading the proteſters, did his beſt to bring his own warning true. Some ſixty members having joined him, they formally demanded that their proteſtation might be entered by order of the Houſe; but the growing excitement was happily allayed by the art with which Pym, in appearing to yield to that propoſal, in reality yielded nothing. The demand was turned into an order for an adjournment "to take into conſideration the " matter touching proteſtations in this Houſe;" and, the following Friday having been fixed for the purpoſe of ſuch conſideration, the Houſe roſe at ſeven o'clock.

So cloſed the laſt debate on the Grand Remonſtrance, which then found its way, after a ſucceſſion of ſcenes and ſtruggles as worthy of remembrance, though not until now remembered, as any in our hiſtory, to the audience for whom it was deſigned. Neither Hampden nor Pym ſpoke further, when the day for diſcuſſion of the right of proteſting came.* They

Printing ordered.

Slanning revives claim to proteſt.

Storm allayed by Pym.

Monday, 20th Dec.

* The Friday originally fixed was changed to the following Monday, when the three principal ſpeakers were Hyde,

408   *The Grand Remonstrance.*

Debate on right to proteft.
left it to the King's ex-fecretary, old Sir Henry Vane, to point out how irreconcileable any fuch right would be with the precedents, the ufages, and the proceedings of the Commons' Houfe. They liftened without replying to a long fpeech from Hyde, who, admitting there was no precedent for the claim, yet urged that neither was there a precedent for the printing of a Declaration, and that, a precedent in a cafe unprecedented being nothing to the purpofe, they

Ominous remark by Holborne.
muft act according to reafon. They liftened, ftill unmoved, to the fignificant allufion of Mr. Holborne, who, putting the cafe of an order having paffed the Houfe which might carry grave confequences, enlarged upon the hard pofition of thofe who, having no right to proteft, would be involved in fuch confequences, " and perhaps lofe their heads in the crowd " when there was nothing to fhow who was

Refolution againft Hyde's party.
" innocent." Their part in the affair was done, their weapon thrown, and none of thofe contingent or poffible events had any alarms for them. They called upon the Speaker to put the Refolution, that in no circumftances fhould a proteftation be defired in that Houfe, or admitted if defired; and they voted and carried it.

§ XXIX. IMPOSSIBILITY OF COMPROMISE.

THE incident too furely fhadowed forth in that allufion of Holborne, the blow which fo

Right to proteft rejected.
Holborne, and Vane, and it was finally " refolved upon the " queftion, That in no cafe a Proteftation ought to be " defired by any member of this Houfe, or admitted by this " Houfe, being defired."

§ XXIX. *Impoffibility of Compromife.* 409

soon was levelled at the heads of the five leading men in thefe debates, and which was but the natural and legitimate fequel to the proceedings in connection with them here detailed, clofed all further legitimate difcuffion, and rendered civil war inevitable. But before concluding this Work I may paufe to fhow, by fome brief extracts from letters lately difcovered,* that the fame honourable good faith, abfence of mere perfonal animofity, and honeft defire for a fettlement within the limits of the Conftitution, which had characterifed the Remonftrance Debates, continued to animate leading men in the Parliamentary Party up to the hour when the fword was drawn.

<small>Refult of Remonftrance Debates.</small>

<small>Popular leaders averfe to war.</small>

The letters were written to Charles the Firft's Attorney-General, who had become his Chief Juftice of the Pleas, and, upon the very eve of the unfurling the ftandards, had interpofed his good offices to mediate in the quarrel. The attempt was unfortunate; yet he frankly admits that it might have had other iffue, but for the fatal indecifion of the King. " I have " adventured far," writes the well-meaning Chief Juftice, " to fpeak my mind freely, " according to my confcience, and *what hazards* " *I have runne of the King's indignation in a* " *high meafure you will heare by others; all* " *men give not the fame advice."* Among the remarkable men, high in the councils of the popular party, who perfifted in a final effort to keep the fword ftill fheathed, were

<small>Indecifion of Charles.</small>

<small>Bankes (C. J.) attempts to mediate with King.</small>

---

* Publifhed by the late Mr. George Bankes of Dorfetfhire, defcendant of Charles the Firft's Chief Juftice, in a book entitled *Corfe Caftle.*

Lords Northumberland and Wharton ; Denzil Hollis, one of the five members who were the object of the King's fatal attempt; Lord Say and Seale, leader of the Puritans ; and even the fubfequent leader of the Parliamentary Armies, Lord Effex. None of thefe men viewed with other than a fad reluctance the ftrife which was about to begin; none of them was eager to exaggerate or precipitate the quarrel. But their frank and unreferved expreffions elicited no return.

Like attempts of leaders in both Houfes.

In a letter of fingular earneftnefs, Lord Wharton warns Sir John Bankes that he is intimate with many popular leaders, " and I do ferioufly " profefs, I dare not in my private thoughts " fufpect or charge any of them for having " difloyal hearts to his Majefty, or turbulent " hearts to this State." In a letter written from that very place in the Houfe of Commons which he occupied in clofe vicinity with Pym and Hampden, Denzil Hollis tells the Chief Juftice that the Houfe of Commons only waits " the firft appearance of change in his Majefty " that he will forfake thofe councils which " would divide him from his Parliament and " people, and make them deftroy one another," to return in duty and affection to his perfon. In reply to a letter from the Chief Juftice foliciting his opinion, Lord Say and Seale more fternly warns him " that your cavaliers " (as they are called) do much miftake in per- " fuading themfelves or others, that there is " any fear among thofe who defire the King's " wealth and greatnefs as it may ftand with " their own rights and liberty, and the end of

Lord Wharton.

Denzil Hollis.

Lord Say and Seale.

§ XXIX. *Impoffibility of Compromife.*

"his government." In rough and unlettered but manly phrafe, Lord Effex communicates thus to Sir John Bankes the grief with which he is about to unfheathe his fword: "The great "misfortunes that threaten this kingdom, none "looks upon with a fadder heart than I; for "in my particular, my confcience affures me I "have no ends of my own, but what may tend "to the public good of the King and the "kingdom." And finally, in two as impreffive fentences as were ever written on the caufes of the conflict, Lord Northumberland tells Sir John Bankes, that Parliament is arrayed againft the King becaufe of the peril of "lofing that "liberty which freeborn fubjects ought to en- "joy, and the laws of the land do allow; and "becaufe thofe perfons who are moft power- "ful with the King, do endeavour to bring "parliaments to fuch a condition that they "fhall only be made inftruments to execute "the commands of the King."

Lord Effex.

Lord Northumberland.

Objects of Court party.

That laft remark is the ftriking and fufficient comment upon the fcenes which have been defcribed in thefe pages. The continued feries of efforts herein prefented were the prelude to yet another, a more defperate, and a final endeavour, to bring parliaments to fuch a condition that they fhould be made only inftruments to execute commands of the King. Happily for us, this laft attempt fucceeded no better than its fore-runners; and it might have become the Chief Juftice's defcendant to remember, as he ftudied thefe letters before giving them to the world, that it mainly had arifen from the failure of the King which apparently

To weaken and degrade Parliaments.

he so much deplores, that he found himself
indebted for the liberty he has not very gene-
rously employed in exalting his anceftor as
unduly as he depreciates unworthily the greater
men who baffled the King's defign. The
part allotted to Sir John Bankes in the momentous fcene was in reality a very fmall one,
though he played it creditably. He was a
refpectable lawyer of honeft intentions and very
limited views, who interfered occafionally with
good effect to moderate both parties, until
both became committed to extremes; but
when the fword flafhed out as arbitrator, he
turned afide helplefs and ufelefs, and, dying
while yet the victory neither way inclined, he
feems to have died in the perfuafion that the
difsavour of Heaven muft fall heavily on both,
and that both would be deferving of overthrow.
There is always much to be faid for a temper
fuch as this, even when moft unfitted to its
occafions; and undoubtedly a difpofition in
itfelf fo kindly and pleafing might, at any other
time than one of neceffary conflict, have done
even ufeful public fervice. Sir John's defcendant was quite entitled to refer to him,
therefore, as a favourable fpecimen of a lawyer
in that age: but it was lefs difcreet, as well as
lefs generous, to contraft his alleged upright
afcent to worldly rank, with the "unfeemly
" intrigues and courtly ftruggles" by which
Sir Edward Coke is declared to have clambered
thither. Allufions not ftrictly untrue may
yet convey an impreffion fingularly falfe.
Whatever his former failings may have been,
to the ftudent of our Civil Wars the Lord

Small part in a great scene:

creditably played.

Character of Bankes (C. J.)

unwisely compared with Coke (C. J.)

§ XXIX. *Impossibility of Compromise.* 413

Chief Justice Coke presents himself in one aspect only. So far, his age redeems his youth and his manhood. It was he who gave to the opening of the struggle that stamp of ancient precedent and legal right, of which it never afterwards, in all its varying fortunes, lost the trace; and, in the presence of any attempt to compare such a man disadvantageously with one immeasurably his inferior, it is impossible not to remember that while, in the Petition of Right, Sir Edward Coke has left a monument of his exertions for English liberty as imperishable as that which the Institutes contain of his knowledge of English law, Sir John Bankes has left no more durable record of either than an elaborate argument against Hampden in the case of ship-money.

<small>Coke's claims.</small>

<small>The Institutes and Petition of Right.</small>

Let me simply repeat in this place what I have formerly hinted,* that to renew anything like the vehemency of the old Civil War disputes, maintained with unhesitating and uninquiring zeal while yet the authority of Clarendon was implicitly accepted, it is now become needful to pass to a " more removed ground" than that which preceded the war. Sir John Bankes was in his grave, and his correspondents diversely and sadly scattered; my Lord Northumberland was sulking at his country-house, Mr. Denzil Hollis was fretting that he had ever so largely helped to turn out the Stuarts, and my Lord Essex had been borne in funeral pomp to the Abbey of Westminster; before that greater and sterner figure had fully

<small>Party views for and against Charles.</small>

<small>A plain case up to the war.</small>

---

* See *ante*, p. 147.

emerged, whofe "rude tempeftuous" qualities, perplexing in early days to Mr. Hyde, were hardly lefs to perplex and trouble all future hiftorians. And it is lefs with the hope of contributing anything to its illuftration that fhould be entirely worthy of the fubject, than to confefs how much in former years it perplexed and troubled myfelf, that I have lately taken occafion to exprefs* to what extent the views I once held have fuffered change in regard to the conduct and character of Cromwell.

A cafe more perplexing.

§ XXX. CONCLUSION.

THE confequences hinted at by Holborne (in the debate of the 20th December on the right of the Minority on the Remonftrance to proteft againft the decifion of the Majority), which had fo fatal a recoil upon the King, do not fall within the fcope of this work. The Arreft of the Five Members is a fubject too large in itfelf to be treated as a portion of that theme which I now bring to a clofe. My object was to reftore a page of the Englifh hiftory of fome importance, which time had been permitted to efface ; and this has been accomplifhed. It is for the reader to apply the details here given to their further ufe, in illuftration of already exifting records, and determination of their value. It would lead the writer too far from

Limited fcope of prefent work:

to reftore an effaced page in Hiftory.

---

* In the *Edinburgh Review*, January, 1856. See Biographical Effays (*Oliver Cromwell, Daniel De Foe, Sir Richard Steele, Charles Churchill, and Samuel Foote*), now publifhed by Mr. Murray in a feparate volume.

§ xxx. *Conclusion.* 415

the defign to which he had purpofely reftricted himfelf, to attempt in this place any fuch application. Every one may do it, within the range of his acquaintance with the general hiftory of the time; and to help to extend this range for all, fome pains have here been taken to render the notes appended to the Abftract of the Remonftrance, as well as to the Debates, both a guide to refearch out of the common track of hiftories, and a warning againft too ready or implicit belief in the moft refpected authorities. It is not defirable, even if it were poffible, that Clarendon's *Hiftory of the Rebellion* fhould be depofed from the place it holds in our literature. Its rare beauties of thought and charm of ftyle, the profound views of character and life which it clothes in language of unfurpaffed variety and richnefs, its long line of noble and deathlefs portraits through which its readers move as through a gallery of full-lengths by Vandyke and Velafquez, have given and will affure to it its place as long as literature remains. But, for the purpofe to which it has mainly been applied by many party writers fince Clarendon's death, as well as by writers not prejudiced or partial, it fhould never have been ufed. The authority of its writer is at no time fo worthlefs, as when taken upon matters in which he played himfelf the moft prominent part; and his imputations againft the men with whom he was once leagued as clofely as he was afterwards bitterly oppofed to them, are never to be fafely relied upon. With the very facts he laboured to mifreprefent, he has been here confronted; and with the antagonifts to whom he

Object of notes appended.

Clarendon's Hiftory.

Its beauties.

Its demerits.

Its author stood actually opposed upon the floor of the House of Commons, he has been here again brought face to face. The Grand Remonstrance has itself been heard after long and unmerited oblivion, and Sir Simonds D'Ewes has spoken to us after a silence of more than two centuries. The result is decisive against Clarendon. It is not merely that he turned King's evidence against his old associates, but that his evidence is completely disproved.

An opinion has been expressed, in the course of this Work, upon the importance of the Grand Remonstrance merely as a contribution to history, and upon the improbability of its being again displaced from the position here assigned to it. Certainly it is impossible that any one should speak of it hereafter as it has been described heretofore. In Mr. D'Israeli's *Commentaries*, for example, a book which after his death was with final and scrupulous correction republished by his son, it is characterised as an historical memoir of all the infelicities of the reign, " *with a very cautious omission* " that all those capital grievances had no longer " any existence."* That such an assertion should be hazarded again is at least not conceivable. Amid much, too, that in the same book is as gravely passed off for truth, the Remonstrance is said to have been smuggled through the House of Commons by a trick. Its authors, we are informed, " assured the " moderate men that its intention was purely

Its author confronted with contemporaries.

Result decisive against him.

Misstatements no longer possible.

Ludicrous errors.

---

* *Commentaries on the Reign of Charles I.* By Isaac D'Israeli. Ed. 1851, ii. 290.

§ XXX. Conclusion.

"prudential; it was to mortify the Court, and nothing more; after having been read, it would remain in the hands of the Clerk, and never afterwards be called for; and so, when it was brought forward, to give it the appearance of a matter of little moment, the morning was suffered to elapse on ordinary business, and it was produced late; but they overshot the mark," &c. &c. with much more to the same incredible purport! Surely not again can Clarendon lead his followers into such a quicksand of "history" as that; nor, with the Remonstrance itself in evidence, can the signal misrepresentation he left of its contents, and of the conduct and objects of its authors, be in future accepted against his own frequent and unconscious testimony to its deep and ineradicable impression upon the mass of the English people.

D'Israeli's *Commentaries*, ii. 294.

Effect of Remonstrance on the people:

That, after all, is its final and lasting vindication. It had become a necessity so to make appeal to the people. It may be true, or it may be false, that Cromwell would have sold all he had the next morning if the Remonstrance had been rejected, and would never have seen England more: but that Falkland heard him say so would seem to be undoubted, and the fact is a singular proof of the gravity of the conjuncture which had arisen. Measured also by the effects produced, the same conclusion is forced upon us; though in the presence of the document itself, these may well appear less surprising. To do Clarendon justice, he never affects to conceal the momentous influence exerted by the Remonstrance over the

its vindication:

and measure of its importance.

subsequent course of affairs. He puts it in his own language indeed: but when he refers to "that dreadful," "that fatal," Remonstrance; when he speaks of it as having "poi-" "soned the heart of the people;" when he recurs to it as "the first inlet to the inunda-" "tions that overwhelmed" his party; when again and again he dwells upon it, as "the first" "visible ground and foundation of that rage" "and madness in the people of which they" "could never since be cured;" no gloss or comment is needed for such expressions. They are so many tributes to the vigour and capacity of his opponents, and to the largeness and wisdom of the outlook they had taken when they launched that Great Remonstrance. Parliament had no such recruiting-sergeant through the after years of civil war. It might have fallen, indeed, comparatively without effect, if Charles the First had been able at any time to accept honestly the consequences of his own acts; but its authors knew that this was not in his nature, and if we would condemn in that respect their policy, we must have satisfied ourselves, that, with a man so essentially and deliberately false as the King was to all the engagements made with him, it was in any manner possible, without direct appeal to the People as a part of the State, to bring about a lasting adjustment of right relations between the Commons and the Crown. The Remonstrance constituted that appeal; and not the least of the claims which in my judgment it possesses to the attention and respect of all students of history, is the proof which it affords

§ XXX. Conclusion.

that English Puritanism had in itself no necessary antagonism to English Institutions and Government. The ancient limited monarchy, and a reformed church establishment, would have satisfied its authors. They were devout, religious men, who claimed free exercise for their religion; but inseparable from the Protestant Reformation, and its overthrow of Roman Catholic bondage, to whose immediate inspiration they owed their greatness, was the passion for civil freedom no less than for religious liberty. The writers who would separate the religious from the political movement in the seventeenth century, and so strive to underrate the earnestness of the effort it included for political as well as religious emancipation, have their answer in the Grand Remonstrance. Liberty of conscience and of worship has its leading place therein, but only as the very basis and condition of such other claims, constituting civil government, as the right not to be taxed without consent, the right to enjoyment of what is lawfully possessed, the right to petition, the right to choose representatives, the right of those representatives to freedom of debate, the right to pure administration of justice, the right to individual freedom under protection of the laws.

To save the ancient monarchy.

Civil and religious freedom not separable.

Rights demanded by Remonstrance.

Of the men by whom these great rights were so asserted in the old English house of legislature, and to whose exertions and sacrifices in the Long Parliament, their ultimate though less complete acceptance by the Convention Parliament is due, perhaps a nearer view is afforded in this Work than hitherto has been

Leaders of the Long Parliament.

attainable in any printed record. It might indeed have been too near if the men had been lefs great. But they do not fuffer by that clofer infpection. Their greatnefs, too, is affumed fo eafily and fo naturally exerted, as to raife no feeling of furprife but that in an age which produced them fuch a tyranny fhould have been poffible. To find, in the party ftruggles of two hundred years ago, a full and perfect anticipation of parliamentary conflicts of more modern days, may probably aftonifh not a few; but ftill more ftartling is it to reflect, that, during the whole fifteen years defcribed in the Grand Remonftrance, while England lay gagged, imprifoned, mutilated, and plundered, under the moft vexatious and intolerable tyranny that ever tortured body and foul at once, fhe yet contained thefe men. But they had profoundly ftudied her hiftory; and they had an immovable faith that her civil conftitution, outraged as it was, yet held within itfelf the fufficing means of recovery and retribution. Nor, happily for us, did they quite lofe this patient belief, until the fword was actually drawn; and hence it was that all the old laws and ufages of the land, all the old ways and precedents of parliament, all the ancient traditions of the rights of the three eftates, fucceffively drawn forth from their refting-place in records, charters, old books, and parchment rolls, were appealed to on either fide, were claimed by both fides, were tried, tefted, and made familiar to all, in fuch debates and conflicts in the Houfe of Commons as thefe pages have defcribed. It was

Their genius and greatnefs.

Their patience and endurance.

Their refpect for old precedents and laws.

§ XXX. *Conclusion.*

for later generations to enjoy what thus was toiled for so gallantly, and only with infinite suffering, and terrible drawbacks, won at last. But the Leaders of the Long Parliament have had their reward in the remembrance and gratitude of their descendants; and it will bode ill to the free institutions of England, when honour ceases to be paid to the men whom Bishop Warburton truly characterised as the band of greatest geniuses for government that the world ever saw leagued together in one common cause.

<small>Reverence due to them.</small>

INDEX.

Abbots.
ABBOTS feasting and Monks fasting, 48.
A'Becket, Thomas. See Becket.
Agricultural Labourers, condition of, under Henry VI, 57.
Alfred, feudal institutions in the reign of, 5.
Alford, Sir Edward (Arundel), a note-taker, 124 *note.* Ordered to give up his notes, *ibid.*
America, first expedition to, 71. Its fruits, *ibid.*
Anglo-Saxon sovereignty not heritable, 11. See *Saxons.*
Anne, Queen of James I, and her husband, 95. "Some affection" between her and Gowrie's brother, 96.
Aquinas, disciples of, 73.
Argyle and the Hamiltons (Covenant leaders), proposed assassination of, 165. Implication of the King in the plot, 165 *note.* 167. The incident turned to account by Pym, 197.
Aristocracy of England, state of, on accession of Henry VII, 68.
Aristotle, studied by D'Ewes, 120.
Army not to be depended on by Parliament, 154. Tampered with by Charles's party, 155. 263. Disbanding of troops in the North prevented by Charles, 164. Hyde's motion relative to undisbanded troops, 166. Germ contained in Cromwell's resolution, 199. Ordinances *minus* the King, 200. Resolution as to second army plot, 210. Nicho-

Ashburnham.
las's fear on this head, *ibid.* Billeting grievances, 218. 221 *note.* 251 *note.* Wentworth's passionate speech thereon, 218, 219 *notes.* Monthly pay of the two armies, 254. 259. Plot in which Courtney was implicated, 356. Suggestion for defence of kingdom, 357. 385. King's design, 357 *note.* Proof of disaffected spirit and of second army plot, 384. Resolution for disablement of officers implicated therein, 384, 385. Their expulsion, 393. Consequences of King's interference with Impressment Bill, 399, 400. See *Militia. Trained Bands.*
Armyn, Sir William (Grantham), Teller on Militia Bill Division, 388. 392.
Arran, Lord, 95.
Arrest of the Five Members. See *Forster.*
Arthur, Prince, not entitled to Crown as of mere right, 11. Why John was preferred, 12.
Arundel, Lord, Cromwell's charge against, 384.
Ashburnham, John (Hastings), Teller in last Remonstrance debate, 406.
Ashburnham, William (Ludgershall), and Percy, Pollard, and Wilmot, members of House and army officers, why disabled from their seats, 384, 385. How rewarded by the King, 385. Expelled the House, 393.

424   *Index.*

Bacon.

BACON, Francis, Lord, character of Richard III by, 62. The *tres magi* celebrated by him, 64. His character of Henry VII 69, 70. 77. 78. 82. His first interview with James I, 100. His suggestion to James for raising money, 105. Referred to by D'Ewes, 338.
Bagshaw, Edward (Southwark), denounces Ecclesiastical Courts, 237 *note* *. His subsequent defection, *ibid.* His speech against the Remonstrance, 299. Pym's reply thereto, 304. Defends Palmer, 348.
Bainton. See *Baynton.*
Balfour, Col. Sir W., Tower Governor, superseded by Charles, 356. 371. Why displaced, 372 and *note.*
Ballads, Political. See *Political Ballads.*
Baltimore, Ireland, Turkish manstealing at, 228 *note.*
Bancroft, Bishop of London, adulation of James I by, 107.
Bankes, George, Privy Councillor, unwise comparisons and contrasts of, in his *Story of Corfe Castle,* 126 and *note,* 127. His misreading of Clarendon's doings, 127. 129. His extravagant parallel, 146. Instance in which the parallel fits, 176. Reference to letters printed by him, 409 and *note.* Reflection which should have occurred to him while compiling his book, 411, 412. Indiscreet in pitting his ancestor against Sir E. Coke, 412, 413.
Bankes, Sir John, Chief Justice, 126 *note.* Opposed to proclamation for call of House, 164. Attempts to mediate between King and parliament, 409. Letters to him from popular leaders, 410. 411. Manner in which he played his part, 412.

Baxter.

His character, *ibid.* Unwise comparison between him and Sir E. Coke, 412, 413. His most memorable act, 413.
Barbary corsairs in English waters, 228 *note.*
Barère, no parallel in English Revolution to, 146.
Barnardiston, Sir N., affection of D'Ewes for, 121.
Baronetcies invented to raise money, 105. D'Ewes a purchaser, 120.
Barons, new relations between the throne and the (temp. Ric. I), 10. Source of their increased strength, *ibid.* What their triumph over John involved, 14, 15. Cause of their indifference to John's loss of his French possessions, 15. Growth of national feeling in them, 15, 16. 25. Make common cause with the citizens, 16. What brought the people over to them, *ibid.* Their disputes with Peter des Roches, 24, 25. Knights of shires associated with them, 37, 38. Royal boroughs created to combat their influence, 40. Their share in deposing Richard II, 43, 44. Commons often deserted by them, 61. Their position after Bosworth fight, 67. 68. See *Lords, House of.*
Barrington, Sir Thomas (Colchester), an "ancient parliament man," 283 *note.* Divisions on which he was a teller, 209. 257. *note.* 309 *note.* 341. 352. Supports motion for defending the kingdom, 357. Opposes Haselrig's Militia Bill, 386.
Bastwick, Burton, and Prynne, brutal treatment of, 236 *note* †. May's comment on their mutilations, 237 *note.*
Battle, style of living of the Abbot of, 48.
Baxter, Richard, mistake of, rela-

Index.   425

Baynton.

tive to Strafford's attainder, 153, 154, *notes.*
Baynton, Sir Edward (Chippenham), complains of furreptitious communications to King, 366 *note.*
Beaumont, M. de, on pofition of James I in his people's eyes, 109.
Becket, Thomas à, theocratical fcheme contended for by, 7, 8. His conflicts with Henry II, 8. Their ultimate refult, 9.
Bedford, Earl of, joins in Lords' petition for a parliament, 251 *note.*
Beecher, Sir William, why committed to Black Rod's cuftody, 245 *note.*
Bellafis, Henry (Yorkfhire), named on Remonftrance prefentation committee, 367.
Benevolences tried by James I, 105. See *Loans.*
Bennet, one John, "a Poet," fabricates a fpeech in D'Ewes's name, 289 *note.*
Berkley, or Berkeley, Sir Robert, Judge, taken from the Bench to prifon, 182 and *note.* Rebukes Holborne for pleading againft Ship-money, 227 *note.* In the Tower, 256.
Bible brought within reach of the people, 85.
Billeting grievances. See *Army.*
Bills in Parliament, how originally dealt with, 50. Evafions of the Sovereign in regard thereto, *ibid.* Abandonment of the fyftem, 51. Enactment on the occafion, 52. Order of Commons as to reading them, 206 *note.*
Bifhops. See *Church.*
Blacknall, Mrs. Mary, and her relatives fubjected to Wardfhip extortions, 225 *note.*
Blany, Mr., ill-reported of, 274.
Bolingbroke, Henry Plantagenet Earl of. See *Henry IV.*

Buckingham.

Bolingbroke, Henry St. John, Lord, views of, regarding Henry VII, 66.
Bolingbroke, Oliver St. John, Earl of, refufes to fubfcribe to loan to Charles I, 220 *notes.* Joins in Lords' petition for a parliament, 251 *note.*
Book of Sports, 303.
Bofworth, focial condition of England after battle of, 67, 68.
Bracton on the limits to kingly power, 28.
Bramfton, Sir John, on Ship-money, 227 *note.*
Bridgman, Orlando (Wigan), a feceder from Strafford's attainder, 154 *note.* Heads oppofition againft Pym, 198. His fpeech in Remonftrance Debate, 305, 306. His pofitions combated by Hollis, 310.
Briftol, Earl of, joins in Lords' petition for a parliament, 251 *note.* Receives King's anfwer to Proteft of Lords and Commons, 402 *note.*
Brooke, Lord, pockets of, fearched by King's order, 245 *note.* Joins in Lords' petition for a parliament, 251 *note.*
Bruce, John, on value of D'Ewes's MSS, 118, *note* ‡. Sir R. Verney's Notes edited by him, 130 *note.* 219 *note.* 228 *note.* 235 *note.* 290 *note.* His erroneous inference on Militia Bill divifion, 393 and *note.*
Buchanan, George, and his pupil James I, 92.
Buckhurft, Lord, feized for wages due by James I, 104.
Buckingham, George Villiers, Duke of, James's favourite, 95. 101. 311. Caufe of his rife to royal favour, 102, 103. His antics how rewarded by the King, 103. His extravagance, 105. His late fecretary, 167 *note.* Coft and luxurious inci-

Index.

Building.
dents of a banquet given by him, 220 *note*.
Building in London, extortionate interferences with, 230.
Burghley, Lord, entertains James I, 100.
Burke, Edmund, on the spirit of English freedom, 1. 2.
Burnet, Bishop, on Chureh covetousness, 48.
Burton. See *Baſtwick*.

CABOTS, expedition and diſcoveries of the, 71.
Cade's Rebellion contraſted with Wat Tyler's, 56.
Cage, Mr. (Ipſwich), "My old neighbour," 283 *note*.
Cambridge Univerſity characteriſed by D'Ewes, 119, 120. Firſt appearance of the town's M.P. 130.
"Candles called for," 205. D'Ewes thereon, 206.
Capel, Arthur Lord, laſt remembrance of on the ſcaffold, 128.
Car, Earl Somerſet. See *Somerſet*.
Carlyle, Thomas, 113. Uſe intended to be made by him of D'Ewes's MSS. 118. Teſtifies to their value, *ibid. note* †.
Cartwright's Cambridge Lectures, Puritan zeal kindled by, 87.
Cary, Sir Robert, entertains James I, 99.
Catholics, Roman. See *Papiſts*.
Caxton, William, diſcovery of Broadſide printed by, 66. How employed by Henry VII, 77.
Cecil, Robert Earl of Saliſbury. His Coach mobbed, 89. His warning to the Commons, 90. His ſervices in ſeating James on the throne, 90, 91. Opportunity then loſt by him, 91. His firſt interview with James I, 100, 101. Impreſſion then made upon him, 101. Exclamation uttered by him at a later period, *ibid*. His complaint as to

Charles I.
James's laviſh expenditure, 104.
James at a Maſque given by him, 108.
Chambers, Richard, Star Chamber perſecution of, 229.
Charles the Firſt, preliminaries to due underſtanding of poſition taken up by opponents of, 1. Why he impriſoned Selden, 2. Anti-conſcription Statutes cited during conflicts with him, 41. Anceſtors of the men of his day, 86. Rumours antecedent to his birth, 95. His infirmities in infancy, 96. Their poſſible influence on his after career, *ibid*. Sir P. Warwick on reſult of propoſed City entertainment to him, 112. Grand Remonſtrance a Juſtification of Rebellion againſt him, 114. His interference a death-blow to Strafford's hopes, 127 *note*. Clarendon's ſtrategy in his behalf, 129. When Culpeper entered into his ſervice, 141. Parliament's Acts prior to war juſtified by his character, 147. Condition of England during war between Commons and him, 148. Greateſt man on his ſide, 149, 150. Intrigued againſt his own viceroy, 151. Policy adopted by his friends after Strafford's death, 153. Cauſe of reaction in his favour, 153, 154. Pretext on which he was prepared to revoke his own acts, 155. Points which told in his favour, 156, 157. Warning of intention of Parliamentary Leaders given him, 158, 159. Biſhop Williams's advice to him, 159. His ſcheme how baffled, 159. 160. Differences between him and Parliament deepened, 160. Remonſtrance againſt him taking ſhape, 161. Departs for Scotland, *ibid*. His ſignificant interview with Hyde, 161, 162. Hopes baſed

Charles I.
on his Scottish journey, 162. 163. Prevents disbanding of Northern army, 164. His implied toleration of Montrose's Assassination plot, 165 *note*. 167. Falkland's loyalty to him based on the law, 172. Seceders won over to him by no amendment on his part, 183. His hopes from reappearance of the Plague, 184. Plots of himself and Queen against Pym, 185, 186. Mixed up with abettors of Irish Rebellion, 190. What Pym would have told to him, 190, 191. His supporters recommended to him, 193. His thanks to Hyde, 193, 194. Insists on investiture of new Bishops, 195. Reception of his scheme by the Commons, *ibid.* Other questions on which his views were thwarted by the Commons, 197. Hopes inspired by Irish Rebellion, 198. Interim power over Army given by him to Essex, 199. Claim of both Houses to make ordinances during his absence, *ibid.* Correspondence of Nicholas and Queen thereon, 199. 200. Receives news of introduction of Remonstrance, 201, 202. Importunities of his Secretary, *ibid.* His commands to his "Servants," 202. 203. Effect of Pym's Resolution as to second Army plot, 210. Nicholas's fears hereon, and on the Remonstrance, 210, 211. Appeal of his friends in the House, 212. Loan demanded in 1626 by him, 220 *note*. Projects for plundering his subjects, 221 *note*. Strafford's fatal advice, 243, 244. Ride through Royston, 243 *note*. Subscriptions for his aid, why ineffectual, 250. People imprisoned for refusing loans to him, *ibid. note* *. Nobility's petition to him for a parliament,

Charles I.
250—252 and *notes*. His first resolve on receiving the petition, 252 *note*. His scheme for setting up his own church by Popish aid, 271 *note*. What the Commons required of him respecting Popery, 271, 272. And as to removal of evil counsellors, 272, 273. Final prayer of the Remonstrants to and for him, 273. Why so anxious to be back from Edinburgh, 274. Objection taken to his indorsement of Moniers' petition, 274, 275. In Westminster Hall, 277. Informed of Royalist tactics for impeding Remonstrance, 313. Congratulated by Commons on his return from Scotland, 344. Clarendon's significant remark on his "logic," 347 *note*. His reception and acts on his return, 355, 356. Plot proved against his officers, 356. His message for dismissal of Trained Bands, *ibid. note*. Proceedings of Commons thereon, 357. 357—359 *notes*. Remonstrance petition to be presented to him, 359. Abstract of its contents, 359—362. Proofs of surreptitious communication of same to him, 365, 366 *notes*. Deference to his feelings in the matter, 367. Petition and Remonstrance presented, 368. His exclamation at clause relating to religion, *ibid.* His pleasantries on the occasion, 369. His insinuating questions, *ibid.* Message returned by him, 370. Acts showing his hostile intents, 370, 371. His admitted object in appointing Lunsford Tower Governor, 372 and *note*. Consequences of his giving command of guard to Dorset, 373 and *note*. Selden on use made

Charles II.

by him of "Pym and his company," 374 and *note* †. Plea for his intended revocation of unpalatable parliamentary acts, 375, 376. Tactics, towards that end, of his party in the House, 376—378. Godolphin's novel suggestion in same direction, 382, 383. Breach of privilege by Charles himself, 383. *note*. Allusions to him and his rights in Eighth Debate on Grand Remonstrance, 287. 292. 294, 295. 301. 302. 303. 304. 305. 311. 312. 321. His Queen.—See *Henrietta Maria*.

Charles II when Prince, 165 *note*.

Charter, Great. See *Great Charter*.

Charter of Henry I a precedent for the Great Charter, 2.

Charters and royal concessions difficult to suppress, 2, 3. Violations under Charles I, 225.

Chatham, Lord, on "Nullus liber homo," 21.

Chaucer, the Poet, rise of, 43.

Chillingworth, Dr. William, ominous disclosure made by, 374. Resolution of House thereon, 375. Suspicions let loose thereby, *ibid*. One of Clarendon's great little men, 405 and *note*.

Cholmley, or Cholmondeley, Sir Hugh (Scarborough), teller on clause against Bishops, 209. Why grateful to Hyde, 330.

Christianity and the Crusades, 6.

Christie, Mr. Shaftesbury Papers published by, 253 *note*.

Church, usurpations of, resisted by Henry II, 7. Seizure of its temporalities proposed by the Commons, 48. Its luxurious Abbots and starved Monks, *ibid*. Grounds of proposed seizure, 48, 49. Revenge taken by its dignitaries, 49. Failure of project a source of regret, *ibid*. Bishops and Bishoprics in danger, 155.

Church.

Historian May on this topic, 156 *note*. Hyde's services and promise in relation thereto, 162, 163. Anti-Episcopacy Bill under discussion, 167. 195. Defection of its previous supporters, 168. Thirteen Bishops impeached, 194. King's proposal for investiture of new Bishops, 195. How received by the Commons, *ibid*. Debate on Bishops' demurrer to impeachment, 195, 196. Conference with the Lords demanded, 196. Altered views of Dering and Falkland regarding Bishops, 207, 208. Division on clause against Bishops, 209. Falkland's Speech on Laud's propapist experiments, 217 *note*. Ecclesiastical tyranny, 237 and *notes*. Enormities of Laud's proceedings, 238. 239. Result of Episcopal Persecutions, 238, 239. Passports to Preferment, 239. What was preached as Gospel, *ibid. notes*. Attempt to force Liturgy on Scotland, 242. 247. Unusual Prayer for the Sick, 243 *note*. Continued obstinacy of Laud and the Bishops, 246. Clergy taxed for King's supply, 247. Harbottle Grimston thereon, *ibid. note* *. Absence from Church more heinous than attendance at Mass, *ibid. note* ‡. Lord Falkland on this grievance, 248 *note*. Repressive measures of Long Parliament, 257. Reforms introduced, 258. Reply of Commons' Leaders to their slanderers on Church matters, 266, 267. What their real designs were, 267—269. Struggles and divisions on the Bishops' Bill, 267 *notes*. Papist help invoked to set up Protestant Church, 271 *note*. Division on Bishops' clause in Remonstrance,

Index. 429

Circuits.

309, 310. Proclamation of King on return from Scotland, 355. 370. Further on abridgment of Bishops' power, 361. 363. What D'Ewes said thereon, 364. 365. Mr. Coventry's suggestions, 361. *note* 364. Question raised by King's use of words not in "Religious Oppressions" clause, 365, 366, *notes*.

Circuits of Judges appointed, 9.

City, alleged counter-projects to entertainment of Charles I by, 112. 357. Indication of its temporary lukewarmness in popular cause, 156. Train-bands ordered to guard Houses of Parliament, 166. One year's Ship Money, 227 *note*. City loan for Irish exigencies, 328. 329. Entertains the King, 355. Uneasy feeling of Citizens, 372. Citizens fired on by King's Guard, 373, and *note*. Unconstitutional plea grounded on expected City Petition, 394. Intention of originators of petition, 396. Aspect of City 220 years ago, *ibid. note*. Arrival of petition at House of Commons, 397. Deputation with same called in, 397, 398. Dimensions of petition and number of signers, 398. Address of deputation, and Speaker's reply, *ibid*.

Civil War. See *Great Civil War*.

Clare, Earl of, refuses to subscribe to loan to Charles I, 220, *note*.

Clarendon, Edward Hyde Earl of, on rise of Villiers, 102. His misleading account of Debates on Grand Remonstrance, 111, 113. Picture drawn by his friend Sir P. Warwick, 112. Test for his honesty, 117. His votes on Strafford's Attainder and Parliament Perpetuation Bill, 126, 127. Signed the Protestation, 127. His share and associates in Strafford's destruc-

Clarendon.

tion, 128. Himself the cause of the confusion hitherto existing on this subject, 128, 129. His reasons for declining office, 129. Duplicities confessed to by him, 129, 130. His first encounter with Cromwell, 130. His disingenuousness relative to Falkland's support of Strafford's attainder, 142. What excuse for himself? 142, 143. Inference deducible from his *only* disagreement with Falkland, *ibid. note* †. What emboldened him to falsify facts, 143. Acts of Charles condemned by him, 155. Among the traitors to the Commons, 156. Ready to counsel deceptive courses to the King, 157. Surprised at being sent for by Charles, 161. His account of the interview, 162. His promise to the King, 163. On absence of Members from the Commons, *ibid*. Attempts to turn debate on plots against Parliament, 165. What he says on Montrose's assassination plot, *ibid. note*. Outvoted on his proposition, 166. His character of Secretary Nicholas, *ibid. note* *. On complaints of " indirect way of the Court," 167 *note* *. His tribute to Falkland, 170 and *note*. Effect of his influence over him, 172. Sir E. Verney's reply to him, 172, 173. Anecdote told by him of Falkland, 175, 176. On Falkland's charities and hospitalities, 178, 179 and *notes*. Chosen by Falkland as his new leader, 181. His party no waverers originally, 182. Their desertion never accounted for, 182, 183. His low estimate of Strode and Haselrig, 187 *note*. Advantage taken by him of Strode's violence, 189, 190. Another Hyde more Royalist than he,

Clarendon.

189, *note.* Check to his eagernefs in the King's defence, 190. His reply to Pym's fpeech on evil counfellors, 191. Recommended to the King for "encouragement," 193. King's thanks communicated to him, 193, 194. His fneer at Dering: the Ovid Story, 207, 208 *notes.* His urgent appeal againft the Remonftrance, 212. Pym's homethruft reply, 212, 213. Charge made by him againft Pym, 214. His fpeech againft the Judges on Ship Money, 229, *note.* On Rule of conduct at the Council Board, 235 *note.* How Commiffions interpreted the "difcretion" permitted to them, 239 *note.* In trouble at York, 240, 241 *notes.* Another fling at Strode and at Southwark Rioters, 245 *note.* Right in his fact, but wrong in his inference, 246 *note.* On favours granted to Papifts, 248 *note.* On Maffacre of Proteftants in Ireland, 265 *note.* On authorfhip of Remonftrance, 268 *note.* A device to gain time, 275, 276. His converfations in Weftminfter Hall, 276. Still waiting to fpeak, 282. At Pym's dinner parties, 282 *note.* Fiennes' attempt to convert him, *ibid.* His place in the Houfe, 284. His fpeech in eighth debate on Remonftrance, 286, 287. His wordinefs, 286 *note.* His incorrect quotation of paffage relating to Eliot, 287 *note.* On Culpeper's manner and character, 300 and *note.* Pym's reply to his fpeech, 302. Tactics of his Party communicated to Charles, 313. His ftatements as to how the Remonftrance was carried, 314, 315. His misftatement relative to Hampden, 317. Protefts againft printing of Re-

Clarendon.

monftrance, 318, 323. Other misftatements of his, 319. Point in his eftimate of Hampden fupported by D'Ewes, 320 *note.* Further paffage from his Hiftory on fame fubject, 321 *note.* On Cromwell's words to Falkland at clofe of Debate, 327. Wrong as to time of Houfe's next meeting, 327. 329. His charge againft Pym and party in connection therewith, 329, 330. Why the "Northern Men" refufed to join againft him, 330. Reafons for difbelieving his ftatements, 330, 331. Diftinction admitted by himfelf, *ibid. notes.* Alleged difpute between him and Palmer, 333 *note.* His fpeech in defence of the Proteft, 333, 334. Strode's fuggeftion regarding him, 334. His defence of Palmer, 335, 336 and *notes.* Calls for a divifion, 340. Teller thereon, 341. "Lets himfelf loofe," 347. *note.* His fignificant admiffion relative to Charles's "logic," *ibid.* Refutation of his misftatements relative to treatment of Palmer, 353—355. His ftatements *verbatim*, 354 *note.* Sees the King privately, 355. His objections to Remonftrance-Petition, 364. Difcreditable acts brought directly home to him, 366 *note.* His charge of violation of compact againft Remonftrants, 370. Taken into King's fecret council, 371. His admiffion of Lunsford's evil antecedents, 372. And of Charles's object in felecting him, *ibid. note.* His obfervation on Commons' difmiffal of King's Guard, 373. His doctrine on Peers' interference at elections, 384. His misftatements and felf-contradictions concerning Hafelrig's Militia Bill, 385. 389—392. Point on which he was right, 392. His

Clergy.

text milread by Hallam, 393. His charge againſt St. John, 400. His character of Slanning, 404. His pictures of great men of little ſize, 405, 406 *notes*. Speaks on right of proteſt, 408. Merits and demerits of his Hiſtory, 415. His contemporaries and himſelf brought face to face, 416. Reſult thereof, *ibid*. His eſtimate of the Grand Remonſtrance, 417, 418. See alſo, 199. 208. 237 *note*. 262 *note*. 271 *note*. 277. 285. 317 *note*. 322. 362. 374 *note* †. 407 *note*. 413. 414.

Clergy, why difaffected to Parliament, 156 *note* *. See *Church*.

Clerk of the Market extortions aboliſhed, 257.

Clotworthy, Sir John (Malden), takes part in Grand Remonſtrance, 203. Amendments on Remonſtrance by "J. C.", 220 *note* *. On gunpowder monopoly, 232 *note*. On lands between high-water and low-water mark, 233 *note*. Diviſions on which he was a teller, 257 *note*. 309 *note* †. 317. 352. 406.

Coat and Conduct money extortions, 225 and *note*. 251 *note*. Aboliſhed, 254.

Cockpit ſports revived by James I, 104. One Maſter of the Cocks equal to two Secretaries of State, 104.

Coinage, projected debaſement of the, 231 and *note*.

Coke, Sir Edward, Chief Juſtice, 23. 24. Contraſted with Sir John Baukes, 412. Services of his later days, 413. His Inſtitutes and the Petition of Right, *ibid*.

Cole, the haberdaſher's apprentice in Diſtaff Lane, 377 and *note*.

Coleridge, S. T., opinion of, relative to war with Charles, 148.

Commons.

Colet aſſociated with Eraſmus, 74. 75. 77.

Comines, Philip de, why England the beſt governed ſtate, 58.

Commerce, ſeeds of, ſown by the Cruſades, 6. Riſe of merchants and tradeſmen, 25. Rights and privileges inſured to them by guilds and charters, 25, 26. Effect of commerce on ſocial diſtinctions, 57. Its condition during the wars of the Roſes, 62, 63. Growth of guilds, 63. Effect of Charles's oppreſſive extortions, 226. Defenceleſſneſs of merchant ſhips in the Channel, 226—228 and *note*. Effect of Star Chamber perſecution, monopolies and reſtraints on enterpriſe, 229—231.

Commiſſions of Inquiry under the Norman Kings and their ſucceſſors, 33. See *Cottagers*. *Depopulations*. *High Commiſſion*. *Sewers*.

Commonalty, poſition gained by the, 38. A recogniſed power in the State, 39. Ill-ſupported by the Commons under Henry VII,'66. See *Commons, Houſe of*. *Parliament*. *People*.

Common, poor deprived of their rights of, 233 and *note* †.

Commons, Houſe of, origination of the, 29. Vague formation of its authority, 34. Knights of Shires ſummoned, 34, 35. Writs iſſued for firſt Houſe, 38. Gradual growth of power of Commons, 39. Statutory recognition of their legiſlative equality, 40. Bearing of Edward III towards them, 42. Courſe taken by them on depoſition of Richard II, 44. Their demands on Henry IV relative to the ſucceſſion, 46. Conditions annexed by them to ſupplies granted to him, 47. They compel him to change his offi-

Commons.

cers, *ibid.* Their propofal to him refpecting Church Temporalities, 48, 49. Advantages derived from neceffities of Henry V, 51. Further rights and exemptions gained, 52, 53. Their privilege afferted in Thorpe's cafe, 53. Source of their ftrength, 61. Their neglect of the people's interefts under Henry VII, 66, 67. What made them his inftrument, 68. Their pofition under the Tudors, 82. Conceffions by Henry VIII, 83. Powers exclufively their own, 84. Peter Wentworth's declaration, *ibid.* Reduction of their authority by Elizabeth, 85. Puritan leaders in the Houfe, 87. A prerogative-loving ferjeant filenced, 89. Cecil's warning and its fequel, 90. What took place when the "Proteftation," was drawn up, 127 *notes.* Confufion hitherto prevailing as to their conduct on Strafford's attainder, 128. Verney's report of debate thereon, and queftion thence arifing, 130—132. Difpute of 10th April, 134. Sitting of 12th April, 136, 137. D'Ewes's report of fame, 137—141. Side on which moft wealth was ranged, 148. Deferters from the popular fide, 163, 164. Strode's propofition for enforcing attendance, 163. Report laid before Houfe by Pym, 164. Proceedings thereon, 165, 166. City train-bands ordered up to guard Houfe, 166. Deferters on the Bifhops' Bill, 168. Break up of the Liberal phalanx, 182. Seceffion of fupporters never accounted for, 182, 183. Effect of threats againft Pym, 185. Waller's unparliamentary efcapade and its refult, 191, 192. Journal entry thereof, 192 *note.*

Commons.

Debates about the Bifhops, 194 —196. About evil counfellors, 197—199. About command of Army, and levying of Volunteers, 199. 200. Proceedings on Grand Remonftrance, 201 *et feq.* [See *Grand Remonftrance.*] Candles moved for, 205, 206. Shilling fines: Procedure on Bills. *ibid. note* †. Unauthorised reports fuppreffed, 209. Refolution as to fecond army Plot, 210. Imprifonment and maltreatment of members complained of, 222, 223. Slanders levelled againft the Houfe, 261, 262. Reply of its leaders to their affailants, 266, 267. What they contemplated in their dealings with Church abufes, 267— 269. Their intentions relative to learning, 269. The old Commons Chamber, 276. Average number of Members prefent during Debates on Remonftrance, 316 and *note.* Attacks on authority of Houfe contemplated, 321. 323. Scene occafioned by Palmer's Proteft, 323 —326. 345. [See *Palmer*]. King's Guard under Dorfet difmiffed, 373. Members to bring their own fervants armed, 374. Selden on King's ufe of Pym and Party, *ibid.* Dr. Chillingworth's difclofure, 374, 375. Charges againft Members ,by Strangways and Kirton, 376, 377 *note*, 378. Pym's fignificant queftion to Speaker, 379. Strode, Waller, and Culpeper's altercation, *ibid.* Difpute between D'Ewes and Culpeper, 380, 381. Pym's complaint of the Lords, 381, 382 and *notes.* Godolphin's retaliatory fuggeftion and reprimand, 382, 383, and *note.* Mr. Speaker defponds, 383 and *note.* Cromwell on breach of privilege by a Peer,

Index. 433

Comus.

383, 384. Hyde's defenfive rejoinder, 384. Apprehended dangers, 384, 385. Scene on introduction of Hafelrig's Militia Bill, 385, 386. Cook's way of citing precedents, 386. His blunder expofed by D'Ewes, 387. Admonifhed by Mr. Speaker, 388 and *notes*. Hafelrig's Bill read firft time, 388. Divifions thereon and confufion relative to fame, 388. 392. Clarendon's miſstatements and felf-contradictions on this fubject, 385. 389—392. Hollis's motion as to the "three reverences," 393, 394 *notes*. New guard of Halberdiers placed at door of houfe, 394. Alleged grounds for fuch guard, *ibid*. Their inftant difmiffal refolved on, 395. Text of order for same, *ibid. note*. A "fhut the door" incident, 395, 396. Punifhment of underfheriff and magiftrates, 396. Arrival of City Petition, 396. 397. Deputation therewith called in, 397, 398. Dimenfions of petition and number of petitioners, 398. Mr. Speaker's reply to the deputation, *ibid*. Houfe fummoned before the King, 399. Unconftitutional courfe taken by him, 399, 400. Refolve of Houfe thereon, 400. Proteftation of Lords and Commons carried to King, *ibid*. His reception of and anfwer to their deputation, 400, 401 *notes*. See *Grand Remonftrance. Long Parliament. Parliament. Saint Stephen's Chapel*.

Comus and his crew, James's court likened to, 103.

Conceffions not refumable, 3.

Confcription for military fervices, acts againft, 41, 42. See *Army*.

Cook, Sir Robert (Tewkefbury) would expel Palmer, 347. Liable to expulfion himfelf, 348.

County Courts.

Cook, or Coke, Thomas (Leicefter) cites precedent againft Hafelrig, 386. Ordered to withdraw, 387. D'Ewes makes merry with him, 387, 388. Admonifhed by Mr. Speaker, 388. Record of the incident from Commons Journals and Verney, *ibid. note*.

Corbet, Sir John (Shropfhire) named on Remonftrance Prefentation Committee, 367.

Corn, foreign, importation prohibited under Edward IV, 62.

Cornwall, children carried off by Turks from, 229 *note*.

Cornwallis, Sir F. (Eye) teller on important divifions, 257 *note*. 309 *note*. 310 *note*. 317. 341. 388. 392.

Cottagers, object of Commiffion againft, 233 *note*.

Cottington, Francis Lord, implicated in Strafford's Treafon, 135. 138. 139. 140. 141.

Cotton, Sir Robert, 24. Story told of him and his lady, 316.

Cottrell, Elizabeth, capital conviction of, 235 *note*. How brought about, 236 *note*.

Council, Great. See *Great Council*.

Council of the North, or Court of York, 182. Hyde's fpeech on its indifcreet 'difcretion,' 239, *note*. How the Court brought him into trouble, 240 *note*. Abolifhed, 256.

Council Table, abominations of the, 235. 238. 239. 245. 250. Hafelrig's recollection of its vagaries, 235 *note*. Character of thofe who fat at it, 241. Not Councillors but Countenancers, 242. Deprived of its powers, 257. Effect of its fentences in Elizabeth's days, 350.

County Courts, 26. Had power to iffue Commiffions of Inquiry, 33. Leaft feudal remnant of modified Feudality, 37. Of whom comprifed, *ibid*.

County.

County rates as connected with county reprefentation, 36, 37.
County reprefentation, beginning of, 33. Statutes for regulating elections, 47. 54, 55. See *Elections. Parliament.*
Court of the North. See *Council of the North.*
Court of Requefts Divifion, 257 *n.*
Courts of Law degraded into Courts of extortion, 231. See *Council Table. High Commiffion. Houfehold. Judges. Juftice. Star Chamber.*
Courtenay, Sir William, houfe of, robbed by pirates, 228 *note.*
Courtney, Adam, charged with participation in army plot, 356.
Coventry, John (Evefham), place in the Houfe of, 284 and *note.* His fpeech in debate on Remonftrance, 312. Suggeftion of his adopted, 361 *note.* Objection raifed by him, 364. D'Ewes " looks towards" him, 365.
Cowley, the poet, and Lord Falkland, 170 *note.*
Cox, Sir Henry, entertains James I, 100.
Crane, Mr., Victualler of the Navy, 275.
Crane, Sir Robert (Sudbury), teller in Remonftrance Debate, 326.
Cranmer, Edward VI an inftrument in the hands of, 80, 81.
Crew, John (Brackley), pofition and principles of, 348. His conciliatory fpeech on Palmer's cafe, 348, 349. His miffion at Uxbridge, 348 *note.*
Crewe, Sir Randall, Chief Juftice of England, caufe of difplacement of, 220 *note.*
Cromwell, Oliver (Cambridge Town), 86. His firft fight of James I, 100. His firft encounter with Clarendon, 130. His coufin Waller, 191. Carries refolution againft inveftiture of

Crufades.

new Bifhops, 195. His fignificant addition to Pym's refolution, 199. Moves amendment on Grand Remonftrance, 203. His queftion to Falkland, 213. His rejoinder to Falkland's reply, 214. Clarendon's deductions from the anecdote, 214 *note.* Claufe in Remonftrance inferted on his reprefentation, 234. Notice given by him, *ibid. note.* His place in the Houfe, 285. Carries refolution to burn Dering's Book, 289 *note.* His deportment and alleged expreffions at clofe of debate on Remonftrance, 327. 417. Complains of flander againft the Houfe, 357. His charge againft Lord Arundel, 383, 384. His " greater and fterner figure," 413. Perplexing features of his character, 414. Change of author's views in regard to him, *ibid.* and *note.* See alfo 182. 274. 348.
Cromwell, Sir Oliver, regales James I, 100.
Crooke, Judge, on Ship Money, 227.
Crown, oppofition of the Barons to the (temp. Ric. I), 10. Not heritable property, 11. Principle on which the Norman kings received it, 11, 12. Same confirmed on John's coronation, 12. Bracton's enumeration of powers fuperior to it, 28. Power of the people to difpofe of it, 44. Amenability of its officers to the Laws, 59. Evafions and encroachments poffible, 60. Control over the public purfe yielded by it, *ibid.* Long Parliament not defirous permanently to abolifh its Prerogatives, 147.
Crufades, injurious effects of the, 5. Their redeeming features, 6. Their influence on commerce and literature, *ibid.*

Index. 435

Culpeper.

Culpeper, Sir John (Kent), an eager fupporter of Strafford's attainder, 128. 134. 154 *note.* Why Clarendon declined to take office with him, 129. Againſt hearing Strafford's Counſel, 131. Why, 144. Advocated conference with Lords, 140. His courſe after Strafford's death, 141. His aſpect at the Commons' bar, 177. How the Queen joined his name with that of Pym, 186 *note.* Added to Remonſtrance Committee, 209. 267 *note.* His denunciation of Ship Money, 227, *note.* On the Gunpowder Monopoly, 232 *note.* His characteriſtic ſpeech on monopolies, 255 *note.* His place in the Houſe, 284 and *note.* His manner of ſpeaking, 300. Hyde and Warwick on his character, *ibid. note.* His ſpeech in eighth debate on Remonſtrance, 301. Pym's replies thereto, 303. 304. His poſitions combated by Hollis, 310. Oppoſes printing of Remonſtrance, 323. Claims leave to proteſt, *ibid.* Againſt calling Palmer to account for his Proteſt, 335, 336. Clamorous for diviſion thereon, 340. Sees the King privately, 355. Objects to Pym's reaſons, 362. Anſwered by Pym, 363. Reiterates charge againſt citizens, 379. Interrupts Sir S. D'Ewes, *ibid.* Proved to be in the wrong, 380, 381. His doctrine on Peers' interference with elections, 384. Moves rejection of Haſelrig's Militia Bill, 386. Teller on diviſions, 388. 392. 406. See alſo 199. 354. 376.

Cumberland, Lord, entertains James I, 100.

Curia Regis—the King's Cabinet —how conſtituted, 28, 29.

D'Ewes.

DANTON and Falkland, parallel traits of character in, 176.

Dean Foreſt, public loſs by break up of, 233 and *note.*

Depopulations, Commiſſion for, 234 *note.*

Dering, Sir Edward (Kent), joins the King's party, 168. His change of tactics regarding Biſhops, 207, 208. His Ovidian motive for oppoſing them, *ibid. notes.* Diviſions on which he was a teller, 209. 326. Characteriſtic paſſage from a ſpeech of his, 211 *note.* His prophecy relative to Grand Remonſtrance, 215. His place in the Houſe, 285. His ſpeech in eighth debate on Remonſtrance, 289. Conſequences of his printing ſame *ibid.* and *note.* Character of the ſpeech, 290, 291. What his conſtituents wanted, 291. His views on church matters, 292, 293. Spoon and moon ſimiles, 293. Sydney Smith's debt to him, *ibid. note.* Final reaſon for his adverſe vote, 293, 294. His colleague's ſpeech, 300, 301. Pym's reply to his ſpeech, 303. His moon ſimile diſpoſed of, 307, 308. Named on Remonſtrance Preſentation Committee, 367. Evades an honour intended for him, 367, 368. D'Ewes's confirmatory entry, 368 *note.*

Derivale, John, and the "Gracious" ſtreet ſcene, 377 *note.*

D'Ewes, Paul, father of Sir Simonds, 119. 120.

D'Ewes, Sir Simonds (Sudbury), deſcription of MS Journal of, 117, 118. Mr. Carlyle and Mr. Bruce on its hiſtorical value, 118 *notes.* His parentage and education, 119. His ſtudies: What he deemed the "moſt raviſhing" part of knowledge, 120. Marries: buys a baronetcy, *ibid.* Why Laud put him

D'Ewes.

into the Star Chamber, 121. Elected M.P., *ibid.* Renders good service with his Records: his first speech, 121, 122. Fruit of his love for note-taking, 122, 123. How he took his notes, 123. Condition of his original MS. 123, 124. Confused present state thereof, 124, 125. His reply to an objector to note-taking, 124 *note*. Character of pages selected for fac-simile, 125. 136. His account of what led to the Protestation, 127, 128 *notes*. His evidence decisive as to presumed disagreement between Pym and Hampden, 133. 136, 137. His minute on procedure against Strafford, 134. His notes of sitting of 12th April (pages in *fac simile* set out) 137—141. His own speech on that occasion, 140. His notes a corrective of Clarendon's falsifications, 143. Reports Pym's speech, 145. Acts and motives of parliamentary leaders first discernible from his notes, 149. On Strode's proposal for fining absent members, 163. 316 *note*. His zoological parable, 166. His portraiture of Falkland at the Commons' bar, 177. His allusions to Strode as a young man, 188. 189 *notes*. Testifies to earnestness of debate on Bishops' investiture, 195. How he raised a laugh at Holborne's expense, 196. On Strode's motion for a shilling fine, 205 *note* †. Supports motion for candles, 206. Not over-respectful to Mr. Speaker, 280 *note* †. Lectures Mr. Speaker on point of order, 281 *note*. His seat and deportment in the House, 283, 284. How referred to there, 283 *note*. His opinion of, and sensible objection to calling in Dering's

D'Ewes.

book, 289 *note*. On publication of fabricated and falsified speeches, *ibid*. On forged Royalist petitions, 289 *note*. Why he left House during debate on Remonstrance, 308. His remark on Yelverton's communication, 309 *note*. On rule of precedence in debates, 311 *note*. On number of members absent from House, 316 *note*. On Hampden's "serpentine subtlety," 320 *note*. On Palmer's motion to take down protesters' names, 323. Describes excitement which followed, 324, 325. On Hampden's conciliatory suggestion, 326. On rising of House, 327. On time of meeting next day, 329 and *note*. Inference from his silence on matters made much of by Clarendon, 330. Named on committee for abuses of printing, 332. On vehemence of Palmer's friends, 335. His speech in debate on Palmer's Protest, 337—340. On addition proposed by Palmer's friends, 340, 341. His votes in the two divisions thereon, 341. Further notes on the Palmer dispute, 344. 345. 350. On usages of House in reference thereto, 351. On final division thereon, 351. 352. Settles point of order in Debate on Remonstrance Petition, 362, 363. His notes of the debate, 363. Defends clause relating to Bishops, 364. His views adopted, *ibid*. Suggestion of his not agreed to by Pym, 365. Named on Remonstrance presentation Committee, 366. Receives Petition and Remonstrance from Speaker, 378. His Journal Entry, *ibid, note*. On Dorset's "indiscreet rashness," 373 *note*. On Chillingworth's disclosure, 374, 375. On the "Gracious"

Index. 437

Digby.
street scene, 376 note. On Dorset's order to fire on citizens, 379. Called to account by Culpeper, ibid. About what? 380. How he disposed of Culpeper's explanation, 380, 381. His notes of debate on Haselrig's Militia Bill, 386. Speaks in support of bill, ibid. Chuckles over Cook's mis-citation of a precedent, 387, 388. His minute of Hollis's motion on form of entering and leaving House, 393, 394 notes. On Newport's attempt to quit House without leave, 395, 396. On dimensions and number of signatures to City Petition, 398. Named on deputation with protest to King, 400 note. His account of King's reception of and answer to same, 401, note. "Great Silence" in the House, 402. His surprise at Purefoy's proposal, 403. Leaves House in midst of debate, 403, 404. Returns in the nick of time, 406. Result of his confrontation with Clarendon, 416. 213. 331 margin, 332 note. 400 note*.

Digby, George Lord (Dorset), vote of, on a resolution relative to Strafford, 131. Not yet Strafford's friend, ibid. A seceder on question of attainder, 153, note. His principal fellow seceders, 154 note. First mover of a Remonstrance, 158. 161. Goes over to the King, 158. His convenient elevation to the peerage, 279. Selden thereon, 280 note. Made a scapegoat by Clarendon, 372 note.

Digby, Hon. John (Milborne Port), guilty of disrespect to the House, 279. Rebuked by Mr. Speaker, 280. Selden's sarcasm on his conduct, 280 note.

Digby, Sir Kenelm, 332.

Disraeli, Isaac, character of his

Edward I.
notice of Grand Remonstrance, 113. His misstatement regarding it, 416, 417.

Distaff Lane, haberdasher's apprentice of, 377 and note.

'Divine Right,' death-blow given to, 44.

Dorset, Earl of, command laid by King on, 358 note. 373. Himself and guard dismissed, 373. His "indiscreet rashness," ibid. note. What followed on his dismissal, 374. 376. His conduct justified by Waller, 379. Blamed by D'Ewes, ibid.

Drake, Sir Francis, 85.

Dudley and Empson. See *Empson and Dudley.*

Durham, bishop of, entertains James I, 100.

Dutch, ships taken in English Channel by the, 228 note.

EARLE, Sir Walter (Weymouth), complains of note-takers, 124 note. Supports motion for conference, 166. Drags Strode out of House, 188 note. His resolution on business of House, 208 note. His place in the House, 285. Moves to call in Dering's book, 289 note. Supports motion for defence of kingdom, 357. Defends D'Ewes on point of order, 380. Divisions in which he was a teller, 310. 327. 406.

Eden, Sir Frederick, on distinction between demands of Wat Tyler and Jack Cade, 56.

Education, popular, endowments for, *temp.* Henry VI, 63. Impetus given by labors of Erasmus and his associates. See *Erasmus.*

Edward I, important statutes passed in reign of, 39. 40. Foiled in attempts to impose taxes independently of parliament, 41. Decline of feudal tenures with his accession, 55.

G G

Edward II.

Edward II, royal boroughs created by, 40. Conditions annexed to fupplies granted to him, 41.
Edward III foiled in attempts to impofe taxes without parliamentary fanction, 41. Statutes of conftitutional import paffed in his reign, 41, 42. His character: Intellectual influences of his reign, 42. Chaucer his contemporary, 43. Length of his reign and number of his parliaments, *ibid.*
Edward IV, commercial reftrictions impofed under, 62. Formalities on his daughter's marriage, 65, 66.
Edward VI the inftrument of Cranmer, 80. Confequences of his forcing on Cranmer's defign, 81.
Eldred, M., a "penner" of forged Royalift petitions, 290 *note*.
Election, Statute of Edw. I for fecuring freedom of, 39. Statute of Henry IV for regulating county elections, 47, 54. Statute of Henry VI, 54, 55. Peers' interference complained of, 384. See *Parliament.*
Eliot, Sir John, fufferings of, 223. 287. Pym's refentment at his fate, *ibid. note.* References thereto in Verney's Notes and Grand Remonftrance, 287 *note.*
Elizabeth, Queen, 68. 71. Her affigned tafk, 81. Direction in which fhe gave way, 82. What Peter Wentworth faid in her reign, 84. Authority of Parliament reduced by her, 85. fpirit in which fhe treated the people, *ibid.* Influences needed to infure downfall of her fyftem, 85, 86. Even partiality of her religious perfecutions, 86. Dangers of her repreffive fyftem, 86, 87. Refult of her attempts to fubdue Puritan leaders in the

Erafmus.

Commons, 87. Extent of her antipathy to Puritanifm, 88. Fate of the Reformation in her hands, 89. Her mifapprehenfion of Puritanifm, *ibid.* Views of her Minifters as to monopolies, 89, 90. Her laft appearance in Parliament and final act there, 90. Her death, 90. 97. Her court contrafted with that of James, 103. Cruel fports prohibited by her, 104.
Elizabeth, Queen of Bohemia, birth of, 95. Caufe identified with her name, *ibid.*
Ellefmere, Chancellor, on union of prieft and king, 107.
Ellyng, Henry, clerk of Houfe of Commons, 278.
Empfon and Dudley, extortioners for Henry VII, 78. Means reforted to by them, 78, 79. Their fate, 79.
England contrafted with France, *temp.* Henry VI, 58. Its ftate during Wars of Rofes, 62, 63. Free from influences potent in France and Spain, 64. Social changes confequent on Battle of Bofworth, 68, 69. Its condition during war between Charles I and the Commons, 148.
Englifh language adopted in Parliamentary Rolls, 43.
Englifh laws, Sir John Fortefcue on the, 58, 59.
Englifh Revolution compared to French Revolution, 146. Folly of the comparifon, 146, 147.
Erafmus brought into England, 71. His ftudies at Oxford, 71, 72. Quaint mention of his poverty, 73. His part in the downfall of the fchoolmen, 73, 74. Source of his power, 74. Luther on his cavilling and flouting, 75. His title to refpect, 75, 76. What he accomplifhed: England's obligation to him, 76. 85.

Essex.

Essex, Robert, Earl of, Lord Chamberlain, 129. Parliamentary guard placed under him, 166. On "indirect way of the Court," 167 *note*. Cromwell's motion for investing him with command, 199. Character of the power thus given to him, *ibid*. Refuses to subscribe to loan to Charles I, 220 *note*. Joins in Lords' petition for a Parliament, 251 *note*. Surrenders command of guard, 356 *note*. His continuance in command insisted on, 358 *note*. Writes to Sir John Bankes, 410. Impressive passage from his letter, 411. His end, 413.
Evelyn, Sir John (Bletchingley) "my very worthy friend," 283 *note*. On number of members attending the House, 316 *note*.
Exchequer Chamber, 235.

FAIRFAX, Ferdinando, Lord, named on Remonstrance Presentation Committee, 367.
Falkland, Lucius Cary, Lord (Newport, Hants) a resolute promoter of Strafford's attainder, 128. 134. 143 *note*. 154 *note*. Why Clarendon did not take office with him, 129. Supposed motive for his animosity to Strafford, 142 and *note* *. Clarendon's untenable statements on this head, 142, 143. Why he objected to hear counsel for Strafford, 144. Baxter's mistake relative to seceders from the attainder, 153 *note*. Attempts (with Hyde) to turn debate on Pym's motion, 165. Outvoted, 166. Changes sides in the House, 168. His rejoinder to Hampden's expression of surprise, *ibid*. Popular misapprehension as to his character, 169. Why more of an apostate than Strafford, 170. Clarendon's tribute to his memory, *ibid*, *note*.

Farlow.

Specimens of his eclogue on Ben Jonson, 170, 171 *notes*. Hyde's influence over him, 172. Warburton's remark on him, *ibid*. *note*. Source of admiration surrounding his name, 173. Lord Macaulay's estimate of his character, 174 and *note*. Instances of excitability of temper, 175. Anecdote told by Clarendon, 175, 176. Resemblances and contrasts, 176. His last appearance in the House of Commons, 177. His possible reflections at that time, 177, 178. Nobler side of his character, 178. Clarendon's happy eulogy, *ibid*. *note* †. 405, 406 *notes*. His unsectarian hospitality, 179 and *note* *. Special characteristics entitling him to highest eulogy, 180, 181. Desertion of himself and party never accounted for, 182, 183. Recommended to the King, 193. His former attack on and present defence of Bishops, 208. 288. Added to Remonstrance Committee, 209. 267 *note*. His dialogue with Cromwell, 213, 214. Deduction therefrom, 417. His speech against Laud, 217 *note*. Speech on brass coinage, 231 *note*. Objects to passage in Remonstrance, 247 *note* †. On encouragement to papists and persecution of protestants, 248 *note*. On large hate and little love for Bishops, 282 *note*. His place in the House, 284. His speech in eighth debate on Remonstrance, 287—289. Pym's reply, 302. Cromwell's words to him at close of Remonstrance debate, 327. Teller on Palmer punishment division, 352. Sees the King privately, 355. See also, 199. 292. 300. 354. 377.
Farlow, Mr., story told by Kirton of, 377 *note*. 378.

G G 2

440   *Index.*

Ferdinand of Spain.
Ferdinand of Spain, 64.
Ferrers, cafe of, 83
Feudal Syftem, origin of the, 4. Its progrefs under the Saxons, 4, 5. Its development under the Normans, 5. Vaffalage extinguifhed, 5. 7. Effect of the Crufades on Feudalifm, 6. Its condition at acceffion of Edward I, 55. Villenage no part of it, 56. Its tendency to decay, *ibid.* Its rapid fall, 57. Doomed before Wickliffe's preaching began, 61. Revival of feudal ftatutes under Charles I, 224, 225 and *notes.*
Fiennes, Nathaniel, (Banbury) Commiffioner on Scotch affairs with Hampden, 165. 167 and *note* †. His evening ride with Hyde, 282 *note.*
Finch, John, Lord, C.J. in Eyre and Lord Keeper, againft proclamation for call of Houfe, 164. Driven into exile, 182, 256. His oppreffive conduct, 226 *note.* His rule of conduct at Council Board, 235 *note.* Unconftitutional writ iffued by him, 394. 395 *note.*
Florida coafted by the Cabots, 71.
Foreft of Dean broken up, 233 and *note.*
Foreft Laws, complaint againft rigid execution of, 225 and *note.* 226 *note.* Reformed, 257.
Forfter's *Arreft of the Five Members*, references to, 124. 160. 165. 185. 188. 197. 206. 281. 289. 321. 366. 372. 383. 396, 397 *notes.* *Statefmen of the Commonwealth*, 119. *Biographical Effays*, 414 *note.*
Fortefcue, Sir Faithful, Pym prefents petition of, 275.
Fortefcue, Sir John, on fpirit of Englifh Laws, 58. 59. 81.
Fouke, Mr., heads deputation with City Petition to Commons, 398. His addrefs to the Houfe, *ibid.*

Godolphin.
Fouquier-Tinville, not paralleled in Englifh Revolution, 146.
France, violation of neutrality by, 228 *note.*
Freedom frequently outraged but not loft, 53, 54.
Freeholders, elective rights exercifed by, *temp.* Henry III, 37. Limit put on their rights by ftatute of Henry VI, 54, 55.
French and Englifh governmental fyftems contrafted, 58.
French Revolution, See *Englifh Revolution.*
Frobenius, 74.
Fuller, Thomas, fallacious deduction of, 57.

GARRARD, Mr., (Strafford's Newsletter writer) fet at 40s. for fhip money, 227 *note.* On plunder of the poor, 233 *note.* On enormities of foap monopoly, 248 *note.*
Gerrard, Sir Gilbert (Middlefex) moves to congratulate King on fafe return from Scotland, 344.
Glanvile, Ranulf de, fervice rendered to Henry II by, 9.
Glaftonbury, ftyle of living of the Abbot of, 48.
Glenham, Lady, confideration for bribe taken by, 103.
Glyn, John (Weftminfter), mode of procedure againft Strafford advocated by, 133. 134. On Lord Cottington's complicity, 141. His treachery towards Vane at the Reftoration, *ibid.* His place in the Houfe, 285. His fpeech in favour of the Remonftrance, 311, 312. Houfe's requeft to him and Wheeler relative to guard, 374 *note.*
Godolphin, Francis (St. Ives), ftartling fuggeftion of, 382. Reprimanded, 383. Entry from Commons' Journals, *ibid. note.*
Godolphin, Sidney, one of Clarendon's great little men, 405 *note.*

Index. 441

Godwin.

Godwin, William, Grand Remonſtrance paſſed over by, 113.

Goodwin, Ralph (Ludlow), complains of a ſcandalous pamphlet, 331, 332.

Goodwin, Robert (Eaſt Grinſtead), moves reſolution for ſuperviſion of King's appointments, 186, 187.

Goodwyn, Arthur (Bucks), teller on diviſions, 310 *note.* 317.

Goring, Geo. (Portſmouth) Plot of, diſcovered, 164.

Gowrie Conſpiracy and its antecedents, 96.

" Gracious" ſtreet, a ſcene in, 377 *note.*

Grammar Schools, riſe of, 63.

Grand Remonſtrance, moſt exciting and moſt neglected incident before the Great Civil War, 110. Means for forming judgment thereon, 110, 111. Effect of Clarendon's miſſtatements, 111. Sir Philip Warwick's animated account, 112. Reſults of Hampden's influence, *ibid.* References of previous hiſtorians to the ſubject, 113. Clarendon generally followed, *ibid.* Purpoſe and ſource of this Work, 113, 114. What the Remonſtrance was, 114. Character of its contents, 115, 116. Its length: difficulty of reproducing it, 116, 117. Clarendon's honeſty teſted by it, 117. Its origin, 158. Formally brought forward, 160. Extent to which it was openly diſcuſſed, 161. Its firſt ſubmiſſion to the Houſe, 201. Troubles of Nicholas and commands of his maſter thereon, 201, 202. 203. Its progreſs in the Commons, 203, 204. Impeded by Iriſh Rebellion neceſſities, 204. Its ultimate deſtination, 204, 205. Fight on Clauſe againſt Biſhops, 207—209. 310. Preparations for final vote, 210

Grand Remonſtrance.

—213. Engroſſed : final debate fixed, 213, 214. Miſſtatement of Clarendon on this point, 214 *note.* Dering's prophecy, 215. *Abſtract of Remonſtrance*: 1. Preamble : Purpoſe aimed at, 215—218. 2. Firſt, ſecond, and third parliaments of Charles, 218—223. 3. Government by Prerogative : Third parliament to pacification of Berwick, 224 —244. 4. Short Parliament and Scottiſh invaſion, 244—253. 5. Acts of Long Parliament, 253—258. 6. Practices of the court party, 559—265. 7. Defence of popular leaders, 265—269. 8. Remedial meaſures demanded, 269—273.

Speeches on Eighth Debate : Supporters : ſee *Glyn, Hampden, Hollis, Maynard, Pym, Rudyard.* Opponents : ſee *Bagſhaw, Bridgman, Clarendon, Coventry, Culpeper, Dering, Falkland, Palmer, Waller.* Members calling for reſumption of debate,˙ 275. Hyde's motion to gain time, 275, 276. Authorities for report of eighth debate, 290, *note.* Diviſions on verbal alterations and on Biſhops' clauſe, 309, 310. Precedents for Remonſtrance, 311. Nicholas communicates Royaliſt tactics to the King, 313. Which ſide gained by protraction of debate ? 314, 315 and *note.* 316 and *note.* Numbers on final diviſions, 316. 317. Debate on printing, 317, 318. Proteſting members, 318. Clarendon's miſſtatements thereon, 319. Real mover of the printing, 319, 320. 323. True object of "Proteſters," 321, 322. Excitement conſequent on their proceedings, 323, 324. 'D'Ewes's Memoranda of the ſcene, 324, 325. Warwick's Old Teſtament parallel,

Index.

Grand Remonſtrance.
325. Hampden's pacificatory ſpeech, 325, 327. Diviſion as to poſtponement of printing, 326. Houſe up at laſt, 327. Cromwell's deportment and alleged expreſſions, *ibid.*
Petition to accompany Remonſtrance agreed on, 343, 344. Referred to committee to prepare, 344. Report ready, 355. Petition brought in, 359. Abſtract of its contents, 559—362. Objections by Hyde's party, 362. Queſtion raiſed as to Pym's right to anſwer ſame, *ibid.* Uſage of Houſe explained by D'Ewes, 362, 363. Petition read again, 363. Clauſes impugning Biſhops' conduct, diſcuſſed, *ibid.* D'Ewes's views adopted, 364. Stand made by Hyde and Coventry, *ibid.* Precedent cited by D'Ewes, 365. Moderate courſe taken by Pym, 365, 366. Proof of unauthoriſed communication of Petition to the King, *ibid. notes.* Arrangements made for preſentation to King, 366—368. Reception of deputation by Charles, 368. His queſtions parried by Hopton, 369. King's anſwer and dimiſſory meſſage, 369, 370.
Laſt Debate. Motion for printing Remonſtrance, 402—405. Numbers on diviſion, 406. Revival of claim to proteſt, 407. Reſult of adjourned debate thereon, 408 and *note.* Importance of Grand Remonſtrance as a contribution to hiſtory, 416. How characteriſed by Iſaac Diſraeli, 416, 417. Clarendon's opinion of its influence, 417, 418. Its effect on the Civil War, 418. The oneneſs of civil and religious freedom proved by it, 419. Rights demanded by it, *ibid.*

Grievances.
Great Charter, precedent adduced by Langton for the, 2. Langton's ſervices in obtaining ſame, 17, 18. Points conſtituting its great value, 18. Principles latent in it, 18, 19. Its remedial proviſions and guarantees, 19. Hatefulneſs to ſucceeding princes of its proviſions for Great Council, 20. Lord Chatham's appreciation of its "nullus liber homo" clauſe, 21. Its effects in later times, 22. Expanſiveneſs of its proviſions unforeſeen by its framers, 22, 23. Great truth embodied in it, 23. Number of its violations and reaſſertions, *ibid.* Boons ſecured by it to the middle claſſes, 26. Its confirmation 9 Henry III, 32. Its proviſion for inquiring into foreſt abuſes, 33. Confirmations and additions under Edward II and III, 40, 41.
Great Civil War, moſt exciting incident prior to the, 110. How it was conducted, 148. Its real character, 149.
Great Council, part borne by the, in the beſtowal of the crown, 12. Its memorable meeting in May 1258, 29. Its conſtitution under the early Norman kings, 29, 30. Break-up of its elements, 30. Writs of ſummons, how regulated, 30, 31. Peculiarities of feudal repreſentation, 31, 32. Compoſition of Council on gradual withdrawal of inferior tenants in chief, 32. Its initiation of county repreſentation, 33.
Greenſmith, John, alleged forger of Royaliſt petitions, 290 *note.*
Grey of Groby, Lord (Leiceſter), named on Remonſtrance Preſentation Committee, 367.
Grievances leading to Grand Remonſtrance, ſamples of, 220—

Grimston.

222 *notes.* 224, 225 *notes.* See *Ship-money. Wardships.*

Grimston, Harbottle (Colchester), on denials of justice, 231 *note*, 234 *note* ‡. On synodical meddlings with taxation, 247 *note*.

Grocyn associated with Erasmus. 75, 77.

Guilds and Charters, 25, 26, 63. See *Charters. Commerce. Great Charter.*

Gunpowder monopoly, effects of, 232. Clotworthy and Culpeper's protests, *ibid. note.*

HALES, Mr., of Eton, estimable character of, 405 *note.*

Hallam, Henry, on articles for regulation of King's affairs, 49. On condition of agricultural labourers under Henry VI, 57. Character of his notice of Grand Remonstrance, 113. Verney's notes used by him, 130 *note.* 291 *note.* In error on Haselrig's militia bill, 393.

Hamilton, Duke of, and Lord Strafford, story told by 1st Lord Shaftesbury of, 252, 252 *notes.*

Hamiltons, the. See *Argyle.*

Hampden, John (Bucks), escapes a purchased Peerage, 106. His influence in debate on Grand Remonstrance, 112. Question raised by a speech of his in the Strafford debates, 131. Lord Macaulay's interpretation, 132. Line really taken by him, 133. Course advocated by himself and Pym, 133, 134. Outvoted on proposed Conference with the Lords, 135, 136. Supposed disagreement between himself and Pym set at rest by D'Ewes's notes, 137. Sent with message to the Lords, 141. Consistency of course taken by him and Pym 143, 144. Point on which his, speech (in Verney's notes) was made, 144. Stands his ground, *ibid.* His suggestion relative to the lawyers, 144, 145. Opposes Charles's Scottish visit, 159. Offices with which he was to be tempted, 159. 160. Communicates discovery of assassination plot, 165. His return from Scotland, 167. 181. His leadership disowned by Falkland, 168. 181. 182. His cousin Waller, 191. Mistake of court lawyers in selecting him for ship money fight, 227 *note.* Opposed ship money not as a light grievance, 228 *note.* At Pym's dinner-parties, 282 *note.* His place in the House, 285. His speech in eighth debate on Grand Remonstrance, 306, 307. Disposes of Dering's moon simile, 307, 308. State of House at his sitting down, 308. Alleged mover of order for printing Remonstrance, 317. Proof of this allegation's untruth, 319. Reasons for wonder at Clarendon's so alleging, 319, 320 *notes.* What Clarendon and D'Ewes say as to his "serpentine subtlety," 320 *note.* Why he was likely to be misjudged, *ibid.* His character further analysed by Clarendon, 321 *note.* How he quelled storm raised by protesters, 325, 326. His question to Palmer, 326. 342. Extent to which he would punish Palmer, 347. Brings charge against Adam Courtney, 356. Defends Pym on point of order, 362. Joined in message to Lords for discharge of King's guard, 373. See also, 178. 195. 231.; 274. 296. 348. 371. 407. 410.

Hampton Court, Conference under James I at, 106, 107. Remonstrance presented to Charles there, 367—370.

Hanoverian succession, precedent for the, 46.

Hanoverian succession.

Harley.

Harley, Sir Robert (Herefordſhire), follows Hampden's bidding. 320 *note*.
Harold, beſtowal of the Crown after defeat of, 11.
Harrington, Sir John, entertains James I, 100. Deſcribes the King at a maſque, 108.
Harriſon's libel on Judge Hutton, 227 *note*.
Haſelrig, Sir Arthur, (Leiceſter-ſhire), 354. Clarendon's eſtimate of him, 187 *note*. His ſpeech on the tyranny of the Council table, 235 *note*. Encounter with Lenthal, 281. His place in the Houſe, 285. Named on Remonſtrance Preſentation Committee, 367. Introduces Militia Bill, 385. Reception given to it, 386, 387. Diviſion on firſt reading, 388—392. Simile applied to him by Clarendon, 391.
Hat, Servandony's, 176. Bag-ſhaw's ſtory, 237 *note*.
Hatton, Sir Robert (Caſtle Riſing), out of order, 341. Teller for adjournment of laſt Remonſtrance Debate, 406.
Hawes, Joſeph, Prayer of Petition of, 273 *note*.
Heath, Chronicler, Rudyard libelled by, 296.
Henri Quatre, epithet beſtowed on James I by, 92, 93. On effect of contempt on a King, 109. Cauſe of his murder, 271 *note*.
Henrietta Maria, Queen of Charles I, unauthoriſed viſits of Prince Charles to, 165 *note*. Plots of herſelf and the King againſt Pym, 185, 186. Stratagem adopted by her towards that end, 186 *note*. Her communication relative to parliamentary ordinances, 200. Scheme for obtaining Papiſt help to ſet up the Proteſtant Church, 271 *note*.

Henry IV.

Her confeſſor in trouble, 328. [See *Philips, Father.*] Pointed at in Remonſtrance Petition, 360.
Henry I, (Beauclerc) Charter of, a precedent for the Great Charter, 2. Futility of his ſub-ſequent attempts to depreſs the people, *ibid*. His chief juſti-ciary's appreciation of his commendations, 2, 3. Judicatory ſyſtem initiated by him, 9.
Henry II, advance of civilization under 7. His reſiſtance to Becket's Church-aggrandizing ſchemes, *ibid*. Intereſts involved in the ſtruggle, 8. Character of Henry, *ibid*. Ultimate reſults of the conflict, 8. 9. His aſſociate in legal adminiſtration, 9. Enduring character of the judicatory ſyſtem eſtabliſhed by him, 9. 10. His policy unſettled by his ſons, 13.
Henry III, Great Charter violated by guardian of, 23, 24. His appeal to the people, 24. Refuſal of parliament to aſſemble at his bidding, 26. Diſmiſſal of his favourite and miniſters, 27. Confirmation of Great Charter, 32. Knights of the ſhire ſummoned by his Queen, 34. Language of the writ, 34, 35. Year of his reign in which the principle of repreſentation became part of the conſtitution, 35, 36.
Henry IV, of Lancaſter (Bolingbroke), 43. Share of the people in his elevation to the throne, 44, 45. Shakeſpeare on his "crafty courteſies" to the people, 45. His politic conſultation of popular feelings, 46. Precedent of ſucceſſion to the Crown agreed to by him, *ibid*. Conditions annexed to ſupplies granted to him, 47. Seizure of church temporalities propoſed to him, 48, 49. Articles preſcribing

Henry V.

mode of government to him, 49. His legiflation contrafted with that of Henry VI, 54.
Henry V, 50. Advantages of his wars to the Commons, 51. Diftinction of his reign in conftitutional hiftory, 51, 52.
Henry VI, legiflation of, contrafted with that of Henry IV, 54. Object of his County Elections Statute, 54, 55. Comforts of labouring claffes in his reign, 57. Condition of England and its laws, 58, 59. See alfo pages 62. 93.
Henry VII, fteps taken to confirm fucceffion of, 65. Inducements to his marriage with Elizabeth of York, *ibid.* Pope's refcript, and ufe made of fame, 65, 66. Difcovery of the Caxton broadfide, 66. Lord Bolingbroke's defcription of him, *ibid.* His defpotifm, how achieved, 67. Social refults of his victory at Bofworth, 67, 68. Scantinefs of his firft Houfe of Lords, 68. His motive in creating the Star Chamber, 69. Confequences then unfeen by him, *ibid.* Lord Bacon's eftimate of his character, 69, 70. 77. 78. 82. Leading acts of his reign: Perfecutes Wycliffe's followers, 70. Characteriftics of his reign, 71. An equivocal friend to commerce and learning, 76, 77. Nobles disfavoured by him, 77. Claffes from which he chofe his friends, *ibid.* Caufe of the increafe of his revenues, 77, 78. His extortioners, their devices, and their fate, 78, 79.
Henry VIII, ftate of exchequer at acceffion of, 79. His appointed tafk, 80. His religious perfecutions and confifcations, *ibid.* Direction in which he met with checks, 81. Privileges won from him, 83.

Hollis.

Henry, fon of James I, 109.
Henry III of France, why murdered, 271 *note*.
Henry IV of France. See *Henri Quatre*.
Herbert, Sir Edward, Attorney-General (Old Sarum), pernicious notion inftilled into Charles by, 155. His place in the Houfe, 284.
Herefy, confequences of perfecution of, 70.
Hertford, W. Seymour, Marquis of, 166 *note*. Joins in petition for a parliament, 251 *note*.
Hexey's cafe cited as a precedent, 386. 387. 388 *note*.
Heyle, Queen's Serjeant, coughed down by the Commons, 89.
High Commiffion Court abolifhed, 182. 256. 260. Confequences of its enormities, 238. Barren of revenue, fruitful in oppreffion, 261.
Hildebrand's definition of Papal authority, 7.
Hiftory, imperfect judgments in, 3.
Holborne, R. (St. Michael's), fpeech of, minuted by D'Ewes, 124 *note*. A feceder from Strafford's attainder, 154 *note*. Recommended to the King, 193. Supports the bifhops' demurrer, 195. Laugh raifed againft him by D'Ewes, 196. Pleads againft Ship-money, 227 *note*. His place in the Houfe, 285. Speaks on right to proteft, 408 *note*. Hard cafe put by him, 408. 414.
Holland, Englifh flag infulted by, 228 *note*.
Holland, Earl of, complains of "indirect way of the Court," 167 *note* *.
Hollis, Denzil (Dorchefter), defignated for office, 159. A "worthy gentleman," 283 *note*. His place in the Houfe, 285. His fiery fpeech in favour of Remonftrance, 310, 311. Further on

446   Index.

Homer.
fame fubject, 323. His charge againft Palmer, 337. On Pym's Irifh Committee, 343. His reminder to the Houfe, *ibid*. His motion adopted, 344. Joined in meffage to Lords for difcharge of King's guards, 373. Teller in divifions, 388. 392. 406. Motion carried by him as to points of form and order, 393, 394 *notes*. Correfponds with Sir John Bankes, 410. Paffage from his letter, *ibid*. A glance at him in later days, 413. See 182.

Homer, revival of ftudy of, 72.

Hopton, Sir Ralph (Wells), an "ancient parliament man," 283 *note*. How he would have the Palmer punifhment queftions put, 350, 351. Replied to by D'Ewes, 351. Named on Remonftrance Prefentation Committee, 367. Deputed to read it to the King, 368. How he performed his tafk, 368, 369. Parries the King's queftions, 369. Reports King's meffage to Houfe, 370.

Hotham, Sir John (Beverley), courfe taken on Strafford's attainder by, 134. Why grateful to Hyde, 330. His ultimate fate, 334. For expulfion of Palmer, 347. 350. Hands in report on public debt, 394.

Hotham, John (Scarborough), courfe taken on Strafford's attainder by, 134. 139. His ultimate fate, 141. 334. His fharp attack on Palmer, 334. His motion on the fubject, 335. Repeats his charge, *ibid*.

Houfehold, Court of the, 235. Cafe reported in the Verney papers, *ibid note* †, 266 *note*.

Howard, Lord Thomas, on James's manner towards his favourites, 102.

Howard of Efcrick, Lord, joins in

Ireland.
Peers' petition for a parliament, 251 *note*. Danger incurred in prefenting fame, 252 *note*.

Hulbert, T., a fabricator of forged Royalift petitions, 290 *note*.

Hume, David, his fource of information on Grand Remonftrance, 111. His falfe diftinctions refuted by the document itfelf, 114, 115.

Huntingdon, Earl of, refufes to fubfcribe to loan to Charles I, 220 *note*.

Hutton, Judge, libelled for oppofing Ship-money, 229.

Hyde, Edward (Saltafh). See *Clarendon*.

Hyde, Robert (Salifbury), fometimes miftaken for Edward Hyde, 189 *note*.

IMPEACHMENT, right of, won by parliament, 53.

Impreffment, horror induced by fear of, 258 *note*. See *Army*.

Ingram, Sir Arthur (Kellington, now *Callington*), named on Remonftrance Prefentation Committee, 366.

Innocent III, Pope, Refcript of, to Henry VII, 65, 66.

Ireland, character of Strafford's government of, 150—152. References in Commons' debates to Irifh rebellion, 190. 191. 197. 204. 205. King's hopes as to "this ill news of Ireland," 198. Irifh levies raifed againft the Scots, 244. Difcovery of intended maffacre of Proteftants in Dublin, 263. Extent of maffacres in other parts of Ireland, 264. May and Rufhworth's narratives thereof, 264, 265 *notes*. Irifh bufinefs in Pym's hands, 575. City loan, 328, 329. Committee obtained for examination of fufpected perfons, 343. Defperate Irifh in London, 358 *note*. Neceffity

Italy.

for men and money, 394. Debate on immediate provision for Ireland, 399. Bill for impreffing foldiers againft rebellion, *ibid.* King's unconftitutional conduct with regard thereto, 399. 400.
Italy, confequences of enrichment of ports of, 6.

JAMES I, ground of imprifonment of Selden by, 2. Sir J. Whitelocke's comment on claim made by him, 54. His acceffion to the throne, 90. Evil of feating him without exacting guarantees, 91. His delight on learning the extent of his prerogative, *ibid.* Effect of his abufe thereof, 91, 92. Singularities of his mental conftitution, 92. Ufes to which he put his acquirements, 93. What he regarded as the climax of fin, *ibid.* His early career in Scotland, 94. Circumftances under which his character was formed, 94, 95. His children. [See *Elizabeth of Bohemia : Charles I.*] Rumours of difagreements between him and his wife, 95, 96. Circumftances attending birth of his fon Charles, 96. Effect on his Scottifh fubjects of his near fucceffion to the Englifh throne, 97. Starts to take poffeffion, 97, 98. Rufh of courtiers on the occafion, 98. His perfonal characteriftics: face, figure, fpeech, and walk, 98, 99. Effect of his appearance on the courtiers, 99. His progrefs to London and reception by the way, 99, 100. His interview with Cecil, 100, 101. Cecil's fervices and feeling towards him, 101. Rife of his favourite Car, 101, 102. [See *Somerfet.*] Repulfes Raleigh's wife, 102. His favourite Villiers, *ibid.* [See *Buckingham.*] Afpect of his

Jonfon.

Court, 103. Revives brutalities prohibited by Elizabeth, 104. Straits to which his extravagance reduced him, *ibid.* His difcreditable expedients for raifing money, 105. Sale of monopolies and honours, 105, 106. His theological affumptions, 106. How he difpofed of a conference between Churchmen and Puritans, 106, 107. Adulations of Church dignitaries thereon, 107. His religious perfecutions: dedicates a book to the Saviour, *ibid.* An African parallel to his creed, 108. His alleged complicity in deeper crimes controverted, 108, 109. Affailed in the pulpit, caricatured on the ftage, 109. Henri Quatre's dictum how verified, *ibid.* How he ufed his parliaments, 154.
Jermyn, Sir Thomas (Bury Saint Edmunds), 284.
Joanes, Judge, on Ship-money, 227 *note*.
John, King, refults of ill performance of his viceregal duties by, 10. His nephew not entitled to the crown as of right, 11. Important principle confirmed at his coronation, 12. Points in the difcuffion overlooked by fome critics, *ibid.* Why he was probably preferred to Arthur, 12, 13. Alternately fupported and oppofed by the people, 13. His character, 14. Deferts both fides, *ibid.* How the Barons regarded his lofs of his French poffeffions, 15. Conduct of the people on his furrender to the Pope, 16. Freedom's debt to him on this occafion, 16. 17. Langton's fhare in compelling him to grant the Great Charter, 17, 18. See alfo, 23. 30. 31. 33.
Jonfon, Ben, extracts from Falkland's eclogue on, 170, 171 *notes*. His eulogies on Sir

Judges.

Benjamin Rudyard, 296, 297 *notes.*
Judges prohibited from pleading King's orders, 47. Degrading meafures of Charles I, 234. Confequences of upright conduct, *ibid.* Anecdote of a judge, *ibid, note* ‡.
Jury fyftem, 39. Helpleffnefs of juries under Henry VII, 79. Packed under Charles I, 226.
Juftice, denial of, under Charles I, 229. 234. and *note* ‡. Abufe and enlargement of old judicatories, 235, 236. See *Council Table. High Commiffion Court. Houfehold. Star Chamber.*

King, regulations for council of the, 49.
King Richard (Melcombe Regis), attacks Speaker Lenthal, 279. 210.
Kirton, Mr. (Milborn Port), and his refpectable citizen, 377 *note.* ftory told by him, 378.
Kingcraft in England, France and Spain, 64.
Knighthood, money raifed by grants of, 105. Extortions under Charles I, 224.
Knights of the fhire under the Plantagenets, 34—37. Not commoners but reprefentatives of the Commons, 38. See *Parliament.*
Knightly, Richard (Northampton), teller in divifion on Remonftrance, 327.

LACKLEARNING parliament, 48.
Lancafter, houfe of, evidence of popular impulfe favoured by acceffion of, 49. Its final predominance favourable to popular liberty, 54. Its laft living reprefentative, 65. See *Henry IV. Henry V. Henry VI.*
Land, excefs and variety of charges upon, 225. How alleged flaws

Lenthal.

in titles were judged, 225, 226. proclamation for curing fame, 234 *note* †.
Langton, Stephen de, precedent for the great Charter adduced by, 2. His character and fervices to Englifh freedom, 17. His fhare in wrefting the Great Charter from John, 17. 18. Prefentment of national grievances by his fucceffor, 27.
Laud, William, Archbifhop of Canterbury, D'Ewes put into Star Chamber by, 121. Implicated in Strafford's treafon, 135. 138. 139. Lodged in the Tower, 182. Falkland's charge againft him, 217 *note.* " Souls put on the rack " by him, 235 *note.* Transforms Star Chamber into an inquifition, 238. Refults of his attempts to impofe liturgical yoke on Scotland, 242, 243. Still moving towards Rome, 246. In the Tower, 256.
Laundrefs's hufband knighted, 105.
Lavender, Mr. ftory told by Kirton of, 377 *note.* 378.
Law and lawyers degraded, 235.
Legat, Bartholomew, fent to the ftake by James I, 107.
Leighton's perfecution only a type of others, 237.
Lenthal, William (Woodftock), Commons' fpeaker, on bufinefs of Houfe, 208 *note.* Pleads for refpite from hard work, 213. His feat in the Houfe, 278, 279. Richard King's attack upon him, 279. Incident which led to his rebuke of John Digby, 279, 280. Selden's account of fame, 280 *note.* Unruly fpirits he had to deal with, 280, 281. His altercations with D'Ewes and other members, *ibid. notes.* Scolds thofe who " run forth for their dinners," 282. Pre-

Index. 449

Linacre.

cedence in debate ruled by speaker's eye, 311 and *note*. In an unquiet state of mind, 383. His letter to Nicholas, *ibid.* and *note*.

Linacre, 77.

Lincoln, Earl of, refuses to subscribe to loan to Charles I, 220 *note*.

Lingard, small notice taken of Grand Remonstrance by, 113.

Lisle, John (Winchester), chairman on tonnage and poundage bill, 359.

Literature, and Learning : seeds sown by the crusades, 6. Revival of learning, 70. Alarms thereat, 72. Old English gentleman's condemnation of it, 73.

Littleton, on loyalty from subject to subject, 380, 381.

Loans and Benevolences, 60. Statute of Richard III, against forced loans, 62. Penalty of refusing obedience to Charles's demands, 219, 250 *note*. Instances of, (1) getting, and (2) squandering, 220 *note*. Country gentlemen fined for living in London, 221 *note*. Coat and conduct money required as loans, 225.

Locke's *Common-Place Book* and Lord Shaftesbury, 252 *note*.

Lollards, (followers of Wickliffe), let alone during the wars of the Roses, 62. Persecuted by Henry VII, 70. 76.

London. See *City*.

London and Paris in revolutionary periods, 146, 147.

London and York, instance of fast journeys between, 241 *note*.

Long Parliament, 37. Not desirous to strip the Crown of its prerogatives, 147. 261. Spirit in which it carried on the conflict with the King, 148. Charles's intent to repudiate its measures, 155. Its acts during first twelve

Lunsford.

months of its existence, 253—258. Reproached with having done nothing for the King, 260. Its defence of its measures, 260, 261. Comparison between it and former parliaments, 262. Character and antecedents of its slanderers, 263. Character of its leaders, 419, 420. Their genius, greatness and endurance, 420. Their respect for law and precedent, *ibid.* Reverence due to them, 421.

Lords, House of, share of, in deposition of Richard II, 44. Their interference with taxation resisted by the Commons, 49, 50. Their reduced number at accession of Henry VII, 68. Their defection from the popular cause, 154. 156. Conferences with the Commons, 195. 196. 198. Most popular member of the House, 199. Peers' petition to the King for a parliament, 251. Copy of the petition, 251, 252 *notes*. Alleged murderous resolve of the court on its presentation, 252. 253 *notes*. Pym's complaint of their obstructive conduct, 381, 382. Close of his speech, *ibid. notes*. Godolphin's proposal as to Commons and Lords, 382, 383 *note*. Their surprise at the setting of the new guard, 395. They join Commons in protest to King, 400. Account of presentation thereof by joint deputation, 401 *note*. See *Barons. Commons. Parliament*.

Louis XI, of France, 64.

Lumley, Sir Martin (Essex), teller on clause against bishops, 209. On Palmer's protest, 341.

Lunsford, Col. Sir T., designated for Tower Governorship, 356. His character and antecedents, 372. King's object in appointing him, *ibid. note*.

Luther.

Luther, way prepared for, 75. His complaint of Erasmus, *ibid.*

Macaulay, Lord, on facility of encroachments by the executive, 60. His mention of Grand Remonstrance, 113. His construction of Sir R. Verney's Note, 132, 133. Point not noticed by him. 133. His estimate of Falkland, 174 and *note.*

Machiavelli, 64.

Magdeburg Singing boy, the 75.

Magna Charta. See *Great Charter.*

Mallory, Mr. (Ripon), 386. What he would have done with Haselrig's Militia Bill, 387.

Mandeville, Lord, joins in Peers' petition for a parliament, 251 *note.* Danger incurred by him in presenting same, 252 *note.*

Manly, Sir Richard, 282 *note.*

Mansfield of Distaff Lane and his apprentice, 377 and *note.*

Marshall, Stephen, Parson of Finchingfield, 320 *note.*

Marten, Henry (Berkshire), course taken by, in proceedings against Strafford, 134. 141. His place in the House, 284. 285.

Mary, Queen, share in the tasks assigned to the Tudors, 81. Where she failed, 82. Indocility of her Parliaments, 82, 83.

Mary Queen of Scots (James's mother), 93. Rizzio's murder, 96. 98. Her chief executioner and her son, 101.

Maxwell, Mr., no comfort in comforting words of, 127 *note.* Takes Judge Berkley into custody, 182 *note.*

May, Thomas, parliamentary historian, on cause of clerical animosity to Parliament, 156 *note* *. On fickleness and impatience of the people, *ibid. note* †. On persecutions for conscience' sake,

Monks.

237 *note.* On massacre of Irish protestants, 264 *note.* On Sir B. Rudyard's character, 294 and *note.*

Maynard, John (Totnels) course taken by, in proceedings against Strafford, 133. Recites points requiring settlement, 137—139. Shows what may be done, 139. Eager for the attainder, 141. His treachery towards Vane at the Restoration, *ibid.* Opposes Strafford's right to be heard by counsel, 144. How he met Hampden's suggestion, 145. His place in the House, 285. Controverts Palmer's law in Remonstrance Debate, 312.

Merchants. See *Commerce.*

Middle Ages, break-up of system of, 64.

Middle classes, privileges and rights conceded to the, 26.

Militia, Haselrig's Bill for settlement of, 385. Scene in House on its introduction, 386—388. Read first time, 388. Clarendon's misstatements and self-contradictions, 385, 389—393. Errors of other writers due thereto, 393.

Military services, acts passed against conscription for, 41, 42. See *Army.*

Ministerial responsibility to Parliament, earliest record of, 10. Further advancement of the principle, 27. Its effectual establishment, 49. Insisted on in Grand Remonstrance, 272, 273. Receipt of foreign pensions petitioned against, 273 *note.*

Money, unconstitutional schemes for raising. See *Wardships, Ship Money, Loans, Monopolies.*

Moniers, exemption from taxation claimed by the, 274. Remark made on their petition, 275.

Monks, poverty-stricken condition of the, 48.

Monopolies.

Monopolies, public outcry againſt, 89. "God proſper thoſe that "further their overthrow," 90. Abandoned by Elizabeth, *ibid.* Multiplied by James I, 105. Revived wholeſale under Charles I, 225 *note.* 230. Papiſt monopoliſts, 248 *note.* Enumeration of matters ſubjeƈt to monopoly, *ibid.* Petitioned againſt by Peers, 252 *note.* Aboliſhed, 254, 255. Culpeper's ſpeech on their univerſality, 255, *note.* Pym on folly of raiſing revenue by ſuch means, *ibid.*
Montfort, Simon de, demands a parliament, 38.
Montgomery, Lord, barber of, knighted, 105.
Montroſe's aſſaſſination plot and Charles I, 165 *note.*
More, Sir Thomas, 77.
Morton, Lord, poor plundered for benefit of, 233 *note.*
Moundeford, Sir Edmund (Thetford and Norfolk), illuſtrations furniſhed by family papers of, 221 *notes.*
Mountjoy, Lord, brings Eraſmus to England, 71.
Mulgrave, Earl of, joins in Peers' petition for a parliament, 251 *note.*

NALSON, JOHN, the colleƈtor, 119 *note.* Lenthal's letter printed by him, 383 *note.* His miſreading of diviſion on Haſelrig's Militia Bill, 329. General charaƈter of his *Colleƈtions.*
Neville, Sir Henry, purport of letter of, 95, 96.
Newcaſtle taken by the Scots, 253.
Newfoundland diſcovered, 71.
Newport, Francis (Shrewſbury), quits Houſe without leave, 395. Fetched back and rebuked, 396.
New Teſtament, alarm of the monks at Eraſmus's publication of the, 74, 75.

Norman.

Nicholas, Sir Edward (Newton, Hants) on diſtribution of offices, 159. Date of his announcement, 160. His wife fidelity to the King, 166 *note.* "Well affeƈted "Parliament men" in trouble, 167, 168. When made Secretary of State, 167 *note.* Submits names of ſeceders to Charles, 183. Hopes derived from reappearance of the Plague, 184. Reports attempt on Pym's life, 185. Recommends Hyde and his party, 193. His interview with Hyde, 193, 194. Informs Charles of impreſſion made by his New Biſhop ſcheme, 195. Hopes expreſſed to him by the King, 198. Sends tidings of Remonſtrance to Charles, 199, 200. Written to by the Queen on ſame ſubjeƈt, 200. Sends news of introduƈtion of Grand Remonſtrance, 201. His perplexities and fears concerning ſame, 201, 202. King's futile reply, 202. Reports further progreſs of Remonſtrance, 203. 206. 211. His fears as to effeƈt of Pym's Army Reſolution, 210. His place in the Houſe, 285. Informs Charles of taƈtics of Royaliſt party for defeat of Remonſtrance, 313. What paſſed after he left the Houſe, 314. Abſent from diviſion, 316. Appointed to office, 355. Lenthal's ſervile letter to him, 383 *note.* Reads King's anſwer to Lords' and Commons' Proteſt, 402 *note.*
Nicholſon, John, D.D., diſcourſe of, with a haberdaſher's apprentice, 377 and *note.*
Norman Kings of England, ſafety how purchaſed by the, 3. Saxon juriſprudence adopted by the Conqueror, 4. Forms deferred to by them at their coronations, 11. Conſtitution of their Great

North.

Council, 29. Extent to which reprefentation exifted under them, 32, 33. Conftitutional maxim fometimes ufed by them, 37.
North, Court and Council of the. See *Council of the North*.
Northampton, Great Council at (*temp.* Hen. II), 9.
Northampton, ftatute of, 394.
Northern Counties, votes by Long Parliament for relief of, 259.
Northumberland, Lord, a correfpondent of Sir John Bankes, 410. Impreffive fentences from his letter, 411. A glance at him in later days, 413.
Noy's "new-old way" 227 *note*.

ONSLOW, Serjeant (not D'Oyley), Verney's notes ufed by, 130, *note*. 131. 291 *note*.
Oratory value of preparation in, 191 *note*.
Overbury, Sir Thomas, Car, Earl of Somerfet, convicted for murder of, 102. James no party to the crime, 108, 109.
Ovid's lines and Dering's oppofition to the Bifhops, 207, 208 *notes*.
Oxford, Erafmus at, 71. 72. 73. Greek Profefforfhip founded, 72. Accomplifhment of Erafmus's work, 85.

Pace, Richard, quaint complaint quoted from, 73.
Paget, Earl, joins in Peers' petition for a parliament, 251 *note*.
Palmer, Geoffrey (Stamford), part taken in Strafford's Impeachment and in Grand Remonftrance by, 203. 222 *note*. His feat in the Houfe, 284. His speech againft the Remonftrance, 312. Protefts againft printing it, 323. Uproar created by his conduct, 324. Debate on his proteft, 332—334. Hotham's attack upon him, 334, 335.

Papifts.

Defended by Hyde, 335, 336 and *note*. Hollis's charge againft him, 337. Precedents cited againft him by D'Ewes, 337— 339. D'Ewes would have him fpeak, 340. Divifions called thereon, 340, 341. Required to fpeak, 341. Speaks accordingly and withdraws, 341, 342. What took place after his withdrawal, 342, 343. Refumption of debate, 344. Points urged in aggravation, 345. Extenuatory confiderations, 345, 346. Reafon for punifhing him, 346, 347. Extent of punifhment defired by Pym and Hampden, 347. Severer Meafures demanded by Hotham and others, 347, 348, 350. Bagfhaw's argument, 348. Crew's fpeech and admonitory fuggeftion, 348, 349. Waller's lefs difcreet harangue, 349, 350. Hopton and D'Ewes on points of order, 350, 351. Tower or Expulfion? Queftions put, 351, 352. Receives fentence at Bar of Houfe, 352. His committal and fubfequent releafe, 353. 393. Mifftatements of Clarendon on this topic, 353, 354, and *note*.
Palmer, "one Mr.," plundered by royal proclamation, 221 *note*.
Palmes, Guy (Rutlandfhire), 222 *note*.
Pamphlets, fcandalous, complained of in Houfe, 331, 332.
Papifts, reafons for Falkland's diflike of, 179 *note*. Favours and monopolies granted to projectors profeffing their creed, 233. 247 and *note*‡. 248, *note*. Defign for affimilating Romifh and Anglican Churches, 242. 246. 247. Their fecret meetings and preparations, 248, 249. Their encouragement petitioned againft by the Peers, 251 *note*. Need

Paris.

for curbing their power to do hurt, 270, 271. Meafures required by Pym, *ibid, notes*. Falfe conformifts to Englifh Church for place fake, 272. Their known favourers how to be dealt with, *ibid*. See *Pope.*
Paris and London in revolutionary periods, 146, 147.
Parker, Archbifhop of Canterbury, put on his mettle, 87.
Parliament, earlieft recorded authority for refponfibility of Minifters to, 10. Its refufal to meet on fummons of Henry III, 26. Its meafures when affembled proof of its control over Minifters, 27. Uniformity of its exercife of fuch control, 27, 28. Securities for public faith exacted by the city of London, 28. Bracton's dictum in favour of fame principle, *ibid*. Origination of the Houfe of Commons, 29. [See *Commons, Houfe of*]. What the Great Council really was, 29, 30. [See *Great Council*]. Parliamentary attendance of inferior tenants how difpenfed with, 31. Phafes of Reprefentation under the Norman Kings, 32, 33. Beginning of County Reprefentation, 33. Knights of Shires fummoned, 34, 35. Separate voting of each order a needful condition, 35. When principle of Reprefentation became part of the Conftitution, 36. Why Knights of Shires were paid, *ibid*. Their wages how levied, 37. How and by whom elected, *ibid*. Their ftation and privileges while fitting, 37, 38. Refult of Simon de Montfort's demand, 38. Additional provifions for affembling parliaments, 40. Refult of royal attempts to impofe taxes without its fanction, 41. Englifh language adopted in its

Peachem.

Rolls, 43. Its fhare in depofition of Richard II and elevation of Henry IV, 43, 44. And in the fettlement of the Crown, 46. The "lack-learning Parliament," 48. Original mode of procedure with refpect to bills, 50. Abandonment of fuch procedure, 51. Privilege of parliament gained and afferted, 53. Right of Impeachment won, *ibid*. Conftitution of parliament under Henry VI, 59. Recognition of its checks by the Crown, 60. Its acts on acceffion of Henry VII, 65. Its neglect of the people during his reign, 66, 67. Obftinacy of Mary's parliaments, 83. Effect of Elizabeth's domination, 85. Debates on Grand Remonftrance, 110, 156 *et feq*. [See *Grand Remonftrance*]. On Strafford's Attainder, 126—152 [See *Strafford*]. Reaffembling of Houfes in Oct. 1641. 163—168. Claim of both Houfes for ordinance during King's abfence, 199, 200. Incidents of Charles's firft parliament, 218, 219. The like of his fecond parliament, 219, 220. The like of his third parliament, 220—223. Parliaments a forbidden topic of talk, 224 and *note*. Its reaffembly petitioned for by the nobility, 251, 252 and *notes*. Bill for its continuance paffed, 258. 260. Object of the bill, 261. Character of the party hoftile to parliaments, 263. Alleged intimidation of parliament, 375—385. See *Commons, Houfe of. Long Parliament. Lords, Houfe of.*
Party ftruggles, beginning of, 10.
Patents and Monopolies. See *Monopolies.*
Peachem, the puritan, tortured and martyred, 107

H H

Peard.

Peard, George (Barnſtaple), moves printing of Remonſtrance, 319. 323. 342. 403. His ſocial poſition, 320.

Peerages put up to ſale, 105. Price of each grade, 106.

Peers' interference with elections complained of, 384.

Pembroke, William Earl of, regent, 23. Standard of rebellion raiſed by his ſon, 27.

Pembroke, Philip Earl of, appointment of as Lord Steward demanded, 348 *note*.

Pennington, Ald. Iſaac (London), introduces the city petitioners, 397.

Penny-a-lining, origin of, 289 *n*.

People, Royal Charters and conceſſions to the, not reſumable, 2, 3. Always on the track of their rulers, 3. Sides alternately taken by them in John's reign, 13. Their gain in the Barons' triumph, 14. What carried them over to the Barons, 16. Eſtabliſhment of their power to alter the ſucceſſion, 44. Acknowledgment of their influence by Henry IV (Bolingbroke), 45. Shakeſpeare's reading of his demeanour towards them, *ibid*. Their advance as gauged by the Statutes of the time, 46. Their condition, *temp*. Henry VI, 58. 59. Their fidelity to the Commons, 61. Expedients to keep them at reſt, *ibid*. Leſs at fault than their repreſentatives under the Tudors, 66, 67. Martial duties impoſed upon them, 83, 84. Their power through the Commons, 84. Their poſition under Elizabeth, 85. Their ficklenefs and impatience during ſtruggle with Charles, 156 and *note*†. Robbed of their right of common, 233. Fired on by Charles's guards, 373 and *note*. See *Commonalty*. *Commons*.

Privilege.

Percy. Henry (Northumberland). See *Aſhburnham, William*.

Petition of Right, an affirmation of old time precedents, 2. Violated by Charles I, 220. 222. 226. 230. Securities required for its due obſervance, 272. Coke's ſervices in regard to it, 413.

Petitions, enactment againſt tampering with, 52.

Philips, Father, Queen's Confeſſor, conflict of Lords and Commons relative to, 328. 329. Articles of accuſation againſt him, 331.

Plague, appearance of the, 184.

Plantagenets, political ſtruggles under the, 1—64. See *Henry I. Henry II. Richard I. John. Arthur. Henry III. Edward I. Edward II. Edward III. Edward IV. Richard II. Henry IV. Henry V. Henry VI. Richard III. Commons, Houſe of. Great Charter. Great Council. Parliament.*

Plunder of the ſubject, oppreſſive ſcheme for, 221 *note*.

Political Ballads, 26.

Pollard,Mr. (Beeralſton). See *Aſhburnham, William*.

Poor, rights of common taken from the, 233 and *note*†.

Poor Law, how neceſſitated, 68.

Pope, Nuncio from, reſident in England, 248. Terms on which Charles required help, 271 *note*.

Prerogative, reſtraints on the, 51. 59. Its temporary predominance, 64. How abuſed by Charles I and his adviſers, 224—244. See *Charles I. Council of the North. Council Table. Crown. High Commiſſion. Laud. Monopolies. Star Chamber. Strafford.*

Price, Herbert (Brecon), 285.

Price, Sir John (Montgomeryſhire), complaint by, 274.

Privilege of Parliament, when achieved, 52, 53. Eſtabliſhed againſt the Courts, 53. Invaded

Proclamations.
by forgeries and unauthorised printings, 289, 290 *notes.*
Proclamations, extortionate and despotic, against living in London, 221 *note.* Against speaking of Parliaments, 224 and *note.*
Protest, royalist party in Commons contend for right of, 323—326. Debate thereon, 331—343. Finally rejected, 408 and *note.* See *Palmer Geoffrey.*
Protestantism, vicissitudes of, under the Tudors, 80, 81. 86.
Protestants more rigidly dealt with than papists under Charles I, 247 and *note‡.* Design of the Irish Rebellion, 263. Massacres of Protestants in Ireland, 264, 265. Narratives of May and Rushworth, *ibid, notes.*
Protestation for parliament and religion, 127. Signed by Clarendon, *ibid.* D'Ewes's account of its origin, 127, 128, *notes.*
Prynne, William, 37. Detail of cruelties inflicted on him, 256, 257, *notes.* Further mutilations desired by some of the Lords, 257 *note.* See *Bastwick.*
Purefoy, William (Warwick), on need of money and how best to bring it in, 402, 403. Moves printing of Remonstrance, 403.
Puritan party formed, 87. Elizabeth's attempts to subdue its leaders in the Commons, *ibid.* Extent of her antipathy to Puritans, 88. Light in which their leaders regarded her, 88, 89. Puritanism and political discontent, 89. Conference with churchmen at Hampton Court, 106. James's abuse of the Puritans, 107. Mr. Carlyle's abandoned project, 118. The party joined by D'Ewes, 121. Upholders of right nicknamed Puritans, 217. To be rooted out by force or fear, 242. Rud-

Pym.
yard's characteristic definition of a Puritan, *ibid, note.*
Pury, Thomas (Gloucester), motion of relative to Dr. Chillingworth's disclosure, 374, 375.
Pye, Sir Robert (Woodstock), on Sir S. D'Ewes, 283 *note.*
Pym, John (Tavistock), on Parliaments without Parliamentary liberties, 53. Notes taken of a speech of his, 124 *note.* How spoken of by Privy Councillor Bankes, 126. Followed by Clarendon in the Protestation, 127. His alleged disagreement with Hampden in the Strafford business, 132. Lord Macaulay's interpretation of Verney's Note, 132, 132. Evidence of D'Ewes decisive on the point, 133. 136, 137. Mode of procedure against Strafford advocated by the two friends, 133. 134. Both outvoted thereon, 136. He suggests a conference, 137. Why he objects to attainder, 139. Advocates Strafford's claim to hearing, 145. Result of his appeal, 145, 146. His life threatened, 157. His servant tampered with by Bishop Williams, 159. 161. Effect of his opposition to Charles's Scottish visit, 159. Not to be won over by office, 160, 161. Chairman of Vigilance Committee during recess, 163. Reports discovery of Goring's plot, 164. Produces Hampden's letter, 165. Traces out project of conspirators, 165 *note.* Defeats Hyde's proposition, 166. Secession of Falkland from his party, 168. 182. Will not postpone Parliament for the Plague, 184. Further attempts upon his life, 184, 185. Plots of King and Queen against him, 185, 186, Queen's artful use of his name, 186 *note.* Covenanter Baillie's

Pym.

tribute to his powers as a leader, *ibid.* Effect produced by his speech on evil counsellors, 190, 191. Waller's parallel between him and Strafford, 191, 192. Waller ordered to apologise, 192 and *note.* Heads conference with the Lords on the Bishops' demurrer, 196. Defeats all the Royalist moves, 197. Evidence of his prudence and sagacity, *ibid.* Baffles King's hopes from Irish Rebellion, 198. Division on his Resolution, *ibid.* Steps taken subsequent thereto, 198, 199. What followed his Resolution, 200. Carries a Resolution as to a second army plot, 210. His vindication of course taken by himself and associates, 212. A homethrust, 212, 213. His courtesy to Speaker Lenthal, 213. Yields a point to his opponents, *ibid.* Charge insinuated against him by Clarendon, 214 *note.* His resentment of Eliot's murder, 223 *note.* His denunciation of Ship Money, 227, 228 *notes.* On folly of raising revenue by monopolies, 255 *note.* Authorship of Remonstrance ascribed to him, 268 *note.* His confession of faith, *ibid.* Requires safeguards against popery, 270, 271 *notes.* Hands full of Irish business, 275. His Westminster Hall conversation with Hyde, 276, 277. His sessional dinner-parties, 282 *note.* Respectful mention of in the House, 283 *note.* His place in the House, 284. Clarendon's remark on Culpeper more applicable to him, 300, *note.* His speech in Eighth debate on Remonstrance, 301—305. How he and his party carried the Remonstrance, 314—316. How their proposal to print it was met, 323, 324. Resolution ul-

Raleigh.

timately carried by him, 326. Bids the "Protesters" prepare to defend themselves, 328, 329. Clarendon's imputations against him and his party, 329, 330. Produces accusation against Father Phillips, 331. His speech against "Protest," 332, 333. Obtains committee to examine suspected Irishmen, 343. His regard for the liberty of the subject, *ibid.* Extent to which he would punish Palmer, 347. Suggests Petition to accompany Remonstrance, 355. His report to House concerning dismissal of guard, 356 *note.* Presents reasons for continuance of guard, 357 *note.* Summary of same, 358, 359 *notes.* Brings in Remonstrance Petition, 359. Answers objections to same, 362. His interrupters silenced by D'Ewes, 362, 363. Answers Culpeper's objections, 363. Point yielded by him, 365. Why he was not one of the Remonstrance Presentation Committee, 367. Joined in message to Lords for discharge of King's guards, 373. His significant question to Mr. Speaker, 378, 379. His complaint against the Lords, 381, 382. Memorable close of his speech, *ibid, notes.* His motion relative to guard of halberdiers, 395 and *note.* Rebukes Francis Newport, 396. His motion on King's interference with Impressment Bill, 400. Clause insisted on by him, *ibid, note.* Allays a rising storm, 407. See also 194. 231 *note.* 234 *note.* 245 *note.* 274. 285. 296. 298. 320 *note.* 327. 343 *note.* 348. 371. 406.

Pym, John and W. recusants, 219.

RALEIGH, Sir Walter, 85. His wife repulsed by James I, 102.

Index. 457

Ratcliffe.

Ratcliffe, Sir George, in Selden's story, 374 and *note* †.
Reading, style of living of the Abbot of, 48.
Recufants, list of, from the Verney Papers, 219. Hampden a recufant, 227.
Reeve, Judge, uprightnefs and humanity of, 246 *note*.
Reformation, made way for by Erafmus, 75. Elizabeth its champion, 81. Begun in the Commons, 84. Its refults, 85. Its impulfes reftrained, 86.
Remonftrance, Grand. See *Grand Remonftrance*.
Reprefentation, Parliamentary. See *Parliament*.
Reynolds, R. (Hindon), complains of unauthorifed printing, 332.
Richard I, minifterial refponfibility eftablifhed in the reign of, 10. Advantage taken by Barons during John's viceroyalty, *ibid*. Queftion of fucceffion to throne at his death, 11, 12. Confequences of lawlefs adminiftration during his abfence, 13.
Richard II, conftitutional principles recognifed in the depofition of, 43, 44. Strengthening of popular rights on the occafion, 44, 45. See alfo p. 59.
Richard III, forced loans abolifhed by, 62. Lord Bacon's eulogium on him, *ibid*.
Rizzio, David, parallel to circumftances connected with murder of, 96. Influence of the murder on James, 98.
Roberts, Mr., Diary of Walter Yonge, edited by, 219 *note*. His account of piracies on Englifh fea and foil, 228 *note*.
Robefpierre's Reign of Terror, Bankes's parallel to, 127. 146.
Roches, Peter des, Poitevin Bifhop of Winchefter, guardian of Henry III, 23. Precipitates

Rufhworth.

the King into difputes with the Barons, 24. Political ballads made againft him, 26, 27. Sent away from England, 27.
Roman Catholics. See *Papifts*.
Rofes, ftate of the nation during wars of the, 62, 63.
Rous, John, extracts from diary of: brafs money, 231 *note*. Tubbing's cafe, 237 *note*. Character of diary, *ibid*. John Commonwealth's-man's ficknefs, 243 *note*. Parliament men's pockets fearched, 245 *note*.* Lambeth and Southwark riots, *ibid*, *note*†. 246 *note*. On the impreffment grievance, 258 *note*.
Royalift Party. See *Clarendon. Culpeper. Dering. Falkland. Nicholas. Proteft. Strafford. Warwick, Sir Philip*.
Royalift Petitions, forged, 290 *n*.
Rudyard, Sir Benjamin (Wilton), part taken in debate on Strafford's attainder by, 131. 139. Moves for conference with the Lords, 166. Defines a Puritan, 242 *note*. Noble words on religious matters, 246 *note*. 249, 250, *notes*. His feat in the Houfe, 285. Character given him by May, 294 and *note*. His fpeech in eighth debate on Remonftrance, 294—296. Chronicler Heath's libel on him, 296. Poet as well as orator, 296, 297. Ben Jonfon's poems in his praife, *ibid*, *notes*. Weak points in his character, 297. His fayings and doings, 298. Wifhing for compromife but ftill of Pym's party, 298, 299. No pattern for deferters, 299. Pym's reply to his objection, 304. His comparifon of divifion on Grand Remonftrance, 315 and *note*.
Runnymede, 14. 17. 20. 23. See *Great Charter*.
Rupert, Prince, 332.
Rufhworth, John, Grand Remon-

Ruffell.

ſtrance printed in collections of, 111. Number of pages occupied by it, 116. Alarmed by encloſure in threatening letter to Pym, 185. His ſeat in the Houſe, 278. See 118 *note* ‡. 188 *note*. 393.

Ruffell, J. (Taviſtock), teller on laſt Remonſtrance debate, 406.

Ruthven (Rizzio's affaffin), murder of grandſon of, 96.

SADLER, Sir Thomas, entertains James I, 100.

Saint John, Oliver, Solicitor-General (Totneſs), mode of procedure againſt Strafford advocated by, 131. 133. 134. 141. 144. Suggeſtion of his adopted by Pym, 197. His conſolation to Hyde, 276. His ſeat in the Houſe, 284. Brings in bill on Tonnage and poundage, 343. Preffes it on, 344. Draftſman of Haſelrig's Militia Bill, 385. 390. 391. Clarendon's charge againſt him, 400 *note*.

Saint Stephen's Chapel (old Houſe of Commons), aſpect of, 276. 278. Coſtume of members and ſpeaker, 278, 279.

Saliſbury, Earl of. See *Cecil*.

Salt, patent for, "which will make "us all ſmart," 221 *note*.

Sanford, J. Langton, 188 *note*.

Sandys, Sir Edwin, courageous remark by, 54.

Savage, Sir Arnold, Speaker, heads the Commons in carrying complaints to Henry IV, 47.

Saxons, baſis of Conſtitution of the, 4. Their juriſprudence adopted by the Norman kings, *ibid.* No ſtrangers to feudaliſm, 4. 5. Feudal rights claimed by their Kings, 5.

Saye and Seale, Wm. Lord, refiſts Ship Money, 227 *note*. His challenge to the Judges, *ibid.* His pockets ſearched by royal order,

Ships.

245 *note*. Joins in petition for a parliament, 251 *note*.

Schoolmen, downfall of the, 37, 74.

Scotland and the Scots: Refult of Laud's attempt to force Liturgy on them, 242, 243. Strafford's levies againſt them, 244. Prayed againſt as rebels, 247. Their invaſion of England, 252, 253. Sum voted by Long Parliament for their relief, 259. "Well " and in peace," 369.

Selden, John (Oxford Univerſity), why thrice impriſoned, 2. A feceder on Strafford's attainder, 154 *note*. His ſarcaſm on Digby, 280 *note*. His place in the Houſe, 285 and *note*. "What's the reaſon of it?" appoſite ſtory told by him, 315, 316. On King's uſe of Pym and party, 374 and *note* †.

Separatiſts, Pym on forced exile of, 303. Bridgman's reply, 305.

Servandony, firm as the hat of, 176.

Sewers Commiffion, notice given by Cromwell about, 234 *note*.

Shafteſbury, Lord, ſtory of, relative to preſentation of Peers' petition to Charles I, 252, 253 *notes*.

Shakeſpeare, 45. 85. 297.

Sheriff's office, when elective, 39.

Sheriffs and Ship Money, 221 *note*. 250. 252 *note*. Nefarious ſyſtem of ſelection under Charles I, 239.

Ships and Ship Money: D'Ewes produces evidence of illegality of Ship Money, 121. Judges impeached for fanctioning it, 182 and *note*. Pretence under which it was levied, 226. Its enormity and hardſhip, 227 *note*. Caſes of Hampden and Lord Saye, *ibid.* Pym's denunciation of it, 227, 228 *notes*. Engliſh ſhips at the mercy of pirates, 228. Caſes of piracy and inſults to our flag, 228 *note*. Conſequences of Judge Hutton's

Shrewsbury.

declaration againſt Ship Money, 229 *note.* Sheriffs impriſoned for not raiſing enough, 250. Petioned againſt by the Lords, 252 *note.* Aboliſhed, 254.

Shrewſbury, Lord, entertains James I, 100. Cecil's note to him on James's expenditure, 104.

Sidney, Sir Philip, 85.

Simonds, Richard, 119.

Singleton, Archdeacon, 293 *note.*

Skippon and his Trained Bands, 397 *note.*

Slanning, Sir Nicholas (Penryn), moves adjournment of laſt Remonſtrance debate, 404. Clarendon's portraiture of him, 404, 405 and *note.* Revives claim to Proteſt, 407.

Smith, or Smyth, Henry (Leiceſterſhire), takes part in Grand Remonſtrance, 203. Notices given by him, 236 *note* *. Sat on Charles's trial, *ibid.*

Smith, Rev. Sydney, precedent for Taxation Diatribe of, 255 *note.* Prototype of his defence of "Prizes in the Church," 293 *note.*

Soap, monopoly of, granted to Papiſts, 248 *note.* Complaints of its quality, *ibid.*

Soldiers, Acts againſt compulſory preſſing of, 41, 42. See *Army.*

Somerſet, Car Earl of, James's favourite, 95. His riſe, 101. Honours laviſhed on him: James's manner towards him, 102. Cauſe of his fall, *ibid.* James no accomplice in his crimes, 108, 109.

Sophia, Electreſs of Hanover, 95.

‡Southwark and Lambeth Riots, how brought about, 245. Rous's diary thereon, *ibid. note.* Judge Reeve's uprightneſs, 246 *note.*

Spain, Engliſh flag inſulted by, 228. See *Ferdinand.*

Speaker, Mr. and the Commons in Charles's days, 279. 311 and *note.* See *Lenthal.*

Strafford.

Speeches, fabrications, falſifications, and unauthoriſed publication of, 289, 290 *notes.*

Speed, the Hiſtorian, on ſeed-plots of Treaſon, 12.

Spenſer, Edmund, 85, 120.

Spies, Falkland's hatred of, 180.

Stanhope, Mr. (Tamworth), teller on diviſions, 257 *note*, 309 *note* †.

Stanhope, Sir Edward, entertains James I, 100.

Stannary Courts, 182. Aboliſhed, 257.

Stapleton, Sir Philip (Boroughbridge), fellow commiſſioner with Hampden, 165. 167 and *note* †. Why grateful to Hyde, 330. Calls attention to new guard at doors of Houſe, 394.

Star Chamber Court created, 69. Aboliſhed, 182. 256. 260. Sample of enormities practiſed by it, 229 and *note.* 236, 237 and *notes.* How Laud aggravated its powers, 238. Sheriffs dragged before it, 250. Its monſtrous ſentence on Prynne, 256, 257 *notes.* Fruitful in oppreſſion when barren of revenue, 261. Effect of its ſentences in Elizabeth's days, 350.

Statutes of conſtitutional importance paſſed under the Plantagenets. See *Election. Treaſons. Winchester.*

Sterling, Lord, poor plundered for benefit of, 233 *note.*

Strafford, Thomas Wentworth, Earl of, 125. Folly of adopting his attainder as a teſt of opinion, 126. Mr. Bankes's extravagant compariſons, 127. 146, 147. His laſt hopes deſtroyed by the King's interference, *ibid, note.* Royaliſt ſupporters of his attainder, 128. Clarendon's ſhiftineſs in connection herewith, 128, 129. Diſpute raiſed by Verney's report of debate on a collateral

Strafford.

queftion, 131. Debate as to mode of procedure againft him, 133 — 137. D'Ewes's notes thereof fet out, 137—141. Subfequent courfe of fome of the fupporters of the attainder, 141. Prefumed caufe of Falkland's animofity, 142 and *note*. Pym and Hampden's courfe of action, 143, 144. His right to be heard by counfel infifted on by them, 144, 145. Himfelf the greateft man on the King's fide, 149. Character of his adminiftration in Ireland, 150. Charles's bad faith towards him, 151. Moral of courfe taken by him, 152. Pofition of parties after his death, 152, 153. Richard Baxter's miftake relative to feceders from his attainder, 153, 154 *notes*. Why lefs an apoftate than Falkland, 170. His name a fignal of difunion, 190. Waller's indifcreet parallel between him and Pym, and its refults, 191. 192. Innovation on forms of Houfe during his attainder, 205. His fpeech on billeting grievances, 218, 219 *notes*. Piracies on Irifh coaft, 228 *note*. Denounces Royalift preachers, 239 *note* †. The Crown's laft and beft refource, 243. How he propofed to ufe it, 243, 244. Wrefts fubfidies from Irifh Parliament, 244. Coft to himfelf of his advice to the King, *ibid*, *note*. His ficknefs a foftener of harfh meafures, 245. Story told by Lord Shaftefbury, 252, 253 *notes*. Strafford's end, 256. His efcape prevented by Balfour, 372. Why Selden fubftituted Ratcliffe's name for his, 374 *note* †. See alfo 176. 182. 183. 199. 227 *note*. 233 *n*. 241. 248 *n*. 354 and *note*.

Strangways, Giles (Bridport), teller on divifions, 310 *note*. 317. 352.

Stuart.

Interrupts Pym on point of order, 362. Rebuked by D'Ewes, 363. Strangways, Sir John (Weymouth), recommended to the King, 193. His motion on bufinefs of Houfe, 206 *note*. His place in the Houfe, 284. His reminder to Sir R. Cook, 348. Charge brought by him againft the Citizens, 376. Story of the "lufty "young man," 377 and *note*. Houfe's opinion of his ftatement, 378.

Stricklands and Wentworths, 87.

Strode, William (Beeralfton), propofes fine for abfent Members, 163. 316 *note*. Gives Hyde the advantage, 187—189. His antecedents no warrant for Clarendon's low eftimate of him, 187 *note*. Poffible confufion between two Strodes, 187, 188 *notes*. Refufes to leave the Houfe with his accufed friends, 188 *note*. D'Ewes's allufions to him as a young man, 188. 189 *notes*. Part taken by him in Grand Remonftrance, 203. 204. His blunt avowal as to Scotch army, 205 *note* *. His motion for fining diforderly Members, *ibid*, *note* †. Addition to Remonftrance propofed by him, 221 *note*. Venomous allufion by Clarendon, 245 *note*. Complains of an Order of the Houfe, 274. His place in the Houfe, 285. His fuggeftion relative to Hyde, 336. Moves for putting kingdom in pofture of defence, 357. Alfo for continuance of guard over Houfes, *ibid*. Defends Citizens againft Waller's attack, 379. Supported by D'Ewes, *ibid*. Supports Hafelrig's Militia Bill, 386. His opinion of Mallory and Cook's fpeeches, 387.

Stuart, Arabella, bribed to intrigue for a peerage, 104.

Stuarts.

Stuarts, grounds of refiftance to tyranny of the, 1. Influence of earlier records on the ftruggles with them, 2. Preparative for the decifive ftruggle, 68.
Subfidies, collection of, under Plantagenet Kings, to whom entrufted, 33. Amount raifed in firft year of Long Parliament, 254.
Suckling, Sir John, and Lord Falkland, 170 *note* †.
Supplies, ftipulations for control over, 28. Made conditional, 41. 47.

TACITUS, feudalifm exifting in the time of, 4.
Taxation, interference with by Lords refifted, 49, 50. Reftored to Commons, 256.
Thinne, Sir James (Wiltfhire), named on Remonftrance Prefentation Committee, 366.
Thorpe, Speaker, privilege afferted in cafe of, 53.
Timber Grievance, 233.
Tirrett, Stephen, his nephew Cole, and Dr. Nicholfon, 377 *note*.
Titles and title-deeds, how made fubject of extortion, 225, 226. 234 *note* †.
Tomkins, Mr. (Weobly), courfe taken on Strafford's attainder by, 134. 139. Why expelled, 141.
Tonnage and poundage, 226. 328. Bill for levy thereof brought in, 343. Preffed on by St. John, 344. Bill in committee, 359.
Tower of London, City fear of infecurity of, 372. Its governors. See *Balfour. Lunsford*.
Trained Bands of London ordered to guard Houfes of Parliament, 166. Cromwell's motion, 199. Effect of gunpowder monopoly, 232. King orders their difmiffal, 355, 356. 370. Pym communicates King's meffage to Commons, 356 *note*. Bill for their future command, 357.

Vane.

Reafons to be fubmitted to King, 357, 358. Subftance of report embodying reafons, 357 —359 *notes*. King's Trained Band difcharged, 373.
Treafons the feed-plot of liberty, 12. Conftitutional value of Statute of Treafons, 41.
Tres Magi, the, 64. 65. 68.
Triennial Bill paffed, 258. 260. Not a ftretch of power on the part of the Parliament, 261.
Tubbing's mutilation, 237 *note*.
Tudor, Henry, 60. 64. 65. See *Henry VII*.
Tudors, peculiarity of defpotifm of the, 67. 81. Influence of their reigns, 71. Their characteriftics, 79. Limits to which they confined their tyranny, 80. Their bearing towards the people, *ibid*. Tafk of each fovereign of the race, 80, 81. Feature of their fyftem relative to Romanifm, 86. Point arrived at by the fyftem at James's acceffion, 90. See *Henry VII. Henry VIII. Edward VI. Mary, Queen. Elizabeth, Queen.*
Turks, piracies committed in Englifh waters by, 228. Their Englifh emulators, 228 *note*.
Tyler, Wat, and Jack Cade, infurrections of, contrafted, 56.

UNITARIANS fent to the ftake, 107.
Univerfities hard at work againft the Parliament, 155. 156 *note* *.
Uxbridge, treaty of, 348 *note* †.

VANE, Sir Henry, the elder (Wilton), objects to note-taking, 124 *note*. Notes taken by himfelf, 134. Ufe made of them by the Houfe, 135. 245 *note*. His Secretary examined concerning them, 136. Refufes to explain when called on, 140. Requires time for deliberation, 141. Intercepts difbanding of army by

Vane.

King's orders, 164. His reference to D'Ewes, 283 note. His place in the Houfe, 284. Deprived of office, 355. Oppofes right to proteft, 408 note.

Vane, Sir Henry, the younger (Hull), hands his father's notes to Pym, 135, 245. Speaks with reference thereto, 136. Treachery by which he was brought to the fcaffold, 141. His place in the Houfe, 284. Self-denying Ordinance, 348.

Vaffals and vaffalage, 4. 5. 7. Effect of the Wars of the Rofes, 68. See *Feudal Syftem*.

Ven, Captain John (London), accufation againft, 378.

Verney, Sir E. loyalty of, 172.

Verney, Sir Francis, an alleged Turkifh pirate, 228 *note*.

Verney, Sir Ralph (Aylefbury), a more reliable reporter than Hyde, 13. His notes publifhed, *ibid, note*. Queftion raifed on his report of a fpeech of Hampden, 131, 132. 144. His note on excitement as to Charles's Scottifh Journey, 160 note †. Lift of recufants from his papers, 219 *note*. On wardfhip extortions, 225 *note*. Elizabeth Cottrell's cafe, 235 note †. 236 *note*. Defcribes Prynne's punifhment, 256, 257 *notes*. Error relative to Sir John Eliot, 287 *note*. Ufe made of his notes in this work, 290 *note*. Inference from his nonallufion to matters dwelt on by Clarendon, 330. Proceedings not mentioned by him, 332 *note*. On Cook's mif-citation of a precedent, 388 *note*.

Victoria, Queen, 37.

Villenage, 55. 56. 61. See *Feudal Syftem*.

Villiers. See *Buckingham, Duke of*.

Vintners of London, fum paid by the, for freedom from monopoly, 248, *note*.

Warwick.

Vorftius perfecuted to the death by James I, 107.

WALES, principle enunciated in giving reprefentatives to, 83.

Waller, Edmund (St. Ives), 170 *note* †. Clarendon's eftimate of his oratorical powers, 191, *note*. His indifcreet parallel between Pym and Strafford and its refults, 191, 192. 199. Commons' journals entry of the incident, 192 *note*. His new allegiance : recommended to the King, 193. Objects to form of Pym's refolution, 197. Caufe of D'Ewes's lecture to Speaker, 281 *note*. His place in the Houfe, 285. His fpeech on the Remonftrance, 306. His defence of Palmer, 349, 350. Inveighs againft citizens of London, 379. Oppofes printing of Remonftrance, 403. His colleague in the Houfe, fee *Godolphin*.

War between Charles and Parliament. See *Great Civil War*.

Warburton, Bifhop, on a feature in Falkland's character, 172 *note*. On atrocities of the Court, 222 *note*. On an expreffion of Clarendon's, 347 *note*. On object of Lunsford's appointment, 372 *note*. On the leaders of the Long Parliament, 421.

Wardfhip, right of, claimed by Saxon kings, 5. Oppreffively exercifed under Charles I, 224, 225. Inftances of extortion, *ibid, notes*. Court of Wards, 235.

Warwick, Earl of, refufes to fubfcribe to loan to Charles I, 220 *note*. His pockets fearched by King's order, 245 *note*. Joins in Lords' petition for a Parliament, 251 *note*.

Warwick, Sir Philip (Radnor Town), picture of Debate on Grand Remonftrance by, 112. His criticifm on Hyde, 286 *note*.

Wentworth.

On Culpeper, 300 *note*. His Old Teſtament parallel, 325.
Wentworth, Peter, declaration in the Commons by, 84. Unſubduable, 87.
Wentworth, Thomas Lord, See *Strafford*.
Weſtminſter Hall, 42. 44. Its aſpect and occupants in Charles's days, 276, 277. Incident noticed in Laud's Diary, 277 *note*.
Wharton, Lord, a correſpondent of Sir John Bankes, 410. Earneſt paſſage from his letter, *ibid*.
Wheeler, Mr. (Weſtbury), ſubject of report by, 274. Watch duty impoſed upon him, 374 *note*.
White, Mr. catches the Speaker's eye, 311 *note*.
Whitelocke, Sir James, quaint obſervation of, 54.
Whitelocke, Bulſtrode (Marlow), on Judge Berkley's arreſt, 182 *note*. Takes part in Grand Remonſtrance, 203. Amendment carried by him, 230 *note*. What he ſays as to how the Remonſtrance was carried, 315. Why his "Memorials" are not entirely truſtworthy, *ibid, note*. His plea for Palmer, 342.
Whitgift, Archbiſhop, fulſome compliment to James I by, 107.
Wickliffe, John, 61. Burning of his followers, 70. Their increaſe, *ibid*.
Wilde. See *Wylde*.
William the Conqueror, Saxon inſtitutions adopted by, 4. See *Norman Kings. Saxons*.
Williams, John, Biſhop of Lincoln, afterwards Archbiſhop of York, tampers with Pym's ſervant, 159. His advice to the King, *ibid*. His labour loſt, 161. Reads Lords' and Commons' proteſt to the King, 401 *note*.
Wilmot, Mr. (Tamworth), 285. See *Aſhburnham, William*.
Wincheſter, ſtatute of, 39, 40.

York.

Windebank, Sir Francis, 285. Driven into exile, 182. 256. Object of reprieve ſigned by him, 235 *note*. Apt agent for the Papiſts, 248. His office given to Nicholas, 355.
Windſor Caſtle, 42.
Wingate, Mr. (St. Albans), 203. 224 *note*.
Winwood, Sir Ralph, purport of Neville's letter to, 95, 96.
Witan, the Saxon, 29.
Wolſey, Cardinal, 77.
Worde, Wynkyn de, 77.
Wray, Sir C. (Great Grimſby), named on Remonſtrance Preſentation Committee, 367.
Wrightman, Edward, ſent to the ſtake, 107.
Writs of ſummons, varieties in, 30, 31.
Wycliffe. See *Wickliffe*.
Wylde, Serjeant (Worceſterſhire), 203. On deſtruction of timber in Dean Foreſt, 233 *note*.
Wynne, Sir Richard (Liverpool), named on Remonſtrance Preſentation Committee, 367. Introduces his colleagues, 368.

YELVERTON, Sir Chriſtopher Boſſiney), communications to D'Ewes by, 308. 323. Extract from D'Ewes's journal relative thereto, 309 *note*. On feeling of Lords as to new guard, 395.
Yonge, Walter, Diary of, 219 *note*. Extract ſhowing how moneys were raiſed and ſquandered, 220 *note*. Caſe of land piracy, 228 *notes*. Impriſonments for refuſing loans to the King, 250 *note*.
"Young Man," uſe of the term as marking identity or diverſity in Strode's caſe, 188, 189 *notes*.
York and London, rapid travelling between, 241 *note*.
York, Court of, 182. See *Council of the North*.

THE END.

ERRATA.

Page 47. *Third marginal note.* After "Officers" infert "of."
,, 75. *Line 7 from bottom.* For "Madgeburg" read "Magdeburg."
,, 132. *Third marginal note.* For "Macauley" read "Macaulay."
,, 255. *Second marginal note.* For "Culpepper" read "Culpeper."
,, 291. *Note.* For "D'Oyley" read "Onflow."
,, 363. *Firſt marginal note.* For "Culpeper" read "Strangways."
,, 367. *Line 4.* For "Second son" read "Son and heir."
,, 377. *Note, eight lines from bottom.* For "Stephen came in . . to tell his uncle" read "came in , . . to tell his uncle Stephen."

BRADBURY AND EVANS, PRINTERS, WHITEFRIARS.

BY THE SAME AUTHOR.

Uniform with this Volume poſt 8vo. 12s.

ARREST OF THE FIVE MEMBERS BY CHARLES THE FIRST.
A CHAPTER OF ENGLISH HISTORY RE-WRITTEN.

Alſo, Third Edition, in One Volume poſt 8vo, 12s.

OLIVER CROMWELL, DANIEL DE FOE,
SIR RICHARD STEELE, CHARLES CHURCHILL, SAMUEL FOOTE. BIOGRAPHICAL ESSAYS.

FORTHCOMING WORKS.
TO BE PUBLISHED BY MR. MURRAY.

I.
LIFE OF THE RIGHT HON. WILLIAM
PITT, WITH EXTRACTS FROM HIS UNPUBLISHED CORRESPONDENCE AND MSS. PAPERS. By EARL STANHOPE (LORD MAHON). Portrait. Vols. 1 and 2. Post 8vo.

II.
THE UNITED NETHERLANDS: FROM
THE DEATH OF WILLIAM THE SILENT TO THE DEATH OF OLDEN BARNEVELD. With a Detailed Hiſtory of the Spaniſh Armada. By J. LOTHROP MOTLEY. Portrait. 2 vols. 8vo.

III.
THE DIARY AND CORRESPONDENCE
OF CHARLES ABBOTT, LORD COLCHESTER, Speaker of the Houſe of Commons, 1802—17. Edited by HIS SON. Portrait. 3 vols. 8vo.

IV.
THE PRIVATE DIARY OF GENERAL
SIR ROBERT WILSON. During his Miſſions and Employment in Spain, Sicily, Turkey, Ruſſia, Poland, Germany, &c. 1812—41. 2 vols. 8vo.

V.
LIFE AND WORKS OF ALEXANDER
POPE. *A New Edition.* Containing 300 UNPUBLISHED LETTERS. Preceded by a Critical Eſſay, and a NEW LIFE of the Poet. Edited by the Rev. WHITWELL ELWIN. Portraits. Vol. I. 8vo.

VI.
ANCIENT LAW: ITS CONNECTION WITH THE EARLY HISTORY OF SOCIETY, AND ITS RELATION TO MODERN IDEAS. By H. SUMNER MAINE. 8vo.

VII.
SUNDAY: ITS ORIGIN, HISTORY, AND PRESENT OBLIGATIONS. Being the Bampton Lectures for 1860. By Rev. J. A. HESSEY, D.C.L. 8vo.

VIII.
THE ORIGIN AND HISTORY OF LANGUAGE. Baſed on Modern Reſearches. By F. W. FARRAR, M.A. Fcap. 8vo.

IX.
THE GREAT SAHARA: OR, WANDERINGS SOUTH OF THE ATLAS MOUNTAINS. By H. B. TRISTRAM, M.A. Illuſtrations. Post 8vo.

X.
A RESIDENCE IN JUTLAND, THE DANISH ISLES, AND COPENHAGEN. By HORACE MARRYAT. Illuſtrations. 2 vols. Poſt 8vo.

XI.
THE PERSONAL HISTORY OF LORD BACON; from unpubliſhed Letters and Documents. By W. HEPWORTH DIXON. 8vo.

XII.
ICELAND: ITS VOLCANOES, GEYSERS, AND GLACIERS. Explored in a Summer Excurſion. By CHAS. S. FORBES, R.N. Illuſtrations. Poſt 8vo.

XIII.
ANTIQUE GEMS: THEIR ORIGIN, USE, AND VALUE AS INTERPRETERS OF ANCIENT HISTORY, AND ART. By Rev. C. W. KING. Illuſtrations. 8vo.

Mr. MURRAY'S
LIST OF RECENT WORKS.

I.
RECOLLECTIONS OF THE DRUSES OF
LEBANON. With Notes on their Religion. By LORD CARNARVON. Post 8vo. 5s. 6d.

II.
ON PUBLIC SCHOOL EDUCATION, with
especial reference to Eton. By SIR JOHN COLERIDGE, D.C.L. Fcap. 8vo. 2s.

III.
PLATO'S DOCTRINE ON THE ROTA-
TION OF THE EARTH., and ARISTOTLE'S COMMENT upon that DOCTRINE. By GEO. GROTE. 8vo. 1s. 6d.

IV.
MEMOIR OF THE LIFE OF ARY SCHEF-
FER. By MRS. GROTE. *Second Edition.* Portrait. Post 8vo. 8s. 6d.

V.
HANDBOOK TO THE GERMAN, FLE-
MISH, AND DUTCH SCHOOLS OF PAINTING. By DR. WAAGEN. Illustrations. 2 vols. Post 8vo. 24s.

VI.
THE SUPPLEMENTARY DESPATCHES
OF THE DUKE OF WELLINGTON. Vol. 6. Relating to the EXPEDITIONS TO DENMARK, MEXICO, AND PORTUGAL and the FIRST ADVANCE of the BRITISH ARMY into SPAIN, 1806-10. 8vo. 20s.

VII.
THE GLACIERS OF THE ALPS. A Narra-
tive of Excursions and Ascents; an account of the Origin and Phenomena of Glaciers. By JOHN TYNDALL, F.R.S. Illustrations. Post 8vo. 14s.

VIII.
A HISTORY OF FLEMISH LITERATURE,
AND ITS CELEBRATED AUTHORS, FROM THE 12TH CENTURY TO THE PRESENT TIME. By OCTAVE DELEPIERRE. 8vo. 9s.

IX.
AUTOBIOGRAPHICAL RECOLLECTIONS.
By the late C. R. LESLIE, R.A. With EXTRACTS from his CORRESPONDENCE. Edited by TOM TAYLOR. Portrait. 2 vols. Poft 8vo. 18s.

X.
A DICTIONARY OF THE BIBLE; ITS ANTIQUITIES, BIOGRAPHY, GEOGRAPHY, AND NATURAL HISTORY.
Edited by DR. WM. SMITH. Plans and Woodcuts. Vol. I. Medium 8vo. 42s.

XI.
THE SECRET HISTORY OF EVENTS
during the FRENCH INVASION of RUSSIA, 1812. By GEN$^{L\cdot}$ SIR ROBERT WILSON. *Second Edition.* Plans. 8vo. 15s.

XII.
ON THE INTUITIONS OF THE MIND.
By REV. DR. McCOSH. 8vo. 12s.

XIII.
THE DISCOVERY OF THE FATE OF SIR JOHN FRANKLIN AND HIS COMPANIONS, IN THE ARCTIC SEAS.
By SIR LEOPOLD McCLINTOCK, R.N. 12th *Thoufand.* Illuftrations. 8vo. 16s.

XIV.
ON THE ORIGIN OF SPECIES, BY MEANS OF NATURAL SELECTION; Or, THE PRESERVATION OF FAVOURED RACES IN THE STRUGGLE FOR LIFE.
By CHARLES DARWIN, F.R.S. *Fifth Thoufand.* Poft 8vo. 14s.

XV.
MEMOIR OF THE EARLY LIFE OF LORD CHANCELLOR SHAFTESBURY.
By W. R. CHRISTIE. Portrait. 8vo. 10s. 6d.

XVI.
NEW ZEALAND—PAST AND PRESENT, SAVAGE AND CIVILISED.
By A. S. THOMSON, M.D. Illuftrations. 2 vols. Poft 8vo. 24s.

XVII.
PICTURES OF THE CHINESE, DRAWN BY THEMSELVES.
With Defcriptions. By Rev. R. H. COBBOLD. Illuftrations. Poft 8vo. 9s.

XVIII.
REMINISCENCES OF THE LATE THOMAS ASSHETON SMITH.
By SIR EARDLEY WILMOT, BART. *2nd Edition.* Illuftrations. 8vo. 15s.

JOHN MURRAY, Albemarle Street.

www.ingramcontent.com/pod-product-compliance
Lightning Source LLC
Chambersburg PA
CBHW021420300426
44114CB00010B/574